MANAGEMENT CONTROLS

NEW DIRECTIONS IN BASIC RESEARCH

Papers Given at the
Seminar on Basic Research
in Management Controls,
Graduate School of Business,
Stanford University.

McGRAW-HILL BOOK COMPANY

New York,
San Francisco,
Toronto,
London

MANAGEMENT CONTROLS

NEW DIRECTIONS IN BASIC RESEARCH

Edited by **CHARLES P. BONINI**

Assistant Professor
Stanford University

ROBERT K. JAEDICKE

Associate Professor
Stanford University

HARVEY M. WAGNER

Associate Professor
Stanford University

MANAGEMENT CONTROLS: New Directions in Basic Research

06488

THE AUTHORS

Hector R. Anton
University of California
at Berkeley

Kenneth J. Arrow
Stanford University

F. E. Balderston
University of California
at Berkeley

Charles P. Bonini
Stanford University

Stanley I. Buchin
Harvard University

Abraham Charnes
Northwestern University

Neil C. Churchill
Carnegie Institute of
Technology

R. W. Conway
Cornell University

William W. Cooper
Carnegie Institute of
Technology

Sidney Davidson
University of Chicago

Peter F. Drucker
New York University

Myron J. Gordon
University of Rochester

Chadwick J. Haberstroh
University of Denver

Mason Haire
University of California
at Berkeley

Jack Hirshleifer
University of California
at Los Angeles

Austin C. Hoggatt
University of California
at Berkeley

John L. Kennedy
Princeton University

Jacob Marschak
University of California
at Los Angeles

Thomas A. Marschak
University of California
at Berkeley

Philburn Ratoosh
San Francisco State College
and University of California
at Berkeley

Stanley Reiter
Purdue University

Edward B. Roberts
Massachusetts Institute
of Technology

Trevor Sainsbury
Carnegie Institute of
Technology

Gordon Shillinglaw
Columbia University

Martin Shubik
Yale University

Clay Sprowls
University of California
  at Los Angeles

Andrew C. Stedry
Massachusetts Institute of
  Technology

Arnold S. Tannenbaum
University of Michigan

Gerald L. Thompson
Carnegie Institute of Technology

Harvey M. Wagner
Stanford University

FOREWORD

The concept of a seminar to discuss current research findings in the field of management control was originated and developed by Professors Charles Bonini, Robert Jaedicke, and Harvey Wagner of the Stanford Graduate School of Business faculty. Its implementation was facilitated by encouragement and support from the Ford Foundation.

As an integral part of the university, the graduate business school has, in addition to its responsibility for teaching, an obligation to advance the practice of management through research. Although some 15 billion dollars was spent by our government last year on research and development in technology and science, an almost negligible figure in comparison was allocated to research in social sciences, and a very minor portion of this was directed toward the creation of new knowledge in the field of management. Certainly rapid and pervasive change, augmented by new technology, has demanded of management new knowledge and a degree of intellectual skill exceeding anything regarded as adequate heretofore. The business school is the logical and appropriate place to focus on this problem. It should be ahead of trends, not behind them — it should be the institution to which businessmen look for leadership in the development of the new concepts, new tools, and new skills needed for the management task in the years ahead.

The business schools cannot leave research in the behavioral sciences, economics, mathematics and modern quantitative methods to the other disciplines without expecting a lack of relevance to business problems that will limit its value to the managerial field and postpone its usefulness. Collaborative effort between business and the other disciplines is developing significantly, a fact illustrated by this seminar.

Research directed to the application of new knowledge and techniques to business problems will undoubtedly be of the most immediate usefulness to the administrator, and the business school has an important role to fill in bridging this gap between theory and practice. But some research may not be immediately useful; it may be some time before anything of practical value will emerge. However, when engaged in basic research, we must have faith that new understanding will be useful and that new ideas without immediate usefulness may turn out to have profound effect on future events. Radioactivity was known 40 years before the new science of nuclear physics to which it led.

So we must create conditions and an atmosphere which will nurture the new ideas which will come to fruition tomorrow. Otherwise we may stultify creative effort and foster mediocrity. But we must also communicate, interpret, and sometimes even translate our research in terms of its useful application today whenever it is possible to do so.

The seminar which generated the papers contained in this volume provided an opportunity for scholars doing original, creative work in the field of management controls to present and discuss their findings and, in turn, be stimulated by the ideas of their colleagues. It is hoped that this book will extend this process to a wider and larger audience and thereby accelerate the development of new knowledge and techniques in this significant field of management.

Ernest C. Arbuckle
Graduate School of Business
Stanford University

INTRODUCTORY COMMENTS

Introduction

In the formative days of modern business enterprise, management control presented little problem. Typically, the entrepreneur initiated his own plans, directly supervised his employees to execute those plans, and made modifications when necessary. The goals of the firm were identically the goals of the proprietor. The recorded information needed by the top executive to run the business was minimal.

With the steady growth toward gargantuan organizations, control has become imperative for effective management of such enterprises. Planning, as one facet of control, involves coordinating the efforts of a multitude of individuals in the organization. Execution of these plans must be performed through a hierarchy of managers, supervisors, foremen, and workers. Accurate and timely information is needed to ascertain whether plans are being followed and when they should be modified. The environment for today's firm is not only complex but also subject to rapid change. All these factors amplify the need for methods to control and regulate the business organization.

Exactly what is meant by "management control" in the business firm? Generally it is the process of ensuring that what *ought* to be done *is* done and of detecting when it *is not* done. Because "ought" implies a system of values, control is intimately bound up with the process of determining values for members of the organization. Consequently control has an ultimate connection with recruitment, promotion, training, and also, more generally, the mores of society. Control requires planning, that is, ascertaining the firm's concrete objectives, and, as an illustration, consideration of the research and development activity. Control also covers the operation and execution of the plans. Here coordination and efficiency are paramount (that is, achieving a goal in the best manner as measured by a criterion such as profit, cost, or time lapse). Thus, control is a very broad and pervasive part of a business enterprise. We believe it is *the* major organizational problem faced by large business firms today, equal in importance to the problem of governmental encroachment on private enterprise.

In response to the burgeoning demands for improved decision-making approaches, the *art* of business management has advanced. There is no dearth of elaborate management control systems that are presumably effective. By trial and much error, business organizations have developed procedures that enable the firm to achieve certain goals with partial efficiency and to modify its procedures (and goals) in response to severe environmental changes. There is little doubt that vast improvements are possible. Surely what is required is a fundamental understanding of the "why" and "how" of these systems, and such is just commencing on a serious basis.

The studies undertaken to improve the knowledge of control processes emanate from diverse fields. Accountants have sustained an interest in management control utilizing formal procedures; financial data early became a central means of evaluating performance for the whole firm vis-à-vis outside parties (creditors and stockholders). These same financial measurements are now applied by firm management for internal control. Economists, too, have also examined price theory as a means of internal control of firms. Psychologists have focused on the behavior of individuals in organizational settings. Sociologists and political scientists from their own point of view have studied central aspects of control (for example, power) in organizations. Management scientists have applied mathematical and statistical techniques as aids to the process of control. Computer specialists and systems engineers have adapted information technology to the firm's control needs.

Thus, research on management control is advancing among many disciplines, and surprisingly often with negligible cross-fertilization. Furthermore, the amount of initial progress in these diverse fields in recent years has been so rapid that it has been difficult for most scholars to keep abreast, even within their own area of expertise.

With this in mind, the Graduate School of Business of Stanford University sponsored its Seminar on Basic Research in Management Control in February of 1963. The intention was to bring together over 40 eminent scholars presently engaged in research having a direct bearing on management control. These men represent a variety of disciplines and are on the faculties of many universities throughout the United States. By enabling them to discuss their work with each other on a direct and concentrated basis, we anticipated that these researchers as well as the body of accumulated knowledge would gain significantly in the process.

Sixteen formal papers were presented during the 3-day seminar, each representing a current research effort. In addition, several of the participants were invited to add written discussions of specific papers after the conference. These papers and the related discussion comments constitute this volume.[1] We believe this publication will provide the same high degree of stimulation to other researchers as did the contents to those who participated at the conference.

Two points must be stressed about the papers in this volume. First, their scope and results almost entirely should be classified as *basic* research. Most of the work reported is not concerned with immediate applications of techniques or theories to actually operating business firms. Current practice receives relatively little attention.

Secondly, the research is current. The authors themselves are engaged in expanding the frontiers of knowledge on the problems of management control. The papers were written explicitly for the seminar, and most of the material was not generally available before presentation at the Stanford Graduate School of Business Seminar.

In the following paragraphs, we briefly describe the contents of the chapters of the book. Our aim here is to emphasize the coherence, unity, and central themes that exist in this collection of papers.

---

[1] The paper, "The Use of Administered Price Systems to Control Large Organizations," (Part I) by Myron J. Gordon was not presented at the conference, although Professor Gordon was in attendance. At our request, he consented to include it in this volume because of its importance and direct bearing on the subject of the conference.

PART I   ECONOMIC THEORY AND MANAGEMENT CONTROL

Notions of control in economic systems stemming from the guiding influence of prices as determined by free competition are well established in economics literature. As would be expected, economists have also attempted to adapt these economic theories to resource allocation problems within complex business firms (especially decentralized firms).

The first paper in this section, that by Gordon, discusses extensions of the economic price system to large organizations, in contrast to the use of the more traditional accounting standard cost or administered price systems. The second paper, by Hirshleifer, explores in depth particular aspects of transfer price systems in decentralized business firms. Both of these papers stress the possible values as well as the limitations from such approaches and indicate promising avenues for future research.

The third paper tackles a different albeit related topic. Marschak is concerned specifically with the cost and value of information in organizations. His model formulations aid in analysis and selection of various information channels.

The fourth paper, by Balderston, deals with planning and control by means of linear programming in a business firm comprised of several independent branches.

PART II   SIMULATION AND MANAGEMENT CONTROL

Accompanying the widespread availability of high-speed computers, management scientists have developed simulation of systems as a feasible tool of analysis. The papers in this section are simulation studies of entire business-firm behavior. In such models, the control element becomes a very important factor in three respects. Each of the papers demonstrates primarily one of these aspects.

First, as Bonini demonstrates, individual controls and budgetary procedures are capable of inclusion in a broad-based simulation study. The reactions of individuals and managers to control information have important effects on a firm's economic performance. Thus, behavioral variables, as well as economic and production constraints, can be included in the formulation of a model business system. Bonini describes a model incorporating such procedures, and he discusses the results of his experimentation.

Secondly, overall systems control and stability can be considered in a context similar to that used by systems engineers. The emphasis here is on the study of feedback mechanisms and procedures or "policies" to keep the system under control. This is the approach emphasized by Roberts. He describes several systems which are subject to engineering-type control systems analysis, including an application to research and development activity.

Thirdly, in extending simulation into the realm of management control, it is possible to make use of people (for example, business executives) as the decision makers in a simulated environment. Buchin describes this kind of simulation in his discussion of the Harbets model. While his research is still at an early stage, Buchin suggests some hypotheses to be explored with his experimentation.

These three papers aptly demonstrate how simulation can be used as a powerful research tool.

PART III   THE BUDGETARY PROCESS AND MANAGEMENT CONTROL

The notion of control is often thought of as synonymous with budgets and related financial controls (for example, standard costs and quotas). The first paper in this section deals with these topics but quickly extends the notion in many other directions. Shillinglaw discusses generally the technique of budgetary control, especially as it fits into a divisionalized framework, and presents an excellent summary of enlightened current practice.

Management scientists in the past few years have substantially advanced business decision making in the areas of inventory control, mathematical programming, queuing problems, etc. The question of how to design a control system to monitor in the application of these techniques, especially in the area of inventory management, is raised by Wagner. He examines whether an overall budgetary control is consistent with the operation of scientifically derived inventory policies.

Budgets are often intended by management to be goals toward which subordinates are to strive. Typically there are a multitude of goals (see paper by Haberstroh in the next section) that may receive attention by a subordinate, and he is partially free to decide upon which goals are important and how much effort to expend on each. Charnes and Stedry build mathematical models which focus on this problem.

Finally, the paper by Shubik returns to internal transfer pricing as a means of decentralized contribution evaluation and control — in this instance, from a game theoretic point of view. Shubik argues that the Shapley value solution merits application to these questions.

The strong interrelationship between the papers in this section on the Budgetary Process and those in other sessions is significant.

PART IV   BEHAVIORAL SCIENCE AND MANAGEMENT CONTROL

Laboratory and Field Studies of the Behavioral Effects of Audits,
by Neil C. Churchill, William W. Cooper, and Trevor Sainsbury
Goals, Programs, and the Training Function, by Chadwick J. Haberstroh
Psychological Research on Pay, by Mason Haire

To properly understand control in organizations, it is essential to investigate the psychology of the individual, as it applies to his internal goal-setting procedures, his aspirations, his views of the reward-penalty structure, and his personal feelings. The paper in the previous section by Charnes and Stedry has already introduced this point. Churchill, Cooper, and Sainsbury carry it forward in their report. These authors have conducted laboratory and field studies, analyzing the effects on individual performance of various aspects of auditing and supervising procedures.

Haberstroh turns attention toward the existence and measurement of multiple goals in organizations. He studies the adaption procedures (programs) that these organizations use to ensure achievement of their goals, and classifies control systems in a broad organizational context.

Haire expounds what is generally assumed to be a major motivation in business organization, namely wages or pay. In his pithy paper he reports current research on what he terms the psychodynamics of pay — the interaction of pay with other psychological activities within the person. Haire discusses the possibility of measuring the amounts of pay workers would be willing to substitute for changes in fringe benefits.

PART V   MANAGEMENT CONTROL IN PERSPECTIVE

Controls, Control and Management, by Peter F. Drucker
Control in Organizations: Individual Adjustment and
Organizational Performance, by Arnold S. Tannenbaum
Research in Management Controls: A Critical Synthesis, by Kenneth J. Arrow

The final section of this volume contains three papers and commentaries that view control in organizations and society from a broad perspective. Drucker addresses himself to the proper use of the controls that are being rapidly provided by modern technology. He also characterizes the personnel decisions (hiring and promotion policies) as the most important controls in a business organization.

Tannenbaum looks at control in organizations from a sociologist's point of view, in which control is broadly associated with influence or power. He reports studies in several business organizations (including labor unions) in which the amount of perceived control was measured and related to variables such as productivity.

The culminating paper by Arrow synthesizes the findings of the research reported at the seminar.

Conclusion

As can be seen from the brief descriptions above, the research described in this volume sweeps over a wide range of topics: from philosophical concepts regarding the neutrality of measurement to an awareness of guilt on the part of persons who are led to perceive that they are overpaid; from simulation studies of elaborate business systems to investigations of how individuals behave under the pressure of an imminent audit; from sophisticated mathematical models of goal achievement and information economics to the results of laboratory experiments and field studies; from scientific techniques of game theory, linear programming, and inventory control to modeling economies, business games, and decentralized decision processes. Yet each paper is a contribution to the basic understanding of those factors that are involved in the notion of management control. This wide diversity reflects the fact that the questions requiring study must inevitably lead the enquirers across many disciplines.

It is our belief that this collection represents the first milestone in the current intensive research effort to expand knowledge on management control. It is our intent that the volume will serve as a stimulus to other scholars. And it is our strong conviction that this impetus is merited by the far-reaching significance of the ensuing basic findings.

Charles P. Bonini
Robert K. Jaedicke
Harvey M. Wagner

CONTENTS

MANAGEMENT CONTROLS
NEW DIRECTIONS IN BASIC RESEARCH

1

THE USE OF ADMINISTERED PRICE SYSTEMS TO CONTROL LARGE ORGANIZATIONS[1]

MYRON J. GORDON
University of Rochester

I INTRODUCTION

In the modern large corporation the accounting system is commonly employed to develop periodic reports for subdivisions of the corporation that may be described as pseudo income statements; that is, the reports are analogous in nature and purpose to the income statements prepared for independent firms. Various terms have been adopted to refer to these systems, which employ standard costs, semi-variable overhead budgets, transfer pricing and other techniques to obtain sub-organization income statements. They will be referred to here as administered price systems and the reason for the title will become evident shortly.

The subject of this paper is the design and use of an administered price system for the control of economic activity in a corporation. In the next section we will examine the salient characteristics of the two classical control systems; viz, a market price system and a bureaucratic system, and then outline how a firm may seek the best of both worlds through an administered price system.

Standard costs are probably the most powerful and flexible technique now employed to achieve the objectives of an administered price system, and Section III will review current practice in the design and use of a standard cost system to direct, motivate and evaluate the performance of subordinate levels of management in a decentralized corporation. Such systems are still far from perfect, and their limitations as well as the manner in which they serve their objectives will be examined. Although this material is only a review of existing knowledge, it is likely to be of independent interest. The reason is that non-accountants seem to know very little on the subject, possibly because of the way accountants have dealt with it in their literature.

Section IV will be devoted to modifications in the design of a standard cost system that are intended to make it more effective in measuring purchasing, manufacturing and sales performance. The objective is an income statement for the manager of each of these functions

[1] The research for this paper was made possible by a faculty research grant to the author by the Ford Foundation.

such that maximizing the income reported in his statement will maximize the company's income. The proposals advanced will not realize this ideal, but they do deal with inadequacies found in existing systems that are fairly general in importance. Apart from their intrinsic merit, these proposals may be of interest as illustrations of a fruitful direction for research on decentralized control systems.

Transfer prices represent another class of administratively created prices. They are employed in non-market transactions to secure the behavior that may be realized with market determined prices. Section V will review the literature on transfer prices and examine some of the problems in realizing the objectives they are designed to serve.

II BACKGROUND

Market Control

Economists have long been fascinated with the operation of a free competitive market price system as an instrument for the control of economic activity. Each individual pursues his own self interest free of any regulation or formal direction beyond the minimal functions of the state. Nonetheless, as Adam Smith wrote, "He is led by an invisible hand to promote an end which was not part of his intention. Every individual necessarily labors to make the annual revenue of society as great as he can..." [28, p. 423].

In seeking the most profitable employment of his resources, each individual, in particular each entrepreneur, employs the factors of production, adopts the technology, and produces the products that provide society (the organization) with the most efficient allocation and utilization of his resources. If a different allocation of the resources becomes desirable, factor and product prices change so as to move marginal resources out of the production of goods in excess supply and into the more desired products. Innovation in technology as well as the optimal utilization of the existing technology are secured by the operation of this system in which no formal controls or instructions are employed. Further, by a marvelous calculus the rewards of each individual including the entrepreneurs are made exactly equal to his contribution to society. In this ideal system the accumulation of capital is independent of its administration by entrepreneurs, and the same process that directs and motivates each entrepreneur to employ his resources most efficiently also selects for the task of management those who are most qualified.

The necessary conditions for a market price system to in fact perform in this optimal manner are quite formidable. They are: (1) a large number of buyers and sellers in each market; (2) each buyer and seller possesses complete information; and (3) the activities of each firm are subject to the law of diminishing returns. Although these conditions are only partially realized, the system is not thereby made non-workable. Increased demand for a product raises its price and increases its supply. An improvement in the method of producing a product lowers its price and increases the utilization of the superior method. Competition maintains or reestablishes a reasonable relation between the reward of an individual or firm and his productive contribution. Finally, the distribution of profits and of credit gives the control of capital to efficient producers and denies it to inefficient ones.[2]

Bureaucratic Control

However, uncertainty as to the future and the economies of scale lead inevitably to the growth in the size of firms. The public policy problems created by this development will not concern us here.[3] Within the firm, however, the owner-manager finds that he no longer has the information and time to make and carry out all the decisions involved in the administration of his company. He is forced by the growth in the size of the company to create a hierarchy of sub-organizations and delegate limited authority to each department manager. The company ceases to be an extension of the individual entrepreneur and becomes instead a bureaucracy.

Blau and Scott have done an effective job of summarizing Weber's description of bureaucracy. The following is taken from their summary [6, pp. 32-3]:

(1) Organization tasks are distributed among the various positions as official duties.

(2) The positions or offices are organized into a hierarchial authority structure...wherein each official is responsible for his subordinate's decisions and actions as well as his own to the superior above him in the pyramid and wherein each official has authority over the officials under him. The scope of authority of superiors over subordinates is clearly circumscribed.

(3) A formally established system of rules and regulations governs official decisions and actions. In principle, the operations in such administrative organizations involve the application of these general regulations to particular cases. The regulations insure the uniformity of operations and, together with the authority structure, make possible the coordination of the various activities.

---

[2] For more on the functioning of a competitive system see Robbins [24], Hicks [11], Scitovsky [25], and Little [18].

[3] They are examined in Stocking and Watkins [29], Wilcox [33], and Bain [4].

(4) Officials are expected to assume an impersonal orientation in their contacts with clients and other officials.

(5) Employment by the organization constitutes a career for officials...Officials are appointed to positions...and thus are dependent on superiors in the organization...After a trial period officials gain tenure of position and are protected against arbitrary dismissal. Remuneration is in the form of a salary...

Notice that as a bureaucracy is here defined, an organization's objective or expectations with respect to a department manager's decisions and actions are that they be in accordance with the rules laid down for his office. If these rules are extremely detailed, they completely prescribe his decisions and action. Compliance allows him no discretion, and control procedures involve confirming his compliance with the rules governing his office. It is well known that this method of operation proves to be arbitrary and inefficient if the organization is seeking to maximize the realization of some objective in the face of a changing environment.

The alternative is to make the rules and regulations less detailed. In the case of a business enterprise the department manager is instructed to select the decisions and actions allowed him by the rules that maximize the company's profit. Formally, the position of the department manager then differs from that of a company owner only in degree. The laws or rules he is subject to in managing his pseudo company only reflect a more highly regulated economic environment than that under which the owner operates.

However, the positions of the owner and the manager differ in a very important respect. The owner needs no instruction to maximize his company's profit since his own self-interest dictates that decision criterion. By contrast, the mere instruction to a manager to use this decision criterion does not guarantee he will do so. First, he may not know what decisions and actions open to him in administering his department maximize company profit. To illustrate this difficulty, consider the problem of an entrepreneur who has accepted the goal of administering his firm to maximize the welfare of society. Second, the department manager has goals such as professional excellence, leisure, and the approval of his peers that may conflict with the maximization of company profit. In order to deal with both of the above problems, a manager's superior may establish performance variables such as idle time, scrap losses, accidents, and employee turnover, and then instruct the manager to maximize the values of these variables subject to the rules and regulations governing his office. Insofar as these goals conflict with company profit, he is of course likely to subordinate the latter. Finally, the objective of a manager is in the last analysis his own welfare. His superior specifies more or less clearly rules and goals, provides information on rule conformity and goal realization, and dispenses on some basis penalties and rewards for rule and goal performance. The manager constructs a welfare function with the organization's rules, goals, and rewards as part of the data. His decisions and actions to maximize his welfare also reflect his values and the data of his informal relations in the organization.[4]

Control by Administered Prices

Standard costs and the other techniques of administered price systems may be employed to make effective the instruction to a manager that he manage his department with the objective of maximizing company profit. The accounting system is employed to create a pseudo income statement for each department head. The measurement rules under which his inputs and outputs are identified and priced are established with the following considerations in mind. First, they should reflect the authority that has been delegated to the manager. In other words, he should only be charged with costs over which he has control or administrative responsibility. His allowed costs or revenue in turn should be derived from his output and the costs considered necessary to obtain the output. Second, the pseudo income statement should be so constructed that decisions by a department manager which maximize his profit maximize company profit.

An administered price system that meets the above conditions provides a remarkably effective control system. First, each suborganization head has a clear instruction as to the criterion he should use in choosing among alternative courses of action. Second, both he and his superior are periodically informed on the level of his performance. The superior, in consequence, has the informational basis for distributing rewards among subordinates on the basis of their performance. The subordinate in turn is motivated to maximize his profit both directly via the score card effect and indirectly via the rewards the superior provides. A third control feature of this system is that as long as the subordinate's income is satisfactory, the superior need not concern himself with the administration of the department.[5]

[4] A considerable literature has developed on how people behave in organizations. For an introduction to it see Blau and Scott [6], March and Simon [19], Likert [17], Argyris [1] and McGregor [21].

[5] A number of articles in Thomas [31] present the practitioner's viewpoint on the control use of an accounting system.

III THE CONTROL USE OF STANDARD COSTS

Standard costs are the foundation on which administered price systems are built in American corporations. Our purpose in this section is to illustrate the design and use of such systems and to critically evaluate the effectiveness of the pseudo income statements they provide for the control of large decentralized corporations.

Definitions and Account Structure

Exhibit 1-1 presents the relevant accounts and transactions of a firm that employs a standard cost system. To avoid excessive detail and to focus attention on the system's features that are of interest, a number of simplifying assumptions have been made. In particular, the company is decentralized only to the extent of the three major functions: purchasing, manufacturing, and sales. The system could be elaborated to allow horizontal and vertical decentralization within each of these functions. Also in the interest of simplicity, no distinction is drawn between labor and material as factors of production, and the so-called indirect or overhead costs are for the present ignored.

The notation employed in Exhibit 1-1 is explained below:

x_i = quantity of the i *th* factor of production

a_i = actual cost per unit of the i *th* factor of production

$\bar{a}_i$ = standard cost per unit of the i *th* factor of production

$\bar{b}_{ij}$ = standard usage of the i *th* factor per unit of the j *th* product

y_j = quantity of the j *ih* product

$\bar{c}_j$ = standard cost per unit of the j *th* product

p_j = actual sales price per unit of the j *th* product

The subscripts i and j run from 1 to n and 1 to m with n and m large, being determined by the nature of the firm's operations. It is a multi-factor multi-product firm.

The actual cost per unit of the i *th* factor, a_i, is the amount actually paid for it. The standard cost, $\bar{a}_i$, is arbitrarily established, e.g., the actual cost prior to the start of the year, and it remains unchanged over a large number of accounting periods regardless of the course of a_i. The accounting period is a week or month. The standard usage of the i *th* factor per unit of the j *th* product, $\bar{b}_{ij}$, is the best estimate of what the usage should be under the most economical method of production. The estimate is made before the start of the year. The standard cost per unit of the j *th* product is

$$\bar{c}_j = \sum \bar{a}_i \bar{b}_{ij}.$$

Exhibit 1-1. Account structure and transactions under
a standard cost system.

	Money				Raw Material		
(SB)	$\sum_{(B)} m$	$\sum_{i(1)} x_i a_i$	(1)	(SB)	$\sum_{i(B)} x_i \bar{a}_i$	$\sum_{i(2)} x_i \bar{a}_i$	(2)
	$\sum_{j(6)} y_j p_j$	$\sum_{(B)} m$	(EB)	(1)	$\sum_{i(1)} x_i \bar{a}_i$	$\sum_{i(B)} x_i \bar{a}_i$	(EB)
(SB)	$\sum_{(B)} m$			(SB)	$\sum_{i(B)} x_i \bar{a}_i$		

	Materials in Process				Finished Goods		
(2)	$\sum_{i(2)} x_i \bar{a}_i$	$\sum_{j(3)} y_j \bar{c}_j$	(3)	(SB)	$\sum_{j(B)} y_j \bar{c}_j$	$\sum_{j(5)} y_j \bar{c}_j$	(5)
		$\sum_{i(2)} x_i \bar{a}_i - \sum_{j(3)} y_j \bar{c}_j$	(4)	(3)	$\sum_{j(3)} y_j \bar{c}_j$	$\sum_{j(B)} y_j \bar{c}_j$	EB
				(SB)	$\sum_{j(B)} y_j \bar{c}_j$		

Equity

	Factor price variance		Sum of all debit balances	(SB)
(1)	$\sum_{i(1)} x_i (a_i - \bar{a}_i)$			

	Factor usage variance		Sales revenue	
(4)	$\sum_{i(2)} x_i \bar{a}_i - \sum_{j(3)} y_j \bar{c}_j$		$\sum_{j(6)} y_j p_j$	(6)

	Cost of goods sold	
(5)	$\sum_{j(5)} y_j \bar{c}_j$	

Number	Description
(1)	Factors purchased during period
(2)	Factors put in production during period
(3)	Output produced during period
(4)	Excess of actual over standard usage during period
(5)	Products sold during period
(6)	Products sold during period

Notice that both the standard usage rates and the standard factor costs are used to arrive at $\bar{c}_j$.

The entries on the left side of each account with the exception of the equity account represent debits or inputs to the indicated asset. The entries on the right side are credits or outputs. A transaction is a collection of two or more inputs and outputs and their algebraic sum is always zero. The symbol in parentheses to the left of each input and the right of each output identifies the transaction of which it is a part. The terms SB and EB refer to balance in the account at the start of the period and the end of the period respectively. The EB at the end of each period is equal to the SB of the subsequent period.

The equity account is introduced to keep the system in balance. At the start of the period, it is equal to the sum of the balances in the asset accounts. Transactions which result in a net increase in assets, i.e., a gain to the system are balanced by a credit to the equity account, while a net credit to the assets or loss to the system is offset by a debit to or reduction in the equity.

Transactions

Exhibit 1-1 presents the transactions of a firm during one accounting period. The transaction code number in each case identifies the summation that is to be carried out. For instance, in Transaction (2) the summation is over all factors of production put into production during the period. Similarly, the SB of the Raw Material Account is the summation over all factors on hand at the start of the period.[6] The starting balance in the money account is simply the amount on hand. Transaction (1) reduces cash by the actual cost of the factors purchased and increases raw material by their standard cost. The excess of the actual over the standard cost of purchases is a system loss, and the amount, called the Factor Price Variance, is a debit (reduces) the equity account.

Transaction (2) credits raw material and debits material in process with the standard cost of the factors put into production. The SB of the raw material account is the weighted sum of all factors at the start of the period with the standard cost of each its weight. The result of transactions (1) and (2) is that the EB of the account is the sum of all factors at the end of the period similarly weighted.

Transaction (3) transfers the production of the period, valued at the standard unit cost of each product from material in process to finished goods. Another assumption made in the interest of simplicity is that the material in process has a zero balance at the start and end of the period. Therefore the difference between the account's input and output is a weighted sum of the excess (positive or negative) of

---

[6] The identification of the items in a class over which the summation is to be carried out appears below the summation symbol as well as alongside the entry.

the actual over the standard usage of factors for the period's output. This is clearly demonstrated by considering just one product. The x_i, $i = 1...n$, consumed in producing the j *th* product are aggregated with $\bar{a}_i$ the weights. The actual output of the j *th* product y_j is credited at $\bar{c}_j$, and $\bar{c}_j$ is obtained by aggregating the $\bar{b}_{ij}$, $i = 1...n$, with $\bar{a}_i$ again the weights. Therefore, if the actual consumption of each factor per unit of the j *th* product is $\bar{b}_{ij}$, $i = 1...n$, we have

$$\sum_i \bar{a}_i x_i = \sum_i \bar{a}_i \bar{b}_{ij} y_j = y_j \bar{c}_j$$

The extension to two or more products is obvious.

Transaction (4) carries the excess of the actual factor usage over the standard usage for the period's output from the Materials in Process Account to the Factor Usage Variance Account. The remaining transactions, (5) and (6), transfer out of the system the standard cost of the goods sold and transfer in the actual revenue on the sales.

For the company, the period's income at standard is the sales revenue less the balance in the cost of goods sold account. The net income at actual under this standard cost system is the income at standard less the two variances—the excess of the actual over the standard cost of factors purchased and the excess of the actual over the standard usage of the factors employed in production during the period. When the factors purchased, the factor content of production, and the factor content of sales are all equal, the income is sales revenue less the actual usage at actual current cost of the factors employed to generate the revenue.[7]

Purchasing Department

Let us now consider the system's effectiveness for realizing decentralized control over the three sub-divisions of the company—purchasing, manufacturing, and sales. The task of the purchasing department is to satisfy the company's material requirements at the lowest possible prices for the factors of production. The price variance account contains the amount by which the actual cost of the purchases during a period exceeded their standard cost. The standard costs reflect the prices prevailing at the start of the year, while the actual costs reflect current market prices. Since a purchasing department typically has little or no influence on the movement of factor prices over time, the resultant variance does not provide a satisfactory measure of the department's performance. Furthermore, minimizing the (unfavorable) value of the Factor Price Variance is not an operational instruction to the manager. When actual prices are above standard, he minimizes his variance by not making any purchases.

---

[7] Actual practice in the design and use of standard cost systems varies among firms. For more detail on this and related questions see Shillinglaw [26], Henrici [10], Bennett [5], and the National Association of Accountants [23].

The Factor Price Variance is nonetheless a useful piece of information for top management. It is an objective and desirably weighted
average of the difference between the prices actually being paid for
factors of production and the prices used in formulating company
plans at the start of the year.[8] Changes in the variance call to management's attention the need for reconsidering prices and indicate the
magnitude of the problem.

Before proceeding it should be emphasized that the purchasing department does not make a production decision, i.e., it does not determine the level of its activity. Given an independently determined level
of activity, the department's task is to procure the material required
at the lowest possible cost. The requirements for the system to be an
effective control instrument are: (1) the costs incurred by the company that are charged to the purchasing manager should vary with the
manager's decisions, and (2) the manager's standards or allowed
costs should reflect what the costs are expected to be given the independently determined production decisions and other relevant variables. It is evident then that the system is not a very effective instrument for providing control information on the operation of the purchasing department.

Manufacturing Department

The task of the manufacturing department is to produce the products required by the company's sales by the most efficient utilization
of materials possible. It also does not make an output decision. The
Factor Usage Variance provides a measure of the department's performance. Recall that the $\bar{b}$ represent the standard consumption of
each factor for each product on the basis of the technology and the
factor prices prevailing at the start of the year. Further, recall that
the department is charged with its actual material usage at the standard prices $\bar{a}$, and it is credited with the actual output at prices $\bar{c}$
which reflect these $\bar{a}$ and $\bar{b}$. Hence, the variance is the excess of
actual over optimal usage on the assumption that the $\bar{b}$ represent the
optimal technology.

The control usefulness of a standard cost system lies for the most
part in the information contained in this variance. If the manager dis-
covers and introduces a more efficient method of production than that
reflected in the $\bar{b}$ given the $\bar{a}$, favorable variances will result and he
can be rewarded. Conversely, if poor management on his part or
events beyond his control give rise to unfavorable variances, this

---

[8] If purchases equal the material content of the sales, the variance is a
price index with the quantity weights reflecting the relative importance of
each factor of production. If purchases differ from sales, the weights depart
from the desired values.

departure from expectations is immediately called to his superior's attention through the routine operation of the system.

However, the system is still far from perfect as an instrument for directing, motivating, and evaluating the performance of the manufacturing manager. For instance, the manager never finds it profitable to change the relative use of the various factors of production in response to changes in factor prices. Assume that at the start of some period, the a_j differ from the $\bar{a}_j$ so that it is more economical for the company to produce y_j of the j th product using different factor proportions than the b_{ij} established at the start of the year. The department manager is still being charged with the x_j at the same prices $\bar{a}_j$, and he is being paid at the same prices $\bar{c}_j$; hence, he would impair his performance by changing the method of production he employed.

Sales Department

The task of the sales department is to establish prices and achieve a sales volume for the company's products that maximize the company's profit. A possible measure of the department's performance is obtained by ignoring the variances and taking the amount by which the actual sales revenue during a period exceeds the standard cost of the goods sold. Ignoring the usage variance seems reasonable on the grounds that sales is not responsible for the performance of the manufacturing department, but ignoring the factor price variance is open to question. Sales has no control over factor prices, but it can be argued that the prices it obtains for its products should reflect current factor costs, and its profit should be measured on the basis of current factor costs. This would support raising the standard cost of goods sold by the factor price variance. However, the standard cost of goods sold plus the factor price variance on purchases is only an approximation of the current cost of goods sold. The two may differ insofar as the factors purchased during a period differ from the factor content of the products sold.

Sales revenue less the cost of goods sold measured on the basis of standard usage and current prices of the factors required for the sales is a measure of the sales department's profit. It should be noted, however, that unlike the other departments, a zero profit here is not satisfactory performance. When a sales organization is judged on the basis of profit, a budgeted profit figure not incorporated in the accounts is used, but the criteria for establishing the optimal price, output and profit in arriving at the budget have not been well-defined.

To summarize, the sales department performances report stands up well under the criterion that given the authority of the department head, decisions to maximize department profit maximize company profit. Product revenue and costs charged to the department are defined so that they respond to the manager's decisions in the same manner as the company's actual product revenue and costs. The design of the performance report is motivated largely by this objective. The limitation of the system is that standard output, effort, and profit information are not generated for comparison with actual results. This limitation is due in large measure to the fact that the sales department differs from the other two in that it makes an output decision. This is evident if the sales department sets product prices, but it is no less true if top management sets product prices and the department makes sales effort decisions—number of salesmen, advertising, technical services etc. The standard sales or output response to these price and input decisions are difficult to evaluate.

Bookkeeping Economy

Before proceeding it is worth noting that the widespread use of standard cost systems has been due as much if not more to the bookkeeping economies they have allowed as their control advantages. With the combination of manual and tabulating equipment methods of data processing in use prior to the last war, standard cost systems were far more economical than actual cost systems. This is made evident by noting that a firm with a standard cost system would require few more accounts than those appearing in Exhibit 1-1 in order to obtain from the accounts the balance of each major category of inventory and the cost of goods sold. Under an actual cost system the firm would require a separate account for each factor of production, for each production order, and for each product.[9]

An argument advanced in favor of actual cost systems is that they provide the actual cost of each production order. It should be noted that Exhibit 1-1 does not provide the actual cost of the i *th* factor in producing the j *th* product. Neither does it provide $c_j y_j$, the actual cost of the actual output of the j *th* product. An actual cost system provides this information, but the information is of value to management only if the costs on each production order are developed at a level of detail, accuracy, and structure that is rarely if ever achieved.[10]

IV REFINEMENTS IN THE SYSTEM

This section is devoted to developing refinements in the system just presented that are designed to make it a more effective instru-

---

[9] For the detail required by an actual job cost system see Shillinglaw [26, pp. 112-170].

[10] See Hill and Gordon [12, pp. 395-412].

ment for directing, motivating, and evaluating the performance of each of the three department managers. The resultant system requires some increase in data processing, and a company is unlikely to find the changes profitable unless it uses a modern computer for its data processing.

Purchasing Performance

As a basis for arriving at a set of measurement rules that are considered useful for evaluating the performance of a purchasing manager, the following propositions are assumed to be true.

1. The primary function of the purchasing department is to provide the materials needed to meet the firm's production requirements.
2. The department is expected to accomplish (1) at the lowest possible cost.
3. To satisfy (1) it is necessary or at least economical to carry material stocks at all times. Further, given a forecast of the firm's operations for the year, it is possible to establish a *normal* level of raw material inventory, a level that would prevail under normal conditions.
4. In each period it is possible to establish independently of the prices that the firms actually pay for purchases, the current price of each factor of production.

Through bargaining, volume purchases, buying in primary markets, and other means, a purchasing department will be more or less successful during a period in buying at prices below the prices generally prevailing in the period. Beyond this, the department may influence the cost of the material it purchases by speculating. Speculation, however, is different for a firm with a non-speculative interest in a commodity than it is for other persons. For the person that ordinarily has no reason for owning a commodity, a positive or negative position in the commodity is speculating on the change in its price. In contrast, a firm that buys a commodity for the profit on selling it in fabricated form ordinarily has some position in the commodity. Speculation in a commodity by such a firm may be defined as a position in the commodity above or below the inventory level considered normal.[11]

The implication of the above observation is that during a period when the purchasing department does not wish to speculate on a change in material prices, it buys in the quantities needed to main-

---

[11] With respect to the inventory equal to its normal position, the firm is speculating on what the price will be on that date in the far distant future when the firm will be liquidated.

tain or reestablish a normal inventory. The department speculates on a rise in price by establishing or maintaining an inventory in excess of the normal level, and the opposite if it speculates that price will fall.

Exhibit 1-2 illustrates a set of procedures for measuring the performance of a purchasing department ... eting requirements at prices that compare favorably wi... current market and in speculating successfully in so far as it does speculate.

Exhibit 1-2. System design to provide information
on purchasing performance.

Money	
$\sum_{i(1)} x_i a_i$	(1)

	Raw material		
(SB)	$\sum_{i(B)} x_i \bar{a}_i$	$\sum_{i(2)} x_i \bar{a}_i$	(2)
(1)	$\sum_{i(1)} x_i \bar{a}_i$	$\sum_{i(B)} x_i \bar{a}_i$	(EB)
(SB)	$\sum_{i(B)} x_i \bar{a}_i$		

Material in process	
(2)	$\sum_{i(2)} x_i a'_i$

Factor price variance	
(1) $\sum_{i(1)} x_i (a_i - \bar{a}_i)$	$\sum_{i(2)} x_i (a'_i - \bar{a}_i)$ (2)

Transaction code

Number	Description
(1)	Factors purchased during period.
(2)	Factors put in production during period.

The only new symbol appearing there is a'_i, the current cost of material during the period. Material purchases are handled exactly as in Exhibit 1-1, and material issues are credited to the Raw Material Account as before at standard cost. However, material issues are now charged to material in process at their current cost—established in each period independently of the actual cost of purchases. The excess of the current over the standard cost of purchases is credited to the Factor Price Variance Account.

Assume that initially the inventory is at its normal level. If the purchases and issues during the first period are equal, the balance

in the FPV account will be the difference between the actual and current cost of purchases. If the inventory is maintained at normal over
the year and actual cost is equal to current cost in each period, the
account will have a zero balance at the end of the year. If purchases
are below issues one period and the inventory is restored to normal
in a later period, the account will have a credit balance equal to the
excess of current cost in the earlier period over the actual cost in
the later period, assuming that prices fell between the two periods.
In general, at the close of a period when the inventory is at normal,
the FPV account will have a credit balance equal to the amount by
which actual cost of purchases was below current cost for the year
to date due to good purchasing and good speculation.[12]

In implementing the above procedures, it might be found that the
best source of current cost data is a published cost figure and that
for the reasons cited earlier, actual cost is usually lower than current cost. In this event it may be considered appropriate to charge
the purchasing department with the cost of operating the department
—including storage and interest on the inventory.

The only burden involved in obtaining the information described
above is that connected with establishing the current cost of each
factor of production monthly instead of annually. This should not be
difficult if published prices are available and the inventory records
are kept on a computer.

Manufacturing and Sales Performance

Let us now turn to the manufacturing and sales departments. The
procedures proposed below are designed to (1) make the manufacturing manager sensitive to changes in relative factor prices in making
his production decisions, (2) make the sales manager sensitive to
changes in factor prices in making his sales decisions, and (3) control the level of finished goods inventory.

Exhibit 1-3 presents the relevant accounts and transactions. Notice that as in Exhibit 1-2 the material put in production is charged
to the material in process account at the current cost of the factors
issued. The account is credited with the output of the j th product,
$j = 1, 2 \ldots m$ during the period valued at

$$\bar{c}'_j = \sum_i \bar{b}_{ij} a'_i$$

In other words $\bar{c}'_j$ represents the cost per unit of product valued at
the standard usage rates and the current factor prices. It may be

---

[12] If the raw material account balance is not at normal at the close of a
period the performance of the purchasing department to date may be established by hypothesizing the transaction (purchase or issue) needed to bring
the account to normal.

Exhibit 1-3. System design to provide improved information
on manufacturing and sales performance.

Materials in process			Finished goods		
(2) $\sum\limits_{i(2)} x_i a'_i$	$\sum\limits_{j(3)} y_j \bar{c}'_j$	(3)	(SB) $\sum\limits_{j(B)} y_j \bar{c}_j$	$\sum\limits_{j} y_j \bar{c}_j$ (5)	
	$\sum\limits_{i(2)} x_i a'_i - \sum\limits_{j(3)} y_j \bar{c}'_j$ (4)		(3) $\sum\limits_{j(3)} y_j \bar{c}_j$		

Factor usage variance		Cost of goods sold	
(4) $\sum\limits_{i(2)} x_i a'_i - \sum\limits_{j(3)} y_j \bar{c}'_j$		(5) $\sum\limits_{j(5)} y_j \bar{c}'_j$	

Product cost variance		
(3) $\sum\limits_{j(3)} y_j (\bar{c}'_j - \bar{c}_j)$	$\sum\limits_{j(5)} y_j (\bar{c}'_j - \bar{c}_j)$	(5)

Transaction code

Number	Description
(2)	Factors put in production during period.
(3)	Output transferred to finished goods during period.
(4)	Excess of actual over standard usage during period.
(5)	Products sold during period.

called the *standard current cost* per unit of output. The factor usage variance is now

$$\sum_i x_i a'_i \; - \; \sum_j y_j \sum_i \bar{b}_{ij} a'_i$$

The manner in which this variance responds to changes in the method of production will now be examined.

Factor Proportions

Regardless of the extent to which factor prices have changed absolutely or relatively, the department will have no variance if it produces at standard under the original method of production. If the standard quantity of each factor is consumed in producing a unit of the j *th* product, the actual cost is $\sum\limits_i \bar{b}_{ij} a'_i$. Since the allowed cost on a unit of the j th product is $\bar{c}'_j = \sum\limits_i \bar{b}_{ij} a'_i$, the actual and allowed cost will be equal if the actual usage is equal to the standard. In other words if all factors employed in producing the j *th* product are consumed at the standard rates, the actual consumption is

$$\sum_i x_i a'_i = \sum_i y_j \bar{b}_{ij} a'_i = y_j c'_j$$

and there is no variance.

It is possible, however, that with a′ the factor prices, there is a more efficient method of producing the j *th* product than the one using b_{ij}, i = 1...n. Let b'_{ij} be the optimal usage of the i *th* factor in making the j *th* product when the factor prices are a′. A production method b'_{ij}, 1 = 1...n is more efficient when factor prices are a′ and it is less efficient than $\bar{b}_{ij}$, i = 1...n, when $\bar{a}$ are the factor prices under the following conditions.

$$\sum_i b'_{ij} a' < \sum_i \bar{b}_{ij} a'$$

and $$\sum_i b'_{1j} \bar{a}_i > \sum_i \bar{b}_{ij} \bar{a}_1$$

Therefore, if the manager adopts the b′ method of production and his actual usage is b'_{ij}, 1 = 1...n and j = 1...m, his cost will be

$$\sum_i x_i a'_i = \sum_j y_j \sum_i b'_{ij} a'_i < \sum_j y_j \sum_i \bar{b}_{ij} a'_i = \sum_j y_j \bar{c}'_j$$

He will have a favorable variance.

It may be argued that the usage standard in each period should be b′. With b the standard the manager is penalized for failing to adopt the most economical production method only insofar as he forgoes the favorable variance from doing so. There are two reasons for keeping b as the usage standards. One is that the information and computation requirements for changing usage standards periodically are likely to be prohibitive. On the information requirements, the staff department that sets these standards is unlikely to have all the information about production methods that the manufacturing department has. The reason is that the staff communicates its knowledge of production methods to the production manager, but the reverse need not be true. The second reason for not using the b′ is, changing the method of production involves a cost, and perfect accuracy and fairness in standards would require that the standard allow a change in the method of production cost.

Product Cost Variance

Looking back at Exhibit 1-3 we see that while the period's output is credited to material in process at $\bar{c}'$, it is charged to finished goods at $\bar{c}$, the original standard cost. The finished goods inventory like the raw material inventory is carried at original standards. The difference between the output at current and at standard factor prices,

$$\sum_j y_j (\bar{c}'_j - \bar{c}_j)$$

is debited to a new account, Product Cost Variance.

The cost of goods sold is credited to finished goods at $\bar{c}$ but it is charged to equity, the cost of goods sold, at the current cost. The excess of $\bar{c}'$ over $\bar{c}$ on the goods sold is credited to the Product Cost Variance Account. The procedure has two consequences of interest. First, the cost of goods sold is valued at current factor costs. Sales revenue less the cost of goods sold at current factor cost is a better measure of sales performance than sales revenue less the standard cost of goods sold. Under the Exhibit 1-1 procedures, the desired figure is only approximated by adding the excess of actual over standard cost of purchases to the standard cost of goods sold.

The second consequence of this procedure of interest is the information contained in the Product Cost Variance Account. It is evident that if manufacturing output in each period is equal to sales, the balance in the account is zero. If production and sales are not kept equal period by period, the balance is a speculative gain or loss on the finished goods inventory analogous to the factor price variance balance. If it is accepted that manufacturing has the responsibility of adjusting production to sales, this variance is a speculative gain or loss of the manufacturing department.

Control of Fixed Costs

Up to this point it has been assumed that the cost of the manufacturing department is proportional with output, i.e., the marginal cost per unit of output is a constant for each product, and at zero output there is zero cost. As most manufacturing companies perceive their costs, the expected cost of a manufacturing department during a period may be represented by the function

$$\bar{C} = \bar{F} + \sum_j y_j \bar{c}_j$$

where $\bar{C}$ is expected total cost and $\bar{F}$ is expected total fixed cost. Our control system may be elaborated to deal with fixed cost as follows. The manufacturing department is charged with its actual fixed costs and credited with $\bar{F}$. The difference is a variance that measures the success of the department in controlling its fixed costs. This variance is not as contradictory as it might first appear, because the fixed costs are only fixed in the sense that they are independent of the level of output. Management policies and performance influence the level of these costs.

The sales department profit is its sales revenue minus the sum of: (1) the variable cost of goods sold as determined previously; (2) $\bar{F}$ the expected fixed costs of the manufacturing department; and (3) the sales effort costs incurred by the sales department. Economic theory tells us that charging the sales department with a cost such as $\bar{F}$ that is independent of the department's decisions will not influence its decisions, and it therefore serves no useful purpose. However, there are psychological reasons that cannot be explored here, why this conclusion may not be true.

V TRANSFER PRICING

The literature has drawn a sharp distinction between a standard cost and a transfer price. A standard cost is derived from arbitrary factor costs and the existing production technology: one need not go outside the firm to obtain it. Further, standard costs are used to direct, motivate, and evaluate a department manager whose task it is to provide an independently determined output at the least cost. How one derives a transfer price is not as easily stated, but there has been little disagreement on what the criterion should be in arriving at the figure. Its purpose is to control a manager whose task is to optimize with respect to the level of output as well as the cost of securing that output. It also has been clear that establishing a transfer price requires more information, some of it outside the firm, than a standard cost requires.

The firm for which an administered price system was developed in the preceding pages presented no transfer price problem. The pseudo income statement established for the sales department was based on actual factor costs and product prices, i.e., prices obtained from the market. Administered prices were used only to eliminate the distortion if any introduced by the activities of the purchasing and manufacturing departments. The sales department statement provides a valid measure of its performance, and the cost and price data which are used in arriving at the statement are also the data the department should use in arriving at its output decision. By maximizing its profit the department maximizes the firm's profit.

The major limitation of the statement is that it fails to provide a zero base, i.e., the profit one might expect the department to earn given the factor costs, production technology, and product demand. A different and greater problem arises, however, when a market cannot be used to provide prices for the firm's product. In this situation transfer prices may be established and used by the firm to secure the optimal output decision by the sales department.

A Socialist Economy

This paper is not concerned with pricing in a socialist economy, but the problem has many important similarities with the intra-corporation transfer price problem. A brief review of this literature is therefore desirable. Von Hayek [9], von Mises [22], and Robbins [24] argued that the state could not make the millions on millions of calculations needed to achieve the rational allocation of resources that takes place under a market economy. Taylor [30] and Lange [16, p. 87] replied that "prices in a socialist economy can be determined by the same process of trial and error by which prices on a competitive market are determined." Lange [16, p. 86] summarized:

> Let the Central Planning Board start with a given set of prices chosen *at random*. All decisions of the managers of production and of the productive resources in public ownership and also all decisions of individuals as consumers and as suppliers of labor are made on the basis of these prices. As a result of these decisions the quantity demanded and supplied of each commodity is determined. If the quantity demanded of a commodity is not equal to the quantity supplied, the price of that commodity has to be changed. It has to be raised if demand exceeds supply and lowered if the reverse is the case. Thus the Central Planning Board fixes a new set of prices which serves as a basis for new decisions, and which results in a new set of quantities demanded and supplied. Through this process of trial and error equilibrium prices are finally determined. Actually the process of trial and error would, of course, proceed on the basis of the prices *historically given*. Relatively small adjustments of those prices would constantly be made, and there would be no necessity of building up an entirely new price system.

Individuals would sell their services and buy products exactly as they do in a market economy. Each plant manager, however, would be *instructed* to adopt the method of production that minimizes average cost and to produce the output that equates his marginal cost with the product price established by the Central Planning Board. The result is that society obtains both the best allocation of the ultimate productive resources on the basis of the given prices in each period and the movement over time of the prices to their equilibrium and optimal values.

Koopmans [14], Arrow and Hurwicz [3], Kose [15], Whinston [32], and others have used the recent developments in mathematical programming to investigate the convergence of decentralized pricing systems under specific adjustment rules for plant managers (with respect to production) and the central authority (with respect to price). Marschak [20] has formulated and explored the problem of comparing the efficiency of decentralized and centralized control systems. Under the latter system the central authority would obtain cost and demand schedules from the plant managers and make the price and production decisions.

The Control Problem

Although the problem of control as described at the start of this paper has been recognized by some of the writers mentioned above, it has only been raised in passing. In addition to all the other criticisms he levelled at the Lange type model, Hayek asked, "What is to be the independent business unit? Who is to be the manager? What resources are to be entrusted to him and how is his success or failure to be tested?" [9, p. 232]. Hayek did not feel that satisfactory answers to these questions could be found. Arrow has mentioned the motivation problem. He states [2, p. 12]:

> The only remaining problem in decentralization would be to insure that each individual process manager with a knowledge of his own technology should maximize his profits. There may indeed be problems of control to insure that maximization does take place and it is clear that such problems present a challenge to accounting procedures as well as incentive schemes.

Lange was not concerned with whether managers would find that maximizing firm profits maximized their welfare. The problem he noted was that in maximizing profit each manager might make his production and supply decision on the basis of existing price with the influence of that decision on subsequent prices in mind. A monopolist or oligopolist in a socialist economy might use his market position in the same way as his counterpart in a capitalistic economy. After stating "managers certainly can and do influence prices by their decisions," Lange [16, p. 81] proposed

> Therefore, the parametric functions of prices must be imposed on them by the Central Planning Board as an *accounting rule*. All accounting has to be done *as if* prices were independent of the decisions taken. For purposes of accounting prices must be treated as constant, as they are treated by entrepreneurs in a competitive market.
> The technique of attaining this end is very simple: the Central Planning Board has to fix prices and see to it that all managers...do their accounting on the basis of the prices... and not tolerate any use of other accounting.

It must be noted, however, that the problem is not one of accounting

rules. Accountants will record transactions at the prices at which
they take place or at other prices given to them. This will not prevent managers from perceiving the influence of their output decisions
on the prices the central authority will establish and they will receive.

Intra Corporate Transfer Prices

Coincidental with the development of the above literature, the
growth in size and diversification of American corporations has made
transfer pricing a real problem. Large diversified corporations have
found it advantageous to organize their activities in two or more divisions with each doing its own purchasing, manufacturing, and sales,
and in some cases each function is established as a separate division.
For a division that has no transactions with any other division, an
income statement derived from market determined prices is used by
corporate offices to direct, motivate, and evaluate the performance
of the division manager. Intra-division control is achieved by the
means described earlier. However, quite often the product of one
division may be used in manufacturing the product of another, and
the top management generally does not consider it in the corporation's best interest to allow the two divisions to act as if they were
completely independent. The top management therefore concerns itself with the conditions and terms under which the two divisions buy
and sell the commodity.

Cook [7], Dean [8], and Shillinglaw [27] are among those who have
examined existing and alternative practices in dealing with the transfer price problem. Hirschleifer [13] has proposed a solution to the
transfer price problem that arises when the firm in our example
divisionalizes. For a firm that sets up its manufacturing and sales
departments as two divisions, he demonstrated [13, p. 183] that:

> If a single joint level of output is to be determined... one of
> the divisions presents to the other its supply schedule (or de-
> mand schedule, as the case may be) as a function of the trans-
> fer price. The second division then establishes its output and
> the transfer price by a rule which leads to the optimum solu-
> tion specified above for the firm as a whole.

Hirschleifer also examined more complicated relations, including the
case where the intermediate product may be sold on the market as
well as to the buying division. In general, one division gives cost or
demand information to the other (not the central authority) and the
division with the information sets the transfer price under rules established by the corporation with the rules designed to maximize the
corporation's profit.

The inadequacies of the Hirschleifer system from a control point
of view are even more serious than the Lange system's. First, it

must be realized that if a transfer price is to have any meaning, it must be the price at which the revenue of the manufacturing division and the costs of the sales division are determined, and that the objective of each division is to maximize its profit with revenue and costs so determined. Hirschleifer would have the corporation instruct the manufacturing division to give the sales division its marginal cost function as a supply schedule. However, with marginal costs well below average costs over the relevant range of output (certainly as costs are in practice measured in industry), compliance by the manufacturing division would make losses a regular phenomena. In view of this fact and the fact that faithful compliance with this instruction cannot be enforced by the corporation, compliance should not be expected. It can be expected that the manufacturing division will increase its profit by restricting supply. With respect to the selling division, Hirschleifer [13, p. 175] recognized that "One condition must be stipulated: the distribution division must not be permitted to increase its separate profit by finding a quasi-marginal revenue curve...and establishing an output...(which)...would amount to the distribution's division exploiting the manufacturing division by acting as a monopolistic buyer...the firm as a whole would lose thereby." It is clear that we have here a bilateral monopoly with no adequate controls to prevent the adverse consequences to the parent that one might expect.

It is of interest to compare the Hirschleifer control system with that presented earlier, since both deal with the same organization structure, one involving transactions between a manufacturing and a sales organization. It can be argued that the two solutions differ only in consequence of the different assumptions with respect to the manufacturing division's cost function.

For the Hirschleifer firm marginal cost increases with output, so that the output the manufacturing division is willing to supply is a function of the transfer price. If marginal cost had been a constant, the division would have been willing to supply any output demanded by sales at marginal cost. The Hirschleifer firm would then have used the same transfer price and arrived at the same end price and output decision as the firm presented earlier.

The administered price presented earlier—current standard variable cost plus a predetermined lump sum to cover fixed cost—results in the optimum price output decision for the company.[13] However, as a transfer price it is defective in two important respects. First, it is

---

[13] This is true on the assumption that marginal cost is independent of the level of output. The assumption is open to question since it is clear that beyond some level of output marginal product cost increases. However, few firms believe that their unit product costs increase with output over the range that they find relevant.

limited in application to single product firms. If the manufacturing division has two or more customers—real or intra-corporate, an allocation of the fixed cost is necessary. A method of allocation that is neutral with respect to the price output decisions of the sales division does not provide a satisfactory measure of the performance of each and vice versa.

The second and more fundamental limitation of this administered price arrangement is that it does not perform the transfer price function of measuring the profitability of the manufacturing division. The division's profit or loss based on standard cost only provides a measure of the department's efficiency in producing an independently determined output. This profit or loss is independent of whether the division is producing at capacity or fifty per cent of capacity, and it therefore fails to provide a measure of the adequacy and effectiveness of the capital and management invested in the division.

VI CONCLUSION

In conclusion the following observations are worth noting. Market price systems do not in fact provide the optimal allocation and utilization of resources that theory demonstrates is true under perfect competition. Nonetheless, market systems are reasonably effective in securing the efficient utilization of resources, the reallocation of resources in response to changes in technology and tastes, in making the best of the existing allocation as the adjustment takes place, and in securing innovations in technology.

By contrast purely bureaucratic methods of organizing economic activity have been found to be most inefficient outside of special situations and/or limited periods of time. However, the development of technology, uncertainty as to the future, the strategic advantages of size, and possibly other reasons have dramatically increased the size of organizations within which bureaucratic methods of control are employed. Modest as the progress to date has been in the design and use of administered price systems in bureaucratic organizations, it has made a material contribution to their efficiency.

Existing practice in the design and use of administered prices as described earlier is still far from satisfactory as a basis for instructing, motivating, and evaluating the performance of sub-organization managers. In consequence these systems are extensively supplemented and contradicted in the process by more conventional means of bureaucratic control. Control in large business organizations is still exercised predominantly through authority relations—formally by instructions and informally through other forms of interpersonal relations. It is doubtful whether the development of administered price systems can or should ever be carried to the point where the impersonal relations of a perfectly competitive market price system completely replace authority relations. Interpersonal relations, which have been passed over lightly in this paper, will continue to play an important role in the operation of organizations which employ administered price systems.

Research on the control of large organizations will therefore involve the separate and the interrelated study of the distribution of authority, the replication of this distribution in an administered price system, the information processing techniques needed to provide the required data, and the interpersonal relations evoked by the control system in operation.

BIBLIOGRAPHY

1. Argyris, C.: *Personality and Organization*, New York: Harper & Row, 1957.
2. Arrow, K. J.: "Optimization, Decentralization, and Internal Pricing in Business Firms," in *Contributions to Scientific Research in Management*, Los Angeles: University of California, 1959.
3. —— and L. Hurwicz: "Decentralization and Computation in Resource Allocation," Technical Report #54, Project on Efficiency in Economic Decision-making (Office of Naval Research Contract N 6-onr-25133), Department of Economics, Stanford University, 1958. Appears also in *Essays in Honor of Howard Hotelling*, Chapel Hill, N. C.: The University of North Carolina Press (forthcoming).
4. Bain, J. S.: *Industrial Organization*, New York: Wiley, 1959.
5. Bennett, E. D.: *Cost Administration: Cases and Notes*, Englewood Cliffs, N. J.: Prentice-Hall, 1960.
6. Blau, Peter M., and W. Richard Scott: *Formal Organizations*, San Francisco: Chandler, 1962.
7. Cook, P. W., Jr.: "Decentralization and the Transfer-price Problem," *The Journal of Business*, vol. 28, 1955.
8. Dean J.: "Decentralization and Intra-company Pricing," *Harvard Business Review*, vol. 33, 1955.
9. Hayek, F. A. von, "The Present State of the Debate," in *Collectivist Economic Planning*, London: Routledge, 1938.
10. Henrici, S. B.: *Standard Costs for Manufacturing*, New York: McGraw-Hill, 1960.
11. Hicks, J. R.: *Value and Capital*, 2d ed., London: Oxford, 1946.
12. Hill, Thomas M., and Myron J. Gordon: *Accounting: A Management Approach*, Homewood, Ill.: Irwin, 1959.
13. Hirschleifer, Jack: "On the Economics of Transfer Pricing," *The Journal of Business*, vol. 29, 1956.
14. Koopmans, T. C.: "Analysis of Production as an Efficient Combination of Activities," *Activity Analysis of Production and Allocation*, New York: Wiley, 1951.
15. Kose, T.: "Solutions of Saddle-value Problems by Differential Equations," *Econometrics*, vol. 24, January, 1956.
16. Lange, O.: "On the Economic Theory of Socialism," B. Lippincot (ed.), in *On the Economic Theory of Socialism*, Minneapolis: The University of Minnesota Press, 1938.

17. Likert, Rensis: *New Patterns of Management*, New York: McGraw-Hill, 1961.
18. Little, I. M. D.: *A Critique of Welfare Economics*, London: Oxford, 1950.
19. March, J. G., and H. A. Simon: *Organizations*, New York: Wiley, 1958.
20. Marschak, T.: "Centralization and Decentralization in Economic Organizations," *Econometrica*, vol. 27, July, 1959.
21. McGregor, Douglas: *The Human Side of Enterprise*, New York: McGraw-Hill, 1960.
22. Mises, L. von: "Economic Calculation in the Socialist Commonwealth," in Hayek, ref. 9.
23. National Association of Cost Accountants, "How Standard Costs Are Being Used Currently," New York: N. A. C. A., 1948.
24. Robbins, L.: *The Great Depression*, New York, Macmillan, 1934.
25. Scitovsky, Tibor: *Welfare and Competition*, Homewood, Ill.: Irwin, 1951.
26. Shillinglaw, Gordon: *Cost Accounting: Analysis and Control*, Homewood, Ill.: Irwin, 1961.
27. ———: "Guides to Internal Profit Measurement, "*Harvard Business Review*, March-April, 1957.
28. Smith, Adam: *An Inquiry into the Nature and Causes of Wealth of Nations*, New York: Modern Library, 1937.
29. Stocking, George W., and Myron W. Watkins: *Monopoly and Free Enterprise*, New York: Twentieth Century Fund, 1951.
30. Taylor, F. H.: "The Guidance of Production in a Socialist State," B. Lippincot (ed.), in *On the Economic Theory of Socialism*, Minneapolis: The University of Minnesota Press, 1938.
31. Thomas, W. E.: *Readings in Cost Accounting Budgeting and Control*, New Rochelle, N.Y.: South-Western Publishing Company, 1960.
32. Whinston, A.: *Price Coordination in Decentralized Systems*, O. U. R. Research Memorandum No. 99, Graduate School of Industrial Administration, Carnegie Institute of Technology, 1962.
33. Wilcox, Clair: *Public Policies Toward Business*, Homewood, Ill.: Irwin, 1960.

2

INTERNAL PRICING AND DECENTRALIZED DECISIONS

JACK HIRSHLEIFER
University of California at Los Angeles

I NATURE OF THE PROBLEM

Economists have recently become concerned with the use of correct internal prices to guide the allocation of resources within the firm [1, 2, 3, 4]. The problem is of practical interest in view of the wide use of decentralized decision systems in business; internal pricing is a live issue wherever there are internal transactions between autonomous intra-firm decision centers. Furthermore, the fascinating analogies between decentralized decision centers within firms on the one hand, and firms themselves as decentralized decision centers within the macro-system of the economy as a whole, make these practical issues of interest to theoreticians as well. The fact that the analogy between micro-system and macro-system is an imperfect one, failing in various subtle and instructive ways, lends intellectual spice to the enterprise.

However, while I will turn back to this analogy at a later point, I intend for the present to look upon the problem from the practical point of view: to wit, how can internal pricing assist firms to increase revenues or reduce costs? When I return later to the analogy, the interest will be in strictly practical considerations: we will explore the range of higher-level controls available to cope with situations where the "hidden hand" of decentralized profit incentives leads to disfunctional behavior from the system-wide point of view. We shall see that even a ferocious monopoly—a predator firm in the macro-system of the economy—might want to set up an internal "anti-trust" operation to make sure that its component parts do not prey on one another.

II WHY INTERNAL PRICES?

I think it is fair to say that internal price systems—as distinguished from conventional cost accounting valuations of intermediate products—have not been introduced into practical business operations as desirable innovations in their own right. Rather, they have been the by-product of the institution of decentralized "profit centers."

The objective of these latter has been clear enough. If the chiefs of corporate component divisions are given appropriate ranges of authority, and then are themselves judged or rewarded on the basis of achieved division excess of revenue over cost, they will be motivated to find ways of increasing division profit and so, indirectly, corporation profit. While in the abstract an ideal set of instructions from corporate headquarters could achieve a profit optimum, in practice the incentives of sub-chiefs under a completely authoritarian system may be such as not to elicit their best efforts. Furthermore, a great deal of the immediate and direct knowledge of local situations possessed by such sub-chiefs would necessarily be lost in transmission even if an attempt were made to convey all relevant information upward for decision. In short, the "profit center" institution attempts to capture the advantages for the corporation of having division heads acting as they would if they were in business for themselves.

This conception would create no difficulty if a firm were but a conglomeration of independent productive operations that happened to be under common ownership. However, a difficulty was almost immediately observed where, as is normally the case, two profit centers within a firm exchange a product or service internally. Wrangling over the "transfer price" is the inevitable outcome. Other difficulties in the profit-center concept have also been suggested or perceived: there may be direct interdependence between the production functions of two divisions, and there may be interdependence between demand prices for their products or supply prices for factors hired [5]. Finally, it has been noted that it may at times be undesirable to close down a division incurring a negative profit—and in fact, it may be desirable to force a division that could earn a profit to price an internal product so low as to incur a loss. In short, the problem is an imperfect correspondence between division profits and firm profits, or division incentives and firm efficiency. This question is really a special case of a classical problem of welfare economics: under what conditions, and in what senses, does goal-maximization on the micro level lead to a macro optimum?

So far as internal pricing is concerned, there are two main analytical aims that might be pursued: (1) We can regard the function of the internal price as that of conveying information on the valuations of the resources embodied, or (2) We can regard its function as providing a measure of the overall worth of the operation in question. In effect, we can let the price reflect, on the one hand, *marginal*, and or the other, *total* efficiency considerations.

These two will conflict in an example like the following. Suppose that one division of a company has been buying a component externally for $10 per unit. Now, an internal supplier division discovers a way of producing the component at a constant cost of, say, $6 per unit. From the point of view of conveying information on marginal resource valuations, $6 should be the transfer price (under certain simplifying assumptions to be explored in more detail shortly). But this will provide no reward for the innovating supplier division, which only breaks even while the user division reaps all the profit increment. From the reward point of view, to provide incentive for improving efficiency by innovation, the supplier division could make a convincing case for a transfer price of $10. But then the division using the component would have no incentive to reorganize production so as to make more use of the cheapened component or to increase output on account of the reduction in the firm's real costs of production.

The question of abandonment of a division provides another example. Where there are economies of scale, so that a supplier division is operating under conditions of diminishing average cost, a price reflecting marginal valuations of resources (a marginal-cost price) will fall short of average cost. Since under such a price a loss is being incurred, the supplier will be motivated to close down so as to terminate the money-losing operation. This *may* in fact be the correct move from the overall firm point of view, but it need not be— and, it appears, the wide prevalence of economies of scale makes the danger of incorrect signals on this score very serious.

There are ways of at least partially reconciling the two objectives. In our first example, a reward providing incentive to innovate might be worked out as follows: Let the innovating division supply the buyer division with the same number of units the latter was previously buying externally, and at the same price of $10; however, let the buyer division then be permitted to purchase additional units internally at $6. In our second example, the supplier division making negative profit while charging low marginal prices might, each year, negotiate with its internal customers for a lump-sum grant or subsidy as a condition for *not* closing down.

Granted that divisional profit figures resulting from correct marginal valuations of inputs may not be a suitable measure of the worth of total divisional operations, I will waive this for the present to concentrate on the more limited question of how to correctly reflect the *marginal* valuations of resources in transfer pricing.[1]

[1]See Shubik [6] for an approach to the transfer problem from the profit-imputation point of view. Shubik shows conditions that a correct profit imputation must meet in order to reconcile division and firm incentives. It does not appear possible to satisfy these conditions, generally, through simple transfer prices.

III INTERNAL PRICING—THE SIMPLEST SOLUTIONS.

To illustrate the general nature of the solutions obtained for internal pricing under the conditions specified, it will be convenient to start with as few complexities as possible. We will consider a simple model situation, in which the firm has a two-stage vertically-integrated operation, each stage being a profit and decision center. The primary stage produces an intermediate product, turns it over at the transfer price to the secondary stage—which converts the intermediate into a final product and disposes of it on the external market. For example, the primary stage may be a manufacturing division and the secondary stage a distribution division. The productive operations at the two stages are, by assumption, "cost-independent"— a term we will use to rule out any impact of the level of operations in either division upon the cost function of the other, either through technological interdependence or through effects on prices of common factors hired.

Let us as our first case assume, for starkest simplicity, that there is no market whatsoever for the intermediate product—no demand for it, or supply of it, aside from the demand and supply represented by the respective divisions of our firm. In this case, ruling out accumulations of inventory, the primary and secondary stages must coordinate their outputs; by an appropriate selection of units we can say they must produce the same output. In our example, the primary division must manufacture just as much as the secondary division distributes. From the firm's point of view, optimum price and output are where firm marginal cost, MC, equals marginal revenue, MR (see Exhibit 2-1). But, under our assumption of cost independence of the two divisions, MC = mmc + mdc. That is, MC is the sum of marginal manufacturing cost and marginal distribution cost. If the distribution division, selling to the external market after paying a specified transfer price p* for the internal commodity, is directed to maximize its profit, it will autonomously set its output q_d so as to make MR = p* + mdc = MC*—the latter expression being overall marginal cost to the distribution division. And, for a specified p*, the manufacturing division would under autonomous profit-maximizing set its output q_m such that mmc = p*. Thus the firm optimum MR = mmc + mdc will be attained—if divisional outputs are coordinated.

There are a variety of ways in which the optimum solution might be arrived at operationally. Some device like a neutral umpire might be employed to set an initial trial p*—after which the divisions would respond by declaring tentative outputs q_m and q_d. If q_m exceeds q_d the p* should be adjusted downward by the umpire, and the reverse if q_d exceeds q_m—until a p* is found such that the planned outputs are coordinated.

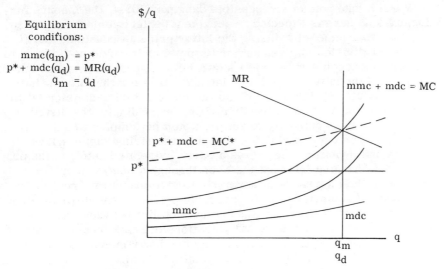

Exhibit 2-1. Best joint level of output.

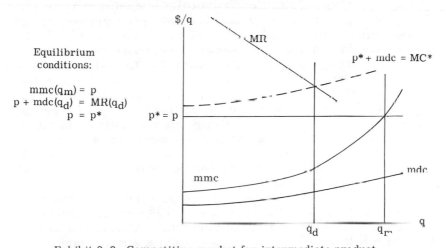

Exhibit 2-2. Competitive market for intermediate product.

We can take note of two possible dangers. First, the manufacturing division here is expected to act like a perfect competitor—to set q_m such that mmc = p*, taking the latter price as constant. But if the seller division is given authority to set p* it would be tempted to act as a monopolist vis-a-vis its own internal customer, since taking account of the latter's declining demand curve for the intermediate product would yield more profit to the manufacturing division (at the cost of an overall loss to the firm). Correspondingly, the distribution division, if given authority to set p*, would be tempted to act as a monopsonistic buyer and take account of the rising supply curve of its internal supplier. Second, as a partially related point, in the process of exchanging information, even through a neutral umpire, it may be in the interest of either party to give inaccurate replies in the hopes of achieving a more favorable price. These difficulties in the simplest case illustrate the radical conflict between internal prices for registering marginal valuations of resources or products, and internal prices as means of assigning departmental profits.[2]

If we turn to an equally simple situation but allow now an external market for the intermediate commodity in addition to internal transfers, the outputs of the two divisions should not, in general, be coordinated. The presence of an external market for the intermediate commodity makes the situation analytically somewhat more complex. But operationally, the problem may become more tractable. Indeed, if the external market for the intermediate commodity is perfectly competitive, the element of divisional conflict under decentralized profit-maximizing disappears. As indicated in Exhibit 2-2, the intermediate supplier (manufacturing division in our example) is motivated to establish its output q_m such that its marginal cost, mmc, equals the given competitive price, p, for the intermediate commodity. On similar grounds the distribution division will set its output, q_d such that its overall marginal cost, p + mdc, equals the marginal revenue MR in the final-product market. Here, no matter which division is given the responsibility for setting the transfer price p*, if any attempt is made to exploit the internal trading partner the latter will turn to the outside market. (We may presume that something like a small saving in transaction cost provides an incentive to trade internally; it would be immaterial to anyone concerned whether any internal transactions took place at all, under a strict assumption of cost independence.) Note that if internal transactions do take place,

[2]These problems have been emphasized by Myron J. Gordon. [See his paper on pp. 1-26 in this book.] They are critical ones since, it will be remembered, the original reason for divisional profit centers was to give some scope to the play of decentralized incentives, in the hope of reaping gains in efficiency thereby. Unfortunately, it may be easier to increase divisional profits by acting as an internal monopolist than by reducing costs and improving efficiency.

the transfer price p* must as before equal mmc—the marginal production cost of the supplier division. This is the crucial information conveyed by the transfer price.

The first case of enough difficulty to be really interesting is the one we shall consider next. Suppose there is an external market for the intermediate commodity, but an imperfectly competitive one such that the marginal cost of the internal supplier, mmc, is less than the ruling market price, p. We may as well assume, for simplicity, that the internal supplier is a monopolist of the intermediate commodity. Then, the external intermediate market is an alternative for the internal supplier, but not for the internal buyer. Nevertheless, some writers recommend use of the external price p as the transfer price p* without reference to the question of the competitiveness of the external price. Such a recommendation would be incorrect here—from our point of view of achieving efficient allocation of the firm's resources. It would entail monopolistic exploitation of the internal (as well as the external intermediate) customer, to the detriment of the firm's overall interests.

The correct solution is indicated in Exhibit 2-3, under a special simplifying assumption that we may call "demand independence"— the analogue of the "cost independence" assumption we have already used. "Demand independence" means that the external demand curves of the divisions of the firm are independent; in this particular context, it requires that additional sales of the intermediate commodity to the internal customer do not adversely affect the external de-

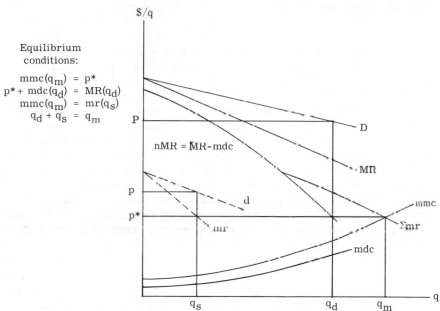

Exhibit 2-3. Imperfectly competitive market for intermediate product.

mands. This would be somewhat unrealistic in general, since the
internal and the external customers for an intermediate commodity
are likely to be in competition in the final-product markets. For
example, a refinery selling unbranded gasoline to an independent
distributor must expect an adverse effect on the demand for its own
brand of distributed gasoline. It may be, however, that geographical
or product-line differentiations are sufficient to make the demands
substantially independent. Under these circumstances, the overall
interests of the firm require monopolistic exploitation of the external
intermediate customers, and of the external final customers, but not of
the *internal* intermediate customer. The solution is found analytically
by a price discrimination technique—in which mmc is equated simultaneously with marginal revenue, mr, in the external intermediate market
(thus determining external intermediate sales, q_s), and with MR-mdc
(which we denote *net marginal* revenue mMR) for the internal customer, thus making mmc + mdc = MR and determining optimal output
q_d in the final external market. The appropriate transfer price p* as
before equals mmc—the marginal cost of the internal supplier. Note
that the external price p for the intermediate commodity exceeds p*—
in fact, external marginal revenue mr = internal price p* = mmc. A
neutral umpire would aim to set p* so as to equate q_m with $q_s + q_d$;
again, he would be concerned to prevent the supplier division's use
of its powerful market position to exploit its internal as well as its
external customers.

   We may summarize this section by noting that—granted the simplifying assumptions of demand independence and cost independence for
the divisions of the firm—the general rule for the transfer price p*
is to set it at the marginal cost of the internal supplier division.
The firm continues to exploit whatever monopoly power it has with
respect to external customers in the intermediate-product or final-
product markets, but does not permit parts of the firm to exploit
other parts. If transfer price p* is set by some device, like a neutral
umpire, so as to be a constant independent of the seller division output and of the buyer division output, then ideally each division will
treat the transfer price as if it were a competitive price for output
in the one case or for input in the other. The result is to convey forward or upward to the final seller division correct marginal-cost information for use in adjusting output in the final-product market.
The correct level of p* for the umpire to set is determined, in the
case where outputs must be coordinated, by the coordination require-
ment; in the competitive intermediate market case, by the competitive external price; and in the monopolistic intermediate market case,
by the condition that transfer price p* to the internal customer should
equal marginal revenue mr from the external customers for the intermediate product. In general, there will be difficulties in that any division with market power will be tempted to use this power against

other parts of the firm either overtly, or through covert devices, including reporting incorrect cost or demand information to the umpire. And, it remains true that the prices here arrived at are correct for marginal allocation decisions only; they will not in general satisfy the function of providing a divisional reward for meritorious achievements like cost reductions; and will not be correct for non-marginal issues like abandonment decisions.

IV INTERNAL PRICING—RELAXATION OF THE ASSUMPTIONS

Limitations of time and space preclude any attempt here to provide formal solutions for optimal internal prices when the special assumptions of demand-independence and cost-independence are relaxed.[3] In a vertically-integrated situation like that described in our previous examples, dependence between the *demands* of the intermediate and the final-product divisions would indicate the desirability of a smaller differential between the prices charged to internal and external customers for the intermediate product—since internal transfers at marginal cost now entail loss of profitable sales at full price. So the rule of marginal-cost pricing to internal customers no longer applies—unless marginal cost is redefined to include the loss of external profit. A rather complex information exchange is necessary to establish the correct price between a buyer and seller division, with the same difficulties and hazards described above.

It is worth mentioning that demand dependence is normally more important for horizontally-integrated than for vertically-integrated concerns. This is true both for products with complementary demands, like cameras and film for Eastman Kodak, and with competitive demands, like Pontiac and Chevrolet for General Motors. However, as divisions on the same horizontal level do not ordinarily exchange products internally, we take no special note here of the problems involved in reconciling the division interests with overall company interests.[4]

Cost dependence between different divisions may represent effects of expanded or decreased operations upon the prices of factors employed in common, or may represent direct dependence between the technological production functions. The former is not usually a substantial consideration, but direct productive interdependence is often very important. The effect is to limit the possibility of having autonomous decision centers. In a refinery, for example, it seems scarcely possible to have any range of autonomy between the decisions to produce gasoline and kerosene, let us say. Here the inter-relationship

[3]For a more complete discussion, see [4] .
[4]A start on this problem is provided in [5] .

between products concerns not only the external market, but the internal productive process. We will not pursue this illustration further,
however, because again it represents a horizontal rather than vertical integration problem. An example of vertical productive interdependence would be a steel mill in which expanded pig-iron production
would make more molten iron available for steel-making, entailing
heat economies as compared with purchased pig iron. As in the case
of demand interdependence, cost interdependence seems to be more
critical for the horizontally-integrated firms than for the vertically-
integrated concerns that typically require internal exchange of an intermediate product.

V PRIVATE OPTIMUM AND GROUP OPTIMUM: CONFLICTS AND CONTROLS

The operational difficulties of an optimal pricing rule have been
alluded to several times. It is difficult to reduce an autonomous center that really has an entrenched monopolistic position within the
firm to the innocuous role of a pure "price-taker." Even with a neutral umpire, the autonomous divisions have an incentive to convey
misleading information in order to secure the benefit of a more attractive price for the transferred commodity. At least in part to control
internal monopolistic exploitation, it is not an uncommon practice in
industry to permit a seller or buyer division to resort to the external
market if the price demanded by the internal partner is too unfavorable. This rule can be unqualifiedly recommended though it sets only
an upper limit upon exploitation. An alternative procedure is the "no
profit, no loss" rule for internal transactions. This is akin to cost-
plus pricing or, perhaps, to a regulated price in the public-utility
sense. It should be roundly condemned as pernicious both in terms of
marginal valuations of inputs and in terms of incentives to improve
efficiency.

There are other devices available, not now commonly used, that
may in certain circumstances have ranges of applicability. The first
and most fundamental might be an attempt deliberately to encourage
internal competition. Rather than reserve a certain protected sphere
to intermediate-product and final-product divisions, laissez-faire
might be given internal sway with divisions being free to enter each
other's bailiwicks. We might even conceive of "anti-trust" regulation
here to prevent collusion among internal competitors, predatory practices, etc.

Alternatively, the opposite tack of permitting a stronger monopoly
might be taken, to make use of the theorem that a perfectly-discrim-
inating monopolist achieves a socially efficient solution (while cap-
turing all the advantages of trade). The ability to discriminate, at

least to some degree, may become almost a necessity in the case of a supplier division with a declining average-cost curve. Here marginal-cost prices necessarily entail producing at a loss. Discrimination would be necessary to recoup costs; ideally, it should be such as to have the marginal prices charged to each internal customer equal to one another and to marginal cost. The ability to make a profit by discriminating on the infra-marginal units provides the clue that the operation in question should not be abandoned. Finally, infra-marginal discrimination would permit a division making an innovation to reap the reward of the consequent cost reduction without distorting the information conveyed on the margin by internal prices.

The main import of this discussion can be briefly summarized. As a fairly straightforward matter, and on the assumption that internal buyer and seller will be pure price-takers, it is possible formally to arrive at pricing solutions based on marginal cost that place correct valuations upon resources transferred internally within the firm. The difficulties considered here were first, the necessity for counteracting incentives to monopolize; and second, possible conflict between the marginal and total conditions for an optimum under simple marginal-cost pricing. This last conflict reveals itself in a lack of appropriate incentives for innovation, and also in failing to give correct signals for abandonment questions (e.g. where marginal-cost pricing leads to negative profits). No full treatment was provided of ways of circumventing the difficulties, which may indeed be to some degree insurmountable. However, two promising possibilities were alluded to: (1) Expanding internal competition within the firm, and (2) Use of more complex discriminatory patterns of pricing that still preserve the relevant resource-valuation information in the prices charged on the margin.

BIBLIOGRAPHY

1. Arrow, K. J., "Optimization, Decentralization, and Internal Pricing in Business Firms," in *Contributions to Scientific Research in Management*, Los Angeles: University of California, 1959.
2. Cook, P. W., Jr., "Decentralization and the Transfer-price Problem," *The Journal of Business*, vol. 28, 1955.
3. Dean, J.: "Decentralization and Intra-company Pricing," *Harvard Business Review*, vol. 33, 1955.
4. Hirshleifer, Jack: "On the Economics of Transfer Pricing," *The Journal of Business*, vol. 29, 1956.
5. ———: "Economics of the Divisionalized Firm," *The Journal of Business*, vol. 30, 1957.
6. Shubik, M.: "Incentives, Decentralized Control, the Assignment of Joint Costs and Internal Pricing," *Management Science*, vol. 8, 1962.

3

PROBLEMS IN INFORMATION ECONOMICS

JACOB MARSCHAK
University of California at Los Angeles[1]

INTRODUCTION

Problems in information economics consist in characterizing optimal "information systems." The microeconomics of information, an extension of the usual theory of the firm, a household, or a government agency considers a single decider with fixed tastes, beliefs, and resources. It is concerned with the choice of an optimal information system under those fixed conditions. An information system may be a simple instrument for collecting observations of the environment, or a complex network (an "organization") of men and machines who make observations, process them, and send messages to each other and finally to those who perform actions impinging on the environment and thus yielding a "payoff." In this complex case, the chooser of the optimal information system can be visualized as the "organizer" (e.g., a management consultant). For brevity, we shall designate all information systems simply as "channels."

Corresponding to our description of micro-economics of information, we can regard the macro-economics of information as an extension of the theory of welfare economics, or public policy. It would attempt to characterize a socially optimal allocation of channels, given the distribution of tastes and beliefs, and given the society's total resources and their initial distribution.

After introducing, in Sections 1 to 6, some useful concepts and propositions, we shall apply them in the rest of the paper to focus on a special micro-economic question, of much relevance to any future macro-economic theory of information. This question is: is there, in any sense, a "law of decreasing returns to information?" In the case of land, labor, and capital, the question is known to be crucial in the discussion of optimal resource allocation methods in a market or a planned economy, at least in a somewhat weaker form, as the "assumption of non-decreasing returns to scale" (rather than to a particular factor of production), also known as the assumption of convexity of the set of possible production plans: see, for example, Debreu [1]. If that assumption is not satisfied the optimal allocation may be a "boundary solution" (rather than an "interior solution"): so that it may be best to use a resource to the limit.

[1] Supported by the Western Management Science Institute under its grant from the Ford Foundation and a contract with the Office of Naval Research, NONR 233(75).

In the case of land, labor, and capital, the discussion of decreasing returns would be simplified if one could, without affecting the results too strongly, replace "bundles" of land plots, of working individuals, and of assets and liabilities, by appropriate aggregates called "factors of production" and represented by real numbers (instead of vectors). But this is possible only in special cases. The same is true of channels, or information systems. As we shall see, a channel is essentially characterized by a joint probability distribution of "messages" and "events." To replace the distribution by a single parameter (e.g., "entropy" as a measure of "information capacity") will, in general, vitiate the results, that is, provide non-optimal solutions. The analogy is particularly strong between economics of information and economics of capital, the latter being a bundle of assets and liabilities characterized essentially by the joint probability of their yields. In fact, an attentive reader will be able to broaden at will the interpretation of our terms in this article, so as to embrace the general question: to find conditions for the optimality of any given arrangement of men, materials and machines, including men, materials, and machines used in gathering, processing, and communicating data. The recent development of "automation" has perhaps added some realism to this generalization of the economic problem.

To familiarize the reader with the relevant concepts and propositions, we shall use very simple examples and accompany them by economic interpretations. In the main "Example 1," more and more assumptions are made as the discussion progresses. They permit us to by-pass the aggregation problem and, in Part II of the paper, to discuss explicitly an important case of increasing returns to information.

I. GENERAL PROBLEM

1. Acts, States, Channels

Given: $A = \{a\}$, the set of possible *acts* of the decision maker; $X = \{x\}$, the set of possible *states* of his environment. Any partition of A will be called a set of *act descriptions;* any partition of X will be called a set of *state descriptions.*

Given: $H = \{h\}$, a set of *channels* available to the decision maker; and, for each channel h, a set $Y^h = \{y^h\}$ of state descriptions called signals or *messages* (these are messages that can be received by the decision maker). Thus y^h is a subset of X.

EXAMPLE 1. Let

$$x = (x_1, \ldots, x_n) \in X; \quad X = \text{real n-space} \tag{1}$$

$$m \leq n; \tag{2}$$

the following channels will be considered with appropriate interpretations:

$$h' : y^{h'} = (x_1, \ldots, x_m) \qquad \text{thus } Y^{h'} = \text{real m-space} \qquad (3.1)$$

$$h : y^h = \sum_1^m x_i \qquad \text{thus } Y^h = \text{real line} \qquad (3.2)$$

$$h^* : y^{h^*} = \begin{cases} 1 \text{ if } \sum_1^m x_i > 0 \\ -1 \text{ otherwise} \end{cases} \qquad \begin{array}{l}\text{thus } Y^{h^*} \text{ consists} \\ \text{of 2 points}\end{array} \qquad (3.3)$$

The following INTERPRETATIONS may be useful to fix ideas:

(a) x_i ($i = 1, \ldots, n$) is the (possibly non-positive) change in the unit price of a security over the next month. Channel h' makes (infallible) predictions of price changes for m selected securities. h predicts the total (possibly non-positive) gain on a portfolio composed of these securities, one unit of each. h^* predicts whether this gain is positive or not; it is a "binary channel." [Instead of a portfolio of securities, we might also consider a list of prices of selected goods and services demanded by the nation, and a price-index based on such a list.]

(b) x_i ($i = 1, \ldots, n$) is the score (measured from some norm) on the i-th test of a prospective employee, $y^{h'}$ is a list of m scores, y^h is their sum, y^{h^*} tells whether the norm is, on the average, exceeded.

Note that of the three partitions $Y^{h'}$, Y^h, Y^{h^*} of X, the first is *finer* than the second, and the second is *finer* than the third in the following sense:

DEFINITION. Let Z and Z' be partitions of X. Z is said to be *finer than* Z' (or alternatively, Z' to be *coarser than* Z) if for every z in Z there is a z' in Z' with $z \subseteq z'$.

The relation "finer than" (the words "a subpartition of" are also used[2]) induces a partial ordering on the set $\{Z\}$ of all partitions of X. Moreover, $\{Z\}$ is a lattice possessing a (unique) finest element, $\{(x)\}$, and a (unique) coarsest element, (X).

2. Payoff-relevant Sets of State Descriptions and Act Descriptions.

We shall continue to denote by $Z = \{z\}$ a partition of X; and we shall denote by $C = \{c\}$ a partition of A. In general, the decision maker associates with a given pair "state description z and act description c" a set of one or more physical outcomes (e.g., the possession of several

---

[2] Birkhoff [2]. Savage's [3] relation "extension of" is also pertinent.

alternative lots of land) and he may or may not attach to these outcomes the same payoff in terms of "utility" (a real number). If he
does not, we say that the set $Z \times C$ of the pairs (z, c) is "too coarse."
On the other hand $Z \times C$ is "too fine" if, for every c in C, some
pairs (z_1, c), (z_2, c) yield identical sets of utilities although $z_1 \neq z_2$; or
for every z in Z, some pairs (z, c_1), (z, c_2) yield identical sets of
utilities although $c_1 \neq c_2$. In the following example (Exhibit 3-1), $Z \times C$
is both too coarse and too fine (the entries are sets of utility-numbers).

Exhibit 3-1. A payoff matrix.

	State descriptions		
Act descriptions	z_1	z_2	z_3
c_1	(1,2)	(1,2)	(1)
c_2	(1,2)	(1,2)	(1)
c_3	(3)	(3)	(0)

   We can assume that the handling of too fine descriptions of states
and acts induces a cost (lowers utility) to the decision maker; while
too coarse descriptions of states and acts make it generally impossible to make choices, either under certainty or uncertainty.
   We must therefore search for a *payoff-relevant* pair $Z \times C$, i.e.,
one that (if it exists) is not too coarse and not too fine. This search
is preliminary to the search for a (jointly) best act description and
best channel; just like the search for the efficient boundary (Irving
Fisher's "Opportunity Line:"[4]) of a given feasible set is preliminary to the search for its optimal point.
   The concepts will be formalized as follows, remembering that a
function (a payoff function in our case) is changed when we change its
domain ($Z \times C$ in our case). For a closer discussion see [5].
   Given: for every partition Z of X and every partition C of Λ, a
set $\Omega = \{\omega_{ZC}\}$ called *payoff condition*, with the following three prop-
ties:

   (i) Each element ω_{ZC} of Ω is a function (called *payoff function*)
from $Z \times C$ to the set of all subsets of the real line R; thus if $z \in Z$,
$c \in C$, then

$$\omega_{ZC}(z, c) \subseteq R \tag{4}$$

   (ii) If $Z = \{(x)\}$ and $C = \{(a)\}$, (these are, of course, the finest par-
tions of X and A, respectively), then

$$\omega_{ZC}\{(x), (a)\} \equiv (u_{xa}) \qquad \text{is a single-element set.} \qquad (5)$$

The number u_{xa} is called the utility of act a at state x. The function ω_{ZC} obeying (5) is called *basic payoff function.*

(iii) All payoff functions in Ω are *consistent* in the sense that

$$\omega_{ZC}(z, c) = \bigcup_{x \in z} \bigcup_{a \in c} (u_{xa}) \qquad \text{all } z, c \qquad (6)$$

The components z and c of the argument of a payoff function ω_{ZC} will be called, respectively, an *event* and an *action.* Hence an action is an act description. An event is a state description. A message (Sec. 1 above) is also a state description, and differs from an event in that a message does not, in general, enter the argument of a payoff function. Rather, it is the argument of the decision function, to be defined in Section 4.

DEFINITIONS. $Z \times C$ is sufficiently fine (or, equivalently, "not too coarse"), given Ω, if and only if

$$\omega_{ZC}(z, c) = (u_{xa}) \qquad \text{all } x \in z, \ a \in c, \ z \in Z, \ c \in C \qquad (7)$$

$Z \times C$ is sufficiently coarse (= "not too fine"), given Ω, if and only if, for every $z_1, z_2 \in Z$, $c_1, c_2 \in C$,

$$\omega_{ZC}(z_1, c) = \omega_{ZC}(z_2, c) \qquad \text{for all } c \in C \text{ implies } z_1 = z_2 \qquad (8.1)$$

and

$$\omega_{ZC}(z, c_1) = \omega_{ZC}(z, c_2) \qquad \text{for all } z \in Z \text{ implies } c_1 = c_2 \qquad (8.2)$$

$Z \times C$ is *payoff-relevant,* given Ω, if and only if $Z \times C$ is not too coarse and not too fine, given Ω.

THEOREM I. *There is one and only one payoff-relevant pair,* $Z \times C$, *given* Ω, (it will be sometimes denoted by $Z^\Omega \times C^\Omega$). The proof is given in [5].[3]

EXAMPLE 1 (Continued). As before, let X = real n-space, $x = (x_1, \ldots, x_n)$. Let

$$A = \text{real interval } (-1 \le a \le 1) \qquad (9)$$

---

[3] Actually, in [5] the author first proves a somewhat stronger theorem. Instead of the *payoff condition,* Ω (denoted there by V), a more general, *outcome condition,* W, is defined: it is a (consistent) set of "outcome functions," from $Z \times C$ to the set of subsets of (physical) outcomes, which are not necessarily real numbers. The uniqueness and existence of an "outcome-relevant" domain $Z^W \times C^W$, given W, is then proved. A real valued utility function u, on the set of outcomes, is then introduced.

By (6), we can define two alternative payoff conditions Ω, Ω' by giving the utilities (u_{xa}, u'_{xa}, say) of each act at each state. Accordingly, define

$$\Omega : u_{xa} = a \cdot \sum_1^n x_i \tag{10}$$

$$\Omega' : u'_{xa} = \delta \left(a \sum_1^n x_i \right) \tag{10'}$$

where δ is the *sign function* in the sense that, for any real r,

$$\delta_r \equiv \delta(r) = \begin{cases} 1 & \text{if } r > 0 \\ -1 & \text{otherwise} \end{cases}$$

[We shall retain this definition and notation for the sign function through the rest of the paper.] Now consider the following sets of state descriptions, each set being an element of the set $\{Z\}$ of all partitions of X:

$$Z^0 = \{(x)\}$$

$$Z^I = \{z^I : x \epsilon z^I \Leftrightarrow \sum_1^n x_i = z^I\}$$

$$Z^{II} = \{z^{II} : x \epsilon z^{II} \Leftrightarrow \delta\left(\sum_1^n x_i\right) = z^{II}\}$$

and the following set of act descriptions (actions), each an element of the set $\{C\}$ of all partitions of A:

$$C^0 = \{(a)\}$$

$$C^{II} = \{c^{II} : a \epsilon c^{II} \Leftrightarrow \delta(a) = c^{II}\}$$

If the payoff condition is Ω as in (10), then clearly $Z^0 \times C$ is too fine, for all C in $\{C\}$, since there exists x, x*, such that $x \neq x^*$ and yet $\sum_1^n x_i = \sum_1^n x_i^*$, and hence $u_{xa} = u_{x^*a}$, for all a. But $Z^{II} \times C$ is too coarse for all C in $\{C\}$, since there exist x, x^* in X with $\sum x_i > \sum x_i^* > 0$. And $Z \times C^{II}$ is too coarse, for all Z in $\{Z\}$, for there exist $a > a^* > 0$ in A. It is easily seen that $Z^I \times C^0$ is the pair relevant with respect to Ω.

If, on the other hand the payoff condition is Ω' as in (10') then the pairs $Z^0 \times C$ and $Z^I \times C$ are too fine, for all C in $\{C\}$; the pair $Z \times C^0$ is too fine, for all Z in $\{Z\}$; and it is easily seen that $Z^{II} \times C^{II}$ is relevant with respect to Ω'.

INTERPRETATION: "Speculator" vs. "sign-matcher."

Every $z^0 \equiv (x)$ in Z^0 is some list of price-changes predicted for the month's end for each of n securities making up a portfolio. Every $c^0 \equiv (a)$ in C^0 is some number of portfolio-units, sold (if $a > 0$) or bought (if $a < 0$) today to be repurchased or resold at month's end. The *speculator's* payoff is u_{xa} in (10) if his utilities are proportional to his money gains. If a is in the interval $[-1, +1]$ it is easily seen that he need not consider other values of a than -1 or $+1$.

The professional adviser to the speculator will be rewarded or penalized, by receiving $+1$ or -1 money units depending on whether he has succeeded or failed to match the sign of the recommended action a with the sign of $\sum_1^n x_i$. The *sign-matcher's* payoff is u'_{xa} in (10') if his utilities are proportional to his money gains.

A Corollary to Theorem I, proved with it in [5], shows how the payoff-relevant pair Z^{Ω}, C^{Ω} of partitions can be constructed when X, A and Ω are known. So far, we have evaded the question whether the decider is assumed to know the sets X and A, i.e., to be able to identify every most detailed description of states and acts. In our interpretation of Example 1 the investor's chosen dinner menu was not mentioned as an attribute of an act description, nor was the position of the planetoid Vesta mentioned among the attributes of a state description. These and many other details were tacitly judged irrelevant to the payoff that consisted of, or depended on, the profit earned on the investor's portfolio, and nothing else. We shall take up this question in Section 5.

It will be understood (because of Theorem I) that to give a payoff condition Ω implies giving a payoff function $\omega_{Z^{\Omega}C^{\Omega}}$ that maps a well defined payoff-relevant pair (Z^{Ω}, C^{Ω}) of description sets into the set of real numbers (utilities).

DEFINITIONS. Consider a payoff condition $\Omega = \{\omega_{ZC}\}$, and hence the basic payoff function u_{xa}, as given. If a_1, a_2 are two acts in A, then a_1 is said to *dominate* a_2 if $u_{xa_1} \geq u_{xa_2}$ for all x in X, and $u_{xa_1} > u_{xa_2}$ for some x in X. The subset $A(\Omega) = \{a(\Omega)\}$ of A consisting of all non-dominated acts $a(\Omega)$, and also every partition $C(\Omega)$ of $A(\Omega)$, will be called *efficient* with respect to Ω. Since, by definition, the decider maximizes utility, one must consider only these efficient sets (of acts or actions, respectively). Replacing every partition of C of A by a partition $C(\Omega)$ of $A(\Omega)$, entails replacing the payoff condition $\{\omega_{ZC}\} \equiv \Omega$ by $\{\omega_{ZC(\Omega)}\} \equiv (\Omega)$ (say). With all the non-efficient action sets eliminated, some pairs $Z \times C$ which are too fine for Ω are not too fine for (Ω). The pair $Z^{(\Omega)} \times C^{(\Omega)}$ "relevant" with respect to (Ω) may be called "efficiently relevant" with respect to Ω. It will, in general, differ from the pair $Z^{\Omega} \times C^{\Omega}$ simply "relevant" with respect to Ω.

EXAMPLE 1 (continued). Clearly, if the payoff condition is Ω as in (10), the efficient set of acts is $A(\Omega) = \{a(\Omega)\} = \{\delta_a\} = (1,-1)$, and its finest partition $C^0(\Omega) = ((1), (-1))$ is the efficient set of actions. The pair $Z^{(\Omega)} \times C^{(\Omega)}$ efficiently relevant with respect to Ω is $Z^I \times C^0(\Omega)$. If, on the other hand, the payoff condition is Ω' as in (10') the efficient set of acts is $A(\Omega') = C^{II}$, and the efficiently relevant pair is $Z^{II} \times C^{II}$.

3. Probabilities of Messages and Events

Given: A probability measure P defined on the set X of states. (The "personal" nature of P will be discussed below, Section 5.)

With P given, the probability distribution over any partition Z of X is determined. In particular, P determines, for a given payoff condition Ω, the probability distribution over the set Z^{Ω} of payoff-relevant state descriptions. Also, given a channel h, P determines the probability distribution over the set Y^h of potential messages that may be received by the decider.

More strongly: the probability measure P on X determines the multivariate distribution over the product space of all partitions Z of X. Therefore P determines the bivariate distribution for each pair of such partitions. In particular, the measure P on X determines the bivariate distribution of (Z^{Ω}, Y^h), for every payoff condition Ω and every channel h.

For simplicity of presentation, we shall assume X finite. The probability $P(x \in z)$ that x falls into the subset z of X, i.e., into the element z of partition Z of X, might be denoted by $p_Z(z)$, as distinguished from $p_{Z'}(z')$ where $z' \subset Z'$. But we shall be able to omit the domain index (Z, Z') if we are careful in denoting the argument of the function by appropriate lower-case letters (z, z') and write $P(x \in z) = p(z)$, $P(x \in z') = p(z')$, it being understood that $z \in Z$, $z' \in Z'$ etc. Thus, we shall define the marginal probabilities

$$p(z^{\Omega}) = P(x \in z^{\Omega}) = \sum_{x \in z^{\Omega}} p(x) \qquad (11.1)$$

$$p(y^h) = P(x \in y^h) = \sum_{x \in y^h} p(x); \qquad (11.2)$$

the joint probability:

$$p(z^{\Omega}, y^h) = P(x \in z^{\Omega}, x \in y^h) = \sum_{x \in z^{\Omega} \cap y^h} p(x); \qquad (12)$$

and the conditional probability:

$$p(z^{\Omega} \mid y^h) = p(z^{\Omega}, y^h)/p(y^h) \qquad (13)$$

All state descriptions with which we shall deal will be either *messages* received by the decider and denoted by y^h; or they will affect the payoff, i.e. occur in the argument of a payoff function $\omega_{ZC}(z, c)$. In the latter case we call them *events*, z. Thus (13) defines the conditional probability of an event, given a message.

The events z will be usually payoff-relevant, and denoted by z^{Ω}; but we shall sometimes be able to remove the superscript Ω for brevity. Also for brevity, we can omit the domain index ZC of a payoff function ω_{ZC}, it being indicated by the corresponding lower-case letters in the argument.

For example, let there be exactly 8 *states* x, labelled $1, 2, \ldots, 8$, and write $p(x) \equiv p_X$. Exhibit 3-2 gives the joint distribution $p(z, y)$ of *events* z (defined in the headings of rows) and of *messages* y (defined in the headings of columns):

Exhibit 3-2. Joint distribution $p(z, y)$.

y: z:	(2,3)	(4,5)	(6,1)	(7,8)
(1,2)	p_2	0	p_1	0
(3,4)	p_3	p_4	0	0
(5,6)	0	p_5	p_6	0
(7,8)	0	0	0	$p_7 + p_8$
$p(y)$	$p_2 + p_3$	$p_4 + p_5$	$p_1 + p_6$	$p_7 + p_8$

From this, the conditional distribution $p(z \mid y) = p(z, y)/p(y)$ can be derived. For example, $P[z = (1, 2) \mid y = (2, 3)] = p_2 /(p_2 + p_3)$.

SUB-EXAMPLE 1.1. (*A finite set of states*). Define the set X of *states* as in Example 1, with $n = 2$. Let each co-ordinate of x have 3 values (so that X consists of $3^2 = 9$ points), and be distributed independently, identically, and symmetrically (in fact, binomially) about the origin, as in Exhibit 3-3. The sets Z^I and Z^{II} of *events* defined in Section 2, Example 1 (continued) will be designated, without danger of ambiguity, as random variables $z^I = x_1 + x_2$ (five-valued) and $z^{II} = \delta(z^I)$ (two-valued). The distributions of z^I and z^{II} are determined by that of x as shown on Exhibit 3-3, where probability numbers corresponding to points in sets are grouped into appropriate subsets.

The distribution of messages y^h and messages y^{h*} also determined by that of states x, is shown in a similar way on Exhibit 3-4. Finally Exhibits 3-5 and 3-6 show the bivariate distributions of events and messages considered, and corresponding conditional distributions

of events, given the messages. All these distributions are derived
from that of states.[4]

Exhibit 3-3. Distributions of states $x = (x_1, x_2)$; events $z^I = (x_1 + x_2)$;
and events $z^{II} = \delta(z^I)$.

$$P(x_i = 0) = 1/2; P(x_i = 1) = 1/4 = P(x_i = -1); p(x_i, x_j) = p(x_i) \cdot p(x_j)$$

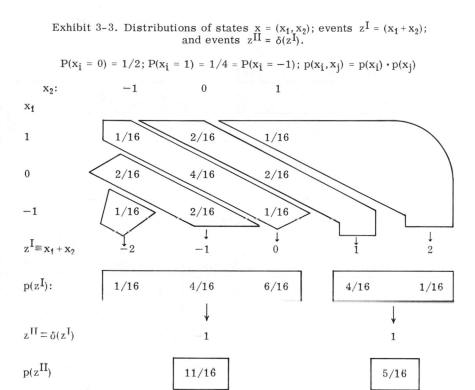

With our definition of states, events and messages, to state an
"error" in a message y —for example, to measure an observation or
transmission error—is to make a comparison between the *state description* y and the *state description* (event) z; not between y and the
state x. The state of the observation or transmission instrument, associated with the error, is itself one of the attributes of the state x of
the world. This idea has been effectively stressed by R. Radner.

[4] yh^* and z^{II} are each distributed asymmetrically (Exhibits 3-4 and 3-3)
because of the way the sign function was defined. This would become less pro-
nounced if each co-ordinate x_i took a larger number of values, thus approach-
ing continuity and making the probabilities $P\left(\sum_{1}^{m} x_i = 0\right)$, $P\left(\sum_{1}^{n} x_i = 0\right)$ approach zero.

Exhibit 3-4. Distributions of states $x = (x_1, x_2)$; messages $y^h = (x_1)$; and messages $y^{h*} = \delta(y^h)$.

x_2:	-1	0	1	y^h	$p(y^h)$	y^{h*}	$p(y^{h*})$
x_1							
1	1/16	2/16	1/16 →	1	4/16 →	1	4/16
0	2/16	4/16	2/16 →	0	8/16		
						→ -1	12/16
-1	1/16	2/16	1/16 →	-1	4/16		

Exhibit 3-5. Distribution of events z^I, jointly with, or conditional on, messages y^h, y^{h*}.

y^h: 1	0	-1	1	0	-1	y^{h*}:1	-1	1	-1
z^I	$p(z^I, y^h)$			$p(z^I \mid y^h)$			$p(z^I, y^{h*})$		$p(z^I \mid y^{h*})$
-2 0	0	1/16	0	0	1/4	0	1/16	0	1/12
-1 0	2/16	2/16	0	1/4	2/4	0	4/16	0	4/12
0 1/16	4/16	1/16	1/4	2/4	1/4	1/16	5/16	1/4	5/12
1 2/16	2/16	0	2/4	1/4	0	2/16	2/16	2/4	2/12
2 1/16	0	0	1/4	0	0	1/16	0	1/4	0
SUM 1/4	2/4	1/4	1	1	1	1/4	3/4	1	1

Exhibit 3-6. Distribution of events z^{II}, jointly with, or conditional on, messages y^h, y^{h*}.

y^h: 1	0	-1	1	0	-1	y^{h*}:1	-1	1	-1
z^I	$p(z^{II}, y^h)$			$p(z^{II} \mid y^h)$			$p(z^{II}, y^{h*})$		$p(z^{II} \mid y^{h*})$
-1 1/16	6/16	4/16	1/4	3/4	1	1/16	10/16	1/4	5/6
1 3/16	2/16 · 0		3/4	1/4	0	3/16	2/16	3/4	1/6
SUM 1/4	2/4	1/4	1	1	1	1/4	3/4	1	1

4. Feasible and Optimal Action Rules.

We use the brief term *action* for the act description c that occurs in the argument of a payoff function. Usually any action we shall deal with will be relevant, c^Ω, or efficiently relevant, $c^{(\Omega)}$; but these superscripts will be often omitted. [The difference will not matter: any action that maximizes expected payoff will turn out to be efficient.] Any function $\gamma_{h,\Omega}$ from the set Y^h of messages (received through channel h) to a set C^Ω of payoff-relevant actions is called a *decision function* (or *action rule*). Thus

$$c^\Omega = \gamma_{h,\Omega}(y^h) \qquad c^\Omega \epsilon C^\Omega, \; y^h \epsilon Y^h \tag{14}$$

The payoff of a given action and given event is then

$$\omega(z^\Omega, c^\Omega) = \omega[z^\Omega, \gamma_{h,\Omega}(y^h)] \tag{15}$$

It follows from (14) that each pair (h,Ω)—a given channel and a given payoff condition—is associated with a unique set $\Gamma_{h,\Omega}$ of action rules. The average payoff of an action rule will be called its payoff, to be denoted by $u(\gamma_{h,\Omega})$. By (15)

$$u(\gamma_{h,\Omega}) = E\omega(z^\Omega, c^\Omega) = E\omega[z^\Omega, \gamma_{h,\Omega}(y^h)]$$

$$= \sum_{y \epsilon Y^h} \sum_{z^\Omega \epsilon Z^\Omega} \omega[z^\Omega, \gamma_{h,\Omega}(y^h)] \cdot p(z^\Omega, y^h) \tag{16}$$

so that by (13)

$$u(\gamma_{h,\Omega}) = \sum_{y \epsilon Y^h} p(y^h) \sum_{z^\Omega \epsilon Z^\Omega} \omega[z^\Omega, \gamma_{h,\Omega}(y^h)] \cdot p(z^\Omega | y^h) \tag{17}$$

The second sum in (17) is the expected payoff conditional upon the message y^h received, and depending on the action rule. The payoff of the action rule is the average of the conditional expected payoffs, taken over all the messages of the channel h. Equation (17) implies that, to maximize $u(\gamma_{h,\Omega})$ over the set $\Gamma_{h,\Omega}$ of action rules, we can maximize separately the expected payoffs conditional upon each of the messages y^h. That is: if $\gamma^*_{h,\Omega}$ is optimal, i.e., if it has maximum utility for a given (h,Ω) then

$$u(\gamma^*_{h,\Omega}) = \sum_{y^h \epsilon Y^h} p(y^h) \max_{\gamma \epsilon \Gamma_{h,\Omega}} \sum_{z^\Omega \epsilon Z^\Omega} \omega[z^\Omega, \gamma(y^h)] \; p(z^\Omega | y^h) \tag{18}$$

or, still simpler (see [14]),

$$u(\gamma^*_{h,\Omega}) = \sum_{y^h \epsilon Y^h} p(y^h) \max_{c \epsilon C^\Omega} \sum_{z^\Omega \epsilon Z^\Omega} \omega(z^\Omega, c) \, p(z^\Omega | y^h) \tag{19}$$

that is, the payoff of action rule is maximized by choosing, for each message y^h an optimal action, i.e., one that will maximize the expected payoff conditional upon this message; the set of pairs "message, optimal action" determines then the optimal action rule, given the channel h and the payoff condition Ω.

The formulations in this section do not differ in spirit or content from those used in the current work in decision theory. The notations are almost identical with those used in the economic theory of teams,[5] except for the lavish use of the indices h and Ω, necessitated by the particular focus of this paper.

5. Beliefs, Tastes and Resources

So far, an optimal rule of action $\gamma^*_{h,\Omega}$ has been defined formally in (18) as that element of the set $\Gamma_{h,\Omega}$ of action rules which maximizes the expected payoff expressed in (16). We assume the decider to be *consistent*, in the following sense: if the channel h and the payoff condition Ω vary, he will choose an appropriately varying optimal rule of action. This is, in fact, implied in the meaning of "personal probabilities" and "utilities:" they are numbers which are assigned, on the one hand, to events and, on the other, to the outcomes of a consistent man's actions, and which have the property that he will always choose the action maximizing the sum of products of these numbers, i.e., the expected utility. The existence of such numbers follows, by logic and mathematics, from a few simple postulates of choice (of which the rules of transitivity and of admissibility are two) which the consistent man will regret not to have obeyed just as he would regret to have disobeyed the rules of logic and arithmetic (see Savage [3]).

Under certainty, an optimal action of a consistent man is determined by two conditions: (1) his *resources*, i.e., the set of feasible actions (e.g., the consumer's resources are given by his assets and the market prices, and the producer's resources are given by his assets and technology); (2) his *tastes*, i.e., the preference ordering on the set of all actions.

In the more general case of uncertainty the preference ordering, or *tastes*, of a consistent man must satisfy the following conditions: there exists a function ω_{XA} on $X \times A$ and a probability function $p(x)$ on X such that, for all a_1, a_2 in A,

a_2 is not preferred to a_1 if $\qquad\qquad\qquad\qquad$ (20)

$$\sum_{x \in X} \omega_{XA}(x, a_1) p(x) \geq \sum_{x \in X} \omega_{XA}(x, a_2) p(x)$$

---

[5] For example McGuire [6], Marschak [7], Radner [8]. In [9] Radner states the relation to the concepts of statistical decision theory.

The two compared averages are called utilities of a_1, a_2, respectively, although this word is sometimes confined only to acts a with $\omega(x, a)$ constant over X. (Note also that in the special case of certainty, $\omega(x, a)$, is indeed constant over X, for every a). The function p on X can then be said to describe the decider's *beliefs*.[6]

The decider's *resources* under uncertainty can be described as the set H of available channels, and the set $\Gamma_{h, \Omega}$ of available action rules, with due attention to the fact that, in general, channels and action rules are not costless. The *cost* of using a channel will depend, in general, on the channel, and on the message actually sent. Accordingly, we define a cost function, κ, from the set Y^h of messages associated with channel h to the set of real numbers (utilities). Henceforth we shall call the payoff $\omega(z^\Omega, c^\Omega)$ of action c^Ω its gross payoff, given the event z^Ω. From the gross payoff, the cost $\kappa(y^h)$ is deducted to obtain the net payoff of the action, given the event and the message. The net payoff is, by (15)

$$\omega[z^\Omega, \gamma_{h, \Omega}(y^h)] - \kappa(y^h) \tag{21}$$

Correspondingly the maximum average payoff $u(\gamma^*_{h, \Omega})$ defined in (18) can be called the *gross payoff of channel* h, *given* Ω. It depends on h and Ω and can be conveniently denoted by

$$v(h, \Omega) \equiv u(\gamma^*_{h, \Omega}) = E_y\{\max_c E_z[\omega(z, c)|y]\} \qquad z \in Z^\Omega, \ c \in C^\Omega,$$

$$y \in Y^h \tag{22}$$

As explained in Section 4., $v(h, \Omega)$ is the average (over all y) of the conditionally expected payoffs obtained under the optimal action rule.

[6] We can now offer at least a conjectural answer to a question raised at the end of Section 2. It is not required that the decider be able to specify the most detailed set of state descriptions and of act descriptions, and the corresponding payoff and probability function. But it is required that consistency be preserved between the different coarser description sets and corresponding payoff and probability functions, that will vary from one decision situation to another and will obey the (appropriately modified) preference condition (20). The sets and functions must be such as to admit the existence of some (unknown), X, A, ω_{XA}, p(X) satisfying the consistency conditions (6) and (12). If such consistency is preserved then it is possible, given a collection of sets Z, Z', ... ,of events on the one hand, and a collection of sets C, C', ... of actions on the other, to construct the two sets X* and A* consisting, respectively of all the intersections

$$x^* \equiv z \cap z' \cap \ldots \qquad \text{all } z \in Z, \ z' \in Z', \ldots$$

$$a^* \equiv c \cap c' \cap \ldots \qquad \text{all } c \in C, \ c' \in C', \ldots$$

and to use X*, A* as if they were the most detailed sets X, A, in order to find the payoff-relevant sets Z^Ω, C^Ω for a given payoff condition Ω, as in [5], Corollary to Theorem I.

The *net payoff of channel* h, *given* Ω, is then

$$w(h, \Omega) = v(h, \Omega) - E_y \kappa(y^h) \qquad (23)$$

To choose an optimal channel is to maximize $w(h, \Omega)$ over the set H of available channels. This operation is preceded by finding the action rule $\gamma^*_{h, \Omega}$ optimal over the set of available action rules.[7]

Regarding the set of available action rules, remember that in Sec. 4 we have defined the whole set $\Gamma_{h, \Omega}$ of functions obtained by associating each possible payoff-relevant action c^Ω with each possible message y^h. In general, only some *feasible subset* of $\Gamma_{h, \Omega}$ will have to be considered, either because some actions are physically incompatible with some messages or because some action rules are difficult to specify or to implement. For example, to specify an optimal decision function of numerical messages may be very difficult unless one limits oneself to the class of linear decision functions. In the last analysis the feasible subset of action rules is chosen on grounds of cost (with infinite cost for physically unfeasible rules). Accordingly, one might redefine the cost $\kappa(y^h)$ to be dependent on the pair $(y^h, \gamma_{h, \Omega})$ and thus to represent the *combined cost of information and of decision making*. This cost, $\kappa(y^h, \gamma_{h, \Omega})$ would replace $\kappa(y^h)$ in (21) and (23). We could go further and interpret h as an instrument that not only produces messages statistically dependent on events, but also transforms messages into decisions. This would take fuller account of automation and of its analogies in the organization problem, but we shall not make this step here. We shall, instead, neglect the cost of decision-making.

---

[7] An unpublished statement by K. Arrow prompts the following important remark. To define the net payoff of an action as a difference (21) *between two utility amounts* and to define, accordingly, the net payoff of a channel (i.e., the maximand!) as a difference (23) *between two utility amounts* is justified in the case when the outcomes of actions and the costs of messages are expressed in money, but only if the utility function of money is linear.

At the end of this paper, we shall interpret Ω as the payoff condition in terms of money, not of utility: that is, $\omega(z^\Omega, c^\Omega)$ is the money profit. Similarly, $\kappa(y^h)$ is the (non-negative) monetary cost of a message. We shall denote by v a general (linear or non-linear) non-decreasing utility function of money. To choose an optimal channel is, then, to maximize, over the set H of available channels, the *expected channel utility* defined as

$$\Upsilon \equiv \Upsilon(h, \Omega) \equiv E \, v[\omega(z^\Omega, c^\Omega) - \kappa(y^h)] \qquad (23^*)$$

where the action $c^\Omega \equiv \gamma^*_{h\Omega}(y^h)$, and where (since v is non-decreasing and κ is non-negative) the best action rule γ^* has been chosen so as to maximize the conditionally expected money profit, given the message y^h.

It would be still more general—but more meager in results—not to assume any monetary measurements and to apply general utility function to the set of outcomes of all feasible pairs of channels and of action rules.

6. Sufficient Channels

In an important case, the ordering of gross channel payoffs is independent of the payoff condition. We give without proof the following Theorem (see also [10, p. 86]):

THEOREM II. $v(h, \Omega) \geq v(h^*, \Omega)$ *for all* Ω *and all* P *on* X *if and only if* Y^h *is finer than* Y^{h^*}.

This is useful in connection with the following definition and postulate:

DEFINITION. A channel h* is said to be sufficient with respect to the payoff condition Ω if, for any available Y^h that is finer than Y^{h^*}, $v(h, \Omega) = v(h^*, \Omega)$.

POSTULATE. If Y^h is finer than Y^{h^*}, the expected channel cost to the decider is larger (or at least not smaller) for h than for h*. (This postulate is to be added to those on consistent behavior of the decider.)

It follows that, if channel h* is sufficient, it cannot be worse than any available channel that is finer or coarser than h*. (The relation to sufficient statistics, a special case, is obvious. See also [12, 13].)[8]

II. A SPECIAL CLASS OF PROBLEMS.
(SUB-EXAMPLE 1.2)

7. Continuous vs. Two-valued Messages; Continuous vs. Two-valued linear payoffs.

As before, we define a *state* $x \in X$ as a real vector

$$x = (x_1, \ldots, x_n)$$

We shall consider two sequences, H and H*, of *channels*; and two alternative payoff conditions, Ω and Ω'. As before, we define a sign function δ of any real number r thus:

$$\delta_r = \delta(r) - \begin{cases} 1 & \text{if } r > 0 \\ -1 & \text{otherwise} \end{cases} \tag{24}$$

The sequence $H = (h_1, \ldots, h_n)$ of channels is defined thus: for every $m (\leq n)$, the message obtained through the channel h_m is

---

[8] The results of this section are not affected in substance by the remark in the previous footnote if gross channel payoff $v(h, \Omega)$ is redefined as $\Upsilon(h, \Omega)$ of (23*), putting $\kappa(y^h) = 0$ and remembering that the money utility function υ is non-decreasing. Similarly, expected channel cost is redefined as $\Upsilon(h, \Omega)$, putting $\omega = 0$ and remembering the κ is non-negative.

$$y^{h_m} = \sum_1^m x_i = y_m, \quad \text{say} \tag{25}$$

Thus Y^{h_m} is the real line.

The sequence $H^* = (h_1^*, \ldots, h_n^*)$ of channels is defined thus: for every $m(\leq n)$

$$y^{h_m^*} = \delta(y_m) \tag{25*}$$

Thus $Y^{h_m^*}$ consists of two points.

In either case messages are about some property of the sub-vector $(x_1, \ldots, x_m)$. In the case H the message is a continuous random variable $y_m = \sum_i^m x_i$. In the case H^* the message is a two-valued random variable: $y_m^* = +1$ or -1. NOTE: *Clearly h_m is finer than h_m^*!*

INTERPRETATION: If we interpret x as the list of future price changes of n securities, a message y_m gives the sum (or, with properly chosen units, the mean) of such changes for a sample consisting of $m(\leq n)$ securities. A message y_m^*, on the other hand, merely states whether the sum (or mean) of the m prices is or is not going to rise. In a more general interpretation, x is a finite population, y_m is the sample mean, and $\delta(y_m) \equiv y_m^*$ is its sign.

We shall sometimes write $y_m = y$ for brevity.
As in (9), (10) and (10′), we define the act a as a point in the real interval

$$-1 \leq a \leq 1 \tag{26}$$

and we define two alternative payoff conditions:

$$\Omega: u_{xa} = a \cdot \sum_1^n x_i \qquad \Omega': u'_{xa} = a \cdot \delta(\sum_1^n x_i). \tag{27}$$

[INTERPRETATION: As before, Ω characterizes a "speculator" with continuous profit variable, and Ω' a "sign-matcher," with a 2-valued profit-variable.]

We have seen (Section 2) that the efficiently relevant pairs of description sets are, in this Example, for the two payoff functions Ω, Ω', respectively:

State descriptions (set of payoff-relevant events):

$$Z^{(\Omega)} = Z^I = \{z^I : x \epsilon z^I \Leftrightarrow \sum_1^n x_i = z^I\};$$

$$Z^{(\Omega')} = Z^{II} = \{z^{II} : x \epsilon z^{II} \Leftrightarrow \delta(\sum_1^n x_i) = z^{II}\}$$

We shall henceforth write $z^I \equiv z$, for brevity. Then

$$Z^{(\Omega)} = \{z\} \qquad Z^{(\Omega')} = \{\delta_z\}$$

Act description (set of efficient payoff-relevant actions):

$$C^{(\Omega)} = C^{(\Omega')} \equiv \{(\delta_a)\} = (1, -1)$$

We shall henceforth write $c = \delta_a$. Then by (27) the two payoff functions to consider are:

$$\omega(z, c) = z \cdot \delta_a \quad \text{and} \quad \omega'(z, c) = \delta_z \cdot \delta_a \qquad (28)$$

where $z = \sum_1^n x_i$.

The two payoff conditions Ω, Ω', combined with the two channel sequences H, H^*, result in four cases which we shall number as on Exhibit 3-7.

Exhibit 3-7. Four cases

Payoff condition:	Channels	
	h_m: message $= y_m = \sum_1^m x_i$	h_m^*: message $= \delta(y_m)$.
Ω: (payoff $= \delta_a \cdot z$)	Case 1.	Case 2.
Ω': (payoff $= \delta_a \cdot \delta_z$)	Case 3.	Case 4.

In all 4 cases, the linear nature of the payoff conditions (27) requires that the set of acts be bounded, as in (26); so that the decider's best action is one of two extremes, $c = +1$ or -1 (e.g., "sell or buy the maximum possible amount").

In Cases 3. and 4., the decider's payoff function is two-valued (the "sign-matcher" case), while in Cases 1. and 2. it is continuous. As to channels: in cases 2. and 4. they send only two-valued ("yes, or no") messages while in cases 1. and 3. the messages are continuous.

For any probability distribution on X we shall characterize the gross channel payoffs on Exhibit 3-8, obtained on the lines of (18), (19), (22), by the following reasoning:

If the payoff condition is Ω [as defined in (27)] and therefore the payoff function is ω [see (28)] then, for any channel h, the conditionally expected payoff, given the message y^h, is

$$E_z[\omega(z, c) \mid y^h] = \sum_z \delta_a z \cdot p(z \mid y^h)$$

$$= \delta_a \sum_z z \cdot p(z \mid y^h) = \delta_a E_z (z \mid y^h);$$

hence optimal action c is $+1$ or -1 according as the conditional expectation $E(z|y^h)$ is or is not positive. Therefore

$$\max_c E_z[\omega(z,c)|y^h] = |E(z|y^h)|,$$

the *absolute value* of $E(z|y^h)$. Hence, by (19), (22), the gross channel payoff is

$$v(h,\Omega) = E_{yh}\{|E(z|y^h)|\} \tag{29}$$

By similar reasoning, if the payoff condition is Ω' then, for any h,

$$\max_c E_z[\omega(z,c)|y^h] = |E(\delta_z|y^h)|$$

$$v(h,\Omega') = E_{yh}\{|E(\delta_z|y^h)|\} \tag{29'}$$

Inserting the definitions of channels h and messages y^h from (25), (25*) we obtain Exhibit 3-8, with the understanding that the inner E-symbol means averaging over events (z or δ_z, as the case may be), while the outer E-symbol means averaging over messages (y_m or δ_{y_m}, as the case may be); and remembering that $z = \sum_1^n x_i$, and that δ is the sign function defined in (24).

Exhibit 3-8. Gross channel payoffs v.

Payoff condition	Channels	
	h_m (message: y_m)	h_m^* (message: δ_{y_m}).
Ω: (payoff = $\delta_a \cdot z$)	Case 1. $E\{|E(z|y_m)|\}$	Case 2. $E\{|E(z|\delta_{y_m})|\}$
Ω': (payoff = $\delta_a \cdot \delta_z$)	Case 3. $E\{|E(\delta_z|y_m)|\}$	Case 4. $E\{|E(\delta_z|\delta_{y_m})|\}$

8. Conditions for Sufficiency of Binary Channels.

In our example so far, we have not yet specified the probability distribution of states, or the probability measure P on X. We shall see in this section that, under a rather weak specification of P, the coarser sequence H* of (binary) channels becomes sufficient with respect to the continuous payoff condition Ω; and that under a somewhat stronger specification of P, H* becomes sufficient also with respect to the binary payoff condition Ω'. The results of this Section will be utilized in the next two sections, enabling us to discuss channel costs relevant to the problem and then, assuming a more special (viz., the normal) distribution of states, take up the question of "decreasing marginal returns," and determine the optimal channel for given channel cost conditions. A similar study was made by McGuire [11].

Our weak specification is this: assume the co-ordinates x_i of the state vector x are statistically independent,

$$p(x_i \mid x_j) = p(x_i) \tag{I}$$

and they have zero means,

$$Ex_i = 0 \quad i = 1, \dots, n \tag{II}$$

We want to show that, under this assumption,

$$v(h_m, \Omega) = v(h_m^*, \Omega)$$

where [see Exhibit 3-8, cases 1. and 2.]

$$v(h_m, \Omega) = E\{|E(z \mid y_m)|\} \tag{30}$$

$$v(h_m^*, \Omega) = E\{|E(z \mid \delta_{y_m})|\} \tag{30*}$$

Since the x_i are independent, and $Ex_i = 0$ $(i = 1, \dots, n)$,

$$E(x_j \mid x_i) \begin{cases} = Ex_j = 0 & \text{if } i \neq j \\ = x_i & \text{if } i = j \end{cases}$$

Hence, writing $y_m \equiv y$ for brevity,

$$E(z \mid y) = E\left(y + \sum_{m+1}^{n} x_j \mid y\right) = y + E\left(\sum_{m+1}^{n} \sum_{1}^{m} x_j \mid x_1\right) = y$$

$$|E(z \mid y)| = |y| \tag{31}$$

Hence by (30)

$$v(h_m, \Omega) = E(|y|) \tag{32}$$

On the other hand, to evaluate $v(h_m^*, \Omega)$ of (30*), note that

$$E(z \mid \delta_y) = \begin{cases} E(y \mid y > 0) \\ E(y \mid y \leq 0) \end{cases} \quad \text{when } \delta_y = \begin{cases} +1 \\ -1 \end{cases}$$

$$| E(z|\delta_y)| = \begin{cases} E(y|y > 0) \\ E(-y|y \le 0) \end{cases} \text{when } \delta_y = \begin{cases} +1 \\ -1 \end{cases}$$

Hence $|E(z|\delta_y)| = E(y|\delta_y) = E(|y|)$, a constant.

$$v(h_m^*, \Omega) = E\{E|y|\} = E(|y|)$$

so that, by (32),

$$v(h_m^*, \Omega) = E(|y|) = v(h_m, \Omega) \equiv v_\Omega(m) \tag{33}$$

Thus when the payoff condition is Ω and the probability assumptions (I), (II) hold, both the coarser and the finer channel yield the same payoff, to be denoted by $v_\Omega(m)$. The coarser channel h_m^* is sufficient with respect to the payoff condition Ω.

Turning now to the binary payoff condition Ω' (cases 3. and 4. of Exhibit 3-8) we shall show that

$$v(h_m, \Omega') = v(h_m^*, \Omega')$$

(so that the binary channel h_m^* is sufficient with respect to Ω') if we replace our previous specifications (I), (II) of the state distribution, by stronger ones: assume all the co-ordinates x_i of x have the same distribution G_1 (say); that is, for any η.

$$G_1(\eta) = P(x_i \le \eta) \qquad i = 1, \ldots, n \tag{III}$$

Also assume G_1 is symmetrical about the origin, i.e.,

$$G_1(\eta) + G_1(-\eta) = 1 \tag{IV}$$

It follows from (III) that the sum of any r distinct co-ordinates has the same distribution G_r. Thus in particular

$$P\left(\sum_{m+1}^{n} x_i \le \eta\right) = P\left(\sum_{1}^{n-m} x_i \le \eta\right) = G_{n-m}(\eta)$$

$$P(y \le \eta) = P\left(\sum_{1}^{m} x_i \le \eta\right) = G_m(\eta);$$

it then follows from (IV) that every G_r is symmetrical about the origin:

$$G_r(\eta) + G_r(-\eta) = 1 \qquad dG_r(\eta) = dG_r(-\eta) \qquad r = 1, \ldots, n$$

and since G_r is a non-decreasing function,

$$G_r(\eta) \gtrless 1/2 \quad \text{if } \eta \gtrless 0, \, r = 1, \ldots, n \tag{35}$$

In this notation,

$$P(z \le 0 \,|\, y = \eta) = P\left(y + \sum_{m+1}^{n} x_i \le 0 \,|\, y = \eta\right) = P\left(\eta + \sum_{m+1}^{n} x_i \le 0\right)$$

$$= P\left(\sum_{m+1}^{n} x_i \le -\eta\right) = G_{n-m}(-\eta) = 1 - G_{n-m}(\eta)$$

so that

$$P(z > 0 \,|\, y = \eta) = G_{n-m}(\eta) = P(z \le 0 \,|\, y = -\eta) \ge \tfrac{1}{2} \quad \text{when } \eta \ge 0 \tag{36}$$

$$P(z \le 0 \,|\, y = \eta) = 1 - G_{n-m}(\eta) = P(z > 0 \,|\, y = -\eta) < \tfrac{1}{2} \quad \text{when } \eta < 0$$

We can now compute the probabilities for each of the four pairs of values of (δ_z, δ_y). Denote $P(\delta_z = 1, \delta_y = 1)$ by $p_\delta(1, 1)$ etc. Then

$$p_\delta(1, 1) = P(z > 0, \, y > 0) = \int_0^\infty P(z > 0 \,|\, y = \eta) \, dG_m(\eta)$$

$$= \int_0^\infty G_{n-m}(\eta) \, dG_m(\eta) = g_{m, n}, \quad \text{say}$$

Since, for η non-negative, both $G_{n-m}(\eta)$ and $G_m(\eta)$ are $\ge 1/2$, $g_{m, n} \ge 1/4$. When $m = n$, $P(z > 0, \, y > 0) = P(z > 0) = 1/2$. Thus we can make the following definition of $g_{m, n}$ (or g, for brevity)

$$g \equiv p_\delta(1, 1) \equiv \begin{cases} \int_0^\infty G_{n-m}(\eta) \, dG_m(\eta) & m = 1, \ldots, n - 1 \\ \\ 1/2 & m = n \end{cases} \tag{37}$$

The quantity g measures the *probability volume over the positive quadrant of the bivariate distribution* of (z, y). The distribution of (δ_z, δ_y) is:

$$1/4 \le p_\delta(1, 1) = g = p_\delta(-1, -1) \le 1/2$$

$$0 \le p_\delta(1, -1) = \tfrac{1}{2} - g = p_\delta(-1, 1) \le 1/4 \tag{38}$$

Now, to evaluate

$$v(h_m, \Omega') = E\{|E(\delta_z \,|\, y)|\} \tag{39}$$

we note that

$$E(\delta_z \,|y) = 1 \cdot P(z > 0 \,|y) - 1 \cdot P(z \le 0 \,|y) = 2P(z > 0 \,|y) - 1$$

and by (36), (35):

$$E(\delta_z \,|y) = 2\,G_{n-m}(y) - 1 \left\{ \begin{array}{l} > 0, \ y > 0 \\[6pt] \le 0, \ y \le 0 \end{array} \right.$$

$$|E(\delta_z \,|\,y\,|) = \left\{ \begin{array}{ll} 2\,G_{n-m}(y) - 1, & y > 0 \\[6pt] 1 - 2G_{n-m}(y) = 2\,G_{n-m}(-y) - 1, & y \le 0 \end{array} \right.$$

Hence $|E(\delta_z \,|\,y)| = 2\,G_{n-m}(|\,y\,|) - 1 \ge 0$

and by (39)

$$v(h_m, \Omega') = \int\limits_{-\infty}^{\infty} [2\,G_{n-m}(|\,y\,|) - 1]\,dG_m(y)$$

$$= -1 + 2 \int\limits_{0}^{\infty} 2\,G_{n-m}(y)\,dG_m(y)$$

$$v(h_m, \Omega') = 4g - 1 \ge 0, \tag{40}$$

g being as defined in (37). On the other hand, to evaluate

$$v(h_m^*, \Omega') = E\{|E(\delta_z \,|\delta_y)|\} \tag{41}$$

we note that

$$E(\delta_z \,|\delta_y) = P(\delta_z = 1 \,|\, \delta_y) - P(\delta_z = -1 \,|\, \delta_y) = 2P(\delta_z = 1 \,|\, \delta_y) - 1$$

$$E(\delta_z \,|\delta_y) = \left\{ \begin{array}{ll} 2P(z > 0 \,|\, y > 0) - 1 & \delta_y = 1 \\[6pt] 2P(z > 0 \,|\, y \le 0) - 1 & \delta_y = -1. \end{array} \right.$$

Now by (38)

$$P(z > 0 \,|y > 0) = [P(z > 0, \ y > 0)/P(y > 0)] = 2P(z > 0, \ y > 0) = 2g$$

$$P(z > 0 \,|y \le 0) = [P(z > 0, \ y \le 0)/P(y \le 0)] = 2P(z > 0, \ y \le 0) = 1 - 2g$$

$$E(\delta_z \,|\, \delta_y) = \left\{ \begin{array}{ll} 4g - 1 > 0 & \delta_y = 1 \\[6pt] 1 - 4g < 0 & \delta_y = -1 \end{array} \right.$$

$$|E(\delta_z |\delta_y)| = 4g - 1 \quad \text{a constant.}$$

And by (41), (40)

$$v(h^*_m, \Omega') = 4g - 1 = v(h_m, \Omega') \equiv v_\Omega(m) \qquad (42')$$

where g is defined as in (37). Thus, under assumptions (III)-(IV), the coarser channel h* is sufficient with respect to the payoff condition Ω'.

Under the same assumptions (III)-(IV) and the payoff condition Ω, the gross revenue of either channel, evaluated in (33), becomes[9]

$$v(h^*_m, \Omega) = 2 \int_0^\infty y \, dG_m(y) = v(h_m, \Omega) = v_\Omega(m) \qquad (42)$$

9. Channel Costs.

Because of our initial, broad definition of a channel as an instrument for gathering, processing, and (not only!) communicating data the expected channel costs $E\kappa(y)$ as defined in Section 5 should include the costs of observing the world, and of formulating (computing, coding) a message and transmitting it.

The theory of information has established a measure of the minimum channel capacity which is required to handle messages at a given rate, when the joint distribution on the set of the channel's inputs (the "source") and the set of its outputs (the set of messages) is known. Presumably channel cost increases with capacity; or, given the capacity, longer time is required per message, and this is again reflected in cost. (See [10].) This seems to be true, however, only if the channels considered are comparable in some sense, still to be defined. Two data-processing instruments of the same capacity are not necessarily associated with the same expected cost per message. Just as two land plots of equal acreage do not necessarily cost the same. Neither acreage nor information capacity solve the aggregation problem present in each case. The channels cannot be, in general, identified by a single (scalar) variable.

However, in the particular case of our example, all sufficient channels h^*_m belong to the sequence H*, ordered according to the unique

---

[9] SUB-EXAMPLE 1.1, continued. Note that the distribution on X given in Exhibit 3-3 satisfies condition (III) of the present section; it also satisfies the symmetry condition, though not in the continuous form (IV). Putting $z^I = z$, $z^{II} = \delta_z$, $y^h = y$, (with m = 1), $y^{h*} = \delta_y$, we can use Exhibits 3-5 and 3-6 to compute directly the gross channel payoffs for each of the 4 cases of Exhibits 3-7 and 3-8.

Cases 1 and 2: $v(h, \Omega) = v(h^*, \Omega) = \frac{1}{2}$

Cases 3 and 4: $v(h, \Omega') = v(h^*, \Omega') = \frac{5}{8}$

Thus, in this discrete sub-example, too, the binary channel (h*) is sufficient under either payoff condition considered.

parameter m, the number of observed co-ordinates x_i of the state vector $x = (x_1, \ldots, x_n)$, $(m \leq n)$. The distribution of x is given, and the joint input-output distributions, and hence the required capacities associated with the several channels, differ only with respect to the free parameter m. In this sense, the aggregation problem is by-passed. We can study the problem of increasing or decreasing returns (marginal gross payoffs to a single information channel parameter which itself increases with cost: just as we can study the problem of increasing or decreasing returns to a single quantitative input (or to a fixed mix of inputs) in a given industry.

The function relating the number m of observations to the minimum required capacity of channel h_m^* will depend on the distribution of the state vector x. It is not necessary to characterize this function explicitly.[10] It is simpler to associate channel cost of h_m^*, not with its capacity, but directly with the number of observations. On empirical grounds, we may know how the cost of observations depends on their number, and we shall regard other contributions to channel cost as fixed.

We shall assume the cost per observation to be constant[11] and denote it by k. Then the net payoffs are:

$$w_\Omega(m) = v_\Omega(m) - km \qquad w_{\Omega'}(m) = v_{\Omega'}(m) - km.[12]$$

The gross revenues v_Ω, $v_{\Omega'}$, evaluated in (42), (42′) depend only on the functions G_m, G_{n-m}. These, in turn, are derived from some given

---

[10] If $x = (x_1, \ldots, x_n)$ is considered the input, and $y_m^* = \delta\left(\sum_1^m x_i\right)$ the output of the channel h_m^*, the minimum required capacity of h_m^* is defined as the difference between U_0 ("uncertainty at source") and U_1 ("uncertainty retained") where

$$U_0 = -\sum_\xi P(x = \xi) \log P(x = \xi)$$

$$-U_1 = P(y_m^* = 1) \sum_\xi p(x = \xi \mid y_m^* = 1) \log P(x = \xi \mid y_m^* = 1)$$

$$+ P(y_m^* \mid -1) \sum_\xi p(x = \xi \mid y_m^* = -1) \log p(x = \xi \mid y_m^* = -1)$$

and ξ is a value of the (finite-valued) vector x. The difference $U_0 - U_1$ is called the "transmission rate" associated with (x, y_m^*). It is conjectured that it approaches a simple function of m as the distribution of x approaches normal distribution.

[11] The unit cost of "search" to the consumer is assumed constant by Stigler [14] in a simple market problem, but he allows non-linearity of cost in another context.

[12] As indicated in Footnote 6, both sides of each of these equations are measured in utility units, and a linear utility function of money is assumed. A more general case will be studied at the end of the next Section.

distribution of states which obeys assumptions (I)-(IV). We shall therefore be able, given any distribution satisfying (I)-(IV), to obtain the functional relationship between the unit cost k of observation and the optimal number of observations, separately for each of the two payoff conditions considered. We can denote these functions by

$$m_\Omega(k) \quad \text{and} \quad m_{\Omega'}(k)$$

respectively.

However, to make these two functions comparable, we must standardize the units. For the speculator (case Ω), the profit unit is \$1. For the sign-matcher (case Ω') profit unit is the fixed money amount gained as reward or lost as penalty. These are also utility units. To compare the functions $m_\Omega(k)$ and $m_{\Omega'}(k)$, relating optimal channel to the cost k per observation, we shall choose as a unit of gain (and of cost) the profit that is yielded by a single observation. That is, we shall impose the standardizing convention,

$$v_\Omega(1) = 2 \int_0^\infty y \, dG_1(y) = 1 \quad \text{using (42)} \tag{44}$$

$$v_{\Omega'}(1) = 4 \int_0^\infty G_{n-1}(y) \, dG_1(y) - 1 = 1 \quad \text{using (42'), (37).} \tag{44'}$$

(Note that in the latter case, the money unit will depend on n.) With the money unit thus standardized, k will measure the cost per observation, expressed as its proportion to the revenue yielded by a single observation.

10. The Case of Normal Distribution of States

We shall analyze completely, not the case of rather weak restrictions (I)-(IV) of Section 8, but only a more special case: the normal distribution. We assume, then, the state vector $x = (x_1, \ldots, x_n)$ to be distributed normally with zero-means and zero-covariances, thus satisfying all restrictions (I)-(IV). For convenience, we measure each x_i in units such that all variances $E(x_i^2) = 1$. To summarize:

$$x_i \text{ normal} \quad E(x_i) = 0 = E(x_i x_j) \quad i \neq j$$

$$E(x_i^2) = 1 \quad i = 1, \ldots, n \tag{45}$$

Since $z = \sum_1^n x_i$, $y = y_m = \sum_1^m x_i$, z and y are jointly normal with

$$E(z) = 0 = E(y) \quad E(z^2) = n \geq 1 \quad E(y^2) = m \geq 1 \tag{46}$$

so that the standard deviations are

$$\sigma_z = \sqrt{n} \geq 1 \qquad \sigma_y = \sqrt{m} \geq 1$$

The covariance between z and y is

$$E(zy) = E[(y + \sum_{m+1}^{n} x_j) y] = E(y^2) + \sum_{1}^{m} \sum_{m+1}^{n} E(x_i x_j) = m \geq 1$$

Hence the correlation, ρ, between z and y is always positive:

$$\rho = E(zy)/\sigma_z \sigma_y = m/\sqrt{mn} = +\sqrt{m/n} \qquad 0 < \rho \leq 1 \tag{47}$$

The gross revenue under the (continuous) payoff condition Ω is obtained immediately from (42). Since $G_m(y)$ is now normal with mean = 0 and $\sigma_y^2 = m$,

$$v_\Omega = +\sqrt{2m/\pi}$$

or, expressed in standard units defined in (44):

$$v_\Omega = +\sqrt{m} = v_\Omega(m) \tag{48}$$

On Exhibit 3-9 the function (48) is plotted for m continuous over the domain $[0, n]$, although only integer values will occur. The function is concave in m; the marginal returns to the number m of observations are decreasing throughout. To find the optimal channel, we maximize the net revenue

$$w_\Omega = \sqrt{m} - km \tag{49}$$

with respect to m, subject to the condition that m is zero or a positive integer not exceeding n. For n large we can treat m as approximately continuous, and let dw_Ω/dm vanish for $m \geq 0$. The optimal number of observations is then,

$$m_\Omega(k) = \begin{cases} 0 & k > \frac{1}{2} \\ 1/(4k^2) & 1/(2\sqrt{n}) \leq k \leq \frac{1}{2} \\ n & k > 1/(2\sqrt{n}). \end{cases} \tag{50}$$

This function is plotted on Exhibit 3-10 for n = 100.

We turn now to determining the gross revenue under the (binary) payoff condition Ω'. By (42'), this requires evaluating g, the probability volume of the bivariate distribution over the positive quadrant. It does not depend on scale. The function G_r defined in Sec. 8,

$$G_r(\eta) = P(\sum_{1}^{r} x_i \leq \eta) \qquad r = 1, \dots, n$$

THE "SPECULATOR"

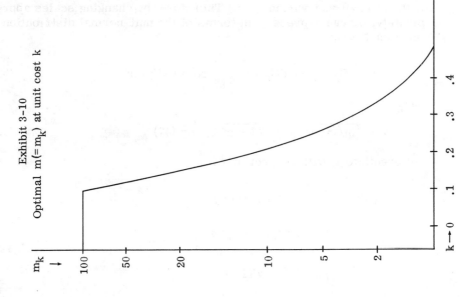

Exhibit 3-10

Optimal $m(=m_k)$ at unit cost k

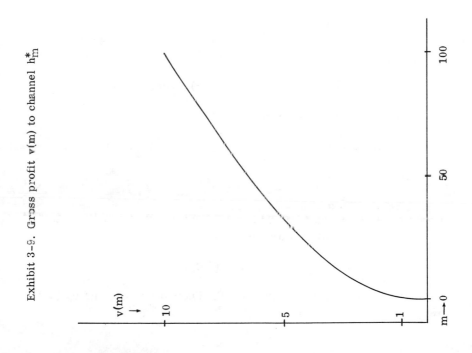

Exhibit 3-9. Gross profit $v(m)$ to channel h_m^*

becomes, under the assumptions (45), the normal distribution function with mean = 0 and variance = r. Therefore, by changing scales appropriately, we can express g in terms of the unit-normal distribution function $N = G_1$:

$$g = \int_0^\infty G_{n-m}(y) \; dG_m(y) = \int_0^\infty N(\tau y) \, N'(y) \; dy \qquad (51)$$

where

$$\tau = \sqrt{m/(n-m)} = \rho/\sqrt{1-p^2} \qquad \text{by (47)} \qquad (52)$$

Differentiate g with respect to τ:

$$dg/d\tau = \int_0^\infty N'(\tau y) \, y \, N'(y) \; dy$$

$$= \int_0^\infty e^{-(y^2/2) - (\tau^2 y^2/2)} \, (y/2\pi) dy$$

$$= (1/2\pi) \int_0^\infty e^{-y^2(1+\tau^2)/2} \, y dy$$

Substitute $t = y\sqrt{1+\tau^2}$; then $ydy = tdt/(1+\tau^2)$;

$$dg/d\tau = (1/2\pi) \int_0^\infty e^{-t^2/2} \, tdt/(1+\tau^2) = (1/2\pi) \cdot [1/(1+\tau^2)] \cdot 1$$

$$dg = (1/2\pi)(1/1+\tau^2) \, d\tau \, ;$$

integrate:

$$g = (1/2\pi) \int d\tau/(1+\tau^2) = (1/2\pi) \arctan \tau + C$$

If we define an angle q by

$$\rho = \sin q$$

then by (52)

$$\tau = \tan q$$

$$q = \text{arc sin } \rho = \arctan \tau$$

$$g = (1/2\pi) \text{ arc sin } \rho + C = g(\rho) \qquad (53)$$

say. To determine C, put $\rho = 0$. Then $q = 0 = \tau$, and by (51)

$$g(0) = \int_0^\infty N'(y) \, N(0)dy = (1/2) \int_0^\infty N'(y)dy = 1/4$$

hence

$$g(\rho) = (1/4) + (1/2\pi) \text{ arc sin } \rho \qquad (54)$$

This gives the probability $g = P(z > 0, y > 0)$ for *any*[13] bivariate normal distribution with zero-means and correlation ρ: for we have not yet used the only restriction (47) on ρ that is imposed in our particular case, viz $\rho > 0$, making $g > 1/4$.

Now, by (42') and (54)

$$v_{\Omega'}(m) = 4g_{m,n} - 1 = (2/\pi) \text{ arc sin } \rho \geq 0 \qquad \rho = \sqrt{m/n},$$

$$0 \leq m \leq n \qquad (55)$$

if we regard m, from now on, as continuous over the whole interval $[0, n]$. Since n is fixed, it is convenient to regard as the variable the ratio $\mu = m/n$ of sample to population size. Then, with q defined as before,

$$\rho = \sqrt{\mu} = \sin q \qquad 0 \leq q \leq \pi/2$$

$$\mu = \sin^2 q = (1 - \cos 2q)/2 \qquad (56)$$

$$\frac{d\mu}{dq} = \sin 2q.$$

With n fixed, the gross revenue will be denoted by

$$V \equiv V(\mu) \equiv v_{\Omega'}(m) = (2/\pi) \text{ arc sin } \sqrt{\mu} = (2/\pi)q \qquad (57)$$

When $\mu = 0$, $q = 0$, $V = 0$;

$$\mu - 1/2, \quad q = \pi/4; \quad V = 1/2;$$

$$\mu = 1, \quad q = \pi/2, \quad V - 1;$$

Moreover,

[13] The result (54) can also be obtained directly from the bivariate normal distribution formula, using auxiliary variables q, u, τ, with:

$$\rho = \sin q \qquad z = u \cos q + y \sin q \qquad \tau = \tan q$$

This leads to (51) and (54). See also [15], [16] for other proofs.

$$dV/d\mu = (2/\pi)/\sin 2q \geq 0 \tag{58}$$

$$d^2V/d\mu^2 = (-4/\pi) \operatorname{ctn} 2q/\sin^2 q \begin{Bmatrix} < \\ = \\ > \end{Bmatrix} 0 \quad \text{when} \quad \mu \begin{Bmatrix} < 1/2 \\ = 1/2 \\ > 1/2, \end{Bmatrix} \tag{59}$$

since $\operatorname{ctn} 2q = (1-2 \sin^2 q)/2 \sin q \cos q = (1-2\mu)/2\sqrt{\mu(1-\mu)}$. By (58), the function $V(\mu)$ is monotone non-decreasing. By (59), it is concave at $\mu < 1/2$, has inflexion at $\mu = 1/2$, and is convex above this point. Thus we have decreasing marginal returns for low proportions of sample to population, but increasing returns when the proportion is high! Doubling the number of observations may more than double the payoff!

On Exhibit 3-11, gross revenue is plotted against the channel variable $\mu = m/n$, when the payoff condition, Ω', is a binary one: the "sign-matcher's" case. To compare with the corresponding Exhibit 3-9, where the assumed payoff condition, Ω, was a continuous one, (the "speculator's" case) we have expressed the revenue in standard units as defined in (44'). Let

$$\nu = 1/\operatorname{arc} \sin \sqrt{1/n} = \text{approx.} \sqrt{n} \text{ for n large. By (55)} \tag{60}$$

$$V_{\Omega'}(1) = 4g_{1,\,n} - 1 = (2/\pi) \operatorname{arc} \sin \sqrt{1/n} = 2/\nu\pi . \tag{61}$$

Dividing this quantity into the payoff expression of (57), we obtain the standardized payoff, denoted by $v(\mu)$:

$$v(\mu) = \nu \cdot \operatorname{arc} \sin \sqrt{\mu} = \text{approx.} \sqrt{n} \cdot \operatorname{arc} \sin \sqrt{\mu} \text{ for n large.} \tag{62}$$

On Exhibit 3-11, $v(\mu)$ is plotted with n fixed at 100, so that $\nu = 10$ approximately, and 100μ = the percentage of sample to population size.

Because of the convex shape of $v(\mu)$ over the upper half of its domain, the optimal value of μ, at sufficiently low unit costs of observation, will not be found anywhere in the interior of the interval $0 \leq \mu \leq 1$, but rather at its upper boundary, $\mu = 1$: a case of "convex programming."

The function

$$\mu_k = m_{\Omega'}(k)/n$$

will express, for n fixed, the effect of varying the (standardized) unit cost k of observations upon the optimal proportion μ_k of sample to population, when the payoff condition is Ω': the "sign-matcher's" case. This function is plotted in Exhibit 3-12. It is to be compared with Ex-

THE "SIGN-MATCHER"

Exhibit 3-11. Gross profit v(m) to channel h_m^*.

(Slope of straight line = critical cost $\bar{k}$ = 1.38. Vertical segments: net profit at $\bar{k}$.)

Exhibit 3-12. Optimal $m(= m_k)$ at unit cost k.

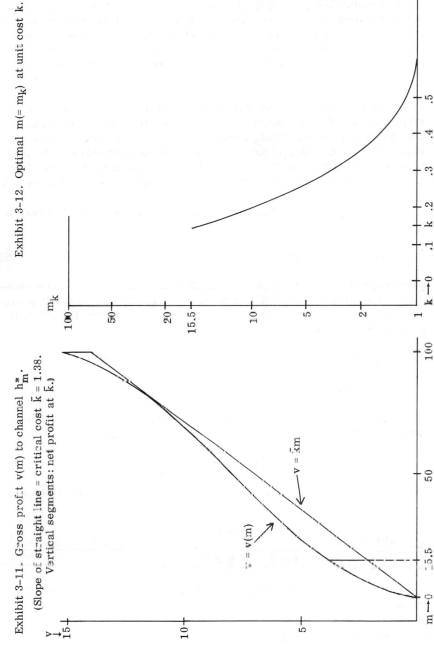

hibit 3-10, plotted correspondingly for the "speculator's" case, Ω. In both cases, we fix n = 100.

On Exhibit 3-10, the optimal number of observations, $m_k = n\mu_k$ is determined—as long as the unit cost k is not prohibitive—by equalizing marginal revenue and unit cost. This follows from the concave shape of the gross revenue function of the channel, which guarantees maximum of the net revenue at its stationary value. When k exceeds the value at which $\mu_k = 1/n$, $m_k = 1$, it becomes prohibitive: m_k falls to 0.

On Exhibit 3-12, by contrast, it is optimal to use the greatest possible number of observations, $\mu_k = 1$, $m_k = n$, for a whole range of unit costs k of observation, reaching from 0 to a certain critical value. Only above this value of k, the "law of decreasing returns" becomes effective, and the optimal decision is obtained by equating marginal return and unit cost; as long, of course, as k remains non-prohibitive.

To plot μ_k (or $m_k = n\mu_k$) as on Exhibit 3-12, we have to maximize the net payoff

$$w(\mu) = v(\mu) - kn\mu \tag{63}$$

with respect to μ for given k, over the range $0 \le \mu \le 1$. We denote by μ_k the optimal value of μ and by v_k, w_k, the corresponding gross and net revenues. We know that, when k is at or below the critical point $\bar{k}$ (say), then

$$\mu_k = 1, \; v_k = v(1) = \nu \cdot \text{arc sin } 1 = \nu\pi/2 \quad \text{by (62)}$$

$$w_k = (\nu\pi/2) - kn \quad k \le \bar{k} \tag{64}$$

On the other hand, when $k \ge \bar{k}$, the optimal value $\mu_k = \mu_k^*$ (say) must satisfy the stationarity condition which by (63) is

$$[dw(\mu)/d\mu]_{\mu=\mu_k^*} = [dv(\mu)/d\mu]_{\mu=\mu_k^*} - kn = 0 \tag{65}$$

The maximum net payoff is, by (64), (65) the following function of k:

$$w_k = \begin{array}{ll} \dfrac{\nu\pi}{2} - kn & k \le \bar{k} \\[2ex] v(\mu_k^*) - kn\mu_k^* & k \ge \bar{k} \end{array} \tag{66}$$

where μ_k^* is defined by (65), and the critical value $\bar{k}$ is determined by setting

$$(\nu\pi/2) - \bar{k}n = v(\mu_{\bar{k}}^*) - \bar{k}n\mu_{\bar{k}}^* \tag{67}$$

We shall now extend the results to the case of a general (linear or non-linear) differentiable non-decreasing utility function υ of money. The question of whether marginal returns to information can be increasing (Exhibits 3-9 and 3-11) must be replaced by the more general question of whether at sufficiently low information costs, the expected channel utility Υ defined in (23*) can achieve its maximum when the number of observations is highest (Exhibits 3-10 and 3-12). It can only if $d\Upsilon/dm \geq 0$ at $m = n$, and $d\Upsilon/dm > 0$ in the proximity of n. Again the answer will be "no" in the "speculator" case, and "yes" in the "sign-matcher" case.

The *"speculator's"* best action rule is $\gamma^*(y) = \delta_y$, and hence his money profit $= z\delta_y$. Since the monetary channel cost is $= km = kn\rho^2$, the expected channel utility is

$$\Upsilon \equiv E\upsilon(z\delta_y - kn\rho^2) \equiv \Upsilon_q \tag{68}$$

say, where $q = \arcsin \rho$. Define a function of z and q:

$$\Phi_q(z) = \upsilon(z - kn\rho^2) \tag{69}$$

Since υ is differentiable and non-decreasing, and excluding the trivial case $\upsilon = \mathrm{const.}$,

$$\Phi_q'(z) \equiv \partial\Phi_q(z)/\partial z > 0 \qquad \text{for almost all } z$$

$$\Phi_u(z) - \Phi_q(-z) > 0 \qquad \text{for almost all positive } z \tag{70}$$

Denote by $f(y, z) = f(-y, -z)$ the joint density of y, z; and by $f(z)$, $f(y|z)$ a marginal and conditional density. With the distribution parameters as given at the beginning of this section, and using the notation of (51) we note that

$$\Pr(y > 0|z) - \int_0^\infty f(y|z) \, dy = N(z\tau) \tag{71}$$

where $\tau = \rho/\sqrt{1 - \rho^2}$ - tan q. Then by (68), (69)

$$\Upsilon_q = \int_{-\infty}^\infty dz [\int_0^\infty \Phi_q(z) f(y, z) \, dy + \int_{-\infty}^\upsilon \Phi_q(-z) f(y, z) dy]$$

$$= 2 \int_{-\infty}^\infty \Phi_u(z) f(z) [\int_0^\infty f(y|z) \, dy] \, dz$$

$$= 2 \int_{-\infty}^\infty \Phi_q(z) N'(z) N(z\tau) dz \qquad \text{by (71)}$$

Now $d\Upsilon_q/dq = I_q + J_q$ where

$$\tfrac{1}{2}I_q = \int_{-\infty}^{\infty} (\partial\Phi_q/\partial q)\cdot N'(z)\, N(z\tau)dz$$

$$= -kn\cdot\sin 2q\cdot\int_{-\infty}^{\infty}\Phi_q'(z)\, N'(z)\, N(z\tau)dz$$

$$\tfrac{1}{2}J_q = \int_{-\infty}^{\infty}\Phi_q(z)\, N'(z)\cdot[dN(z\tau)/dq]\, dz$$

$$= (1/\cos^2 q)\cdot\int_0^{\infty}[\Phi_q(z) - \Phi_q(-z)]\, zN'(z)\, N'(z\tau)dz$$

When $0 < m < n$, $0 < q < \dfrac{\pi}{2}$, $I < 0$, $J > 0$, by (70). Let $q = \tfrac{1}{2}\pi - \epsilon$, ϵ small positive. Then approximately (neglecting ϵ^2 and higher powers) $\rho = 1$, $\cos q = \epsilon$, $\sin 2q = 2\epsilon$, $\tau = 1/\epsilon$, $N(z\tau) = 1$, and

$$I_{\tfrac{1}{2}\pi-\epsilon} = -kn\cdot 2\epsilon\int_{-\infty}^{\infty}\Phi_q'(z)\cdot N'(z)\, dz < 0$$

$$J_{\tfrac{1}{2}\pi-\epsilon} = (1/\epsilon^2\sqrt{2\pi})\cdot\int_0^{\infty}[\Phi_q(z) - \Phi_q(-z)]$$

$$\times z\,\exp[-z^2(1 + \epsilon^{-2})/2]\, dz > 0$$

As $\epsilon \to 0$, both I and J approach zero, J faster than I (because of the exponential term) so that at $q = \tfrac{1}{2}\pi - \epsilon$, $d\Upsilon_q/dq < 0$. Hence at $q = \tfrac{1}{2}\pi$, $m = n$, Υ has a (local) minimum, not a (global) maximum.

The *"sign-matcher"* has the same best action rule and the same channel cost as the "speculator;" but since his money profit $= \delta_z\delta_y$, the expected channel utility is

$$\Upsilon_q = E\upsilon(\delta_z\delta_y - kn\rho^2);$$

then by (69)

$$\Upsilon_q = \Phi_q(1)\Pr(\delta_z = \delta_y) + \Phi_q(-1)\Pr(\delta_z \neq \delta_y)$$

$$= \Phi_q(1)(\tfrac{1}{2} + q\pi^{-1}) + \Phi_q(-1)(\tfrac{1}{2} - q\pi^{-1}) \quad\text{by (54)} \qquad (72)$$

$$\frac{d\Upsilon_q}{dq} = -kn\cdot\sin 2q\cdot[\Phi_q'(1)(\tfrac{1}{2} + q\pi^{-1}) + \Phi_q'(-1)(\tfrac{1}{2} - q\pi^{-1})]$$

$$+ \pi^{-1}[\Phi_q(1) - \Phi_q(-1)]$$

By (70), this is positive both when $q = \pi/2$ and when $q = 0$. Hence, at $m = n$, Υ has a local, and possibly global, maximum. When kn is large the global maximum may be at $m < 1$ so that no observations will be made. On the other hand,

$$\lim_{kn \to 0} \Upsilon_q = \upsilon(1)(\tfrac{1}{2} + q\pi^{-1}) + \upsilon(-1)(\tfrac{1}{2} - q\pi^{-1}) \begin{cases} < \upsilon(1) & q < \pi/2 \\ \\ = \upsilon(1) & q = \pi/2 \end{cases}$$

$$\lim_{kn \to 0} \left(\Upsilon_{\pi/2} - \Upsilon_q \right) > 0 \qquad q < \pi/2$$

so that, for kn sufficiently small, the channel with $q = \pi/2$, $m = n$ may be optimal.

Similar results were also obtained for a non-differentiable utility function of a "satisficer": $\upsilon(r) = 1$ or 0 as $r \geq$ or $< A$, a constant (the "aspiration level"). If this utility function is attributed to the "speculator" it has been shown[14] that Υ_q has a local minimum at $m = n$. But in the case of the "sign-matcher" this utility function results in a global maximum for Υ_q at $m = n$, if and only if $kn \leq 1 - A$.

BIBLIOGRAPHY

1. Debreu, Gerard: *Theory of Value*, New York: Wiley, 1959.
2. Birkhoff, Garrett: *Lattice Theory*, 2d ed., New York: American Mathematical Society (Colloquium publication), vol, 25, 1949.
3. Savage, Leonard J.: *The Foundations of Statistics*, New York: Wiley, 1954.
4. Fisher, Irving: The Theory of Interest, New York: Kelley, 1930.
5. Marshak, Jacob: "The Payoff-Relevant Description of States and Acts," *Econometrica*, vol. 31, pp. 719-726, 1963.
5a. March, James G., and Herbert A. Simon with the collaboration of Harold Guetzkow: Organizations, New York: Wiley, 1958.
6. McGuire, C. B.: "Some Team Models of a Sales Organization," *Management Science*, vol. 7, pp. 101-130, 1961.
7. Marschak, Jacob: "Towards an Economic Theory of Organization and Information," Chap. XIV in Thrall et al. (eds.), *Decision Processes*, New York: Wiley, 1954.
8. Radner, Roy: "The Evaluation of Information in Organizations," *Proceedings of the 4th Berkeley Symposium on Mathematical Statistics*, vol. 1, pp. 491-530, Berkeley, 1961.
9. ———: "Team Decision Problems," *Annals of Mathematical Statistics*, vol. 33, pp. 857-881, 1962.
10. Marschak, Jacob: "Remarks on the Economics of Information," *Contributions to Scientific Research in Management*, pp. 79-100, Western Data Processing Center, University of California, Los Angeles, 1959.
11. McGuire, C. B.: "The Marginal Productivity of a Fully Exploited Bit," (mimeogr.) RAND D-8947, 1961.

[14] In collaboration with T. Ferguson. For our definition of "satisficing" see [5a, pp. 140-141].

12. Raiffa, Howard, and Robert Schlaifer: *Applied Statistical Decision Theory*, Division of Research, Graduate School of Business Administration, Harvard University, Boston: 1961.
13. Feinstein, Amiel: *Foundations of Information Theory*, New York: McGraw-Hill, 1958.
14. Stigler, George J.: "The Economics of Information," *Journal of Political Economy*, vol. 69, pp. 213-225, 1961.
15. Gupta, Shanti S.: Probability Integrals of Multivariate Normal and Multivariate *t*, Technical Report No. 64, *Applied Mathematics and Statistics Laboratory, Stanford University*, 1962. Accepted for publication in *Annals of Mathematical Statistics*.
16. Cramer, Harold: *Mathematical Methods of Statistics*, Princeton, N. J.: Princeton, 1946. p. 290.

4

TWO PROBLEMS IN THE STUDY OF MULTIPLE-BRANCH ORGANIZATIONS: GOAL CONFIGURATIONS AND STRATEGIES OF BRANCH LOCATION

F. E. BALDERSTON
University of California at Berkeley

I INTRODUCTION

We must be cautious in asserting how a structural configuration—whether it is a hierarchy of job assignments according to some rule of span of control, or a series of physical work arrangements in some restricted relation to one another, or some other structural commitment—will affect organizational performance.

At the same time, we may profit by seeking to develop analysis for special cases. In a recent paper, it has been argued that multiple-branch organizations can be identified and certain of their performance characteristics studied in the framework of "activity analysis" [1, pp. 40-57]. I shall first summarize a few points of that argument. Then I shall discuss two modest extensions of the model: first, to the interpretation of relationships between branch goals and the organization's goals, and then to a problem of competitive strategy when multiple branch organizations confront one another in the market.

II POLAR CASE OF MULTIPLE BRANCH ORGANIZATION

Consider the linear-programming formulation of the firm's short-run profit-maximization:

to maximize $R = bx$
subject to $Ax = E$
and $x \geq 0$

where R is total net revenue, b is the vector of unit net revenues, x is the vector of unknown activity-levels, A is the matrix of activity-coefficients, and E is the vector of resource constraints. Then, for branch J, define the following:

its revenue coefficients are $\underline{b}_J \in b$;   (2)
its matrix of activity-coefficients is $\underline{a}_J \in A$ (3)
its activity-vector is $\underline{x}_J \in x$ (4)
and its resource-vector is $\underline{e}_J \in E$.   (5)

The polar case is exemplified, first of all, by complete standardization of all branches. That is, for N branches,

$$\underline{b}_1 = \cdots = \underline{b}_J = \cdots = \underline{b}_N , \tag{6}$$
$$\underline{a}_1 = \cdots = \underline{a}_J = \cdots = \underline{a}_N , \tag{7}$$
$$\underline{x}_1 = \cdots = \underline{x}_J = \cdots = \underline{x}_N , \tag{8}$$
$$\text{and } \underline{e}_1 = \cdots = \underline{e}_J = \cdots = \underline{e}_N . \tag{9}$$

We presume each branch to service a local clientele having no demand interactions with other branches, but identical local demand,
hence (6). Restriction (7) places all branches in equivalent positions
of efficiency with respect to production alternatives. Restriction (8)
shows identical menus of activity-alternatives for all branches, and
(9) shows them all to have identically the same endowments of resources.

In these circumstances, when the organization has solved the sub-
problem of finding the optimal program for one branch, it has found
the overall solution, and the overall problem is in fact degenerate.
Departures from the polar case are of course of main importance.
Any of the four restrictions (6)-(9) may be violated. In addition, the
above formulation has presumed the absence of any special activities,
resources, or autonomous revenues, in a headquarters. The organization exists only through its branches. Headquarters self-main-
tenance requires the definition of a new sub-set of activities. Any
sharing of a resource (e.g., working capital) among all branches and
the headquarters throws the problem back to one of overall maximization.

The headquarters, as these definitions show, can seek to standardize branches by fixing their resource-endowments, $\underline{e}_J$, by specifying
revenue coefficients (fixing the admissible values of one or more elements of $\underline{b}_J$), attempting to control the values of activity-coefficients
in $\underline{a}_J$, or requiring specific performance-levels of certain activities
(elements of $\underline{x}_J$). Each of these standardization policies would require a particular type of headquarters control information from the
branches.

The headquarters may seek to standardize branches for either or
both of the following reasons: (1) Each branch is an embodiment of
the organization's mission; the more sharply defined is this mission,
the greater is the prospect of setting up to perform it in a uniform
manner. (Also important, but outside the present model because of
its implication of demand interdependence between localized markets,
is the possibility of conveying a consistent "image" through uniformity of buildings, signs, brand-names and assortment of goods, etc.)
(2) Standardization appears to facilitate cross-comparisons of branch
performance and is thus an aid to control.

Heterogeneity of local conditions impedes branch standardization
and may in fact make it a costly, sub-optimizing policy. Branch managers can point to such differences of local circumstances as reasons

for deviating from standard policies. The headquarters faces a dilemma. It it insists on standardization policies despite their inapplicability and the consequent resistance to them, this increases the required amount of control activity. If it accedes to the arguments favoring branch differentiation, comparability is made more difficult, and it needs a greater amount of control information in order to understand and evaluate branch performance.[1]

III BRANCH GOALS AND ORGANIZATIONAL GOALS

The configuration of goals in the multiple-branch organization was discussed briefly in the above-mentioned paper [1, pp. 54-55]. Issues of goal formation and goal structure have, of course, received widespread attention in the literature of organization theory. One suggestion is to consider the organization's goal commitments as the outcome of a series of specific processes of coalition formation.[2] Another kind of construct altogether is used by J. Marschak and Roy Radner in the theory of teams, where all participants in the organization are assumed to contribute to an agreed organizational objective, and the problem is one of effective distribution of effort in view of the costs of obtaining, transmitting, and using information.[3]

As was pointed out in my previous paper, a goal statement may be written as a constraint inequation in the linear-programming model. Using this fact, three kinds of goal can be defined in terms of the inequation's coefficients:

> *regular* goals, all of whose coefficients are non-negative;
> *strict avoidance* goals, all of whose coefficients are non-positive; and
> *partial avoidance* goals, at least two of whose coefficients are not of the same sign.

The "resource" limit in such a goal-inequation is a *target value* for minimum or maximum attainment.

A set of goal statements containing any or all of the above types of goals for each branch unit can be incorporated in the activity analysis model. The model can then be used to test the feasibility of plans, and

---

[1] Robert Olsen, a Berkeley doctoral candidate, is now working on modifications of this model to fit an organization consisting of a number of district offices. He hopes to test empirically some of the above propositions concerning efficiency and standardization.

[2] Cyert, R. M., and J. G. March: "A Behavioral Theory of Organizational Objectives," in [2, pp. 76-90].

[3] Cf., for example, J. Marschak: "Efficient and Viable Organizational Forms," in [2, pp. 307-320]; and [3], which contains a short bibliography on this subject.

to consider what total profit may emerge from the combination of technical constraints and goal constraints facing the organization.

The branch manager faces difficulties whenever branch goals and organizational goals are not totally in correspondence with one another. One response to this problem is the demand for managerial autonomy. This demand may be reinforced by the claim that autonomy is needed for faster and more flexible problem-solving [4]. This, however, competes with the branch manager's incentives to cultivate and intensify his representational contacts with headquarters superiors. Effectiveness in this role (aside from its potential benefits to the person in making him visible and hence promotable) enhances the branch manager's value to his own subordinates. Likert discusses this phenomenon under the label of the "linking-pin" function.[4]

It would seem that the branch manager's position contains a high potential of ambivalence. What can be done to represent this situation in the activity-analysis model?

Let us define $\underline{e}^*_J$ a vector of goal constraints for the J-th branch, and a similar vector $\underline{e}^*_H$ for the headquarters. A particular element of $\underline{e}^*_J$ may stand in any of three relationships to $\underline{e}^*_H$:

1. There may be an element of $\underline{e}^*_H$ such that an increase in branch goal attainment will also contribute to an increase in the attainment of that headquarters goal. The two goals are in positive correspondence.
2. There may be an element of $\underline{e}^*_H$ such that an increase in branch goal attainment will *lower* the degree of attainment of the headquarters goal. This is a case of goal conflict.
3. There may be no elements of $\underline{e}^*_H$ which are affected by the level of attainment of the branch goal. This is a case of goal neutrality. (Another case of goal neutrality is that in which there is a headquarters goal which is unrelated to any branch goal.)

We may note the consequences in each of these cases for the problem of headquarters control. In case 1, since branch and headquarters objectives point in the same direction, the only possible arguments may be over failure to meet the goal (violation of the constraint) or over the level at which the target value is set (degree of priority given this branch goal as compared to others). Headquarters needs only minimal control information.

In case 2, headquarters faces a disagreement, a high demand for control, and consequent need for large amounts of control information to resolve the conflict and enforce the solution.

In case 3, where the branch goal affects no headquarters goal, the

---

[4] Likert, R., "A Motivational Approach to a Modified Theory of Organization and Management," in [2, especially pages 200-202].

only possible concern is with secondary and indirect effects: claims on resources arising out of the goal statement which may impede other aspects of goal performance. If there is a reasonable amount of "organizational slack," this problem is likely to be ignored. If headquarters has a goal of its own that is neutral to the branch, it may ask for information at will, facing only the costs of bureaucratic nuisance that arise when the headquarters requires reports for mysterious or (to the subordinate organization) irrelevant reasons.

One more comment is in order concerning the characteristics of the goal inequations themselves. A goal expression relevant only to branch J could contain non-zero coefficients only in association with the elements of x_J, the vector of activity-alternatives for J. A goal statement linking branch J and the headquarters could contain additional non-zero coefficients in association with the elements of the vector of headquarters activities. But branch J might be in a state of rivalry with other branches. This situation would find expression in a partial avoidance goal statement for branch J, in which some negative coefficients were associated with elements of the activity vector of the other branch.

IV STRATEGIES OF BRANCH LOCATION IN THE COMPETITION BETWEEN MULTIPLE-BRANCH ORGANIZATIONS

We have assumed, in setting up the definition of multiple-branch organization, that the clientele is divided into mutually isolated segments. Let us now look briefly at an *external* policy problem, namely, potential patterns of competition between several such organizations which offer competing goods or services and *which agree on the definitions of the market segment boundaries*. One possible strategy is to avoid any local market in which a competitor has placed a branch. If every firm in the industry were to follow this strategy, the aggregate market would be divided into pockets of localized monopoly. At the opposite extreme is the policy of always *seeking* to locate branches in local markets where competitors are present. In the context of our earlier discussion, these radically different policies are expressed in differing target values, set by the headquarters, on the branch goal of "local market share or position."

But the most interesting problem in this competitive interaction, perhaps, is that the multiple-branch organizations are the only vehicle of direct connection between one market-segment and another. They bring about whatever degree of "connectedness" the market as a whole may have.

In certain industries (e.g., commercial banking), regulatory authorities have the responsibility of giving or withholding permission to establish branches. In some such industries, the regulators' tradition has been to foster local shelters from competition. In other cases, the eventual amount of connectedness between markets has been the consequence of whatever policies of branch application the competing firms happened to pursue. Yet it is apparent that resource allocation from the social point of view would be improved through the presence of competitors in every sufficiently large market-segment and through the fostering of the greatest feasible number of interconnections between local markets.

The firm's problem of choosing a branch-location strategy would seem to deserve further study. So would the problem of interpreting the meaning and consequence of market interconnection that is achieved through the *aegis* of the multiple-branch organization.

BIBLIOGRAPHY

1. Balderston, F. E.: "Models of Multiple Branch Organizations," *California Management Review*, vol. 4, 1962.
2. Haire, M. (ed.); *Modern Organization Theory*, New York: Wiley, 1959.
3. Radner, R.; "Team Decision Problems," *The Annals of Mathematical Statistics*, vol. 33, September, 1962.
4. Dill, William R.; "Environment as an Influence on Managerial Autonomy," *Administrative Science Quarterly*, vol. 2, pp. 409-443, 1958.

Discussion

ECONOMIC THEORY AND MANAGEMENT CONTROL

THOMAS A. MARSCHAK

University of California at Berkeley

I shall comment on three papers which, like all useful exploratory papers, raise a number of unsettled questions; the papers of (I) Marschak, (II) Hirschleifer, and (III) Balderston.

I MARSCHAK

1. Channel Costs.

The paper concentrates on the "gross revenue" of alternative channels. Ultimately channels must be ranked with respect to net payoff; the net payoff of a channel is its gross revenue less the average total costs (suitably measured) of operating it. One direction for future research is to explore further the nature of those costs so as to improve the assumptions which the paper makes, as a reasonable first approximation, about them.

Consider the central example of the paper. A state of the world is defined by the n-tuple $x = (x_1, \ldots, x_n)$. The decision-maker is to choose one out of a collection of 2n channels, each yielding information about x: the n "fine" channels yielding the sum of the first m coordinates of x, $m = 1, \ldots, n$, and the n "coarse" channels yielding the sign of this sum. Given a "payoff condition" a channel is best in this collection if it achieves a not lower net payoff than any other.

The total cost of operating a channel following a state x comprises the cost of observing and gathering the m numbers; computing adding up the m numbers and determing the sign of the sum if the channel is a coarse one; coding this information; transmitting it; decoding it; and applying the appropriate rule to the decoded information in order to obtain an action. The total cost can be thought of as a charge made to the decision-maker for the use of equipment that achieves all these tasks. The tasks, and hence the charge, vary from one value of x to the next.

Now the paper shows that for fixed m, under certain assumptions on the probability distribution of x, the coarse channel is no worse than the fine one with respect to gross revenue alone, for both of the "payoff conditions" considered. For the continuous payoff function this is assured when the probability distributions of the x_i (a) are independent, and (b) have zero means. For the "satisficing" payoff function, this is assured if in addition the probability distributions of the x_i are (c) all the same, and (d) symmetric about zero when continuous. As one increases m, moreover, the gross revenue of the coarse (and hence the fine) channel increases or stays the same for all probability distributions of x. In order to study net payoff, the further assumptions are made that (1) for fixed m the expected total cost of operating the coarse channel is less than that of operating the fine one, and (2) as one increases m, the expected total cost of operating either type of channel goes up in proportion to m.

The easiest component of total cost to study is transmission cost. As footnote 9 of Section 9 (p. 00) indicates, this can reasonably be assumed to be a non-decreasing function of the "minimum required capacity" of the channel (measured, say, in bits per time unit).[1] If assumptions (1) and (2) are to be met with respect to total operating cost, it would be reassuring to know that at least the transmission cost component of total cost meets them, or comes close to doing so.

Transmission cost certainly satisfies (1), for any probability distribution of x, at least if we replace "less" by "not greater." For the following general statement is easily proved: suppose we are given two channels and the set of possible inputs is the same for each channel. The possible outputs of the first channel partition the set of inputs in a certain way, while the possible outputs of the second channel partition the set in a way that is coarser, in the sense of the paper. Then no matter what the probability distribution of the possible inputs, the minimum required capacity of the first channel (the reduction in entropy which it achieves) is not less than that of the second.

Assumption (2), however, is not so easily satisfied by transmission cost. If we make assumptions (a)-(d) about the probability distribution of x, and assume the distribution to be continuous, then as we increase m the minimum required capacity of the coarse channels stays the same. For, by the symmetry assumption, the sum of the first m coordinates of x is positive with probability $1/2$ and negative with probability $1/2$. But if we omit assumption (d), or let the distribution

---

[1]An interpretation of "minimum required capacity" is this: Suppose the channel-user is required (for some reason) to choose his actions at a specified average rate, so that he must receive messages about the successive states x at a specified average rate. By choosing the time unit appropriately, this required average rate can be made to be one per time unit. If the channel has "minimum required capacity," in bits per time unit, then it is possible to code the successive states x in such a way that the channel-user receives the messages at an average rate as close as desired to one per time unit—or, more accurately, such a coding is possible provided the successive states x occur at a rate sufficiently fast that the coder never "runs out" of states to code.

of x be discrete, there is difficulty. It may then be that the minimum required capacity of the coarse channel decreases as m increases.[2]

But even if transmitting cost does satisfy (1) and (2), can we expect the other elements of channel cost to do so? It is very likely that they do not. Thus, in the example, for a given m the coarse channel is cheaper than the fine one with respect to transmission, but it requires an extra computational operation—determination of sign—to be performed. Other examples could doubtless be constructed which illustrate much more strikingly the possibility of trading off elaborate computation against cheap transmission. And the same is true of trading off coding, decoding, and observing costs against transmission and computing costs and against each other. At present, unfortunately, only the technology of transmission is sufficiently well understood so that one can conveniently measure the cost of a given transmission task. It would seem an important next step in the economics of information to study, say, the technology of computing as it has so far not been studied: to search for some relatively convenient way in which the cost of a simple computing task (like the summing of m numbers) can be measured.

2. Increasing and Decreasing Returns.

Suppose that only the transmitting task is costly; computing, coding, decoding, and observing are free. Suppose that the minimum required capacity (in bits per time unit) of the coarse channels increases as m increases, and increases, moreover, at a constant rate. Does it then follow that the dollar cost of operating a coarse channel is proportional to m — so that if gross revenue (measured in dollars) increases more (less) than proportionately to an increase in m, then the channel user faces increasing (decreasing) returns to scale? It does not follow at all. For the resources ultimately required for the transmission task are not "channel capacity," but rather the labor and other primary resources that produce the materials and services

---

[2]As the following example shows: Let $x = (x_1, x_2)$, where x_i, $i = 1,2$, equals -10 with probability $4/9$, 8 with probability $5/9$. (Thus assumptions (a)–(c) are satisfied.) Then the sign of x_1 is positive with probability $5/9$, negative with probability $4/9$, and the sign of $x_1 + x_2$ is positive with probability $25/81$, negative with probability $56/81$. The minimum required capacity for the channel yielding the sign of x_1 is greater than that for the channel yielding the sign of $x_1 + x_2$ if and only if the (unconditional) entropy of the sign of x_1 is greater than that of the sign of $x_1 + x_2$, i.e., if and only if

$$-(4/9 \log 4/9 + 5/9 \log 5/9) > -(56/81 \log 56/81 + 25/81 \log 25/81).$$

Take the logarithms to the base 2. After rearranging and simplifying, the inequality becomes

$$62 \log 3 < 5 \log 5 + 56 \log 7 + 96,$$

which is correct.

out of which the transmitting equipment is made. The industry that produces "channel capacity" may have decreasing returns with respect to its own inputs. These decreasing returns may offset any increasing returns with respect to channel capacity that the channel-user experiences. The point applies as well to the other inputs used to produce a channel's output—computing, capacity, coding, decoding, and observing capacity—when these are no longer assumed free.

If one is concerned about the eventual incorporation of the commodity "information" into a general theory of economic equilibrium, then it need not be disturbing that the "production" of information exhibits increasing returns with respect to the inputs into such production, where these inputs are identified and measured in the most convenient way. For the existence of a competitive equilibrium requires, in the present state of the theory, only that the economy's *total* production possibilities be free of increasing returns (non-convexity). Increasing returns with respect to the output and inputs of one firm do not preclude competitive equilibrium if they are cancelled out by decreasing returns in those firms that produce the inputs of the firm in question.

3. The Cost of Delays.

The paper confines itself to a discussion of those costs which are incurred in using equipment that achieves a channel's tasks—dollar charges, say, that the equipment user pays, and that vary with the elaborateness of the equipment and the intensity with which it is used. But there is, in many situations, another type of cost that the decision-maker must worry about—the time it takes him to reach a new action following a new value of x. If the capacities of the equipment he uses are fixed, this time will vary from one x to another. For some values of x the message sent over the channel will take longer to code and decode than for others (a code will be selected such that the more frequently sent messages will take less time to code and decode). Some values of x may require more computing in order to obtain the message to be sent (a computer may have been programmed to handle instantly the most common values of x, while for others it has to be programmed afresh).

In many situations, a long delay imposes a penalty. For until the new action is achieved, an inferior one—either the previous action or some "makeshift" action—will be in force. On the other hand, the average delay, and hence the average penalty, can probably be made smaller by using more elaborate equipment or by using given equipment more intensively. This, however, costs more money.

When he takes delays into account, the decision-maker clearly faces a complex global problem in choosing between two channels. To solve it he must know the probability distribution of alternative sequences of the states x, the probability distribution of the interval between successive states, the payoff enjoyed while a makeshift action is in force, and for each fixed x the alternative probability distributions of task-completion times that can be bought by spending alternative amounts of money on each channel's equipment.

II HIRSCHLEIFER

It may be instructive to spell out an adjustment process by which the proper price p* could be attained in the case of the imperfectly competitive market for the indeterminate product. This will serve to relate Hirschleifer's discussion to recent studies of decentralized adjustment processes that might be used by the parts of a firm (or of some other organization) to reach decisions yielding a high value of a payoff function.[3]

Let $f(q)$ be the *total* receipts of the distributor (the manufacturer's internal customer) when he sells q units. Let $g(q)$ be the manufacturer's total-receipts function in the external market. Let $h(q)$ be the manufacturer's total-cost function, and let $w(q)$ be the distributor's total-cost function. The firm's problem is: choose q_d, $q_s \geq 0$ such that profit, $\pi(q_d, q_s)$, is a maximum, where

$$\pi = f(q_d) + g(q_s) - h(q_d, q_s) - w(q_d)$$

Assume the shapes of the functions f, g, h, and w to be such that (1) π is uniquely maximized at some point (q_d^*, q_s^*) with both coordinates positive, and (2) only at this point are the marginal conditions (the first-order maximum condition) given by Hirschleifer fulfilled.

We want to formulate a process that will eventually attain (q_d^*, q_s^*) *without* requiring the manufacturer to tell anyone else the functions f and w. One such process does not require Hirschleifer's "umpire" and is as follows:

The distributor picks a (positive) initial value of q_d, call it q_d^1, which he announces to the manufacturer. The manufacturer then picks a value of q_s, call it q_s^1, so as to maximize $g(q_s) - h(q_s + q_d^1)$ (his "profit" on external sales of the intermediate profit when he is obliged to deliver q_d^1 units to the distributor). The manufacturer next announces to the distributor the "price" (marginal manufacturing cost) $p^1 = h'(q_s^1 + q_d^1)$. The distributor then picks a new value of q_d, call it q_d^2, so as to maximize $f(q_d) - p^1 q_d - w(q_d)$ (his "profit" on external sales of the final product). He announces q_d^2 to the manu-

[3]See Arrow, K. J., and L. Hurwicz: "Decentralization and Computation in Resource Allocation," in R. W. Phoutts (ed.), *Studies in Mathematical Economics and Econometrics*, Chapel Hill, N.C.: The University of North Carolina Press, 1961.

facturer and a new iteration begins. Clearly the process stops if and only if (q_d^*, q_s^*) is attained and the marginal conditions given by Hirschleifer are met. For appropriate shapes of the functions f, g, h, w, moreover, the process (a difference-equation system) converges to (q_d^*, q_s^*) for an arbitrary initial value q_s^1.

One appealing property of this process, as of others that have recently been studied, is its decentralization with respect to the participants' specialized knowledge. But Hirschleifer concentrates, in a suggestive way, on a second appealing property of processes that use internal prices: they provide us with a fairly good ready-made device for ensuring that the rules of the process are carried out in fact. And for this purpose it does not really matter whether (1) the process is carried out only "on paper" until it terminates, at which point the terminal "paper" outputs become actual new physical outputs; or (2) the distributor's and manufacturer's actual outputs are physically revised after each iteration. We need only tell distributor and manufacturer that each will be rewarded in proportion to the "profit" he earns—in case 1 the profit earned after the terminal "paper" iteration, at which the new physical outputs are obtained; and in case 2 the sequence of successively revised profits actually earned. If, in case 1, each participant never knows whether or not a given iteration will be the final one (which will be true for a number of reasonable termination procedures), then he will want to follow the rules of the process in order that his current paper profit, which might turn out to be his actual profit, be large. In case 2 he wants to follow the rules in order to make his actual profit sequence large. It may be possible, of course, for a participant to disobey the rules in some way that yields him even higher profit than obeying them. But it may be conjectured that the other participant will then have some counteracting way of disobeying his own rules. This would provide policing even in the absence of an umpire. The matter requires much more study.

There are other devices besides profit-based regards, e.g., occasional direct inspection, to insure compliance with the rules. And there are other processes, including the completely centralized computation of (q_s^*, q_d^*). Choice between alternative processes and control devices is a very complicated matter. The equipment costs and the delay costs discussed above will ultimately have to enter it.

III BALDERSTON

The same is true with respect to the choice problem discussed by Balderston. The firm has a collection of resources and linear activities whose levels must be such that the resource quantities required do not exceed the amounts available. The resource collection and the

activities are to be divided up among "branches" each of which is
told to maximize a certain linear function of its activity levels subject to its own resource constraints. The resulting decisions will be
feasible and optimal only if the original matrix is in fact completely
block-triangular. If it is not, the resulting decisions take no account
of interactions (e.g., of the fact that several managers may be jointly
exploiting a central resource), and they may therefore be infeasible
and non-optimal.

A central-office "control" procedure will then be required to
adjust the branch managers' proposed solutions. The question is
whether the labor of control may be diminished if the managers'
payoff functions and resource assignments are identical. This will
depend, presumably, on the extent of the departure from block-
triangularity, on the departure from the optimal solution when the
standardized sub-problems are solved, and on the complexity of the
messages interchanged in the dialogue between central office and
branches, through which the branch managers' solutions are adjusted.

Discussion

ECONOMIC THEORY AND MANAGEMENT CONTROL

STANLEY REITER

Purdue University

In his paper, Professor Marschak distinguishes a class of cases in which optimal choice of an information channel can be handled in the same way economic theory handles optimal choice of a productive input variable in "size" or "quantity." This class is in part identified (implicitly) by the Postulate (on p. 53), which states that if one channel is finer than another, then its expected channel cost is greater. It is interesting to try to see more intuitively what kinds of cases are covered by the Postulate.

Professor Marshak's concept of channel costs includes ". . . the cost of observing the world and of formulating (computing and coding) a message and transmitting it." Suppose the state of the world is represented by a real vector $x = (x_1, \ldots, x_n)$. Consider two channels. The first observes, encodes, and transmits the vector x, to a decision center, preserving, say, 10 decimal digits in each component. And the second channel observes, encodes, and transmits only the first component x_1, accurate to ten decimal digits. The first channel is a refinement of the second and it is quite plausible that the first channel should cost more to operate than the second, when the vector x has more than one component.

Consider now a third channel in which the vector x is observed, a real function f is evaluated at x, and the value $f(x)$ is transmitted, all to ten digit accuracy. The contours of f define a partitioning of the set of states, and it is clear that the first channel is a refinement of the third. Now, it is not hard to think of examples of functions f such that it is more expensive to evaluate the prescribed number of digits of the real number $f(x)$ and transmit that number than to encode and transmit the n components of x. Such channels violate the Postulate.

If the cost of doing arithmetic is large compared to the cost of transmitting real numbers, then all but the most rudimentary and limited computations are likely to cost more than transmitting components of x. Under these conditions it may be that the force of the Postulate is to restrict attention to channels which involve only "almost" directly observable functions of the state x, for example, the projections of x onto coordinate planes.

There is another element of cost not explicitly admitted into the theory, consideration of which also involves some unsettled problems in the theory of decision-making under uncertainty. Without any suggestion that the present paper should solve all problems, it is interesting to notice where these problems come out in Professor Marschak's theory. It will be helpful to carry on the discussion in terms of an example.

Suppose the states of the world, actions and pay-offs are as follows:

States	Actions		
	a_1	a_2	a_3
x_1	2	1	0
x_2	1	2	0
x_3	0	0	2

Suppose further that it is very costly to distinguish state x_1 from x_2, but cheap to distinguish either from x_3. Then, it can easily be arranged that the only candidate for an optimal channel is one with four possible messages, namely $y_0 = \Phi$ (the empty set), $y_1 = \{x_1,x_2\}$, $y_2 = \{x_3\}$, and $y_3 = \{x_1,x_2,x_3\}$, only two of which, y_1 and y_2, are of interest.

Now, in order to select an optimal decision function among those which associate one of the actions a_i, $i = 1,2,3$, with a message y_j, $j = 1,2$, it is necessary to have a (personal) probability distribution $p(x_k/y_j)$, $k = 1,2,3$; $j = 1,2$. This distribution is here, as in other contexts, assumed to be available without cost. It may happen, though, that this is not the case. Interpret this example as follows. Suppose that state x_1 represents infection (of someone) by one of three diseases. The diseases corresponding to x_1 and x_2 have very similar symptoms, although these symptoms are produced by different microorganisms in each case. If one knew which microorganisms were present, one could employ the drugs that work best on that organism, less well on the others. Suppose further, that to find out the probability of having a specified one of these diseases, given that a patient is infected by either of them, involves either expensive chemical analysis or an expensive statistical study of the current incidence of the two diseases in reported cases. (Such a study would of course also involve distinguishing one disease from the other, but the cost might conceivably be borne for other reasons in other cases, still making the results available.) One might then consider that the cost of estimating $p(x_k/y_j)$ should be included in the channel cost. If that is done, and the cost is large, there may be no advantage in making such an estimate. We would then be left either with no way to choose a decision function, or under compulsion to commit perjury in order to rationalize some decision. One way out of this impasse is to enlarge the class of decision-functions to include mixed strategies, i.e., instead of allowing only functions from messages to actions, allow also functions from messages to probability distributions of over actions. This would, in the usual way, allow the possibility of incurring uniform risk by suitable randomizing, when it is too expensive to find out about the distribution p (x_k/y_j).

5

SIMULATION OF ORGANIZATIONAL BEHAVIOR

CHARLES P. BONINI
Stanford University

In the work that has been done on managerial control, there are at least two distinct approaches. I would like to discuss these approaches briefly with the hope of setting the stage for a discussion of the research that will follow.

The first concept of control I shall designate, for want of a better name, as *control-in-the-large*. This is the *designing* of a *system* to achieve the aims of management. It involves the determination of specific procedures, policies, decision rules, internal prices, and so on. In some sense, it is not control at all but, really, organizational planning.

Let me be more specific in describing this notion of control-in-the-large. Those who use the term "Management Control Systems" are proponents of the broad concept of control. Essentially, they aim to find a set of procedures or decision rules by which the firm can maximize its profit, or at least do better than in the past. These decision procedures must be programmable. That is, they must be capable of specifying what decision is to be made in a given situation for every set of circumstances. Such decisions may involve how much inventory the firm should carry, how many workers it should hire (or fire), what its prices should be, etc.; all these as a function, perhaps, of a whole series of other variables. But the crucial element is that the decision rules specify which decision is to be made for each circumstance.

Accounting systems practitioners also are concerned with the broader definition of control. Rules which determine how checks are to be written, what forms are to be utilized in making a payroll or in recording a sale, etc., have as their aim the keeping of accurate records and the prevention of fraud. Note, again, that the rules are very determinate and specific. They specify the procedures for all sets of circumstances, and hence are programmable. Therefore, we can summarize this notion of control-in-the-large by noting that it generally involves a total business systems approach and the specification of certain rules or procedures within the system. In contrast is the notion of *control-in-the-small*. Here, the emphasis is upon only parts of the business, and, by-in-large, non-programmable decision making is involved.

Budgetary control, and, to some extent, cost accounting, illustrate this narrow notion of control. Both involve breaking down cost or expenditures and attaching them to sub-units or accounts within the firm. Some freedom of action for the decision maker as to how he achieves his goal or budget is also implied. Consider, for example, a manager to whom a budget has been assigned. To achieve this budget the manager is primarily concerned with his own sub-unit and not with the effects of his decisions upon the firm as a whole. Also, the manager does not have at his disposal a set of decision procedures that tell him exactly how to behave in all circumstances. So he must use some of his own judgement and depend on his own abilities. The manager is allowed such leeway simply because it is not possible with our present knowledge to program these decisions. This results partly from the fact that there may be too many decisions and too many variables involved in these decisions. Also, many of these decisions are of a human relations nature and offer both moral and practical difficulties to those attempting to specify complete decision procedures. We must also consider the psychology of the manager himself—his goals and aspirations. And, while work is being done in this area (some of which is being reported here) we are not yet able to specify behavior with exactness.

Control-in-the-small, then, involves some sort of standard of behavior and an explicit or implied imperative to the individual to meet or better this standard. The individuals decisions are not rigidly specified, and he can use his own initiative to achieve the goal set for him.

Those who have studied control-in-the-large and those who have studied control-in-the-small, have usually gone their separate ways. And yet, it is important to combine, to some extent, the fruits of the studies of each point of view.

It would be very useful, I think, to include in systems studies certain decisions which are not programmable, particularly control-in-the-small type decisions. For one thing, these include many of the most important decisions in the business enterprise. Also, there are important interactions between decision rules for programmed decisions and control-in-the-small or non-programmed decisions. For example, the types of decision rules employed for inventory may have a very significant effect upon the ability and motivation of a chain store manager to meet his budget.

It would be equally useful to incorporate budgetary and cost accounting procedures in a complete systems analysis. For it is important to know, not only how various budgetary and standard setting procedures affect individuals and their sub-units of the firm, but also how these procedures affect the firm as a whole.

The research that I will describe in this report is a step toward combining notions from the two concepts of control (as I have described them) in one study. I have constructed a model of a management system that includes certain non-programmable control decisions. Thus, this is a first step in a more comprehensive study of business organizational behavior.

CONTROL-IN-THE-SMALL DECISION MODEL

Before describing the over-all model of the business system, we shall first describe the model for control-in-the-small decisions within the firm. It is this sub-model which provides the link between the systems concept of control and the more narrow budgetary-type control decision.

The model has as its center the psychological variable of pressure—the pressure that an individual feels exerted upon him in the performance of his job. To quantify this variable, I have constructed an *Index of Felt Pressure* for each decision maker within the firm. This index involves pressure upon an individual to perform his task up to the level of the standard set for him (e.g., up to quota). It also involves pressure from his superior, pressure from his equals, and could even involve pressure from his personal life. These indexes are of primary importance in our over-all systems model for three reasons:

1. These indexes are the major mechanism through which control-in-the-small is exercised in the firm.
2. These indexes are the major mechanism by which information is converted into action in the model.
3. It is through these indexes that the hierarchial order in the business organization and the procedures related to authority are built into the model.

Before proceeding to discuss these indexes further, the actual construction of the indexes will be presented. Each of these indexes is made up of a series of factors and a weight describing the relative importance of each factor. An example of the index of pressure for one of the firm's salesmen is given below:

Index of Pressure for a Salesman

Factor	Weight
1. Index of pressure of his superior (the district sales manager)	25
2. His quota relative to his sales in the past month	40
3. Sales of the average salesman in his district relative to his sales	10

Index of Pressure for a Salesman (continued)

Factor	Weight
4. .75 + (percentage of his products less than 75% of quota)	10
5. His total quota for the past quarter relative to his total sales for the last quarter	15
	100

While the weights in the above example have been given exact numerical values, the weights used in the model will be experimental variables. That is, we will wish to study the effects upon the business system of different weights in the indexes of pressure.

Note that the above index, as with the indexes for the other decision makers in the firm, is made up essentially of two parts. The first part is the index of pressure of the next higher (i.e. the immediate superior) in the organizational hierarchy. I have called this factor the *contagion effect* of pressure. The greater weight this factor receives, the greater is the contagion of felt pressure from one level in the organization to the next. It is through this mechanism that the salesman, for example, is made to feel some pressure due to the difficulties encountered by the company as a whole, or pressure within the sales division of the company, or even pressure felt by the district sales manager.

The second set of factors in the indexes of pressure include the effect of information upon pressure. Note that I have confined myself to information relating performance to standard. And this information is mainly of the type that would be found on accounting reports. Of course, I could have added a series of informal factors, such as information from the company newspaper, information obtained from the boss's secretary, and so on.

Exactly how these indexes of pressure convert information into pressure (and thence into action) needs some explanation. The weight of a particular factor (e.g., quota relative to sales) indicated the relative degree of importance attached to that piece of information by the individual in the firm. A large weight means that the individuals "felt pressure" is greatly influenced by variations in the indicated factor (i.e., the information). A zero weight means either that the information is not available, or, if available, it is of no concern to the decision maker.

The discussion above has been in terms of pressure. It is now necessary to relate this to the control-in-the-small decision. Such control in an organization is generally considered to proceed from one level in a hierarchy to the one immediately below it. Note first, that all of the factors in an index of pressure (with the exception of the pressure communicated from the superior) are a relationship between actual performance and some standard. Deviation of actual from standard causes an increase in pressure. Hence control is operative in the firm if the individual feels pressure when his performance is below standard. He will react to this pressure by attempting to reduce pressure—either by improving his performance or by some other method.

There are two ways that a superior exercises control over his subordinates. These are:

1. The hierarchial aspect (direct communication of felt pressure to a subordinate)
2. The self-control aspect (when a subordinate feels that his performance is being evaluated by a superior)

Thus, the exercise of control is translated into pressure in the model. But I have yet to describe how pressure is translated into action. I shall proceed to do this now.

For many individuals in the organization, an increase in their felt pressure motivates them to do better. Inversely, when pressure is relaxed, organizational slack tends to build up. Motivation for better performance slacks off, and inefficiencies of all kinds creep into the firm. Individuals (and groups) divert their attentions to other goals. Also, there is only a stochastic relationship between motivation to perform better and actual performance. An increase in motivation will increase only the expected level of performance, with the actual performance in any given period of time determined randomly from a given probability distribution.

However, not all decision makers respond in the same manner to pressure. There are four types of salesmen, for example, each type reacting somewhat differently. As above, some salesmen meet increased pressure by increasing effort and selling more (on the average); others react adversely to pressure and slightly decrease sales effort; others react to pressure by borrowing sales from the future (convincing customers to overstock); and still others react by reducing the variability of sales (calling only on relatively sure customers).

This completes the description of the control-in-the-small decision model. Note that no attempt was made to program the specific ways that an individual would perform his control decisions over the part of the organization under his authority. That is, there are no decision rules specifying the daily tasks and the manner of their performance for the salesmen and others in the firm. Rather, there is a general relationship between the pressure felt by an individual decision maker and the over-all level of his performance.

BUSINESS SYSTEMS MODEL

I propose to discuss now the remainder of the model of a business firm within which the above control model will be included. The systems model is an attempt to build a comprehensive model of a hypothetical business firm, embodying relevant theory from the disciplines of economics, accounting, and the behavioral sciences. In addition, many of the decision procedures are taken from the literature of business administration.

We can view the firm as being made up of a series of decision centers or places in the firm where a decision is made. Associated with each decision center is a set of decision rules. The complete set of all decision rules in the firm is called the decision system of the firm. And since information is necessary for decision making, the complete flow of information within the firm must also be specified. This flow is called the information system of the firm.

Exhibit 5-1 on the following page summarizes the functions performed at each decision center in the firm. The firm is made up of three general parts: a sales department containing a general sales manager, district sales managers, and salesmen; a manufacturing department, containing a vice-president, a plant supervisor, an industrial engineering department, and foremen; and, finally, an executive committee that does the over-all coordination of the firm. In general, it can be seen from this exhibit that the firm plans by making forecasts; it operates by setting price and output, incurring costs and administrative expenses, and making sales; and it exercises control by using standards and quotas.

Space prohibits any discussion of these decision rules.[1] It is sufficient to repeat that some are based upon theory from the disciplines of economics, accounting, or the behavioral sciences; and others have been incorporated from the existing body of business practice.

SOME STUDIES WITH THE MODEL

The general method of experimentation with the model is as follows: I make changes in the information flows within the firm, changes in the decision rules (including different sets of weights for the various factors in the indexes of pressure), and changes in the firm's environment. The effects of these changes upon the behavior of the firm over time is noted.

There are generally two kinds of things that we can achieve with this experimentation. First of all we can *formulate* hypotheses about factors which affect the behavior of the firm. This is the process of

---

[1] These rules are described in detail in [2] .

Exhibit 5-1. Decisions made at various levels in the firm.

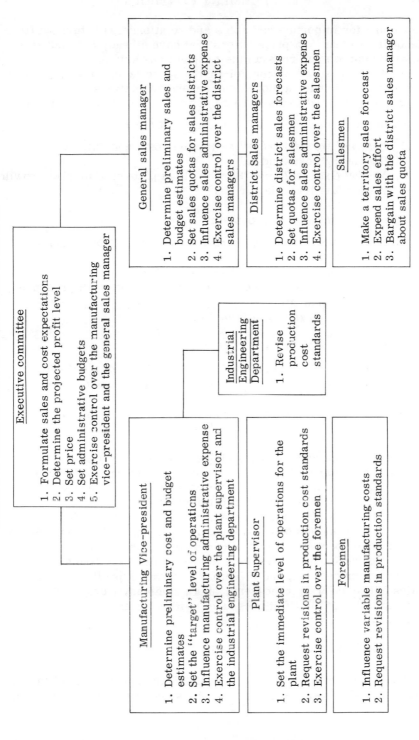

Executive committee

1. Formulate sales and cost expectations
2. Determine the projected profit level
3. Set price
4. Set administrative budgets
5. Exercise control over the manufacturing vice-president and the general sales manager

General sales manager

1. Determine preliminary sales and budget estimates
2. Set sales quotas for sales districts
3. Influence sales administrative expense
4. Exercise control over the district sales managers

District Sales managers

1. Determine district sales forecasts
2. Set quotas for salesmen
3. Influence sales administrative expense
4. Exercise control over the salesmen

Salesmen

1. Make a territory sales forecast
2. Expend sales effort
3. Bargain with the district sales manager about sales quota

Manufacturing Vice-president

1. Determine preliminary cost and budget estimates
2. Set the "target" level of operations
3. Influence manufacturing administrative expense
4. Exercise control over the plant supervisor and the industrial engineering department

Industrial Engineering Department

1. Revise production cost standards

Plant Supervisor

1. Set the immediate level of operations for the plant
2. Request revisions in production cost standards
3. Exercise control over the foremen

Foremen

1. Influence variable manufacturing costs
2. Request revisions in production standards

searching for important variables and relationships within the firm. Secondly, we can *test* propositions that have already been advanced. In particular we can re-examine propositions arising from studies of control-in-the-small or control-in-the-large to see if such propositions are valid under a more comprehensive analysis.

Eight specific changes were selected for this study. They are:

Changes in the External Environment of the Firm:

1. *External World Variability* (Stable costs and sales versus fluctuating costs and sales)
2. *Market Growth Trend* (Slow cyclical pattern of market growth versus fast irregular growth)

Changes in the Decision System:

3. *Loose versus Tight Industrial Engineering Department* (loose or tight standard costs)
4. *Amount of Contagion of Pressure in the Firm* (Degree to which an individual transmits his "felt pressure" to his subordinate)
5. *Sensitivity of Individuals to Pressure*

Changes in the Information System:

6. *LIFO versus Average Cost Method of Inventory Valuation*
7. *Knowledge by the General Sales Manager of the Company Inventory Position*
8. *Emphasis Upon Current Period Information versus Past Information for Control Purposes*

In each of the eight changes above there were two alternative cases. And we are interested in the effects, not only of the changes taken singly, but also the effects of combinations of changes (in the statistical terminology—the interactions).

A 2^8 factorial design was used for measuring these effects. Each run of the model was done then under a different set of changes. In each run 108 periods of time (months) were simulated. The following measures were used to describe the behavior of the firms over time: indexes of price, cost, and inventory; dollars of profits; dollars of sales adjusted for market trend; and a summary index representing a compilation of the "felt pressure" within the firm.

RESULTS OF THE STUDIES

Space prohibits our itemizing in detail the conclusions of the experiment. However, we shall describe some of the most important results.

1. Effect of High Variability in the External Environment:

The firm, in a highly variable environment, had lower costs, higher sales, and greater profits than when the environment was relatively stable. High variability also increases pressure within the firm. This effect was quite significant and was largely independent of the other alterations in the model.

We should first discuss the meaning of "high variability". When the firm is in a highly variable environment, the foremen and salesmen are faced with greater monthly fluctuations in manufacturing costs and sales (i.e. the standard deviations of the probability distributions determining costs and sales are much larger in the highly variable environment). In a relatively stable environment, the fluctuations in costs and sales are more moderate.

Increased variability had a favorable effect upon the profit of the company and caused a significant increase in pressure within the firm. Variability kept the firm more "on its toes" and more likely to take advantage of cost and market opportunities when the occasion arose.

It should also be noted that much the same effect was created by the use of a modified LIFO inventory valuation method. This LIFO method created artificial variability in the profit of the firm and significantly increased the performance of the firm.

While more research certainly needs to be done in investigating this result, there are some questions of importance raised for designers of management control and information systems. For example, accounting methods designed to achieve a stable profit level over time may be of less value to a firm than methods which allow realistic variability. Similarly, many practices of smoothing information and of using average sort of figures possibly should be modified.

2. Effect of "Tight" versus "Loose" Industrial Engineering Department:

Strong effects appeared when the industrial engineering department changed its method of revising production cost standards. *A "tight" industrial engineering department reduced cost in the firm, but it also caused a large decrease in sales. Thus, the profits of the firm did not change significantly.* Hence, we have a counterbalancing effect. When costs are reduced, pressure upon profits and sales is alleviated; and the level of total sales is allowed to fall. On the other hand, when cost standards were "loose" and costs high, the sales department increased its efforts to keep up profits. In general terms, the effect of loose standards in one sector of the organization tended to be counterbalanced by better performance in another sector.

The effect described above was more evident when the firm was in a relatively stable environment than when the firm's environment was highly variable.

Again, this result raised some questions for those interested in management control. It is generally assumed implicitly in determining sales and cost standards that these are independent activities. Hence two separate parts of the organizations often do the goal or standard setting for their respective departments without any thought of over-all coordination. And, yet, the above result indicated that lack of such coordination may impair the effectiveness of the firm.

3. Effects of Changes in the Index of Pressure Weights:

There were two changes involving the weights attached to the various factors in the indexes of pressure in the firm. The first of these studied the effects of differing degrees of contagion of pressure (the degree to which an individual in an organization can transmit his own "felt pressure" to his subordinate).

An increase in the amount of contagion of pressure directly reduced cost. Sales were also affected (increased) when the firm operated in a highly variable environment. This leads to the hypothesis that the effect of contagion is dependent upon the number of levels in the hierarchy through which contagious pressure must pass. Manufacturing, having fewer levels, was affected directly by a change in the amount of contagion; sales, with more hierarchial levels, was affected only when variability was also present. This result, then, introduces a new variable (the ability to transmit pressure) into the question of centralization versus decentralization.

The second change involving the index of pressure weights concerns past versus present data. The use of past data refers to a heavier emphasis upon the performance of an individual over the past quarter than upon his performance in the present period. This change had virtually no effect upon the firm. This is true even though emphasis upon the past data (a three month period) might be expected to have a smoothing effect upon a highly variable environment.

CONCLUSION

A comprehensive approach to management control, utilizing both the concepts of management systems analysis and budgetary and cost control, is very valuable. A model was constructed in an attempt to combine elements of both approaches. Eight changes in the model were proposed and the model was used to study the effects of these changes. Some of the results raise important questions for management control theorists, and establish the value of the comprehensive model as a research tool.

BIBLIOGRAPHY

1. Bonini, Charles P.: *Accounting-Information Systems in the Firm*, O.N.R. Memorandum No. 59, Graduate School of Industrial Administration, Carnegie Institute of Technology, December, 1958.
2. ———: *Simulation of Information and Decision Systems in the Firm*, Englewood Cliffs, N. J.: Prentice-Hall, 1963.
3. Cyert, R. M., and J. G. March: *Behavioral Theory of the Firm*, Englewood Cliffs, N. J.: Prentice-Hall, 1963.
4. ———, "Organizational Factors in the Theory of Oligopoly," *Quarterly Journal of Economics*, vol. 70, February, 1956.
5. Forrester, Jay W.: *Industrial Dynamics*, New York: Wiley, 1961.

6

INDUSTRIAL DYNAMICS AND THE DESIGN OF MANAGEMENT CONTROL SYSTEMS[1]

EDWARD B. ROBERTS
Massachusetts Institute of Technology

I. THE ORGANIZATION AS A CONTROL SYSTEM

Every organization is a control system. Each has direction and objectives, whether explicit or implied. Each has beliefs as to its current status. Each has policies and procedures whereby it reaches decisions and takes actions to attain its goals more closely. Every organization actually contains a myriad of smaller control systems, each characterized by the same goal-striving, but not necessarily goal-attaining, behavior.

The organization as a whole or any one of its component subsystems can be represented by the feedback process shown in Exhibit 6-1. Four characteristics of this diagram are noteworthy. First, the transformation of decisions into results takes place through a complex process which includes a basic structure of organizational, human, and market relationships; this structure is sometimes not apparent because of its numerous sources of noise or random behavior and due to its often lengthy time delays between cause and effect.

The second aspect to be noted is the distinction between the achievements that are apparent in the organization and those which are real. The real situation is translated into the apparent through information and communication channels which contain delays, noise, and bias. These sources of error may be the inadvertent features of an organization's communication system, or they may result from the chosen characteristics of a data-processing system which sacrifices accuracy for compactness. In any event, however, the bases of actual decisions in an organization may be assumptions which bear but little relation to fact.

[1]This article is based on studies supported principally by a grant of the Ford Foundation, which has sponsored Industrial Dynamics Research at M.I.T., and in part by a grant of the National Aeronautics and Space Administration to sponsor research on the management of research and development. The computer simulations were carried out at the M.I.T. Computation Center. The writer is grateful to Professors Donald C. Carroll, Jay W. Forrester, and Donald G. Marquis for their many helpful comments.

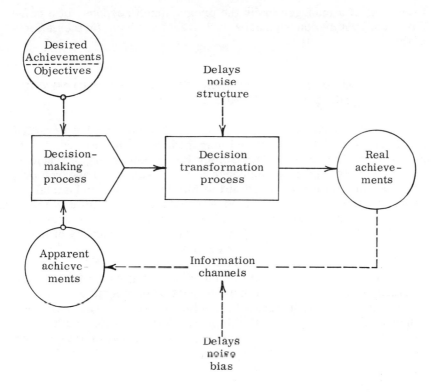

Exhibit 6-1. Control system structure of organization.

The third feature of the diagram is that the decision-making process is viewed as a response to the gap between objectives of the organization and its apparent progress toward those objectives. Although both the objectives and achievements may be difficult to define precisely and measure accurately, such goal-seeking behavior is nonetheless present in all organizations and in every subsystem of the organizations. At any level of an organization, many similar decisions are being made. The real problem of the management control system designer is to recognize these multiple decision loops and their interrelationships, and to develop policies and an organizational structure that will tie these activities into progress toward total organization objectives.

The fourth characteristic of Exhibit 6-1 is the continuous feedback path of decision-results-measurement-evaluation-decision. It is vital to effective system design that each element of this feedback path be properly treated and that its continuous nature be recognized. Whether the decision in the system is made by the irrational actions or logical

deductions of a manager or by the programmed response of a computer, the system consequences will eventually have further effects
on the decision itself.

II. INDUSTRIAL DYNAMICS—PHILOSOPHY AND METHOD-
OLOGY FOR CONTROL SYSTEM DESIGN

Industrial Dynamics is a philosophy which asserts that organizations
are most effectively viewed (and managed) from this control system
perspective. It is also a methodology for designing organizational
policy. This two-pronged approach is the result of a research program
that was initiated and directed at the M.I.T. School of Industrial
Management by Professor Jay W. Forrester. The results of the first
five years of this program are described in Professor Forrester's
book, *Industrial Dynamics*, which also discusses a variety of potential
applications to key management problems.[2]

Industrial Dynamics recognizes a common systems base in the flow
structure of all social-economic-industrial-political organizations.
This perspective ties the segmented functional aspects of formal
organizations into an integrated structure of varying rates of flow and
responsively changing levels of accumulation. The flow paths involve
all facets of organizational resources—men, money, materials, orders,
and capital equipment—and the information and decision-making network that links the other flows.

Industrial Dynamics views decisions as the controllers of these
organization flows. Such decisions regulate the rate of change of
levels from which the flows originate and to which they are sent. In
the flow diagrams drawn as part of an Industrial Dynamics study,
decisions are even represented by the traditional control valve
symbol of the engineer. Exhibit 6-2 shows such a decision, based in
part on information about the contents of the source level, controlling
the rate of flow to the destination level.

The system structures and behavioral phenomena that are
studied by the Industrial Dynamics methodology are present at all
levels of the corporation. The top management of the firm is
involved in a system that can be studied and aided in the same manner
as the middle management of the organization, and again in the same
fashion as the physical operating system of the plant. The potential
payoff from changes derived from systems studies increases greatly,
however, as the study is focused higher up in the organization. For
all studies the pattern of forming a dynamic verbal theory, developing
mathematical equations, computer simulation of the model, and deri-

[2]Jay W. Forrester: *Industrial Dynamics*, Cambridge, Mass.: M.I.T.,
1961.

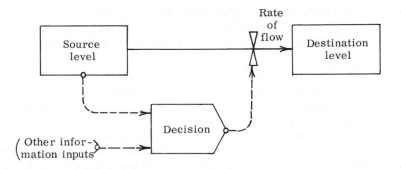

Exhibit 6-2. The decision as a controller.

vation of improved policies is followed. The problems encountered
in these phases do not significantly change as we move from the
bottom to the top of an organization. Only during the final stage of
implementation of system change does the problem complexity get
significantly greater the higher the level of organization involved.
But the impact of improved corporate-level policy on company growth,
stability, and profitability can readily justify this added effort to
renovate top management policy making.

III. PROBLEMS OF MANAGEMENT CONTROL SYSTEMS

The preceding discussion has focused on the nature of organizational
problems as management control system problems, and on the intended
applicability of Industrial Dynamics to these problems. Observation of
several different types of management control systems and a survey of
the literature in this field lead to a belief that a new attack on control
system design is needed. The traditional approaches to management
control systems have mushroomed in number and sophistication of
applications as operations research and electronic data processing
have developed during the post-war era. Although these systems have
made significant and successful inroads, many fail to cure the problems
for which they were designed; other management control systems even
amplify the initial difficulties or create more significant new problems.
All this is taking place even as we derive enhanced but misplaced confidence in the systems.

Several examples will help to illustrate these problems and lead us
to some findings about the design of management control systems.

Systems Inadequate for Their Problems

Sometimes the management control system is inadequately designed
for the problem situation. In such a case the control system may im-

prove performance in the trouble area, but be far short of the potential gains. At times the limited effectiveness may transform a potentially major benefit to the company into but a marginal application.

A Production-Inventory-Employment Control System

As an example, let us take the case of an industrial components manufacturer who initially has no formal production-inventory-employment control systems. Such a firm operates by its response to current problems. It follows the example of the firemen trying to use a leaky hose—as soon as one hole is patched up, another leak occurs elsewhere. A company operating in this manner does not keep sufficiently close tabs on changes in sales, inventories, backlogs, delivery delays, etc. Rather, when customer complaints build up on company delivery performance, people will be hired to increase the production rate and repair the inventory position. Similarly, when a periodic financial report (or the warehouse manager's difficulties) shows a great excess in inventory, workers will be laid off to reduce the inventory position. Despite the obvious faults, the majority of our manufacturing firms have these problems. The dynamic behavior of such firm (as here illustrated by simulation results of an Industrial Dynamics model) has the appearance of Exhibit 6-3, with wide swings in sales, inventories, employment, order backlog, and, correspondingly, in profitability. The potential for a well-designed management control system in such a firm is enormous.

The traditional approach (some may prefer calling it the "modern approach") to the design of a control system for such an organization will recognize that: (1) better information on sales is necessary; (2) such information should properly be smoothed to eliminate possibilities of factory response to chance order-rate variations; (3) inventories should be periodically (perhaps even continuously) checked, and reorders generated when needed to bring stocks into line with target inventories; (4) order backlogs should not be allowed to drift too far from the normal levels; and (5) work force should be adjusted to meet the desired production rate that stems from consideration of current sales volume and the manufacturing backlog situation. Using our earlier company model, we can readily build into the model a management control system that incorporates all these features. The modeled company would then be a leader in its use of management control techniques. And, as Exhibit 6-4 illustrates, the company would have benefited by this approach. With the new control systems installed, fluctuations in the business have in general been reduced in magnitude as well as periodicity. Yet the basic dynamic pattern observed in the earlier diagram is still present—periodic fluctuations in sales, larger ones in inventories, and corresponding variations in production rate and work force. The latter situation is similar in character to that which we encountered at the Sprague Electric

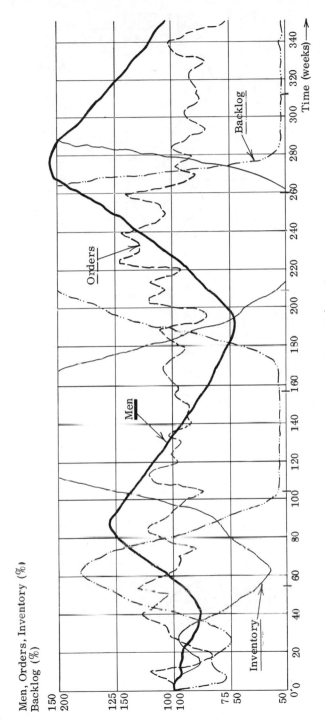

Men, Orders, Inventory (%)
Backlog (%)

Exhibit 6-3.   Management by crises.

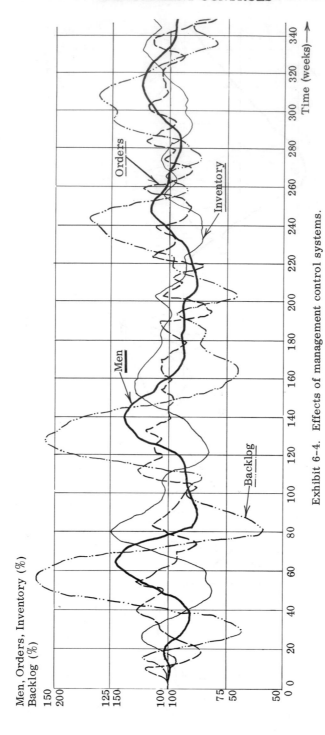

Exhibit 6-4. Effects of management control systems.

Company, at the beginning of our Industrial Dynamics study program
with them several years ago.

Let us briefly review their case. The Sprague Electric Company
is a major producer of electrical components, with an annual sales
volume of approximately 75 million dollars. The particular product
line which was selected for Industrial Dynamics research is a relatively mature industrial component, developed by Sprague several
years ago and now past its market introduction and major growth
phases. The principal customers of the product are manufacturers
of military and high-grade consumer electronic systems. The
industry competition is not price-based, but is rather dependent on
product reliability and delivery time.

The work structure of the company, including its inventory and
manufacturing control aspects, is diagrammed in Exhibit 6-5.
Orders arrive from the customers, and a determination is made
as to whether or not they can be filled from existing inventories.
Orders for those catalogue items not ordinarily stocked, or for those
which are currently out of stock, enter into the backlog of manufacturing orders. The customer orders for which inventory is in stock
are processed and shipped from inventory.

The inventory control system of the company attempts to maintain a proper inventory position for the product line. Target inventories are adjusted to take into account average sales, and inventory
reorders are generated to reflect the shipping rate from inventory
and the desired inventory corrections. The orders for inventory replacements enter into the manufacturing backlog.

Production rate in the company is determined by the level of
employment, with manufacturing output being sent to the customers
or to inventory in reflection of the relative production order backlogs.
Control of both backlog size and employment level is attempted by
means of the employment change decision of the company.

As the curves of Exhibit 6-4 demonstrated, inventory, backlog, and
employment all had sizable fluctuations, despite the existing controls
in these areas. They seemed to reflect, with some amplification, the
variability in incoming orders. Given this situation of fluctuating
sales, the traditional management control designer would either express satisfaction with the system performance or perhaps seek
additional improvement by parameter adjustment. Neither approach
would get at the source of the difficulties, and this source is not the
fluctuations in incoming customer orders.

To determine the real system problem, let us examine our next
diagram (Exhibit 6-6). Here we have duplicated the manufacturer's
organization of Exhibit 6-5 and added a representation of the customer
sector of the industry. The customers receive orders for military
and commercial electronic systems. These are processed through
their engineering departments, resulting in requirements for com-

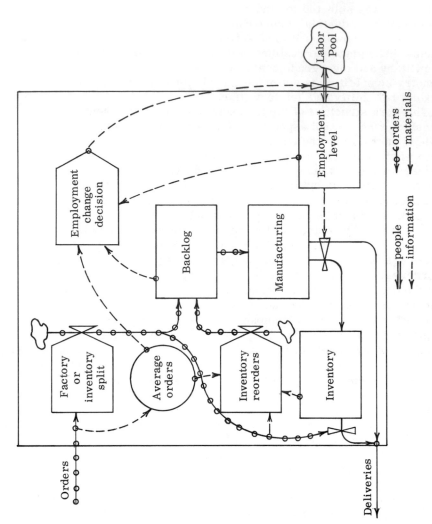

Exhibit 6-5. The manufacturer's organization structure.

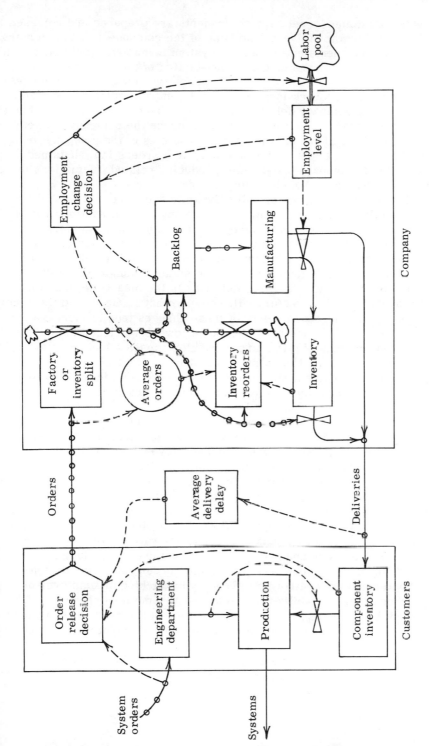

Exhibit 6-6. Company–customers system.

ponents. Customer orders for components are prepared and released as demanded by the delivery lead time of the component manufacturers. Delivered components enter into the system manufacturers' component inventories and are used up during production of the systems.

Having added this sector to our diagram, we now discover the presence of another feedback loop in the total company-customer system: Changes in the company delivery delay will affect the customer release rate of new orders, which in turn will influence the company delivery delay. This loop amplifies the system problems of the company, being able to transform slight variations in system orders into sustained oscillations in company order rate, producing related fluctuations in company inventories, backlog, employment, and profits.

Let us follow through a possible dynamic sequence that will illustrate the full system interactions. If, for any reason, system orders received by the customers temporarily increase, the customers will soon pass this along to the component supplier as an order increase. Since, even under ordinary circumstances, weekly fluctuations in order rate to the component manufacturer are sizable, some time will elapse before this order rate change is noticed. In the meantime, the component manufacturer's inventory will be somewhat reduced, and the order backlog will be increased. Both of these changes tend to increase the delivery delay. The smaller inventory allows fewer incoming orders to be filled immediately; the larger backlog causes a longer delay for the now increased fraction of orders that must await manufacture. As the customers become aware of the longer lead time, they begin to order further ahead, thus maintaining a higher order rate and accentuating the previous trend in sales.

Eventually, the component manufacturer notes the higher sales, larger backlog, and lower inventory, and begins hiring to increase his factory employment. The employment level is set higher than that needed to handle the current customer order rate, so that backlog and inventory can be brought into line. As the increased work force has its gradual effect on inventory and backlog, the changes tend to reduce the delivery time. The information is gradually fed back to the customers, lowering the order rate even below the initial value. This set of system interactions can produce order rate fluctuations unrelated to the basic demand pattern for the customers' products.

To dampen the fluctuations in customer order rate, the component manufacturer must control not inventory or backlog or employment, but rather he must stabilize the factory lead time for deliveries. This can readily be accomplished once the nature of the need is recognized. System behavior can also be improved to a great extent when the component manufacturer becomes aware that his inventory control system does not really control inventory, but it does contribute to production overshoots of any change in orders received.

The details of the Sprague case, the model for its study, and the new policies now being implemented at Sprague are discussed fully in chapters 17 and 18 of *Industrial Dynamics*.[3] It is sufficient for our purposes to show the effects of the new policies applied to the same situation shown earlier in Exhibit 6-4. The curves shown on the next graph (Exhibit 6-7) demonstrate a higher degree of stability achieved in all variables except inventory, which is now being used to absorb random changes in sales. In particular, the employment swings have been dampened significantly. The simulation results forecast significant benefits to the company deriving from the application of this new approach to management policy design. Our experiences during the past year of system usage at Sprague seem to support the initial hypotheses, and the product line is currently benefiting from higher productivity, improved employment stability, higher and smoother sales, and lower inventories.

The Control of Research and Development Projects

Another area in which the traditional approach to control system design has proven inadequate is the management of research and development projects. The intangibility, lack of precise measurements, and uncertain character of R and D results are partly responsible for this failure. But a more basic lack of system understanding has implications of even greater significance. All systems of schedule or budget controls that have been tried till now have failed to achieve success in R and D usage. These techniques have included Gantt charts, milestone schedules, and computerized systems of budgetary and manpower control.

The latest approaches to control of research and development projects are based on PERT (Program Evaluation Review Technique) or PERT/COST. The management control systems implied by the methods used can be represented by the diagram of Exhibit 6-8. As shown here, the basis for the current sophisticated methods is a single-loop system in which the difference between desired completion date and projected completion date causes decisions to change the magnitude or allocation of project resources (manpower, facilities, equipment, priorities). As these resources are employed, they are assumed to produce the progress that is reported during the project. These reports are processed through a PERT-type evaluation and forecasting system to create the projected completion time.

But the design of a management control system based on such a set of assumptions is doomed to failure, since some of the most vital aspects of the real system have been excluded from the underlying analysis. For example, the lack of tangible, precise measurement sources is entirely ignored. Yet these factors contribute much of the error between the *real* situation in the project (its true scope and

[3]Ibid.

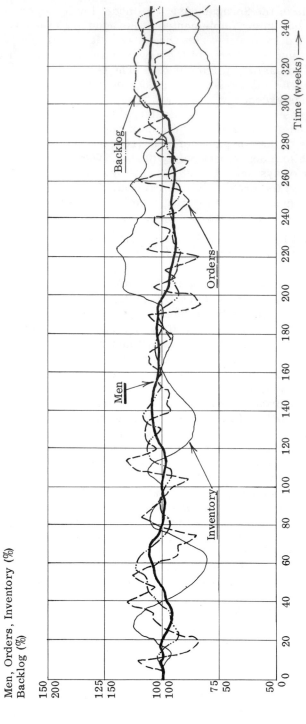

Exhibit 6-7. Effects of Industrial Dynamics policies.

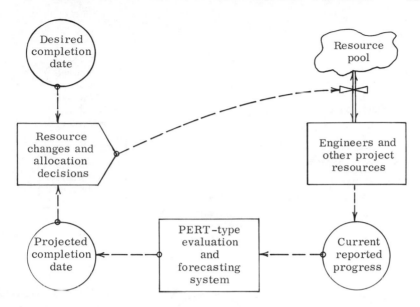

Exhibit 6-8. Assumed basis of current R and D project controls.

actual progress to date) and that which is *apparent* to those doing the engineering work.

Another part of the real system which appears to be ignored by current R and D control system designers is the human element in the project actions and decisions. The attitudes and motivations of the engineers and managers, their knowledge of the schedules and current estimates in the project, the believed penalty-reward structure of the organization—all affect the progress and problems that are reported upward in the organization. Furthermore, these same factors even affect the rate of real progress toward project objectives. All systems of measurement and evaluation (in R and D, manufacturing, government, universities, or what-have-you) create incentives and pressures for certain actions. These interact with the goals and character of individuals and institutions to produce decisions, actions, and their results. For example, a system which compares "actual to budgeted expenditures" creates an incentive to increase budgets, regardless of need, and to hold down expenditures, regardless of progress; one which checks "proportion of budget spent" creates pressures on the manager or engineer to be sure he spends the money, whether or not on something useful. The presence of such factors in research and development ought to be recognized in the design of systems for R and D control.

Adding these two additional sources of system behavior to the earlier diagram produces the more complete representation of a research and development system that is pictured in Exhibit 6-9.

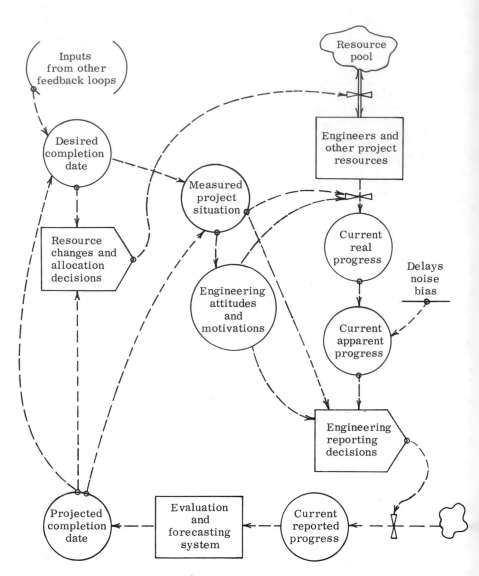

Exhibit 6-9. More complete representation of R and D system.

But even this is an incomplete representation of the complex system which interrelates the characteristics of the product, the customer, and the R and D organization. A proper characterization of research and development projects must take into account the continuous dynamic system of activities that creates project life cycles. Such a system will include not just the scheduled and accumulated effort, costs, and accomplishments. Rather, it will encompass the full range of policies and parameters that carry a research and development project from initial perception of potential need for the product to final completion of the development program. The fundamental R and D project system is shown in Exhibit 6-10, from which we have developed an Industrial Dynamics model of research and development project dynamics.

Some of the results of simulation studies of this model are of particular interest to designers of management control systems. They demonstrate the importance of taking cognizance of the complete system structure in attempting to create and implement methods of system control. For example, one series of simulations of the general project model was conducted in which only the scheduled project duration was changed in the various runs. Within the model the effort allocation process *attempts* to complete the project during this scheduled period. However, the actual completion dates of the projects seem only remotely responsive to the changes in desired completion time.

Exhibit 6-11 demonstrates the nature of this response, using the data of four model simulations. The horizontal axis is an index of the

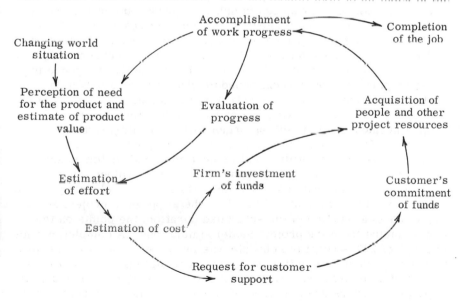

Exhibit 6-10. Dynamic system underlying R and D projects.

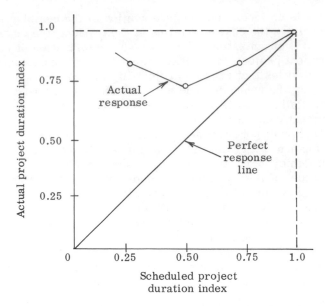

Exhibit 6-11. Scheduled versus actual project durations.

scheduled project duration as a percentage of the maximum schedule
used; the vertical axis shows actual completion time in a similar
percentile manner. If changes in schedule produced corresponding
changes in actual completion dates, the curve of results would have
followed the diagonal "perfect response" line; that is, a 50 percent
reduction in scheduled duration should produce a 50 percent reduction
in actual duration, if control is *perfect*. But the actual response is
far from perfect; a 50 percent schedule change effects only a 25 percent actual change. And at the extreme, the actual change is even in
the opposite direction, taking longer to complete the urgent crash
project because of the resulting organizational confusion and inefficiencies. Of course, this response curve does not present the data
on the manpower instability, total project cost, and customer satisfaction changes that also accompany shifts in the project schedule.

Some of the implications of Exhibit 6-11 are more clearly presented
by the next curve (Exhibit 6-12). Here the slippage in project schedule
is plotted as a function of the scheduled duration, the points on the
curve coming from the project model simulations. A completion time
slippage of 242 percent of schedule was incurred in the crash project,
with a rapid decrease in this percentage completion date overrun as
the schedule is dragged out. When the project is slowed too much, the
slippage increases again as lack of enthusiasm induces further stretch-
out during the project life.

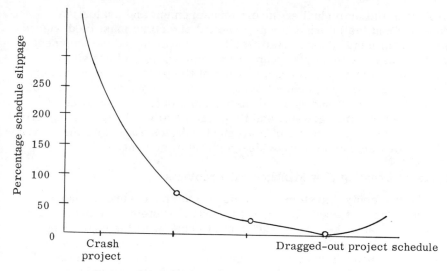

Exhibit 6-12. Schedule slippage as a function of schedule.

The principal point made by these two illustrations is that many factors other than desired schedule determine the resultant actual schedule of research and development porjects. *Control systems for R and D which resort to schedule and effort rate control without full understanding of the system structure of projects are bound to be ineffective*. The current PERT-based project control systems seem guilty of this error in design philosophy. In fact, many aspects of our government contracting program suffer similar faults of inadequate system understanding, producing ill-conceived policies with attendant poor results. For example, increased risk-taking (i.e., greater willingness to invest company funds prior to contract receipt) and higher bidding integrity by R and D companies would act in the best interests of the government customer of research and development. However, our simulation studies show that neither policy is in the short-term best interests of the R and D companies, under existing government regulations and practices. Thus the contracting policies, a government control system for R and D procurement, act to the detriment of national objectives by inducing company behavior which produces unsatisfactory project outcomes.[4]

The proper design of research and development control systems, for both company and customer, should take into account three things: (1) the source of internal action, information, and control in a

[4] A general theory of research and development project behavior, a model of the theory, and extensive simulation studies of parameters and policies influencing R and D outcomes are reported in the author's book, *The Dynamics of Research and Development*, to be published later this year by Harper and Row.

project is the individual engineer; measurement and evaluation
schemes and the internal penalty-reward structure must be designed
with him in mind; (2) the total results of research and development
projects are created by a complex dynamic system of activities,
which interrelates the characteristics of the product, the customer,
and the R and D firm; control systems which ignore vital aspects of
these flows cannot succeed; (3) institutional objectives of R and D
companies (profits, growth, stability) can be aligned with the objectives
of government customers; procurement policies constitute the system
of control which can effect or destroy this alignment.

Systems Creating New Management Problems

The two control system areas discussed above were intended to
demonstrate that many management control systems are designed in
a manner that makes them inadequate to cope with the underlying
problems. In each example, however, certain aspects of the systems
were described which actually aggravated the existing problems. In
the Sprague case, the inventory control system amplified sales
changes to create wider swings in production and employment than
actually existed in orders received from the customers. Our discussion of research and development project control indicated that
government contracting policies often create resulting behavior that
is contrary to the government's own interests. Other examples can
be presented which have similar effects: the attempt to achieve
management control leads to situations in which initial difficulties
are amplified or significant new problems are created.

Problems of Logistics Control

One apparent instance of this type occurs in the Air Force Hi-Value
Logistic System. This inventory control system was developed over a
long period of time at great government expense by some of the nation's
most sophisticated control system designers. The Hi-Value System is
intended to provide conservative initial procurement and meticulous
individual item management during the complete logistic cycle of all
high-cost Air Force material. Yet an Industrial Dynamics study of
this system by a member of the M.I.T. Executive Development Program concluded that the system behavior can result in periodic over-
statement of requirements, excess procurement and/or unnecessary
repair of material, followed by reactions at the opposite extreme.[5]
These fluctuations produce undesirable oscillations in the repair and
procurement work loads and in the required manpower at Air Force
installations, supply and repair depots. The study recommended

[5]Max K. Kennedy: "An Analysis of the Air Force Hi-Valu Logistic System;
An Industrial Dynamics Study," unpublished S. M. thesis, M.I.T. School of
Industrial Management, 1962.

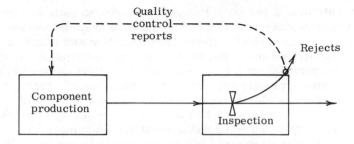

Exhibit 6-13. Theoretical quality control system.

changes in policy and information usage that tend to stabilize the
procurement system behavior.

Quality Control Systems

A commonly utilized management control system has as its purpose
the control of manufacturing output quality. The feedback system
apparent to the designers of such quality control systems is pictured
in Exhibit 6-13. Component parts are produced by a process that has
a certain expected quality or reliability characteristic. The parts
are inspected for flaws and rejects discarded or reworked. Statistically designed control charts determine when the production process
is out of control, and reports are fed back to production to correct the
problem sources.

The effectiveness of such quality control systems becomes questionable when we view the performance curves generated by a typical
system. Exhibit 6-14 plots component production rate and inspection

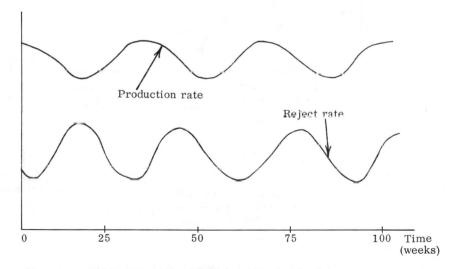

Exhibit 6-14. Quality control system performance.

reject rate over a period of two years. Wide periodic swings in
reject rate produce violations of the control system tolerance limits
which cause machine adjustments in production and temporarily
lower production rates. But what causes the oscillations in the reject
rate? Its periodic nature suggests seasonal fluctuations in production
quality, often strangely encountered in many manufacturing plants.
The manager has almost no way of checking the validity of such an
assumption. Therefore, since the explanation seems reasonable, it
would probably be accepted under most circumstances.

This situation illustrates one of the key problems in quality control
—the lack of an objective confirming source of information. We are
in a more favorable position to understand the phenomenon, however,
since the results were produced by a computer simulation. The
surprising fact is that the actual production quality was held constant,
without even random variations, throughout the two years of the run.
This means that the oscillations of reject rate and production shown
in Exhibit 6-14 are not responses to outside changes, but rather are
internally created by the behavioral system.

Let us examine a more complete picture of the total factory
system, as shown in the next diagram (Exhibit 6-15). Components are
produced, then inspected, rejects being discarded. The accepted
components are forwarded to an assembly operation, where they enter
into the manufacture of complete units. In an electronics plant, for
example, the component production and inspection might correspond
to a grid manufacturing operation, with the assembly operation putting
together complete electronic tubes. When the tube is put through a

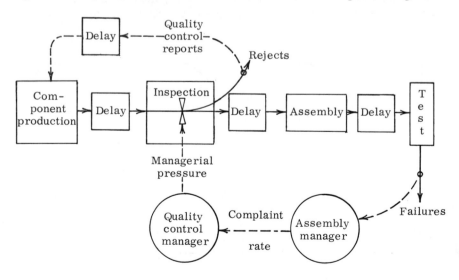

Exhibit 6-15. More complete representation of quality control system.

life test, tube failure and the source of failure are far more obvious
than are the grid imperfections during the component inspection.
Should too many imperfections get through component inspection,
eventual tube failure rate will produce complaints by the assembly
manager to the quality control manager. As these complaints continue
to build, the quality control manager puts pressure on his inspectors
to be more careful and detect more of the poor grids. In response to
this pressure, the inspectors reject far more grids. Without an objective measure of grid quality, the reject rate tends to be a function
of subjective standards and inspection care. Under pressure from the
manager, the inspectors will reject any grid which seems at all
dubious, including many which are actually of acceptable quality. As
the rejects rise, fewer poor grids enter the assembly process, thus
causing fewer tube failures in test. The assembly manager's complaints drop off and, in fact, soon switch to a concern for getting more
grids for his assembly operation. Without pressure from the quality
control manager and with counterpressure to get more grids to the
assembly operation, the grid inspectors tend to slacken gradually
their care and their reject standards. Eventually, the number of
rejectable grids getting into the tube assembly creates the problem
of tube failures again, and the cycle repeats. Given normal delays in
such a process, the entire cycle takes on a seasonal appearance.
Thus, a system intended to assure control of product quality actually
creates serious fluctuations of rejects, component production, and
tube failures, all attributed to unknown factors "out of our control."

The consequences of such a situation are even more serious when
the inspection output is distributed to eventual customers through the
normal multi-stage distribution system. In this case the customer
complaints and store returns also affect sales. These influences
combine after a long delay to produce significant top management
pressure on the quality control manager in reflection of a situation
which existed many months before. In both Exhibits 6-15 and 6-16,
the quality control manager's response is a key to system behavior.
Here the manager of the formal quality control system is himself the
most important aspect of the total system of quality and production
control.

IV. SOME PRINCIPLES OF MANAGEMENT CONTROL
SYSTEM DESIGN

The examples discussed represent a wide range of management
control systems. Study of these applications produces some general
principles of management control system design.

A. The key to effective control often lies outside the boundaries
of *conventional* operational control systems; in fact, it is sometimes outside the *formal* boundaries of the company organization.

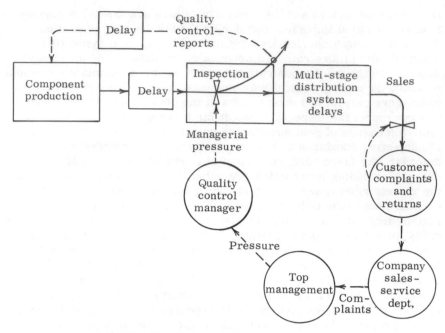

Exhibit 6-16. Total quality control system.

Too many organizations give up altogether too soon the battle for mastering a management problem caused by factors apparently "out of our control." The cyclic swings in customer orders in the production-inventory case, government changes in project funding of research and development, seasonal variations of product reject rate in the quality control problem are all examples of such factors. Yet in each case successful control system management rests within the access of company policy.

In the Sprague case the system requiring control included the ordering decisions of the customer, certainly not part of Sprague's formal organization. But the basis for system control exists in the stabilization of the input to the customer decision, the component delivery delay. Again, project success in R and D is strongly influenced by company integrity and risk-taking. Yet customer, not company, policy can be redesigned to achieve desirable company behavior. And the key to quality control involves recognition of the total system of product flow to assembly (or to customers) and the resulting feedback of complaints and pressures.

The boundaries of a management control system design study must not be drawn to conform with organizational structure merely because of that structure. System boundaries cannot ignore vital feedback channels for information and action if the system is to be effective.

B. The proper design of management control systems often requires inclusion of the effects of intangibles; in particular, the role of decision makers who are part of the total system of control must be treated carefully.

Control system designers who are working with computers often have as their end product a computer model for calculating (or searching for) an optimal control decision. Yet while being willing to model a decision for a machine, they seem unwilling to include in their studies any models of man—of human decision-making within the control loops. In the production-inventory control case, the modeling of aggregate customer decision-makers is a vital part of the system. Our second example emphasized that a properly designed R and D control system should be based on models of engineer and manager decision-making in both the company and customer organizations. Finally, we observed that the decision-making and responses of both managers and inspectors are crucial aspects of the quality control case.

These illustrations emphasize the usual failure to recognize and cope with the nature of human response in organizations. The decision-makers, single or aggregated—their motivations, attitudes, pressures, modes of response—must be included in management control system design. *The man (and manager) is part of the system of control, and management control system design must be viewed as a form of man-machine system design.*

C. A true understanding of total system basis and system behavior can permit effective design of both operational control systems and top management policy, without differences in philosophy or methodology of approach. In fact, most significant control system applications inherently require supra-functional or multi-departmental organization.

In the Sprague case, for example, successful control involved consideration of such aspects as customer service (marketing), inventory and production rate (manufacturing), and employment policies (personnel). Thus what often gets treated as a middle-management problem becomes resolvable only at the top policy-making level of the firm. The important elements in research and development tend not to be middle-management concerns for schedules, but rather top management policy affecting investment planning, customer relations, and company-wide attitudes. Management control systems can therefore seek to achieve the major goals of the organization as a whole, and not just the sub-optimizing aims of individual segments. A great present hazard, in fact, is the common planning and programming of control systems at the wrong level of the company, by people who lack total system perspectives and the authority to achieve broad system integration.

The Industrial Dynamics program has demonstrated the possibilities of examining and treating system problems of great variety and scope of complexity. We have dealt with many situations in which stabilization was needed and more recently with other cases in which balanced growth was the objective of the policy design efforts. The potential advantages to companies who pioneer in this work are significant and may become the basis of our future industrial competition. In this regard, it seems fitting to close with the implied advice of the Japanese scholar who said: "When your opponent is at the point of striking you, let your mind be fixed on his sword and you are no longer free to master your own movements, for you are then controlled by him."[6]

[6]Takawan, as quoted by Charles H. Townes: "Useful Knowledge," Technology Review, p. 36, January, 1963.

7

THE HARBETS SIMULATION EXERCISE AND MANAGEMENT CONTROL

STANLEY I. BUCHIN
Harvard University

I INTRODUCTION

In August 1963, the Harvard Business School and the Educational Testing Service will complete an experimental investigation into executive decision-making behavior begun during the summer of 1962. By that time it is hoped that the decisional behavior of about one hundred business and government executives organized in four-man teams will have been observed and recorded in an environmental setting simulating that found in the real world of business.

II GENERAL DESCRIPTION OF SIMULATED ENVIRONMENT

The task assigned to these executives is the management of a medium-sized manufacturing firm, the Harbets Company, with sales of about $25,000,000 per year of industrial non-durable goods, namely, grinding wheels. Each participant is given a specific role: marketing vice-president, manufacturing vice-president, director of research and engineering, or comptroller. Not only is each participant responsible for the operation of his own part of the company, but each four-man team has been asked by the company president in a memorandum to act collectively as an executive committee. During their two week involvement in the simulation exercise, the executives guide their company through two years of operations with the opportunity to change plans and policies every three months (one day of real time being equal to three months of simulated time).

Management control is performed by written response to various budgets, reports correspondence, and memoranda found by the participants in their "in-baskets" each morning. Some of these materials are generated by a computer model of the firm and its environment (Harbus 2)[1] based on the existing company policies and the current and predicted economic conditions (see Exhibit 7-1). The rest are typical of that found at the prototype company, Bay State Abrasive Products Company and are assigned to particular "in-baskets" ac-

---

[1] See Appendix A for more detailed description of Harbus 2 model.

EXHIBIT 7-1

RESEARCH AND ENGINEERING BUDGET FOR YEAR 1 QUARTER I

Supn. and Engineers - Basic Res.	$ 16,250
Supn. and Engineers - Prod. Dev.	31,250
Supn. and Engineers - Qual. Cont.	36,250
Supn. and Engineers - Ind. Eng.	46,250
Supn. and Engineers - Equip. Des.	23,750
Supn. and Engineers - Genl.	21,250
Supn. and Engineers - Total	175,000
Technicians - Basic Res.	9,000
Technicians - Prod. Dev.	27,000
Technicians - Qual. Cont.	21,000
Technicians - Ind. Eng.	18,000
Technicians - Equip Des.	27,000
Technicians - Genl.	3,000
Technicians - Total	105,000
Pensions, FICA, etc.	35,000
Matl. and Out Serv - Basic Res.	10,000
Matl. and Out Serv - Prod. Dev.	37,500
Matl. and Out Serv - Qual. Cont.	35,000
Matl. and Out Serv - Ind. Eng.	22,500
Matl. and Out Serv - Equip Des.	22,500
Matl. and Out Serv - Genl.	22,500
Matl. and Out Serv - Total	150,000
Equip. Depreciation	0
Bldg. Depreciation	15,000
Total Depreciation	15,000
Total	$480,000

cording to the research design (see Exhibits 7-2 and 7-3). They vary in problem generality, probable impact on company operations, search required for information necessary for solution, and apparent time pressure for a response. Also available to the participants are computer-generated reports on the last three months of operations to provide indications of how successful past decisions were and how competition and customers seemed to be responding to these past decisions (see Exhibit 7-4).

It is the task of each participant to determine what he wants to respond to, how much group advice to solicit, and what decisions to make. The company will continue to run even if the entire team of executives made no decisions at all. All recommendations made in the reports and budgets are assumed to be approved unless they are clearly and specifically changed by the participants.

EXHIBIT 7-2

DATE <u>March 24, 1970</u>

MEMORANDUM

To   <u>Jim Stevens</u>

From   <u>George Evans</u>

    Dick Laity has just left my office after informing me that he has received a job offer from Monsanto and is seriously considering taking it. He has not been unhappy here but feels that this is a good opportunity that he shouldn't pass up. The salary difference is not great—I think they're only offering a couple thousand more—and I think he feels the main value would be a more stimulating atmosphere. Can we offer him something better? He's an awfully good man and we can't afford to lose him. If we could meet their salary and give him some other benefits, such as a little more opportunity to follow his own research interests, I think I could persuade him to stay. Please let me know what I can do as soon as possible. I'd like to give him a counter proposal right away so that he'll feel we are really interested in him.

EXHIBIT 7-3

December 23, 1969

TO: T. Fisher
        L. Fredericks
        W. McLaughlin
        J. Stevens

FROM: Henry Weiss

    I am to see Mr. Paul Enns of the First National Bank tomorrow regarding some matters relating to our employees.
    If it meets with your approval, I would like to ask him at that time if they would consider re-opening the bank for a couple of hours on Friday night so that our employees can cash their checks. Since we are one of their largest depositors and, as most of your employees bank there also, they might be willing to perform this service. I know that many of our employees find it inconvenient to have to wait until Monday to cash their checks.

    All decisions made by the participants affect the computer simulation of the company's operations. The changes made in the budgets, price lists, or other quantitative items of a similar nature are directly fed into the computer. The other decisions are all coded for

EXHIBIT 7-4

HARBUS MARKETING BUDGET AND EXPENSE REPORT
FOR YEAR 1 QUARTER 1 MONTH 3

	Budget Quarter 1	Expenses Month 3	Cumulative Quarter 1	Cumulative Expenses Year 1
Sales Commissions - Region 1	$120,000	$ 40,000	$120,000	$120,000
Sales Commissions - Region 2	$120,000	$ 40,000	$120,000	$120,000
Sales Commissions - Region 3	$ 60,000	$ 20,000	$ 60,000	$ 60,000
Sales Commissions - Total	$300,000	$100,000	$300,000	$300,000
Salesmen in Training	$ -	$ -	$ -	$ -
Salesmen Severance Salaries	$ -	$ -	$ -	$ -
Salesmen Expenses Region 1	$ 66,000	$200,000	$ 60,000	$ 60,000
Salesmen Expenses Region 2	$ 60,000	$220,000	$ 60,000	$ 60,000
Salesmen Expenses Region 3	$ 30,000	$ 10,000	$ 30,000	$ 30,000
Salesmen Expenses Total	$150,000	$ 50,000	$150,000	$150,000
Administrative Salaries	$ 75,000	$ 25,000	$ 75,000	$ 75,000
Clerical Wages	$ 25,000	$ 8,332	$ 24,996	$ 24,996
Pensions, FICA, etc.	$ 50,000	$ 16,667	$ 50,001	$ 50,001
Total Advertising	$120,000	$ 40,000	$120,000	$120,000
Total	$720,000	$239,999	$719,997	$719,997

the concern shown for human relations, organizational efficiency, and competitive market position. These, in turn, influence such computer model parameters as worker productivity, worker quitting, produce quality, and product suitability for customer needs.

To familiarize the participants with the company and jobs they are taking over, about a day is spent in orientation. This includes:

1. A description of the grinding wheel industry and Harbets' position within it
2. A slide tour of the Harbets' manufacturing facility
3. A description of the Harbets' organization, rules, and procedures, especially the president's concept of how the executive committee should operate
4. Tape-recorded talks by the outgoing Harbets' executives whose jobs the participants are taking over (played by the respective Bay State Abrasive Products Company executives)
5. Reports on the operations of the company for the previous five and one-half years (generated by the computer) to provide information on both past activities and the report formats used
6. List of limitations on the actions of the participants ("rules of the game")

III RESEARCH DESIGN OF PROJECT

The research purposes of the project are the following:

1. Identification of the relative effectiveness of alternative ways of arriving at executive decisions
2. Discovery of obstacles, inefficiencies, or limitations which reduce the effectiveness of business decisions
3. Determination of the influence of experiences, abilities, and other personal qualities of the executives on the characteristics of the decisions in which they were involved
4. Validation of psychological test data against a criterion of decision effectiveness, and
5. Production of a set of standard materials which after the completion of the study, would be available for training appraisal, or further research uses

The major variables controlled for the teams are the following:

1. Experience of the team members in the jobs to which they are assigned—high, medium, or low
2. Aggressiveness of competitive activity (within the computer model)—high or low, and
3. Predictability of incoming customer orders (within the computer model)—high or low

An intra-group variable used is the nature of general business conditions. In four of the quarters of play there are improving conditions, in four quarters recessionary conditions.

Available as measures of group effectiveness will be a host of economic indices such as net profits, share of market, net sales, or stock price and the behavioral indices of concern for human relations, for organizational efficiency, and for competitive market position. There will also be available the observations of the group decision-making processes during executive committee meetings and telephone conversations between executives.

The major variables to be studied with respect to individual behavior are the following:

1. Non-computer "in-basket" item categories, namely:
   a. Search required before a reasonable response is believed possible—high or low
   b. Probable impact of item—high, medium or low
   c. Apparent pressure for a response—high, medium or low, and
   d. Problem generality—germane to one business function or to several
2. Biographical data, including experience with task assigned
3. Scores on a series of aptitude and attitude tests; and
4. Effect of the team variables

IV PRELIMINARY OBSERVATIONS ABOUT 1962 EXERCISES AND MANAGEMENT CONTROL

While the detailed statistical analysis of the behavior exhibited in the simulation exercise will not be done until after the 1963 sessions are completed, there are several preliminary observations that may be of interest.

First, the results of an investigation of the simulation reality are shown in charts on pages 133 and 134.

These results have the qualitative characteristics one might reasonably expect. A very cursory analysis indicated that the reasons for these results seem to be the following:

1. The more aggressive competition created the need for more marketing, research and engineering expenditures and stimulated the tendency toward price cutting.
2. Low order predictability made budgeting and planning a more uncertain process. Random changes in the level of incoming orders were mistaken for more permanent changes.
3. The more highly experienced executives coordinated their activities better, devoted their time to the more important prob-

lems, changed policies in a slower, steadier way avoiding wide fluctuations in the marketing and research areas, and generally avoided price cutting except as an extreme defensive marketing strategy.

A much more detailed analysis is needed of a larger number of groups before more conclusive statements about executive behavior can be made.

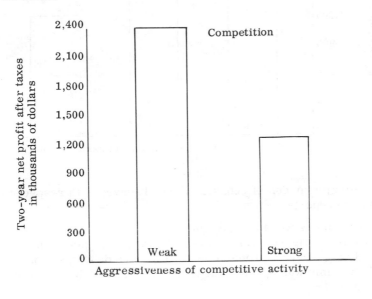

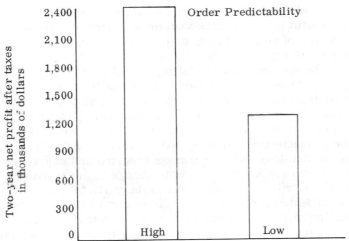

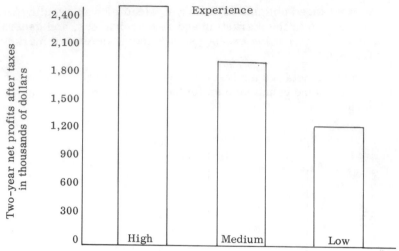

Experience of team members in assigned jobs

Three major modes of behavior were observed with respect to the quantitative reports:

1. The reports were largely ignored.
2. A few key figures were examined and further detail investigated only where a problem seemed to have developed, or
3. Much time was spent in the indiscriminate evaluation of all figures.

The first and third courses of action were associated largely with those people with little previous working experience with quantitative reports. A lack of understanding of quantitative reports was a general weakness of the executives studied. For example, the impact of changing the method of depreciating capital equipment was not often appreciated by the participants. Essentially, adoption of the accelerated depreciation method (sum-of-digits or double declining balance) caused a large increase in the equipment purchased and the accounting depreciation expense. This in turn, increased the full cost of the products manufactured and created an upward pressure on prices. It also lowered the earnings reported and depressed the price of common stock. That a simple change in the accounting rules could do all this was rather startling to the participants.

Despite repeated reminders, the participants had difficulty in differentiating single-shot decisions from those that would affect future recommendations to them. They were told that long-term policy changes would not be assumed from a revised budget amount, unless specific instructions were provided with respect to policy.

Comments received from participants afterwards indicated the exercise was useful in making them think about the difference between decisions and decision rules.

The participants seemed to have found it helpful to have had the following information available for making decisions:

1. Past forecasts and budgets
2. Past actual orders and costs
3. Current forecasts, and
4. Current budget recommendations

In some teams, the process of adjusting current forecasts and budgets by the past errors was very explicit. However, this required a good understanding of the meaning of the reports.

In conjunction with this project a new measure of management control effectiveness was developed. This was a comparison between actual operating results for each quarter and what those results would have been had the team members not changed any of the recommendations made to them at the beginning of the quarter. While this gives only a short-run evaluation of the decisions made, it is possible to get long-range projections of each set of decisions. This information was not made available to the participants until the exercise was completed as part of the "feedback". Even at that time, it was believed helpful for the self-evaluation of the effectiveness of the decisions made.

V   CONCLUSIONS

Even at this stage of analysis, one particularly interesting result that seems to be emerging is the strong relationship between an understanding of quantitative reports and prudent management control (at least in a situation new to an executive). Management planning and control appeared to be an inseparable process assisted by an intelligent use of quantitative information.

A more detailed analysis of how management viewed and responded to controlled circumstances should be of help in the design of future quantitative information systems. This, it is hoped, will be complete by 1964.

APPENDIX A.   HARBUS 2 COMPUTER MODEL

By means of the Harbus 2 mathematical model, the computer generated the response of the Harbets Company and its environment to the decisions made by the participants and generated recommendations for further action by the participants.

The environmental sectors represented in the model included the following:

1. Six customer groups representing two different industries in each of three regions
2. Competition (considered as one collective entity)
3. Labor market for each kind of personnel required by the company
4. Material vendors
5. Factory equipment manufacturers
6. Short term debt market
7. Bond market, and
8. Stock market

Major behavior described within the Harbets Company included:

1. Office and factory order processing
2. Labor requisitioning, hiring, training, firing, quitting, overtime, and undertime in all of the company's divisions (manufacturing, marketing, research and engineering, accounting and finance)
3. Materials ordering, receipt, and usage in the factory (and usage of materials and outside services in the other divisions)
4. Installation and scrapping of factory equipment
5. Cash flows resulting from the above and the participants' financial decisions
6. Changes in the product and process as the result of research and engineering activity
7. Historical and forecasted information about the above including various accounting and cost reports

Among the recommendations for further action were the following:

1. Personnel desired for each of the four divisions of the company
2. Divisional budgets
3. Factory and office order backlogs desired
4. Factory and office normal workday
5. Factory excess capacity desired
6. Factory equipment budget
7. Direct materials reorder levels and quantities
8. Advertising budget
9. Proposed price list
10. Proposed delivery schedules for customer orders
11. Proposed dividend payout, and
12. Proposed sale of long-term bonds and common stock

In addition, competitive price lists and delivery schedules are provided to the participants as auxiliary marketing information.

To accomplish this the Harbus 2 model, which is programmed in FORTRAN for the IBM 7090 computer, contains about 15,000 significant parameters and variables in approximately 10,000 important equation or logical relationships. Some of these relationships are revalued weekly, some monthly, quarterly, or annually. For example, the factory hiring and firing is done once each simulated week, the divisional budgeting once each quarter.

Available to the participants were some 15 reports per month like divisional budget and expense reports, divisional personnel status reports, income statement, balance sheet, incoming order and shipping status reports, an additional five quarterly historical reports on total industry orders, share of market, equipment status, rejections and direct materials out-of-stock.

About fifteen forecasts, planning reports, and budgets were provided each quarter, another five once each year.

The model can be set to run either for a quarter of a year generating recommendations for action for the next quarter or for longer periods of time in which case these recommendations are implemented without change. In the latter way, the computer generated a five and one-half year history of company operations as part of the orientation of the participants.

In addition, this feature made it possible to have available for research analysis a comparison of the actual performance each quarter vs. the projected performance if the participants had not changed any of the actions recommended to them. The immediate impact of the changes made by each team each quarter as compared with what would have happened if nothing had been changed was used as part of the final "feedback" sessions for the participants. See Exhibits 7-5 and 7-6 summarizing the decisions made by one of the teams throughout the exercise and their immediate effects.

A mathematical calculation of an optimum set of decisions within the simulated setting was highly unlikely for three reasons:

1. The difficulty in specifying the criterion or criteria to be optimized (i.e. profits, cash position, market share)
2. The great complexity of interrelationships in the model, and
3. The time lags in the model between stimulus and response

As part of the experimental design of the exercise, the following model values were controlled:

1. Cyclican pattern of customer purchases
2. Randomness of customer purchases, and
3. Aggressiveness of competitive marketing and research activities

The model restricted the freedom of action of the participants to some extent, largely as follows:

1. No more than two different groups of products were possible.
2. No additional markets could be entered.

3. Finished goods inventory was not permitted.
4. No information was available on individual items, except price.
5. No major changes could be made in the production process for the manufacture of all products (sequential through five departments).

EXHIBIT 7-5
SUMMARY OF SIGNIFICANT DECISIONS ARE MADE BY TEAM 34

Team 34 made the following significant changes in the operations of the Harbets Company during the simulation exercise.

Period 1.   (1) Raised prices back up to historical levels
            (2) Showed high interest in factory and office efficiency
            (3) Shifted salesmen from the eastern to the western region
            (4) Eliminated the year-end dividend

Period 2.   (1) Requisitioned a 30% increase in the research and engineering staff
            (2) Shifted more salesmen from the eastern to the western region
            (3) Decreased the proposed factory equipment budget by 15%.
            (4) Retired $1,000,000 debt one year earlier than required
            (5) Restored historic dividend rate
            (6) Changed delivery schedules to the eastern and mid-western regions
            (7) Increased office order processing personnel by 15%.

Period 3.   (1) Laid off several salesmen and shifted still more from the eastern to the western region
            (2) Increased the advertising budget by 10%.
            (3) Showed a large increase in interest in factory and office efficiency
            (4) Increased office order processing personnel by an additional 10%.
            (5) Declared an extra dividend
            (6) Shifted from straight-lined to sum-of-digits depreciation for new factory equipment

Period 4.   (1) Reduced all prices by 3%.
            (2) Reduced advertising to historic levels

Period 5.   (1) Requisitioned a 15% increase in salesmen staff
            (2) Stopped the scrapping of old equipment

Period 6.   (1) Raised prices back to historic levels
            (2) Requisitioned an additional 5% increase in the salesmen staff
            (3) Requisitioned a 10% increase in the research and engineering staff
            (4) Decreased proposed factory equipment budget by 90%.
            (5) Declared extra quarterly dividend
            (6) Showed an additional increase in interest in factory efficiency

Period 7.   (1) Increased wages and salaries by 4%.
            (2) Showed an additional increase in interest in office efficiency

Period 8.   (1) Increased office order processing personnel by 10%.
            (2) Showed still further interest in factory and office efficiency

EXHIBIT 7-6

TEAM 34 RESULTS

The following results were produced by the changes made by Team 34:

Period:	1	2	3	4	5	6	7	8
Share of market:								
Projected*	17.8	18.6	17.1	16.7	18.0	21.9	22.8	22.7
Actual	19.4	19.0	17.2	16.6	18.4	20.7	22.9	22.5
Incoming Orders								
Projected*	6,004,000	6,423,324	5,526,542	5,696,672	5,759,462	6,409,706	6,858,450	7,485,654
Actual	6,723,890	6,553,488	5,576,366	5,669,821	5,915,677	6,351,320	6,876,578	7,396,928
Sales:								
Projected*	5,494,850	6,774,234	6,708,642	6,061,534	5,770,367	6,262,279	6,552,246	7,418,626
Actual	6,864,716	6,562,390	7,085,656	6,951,407	5,794,409	6,645,856	6,620,790	7,647,910
Net profits after taxes:								
Projected*	-66,192	605,256	538,823	376,571	325,279	398,501	610,269	818,232
Actual	540,018	540,986	617,506	311,180	323,538	629,855	599,191	890,829
Cash:								
Projected*	3,453,834	5,630,071	5,598,446	6,504,982	6,687,323	6,745,943	7,926,162	8,656,585
Actual	4,331,417	4,389,015	5,442,000	6,454,715	6,684,475	7,373,079	7,747,810	8,801,664

*Projected values are those which would have resulted in that quarter if the participants had made no changes in the courses of action recommended to them in the beginning of the quarter.

Discussion

SIMULATION AND MANAGEMENT CONTROL

R. W. CONWAY
Cornell University

The use of a digital computer opens many areas to attack by experimental research that would otherwise be closed, by reasons of accessibility or economics. In psychological laboratory work the computer may be used essentially as part of the laboratory environment. It can provide the background of a large and complex organization, against which to study the reactions and decisions of the human laboratory subjects. The study described by Buchin and the RAND Logistics Laboratory are examples of this type of investigation.

Alternatively the computer may provide both the environment and the subject of investigation, as illustrated in the paper by Bonini. This type of investigation may explore alternative structures and policies, under differing imposed loads and circumstances with the experimental advantage of freedom from vagaries of human implementation. Since the real world does not possess this freedom, knowledge obtained in this way is at best conditional and suggestive but properly used this type of simulation should provide an admirable vehicle for preliminary exploration.

In spite of its obvious virtues the use of a computer as an experimental vehicle accentuates the difficult task of interpreting and generalizing from the results of experimental research. In the first place one can only make assertions of a statistical nature about the performance of a specific model, and this requires certain niceties of design, operation and interpretation that are more often overlooked than observed. Secondly, there is a difficult question concerning the generality of results obtained. Even when one constructs a computer model of a specific organization it is a formidable task to evaluate the utility of the representation. When one constructs a model of a hypothetical organization, intended to be representative of a large class of organizations, the evaluation must be entirely subjective. The evaluation is not aided by imprecision in the definition of the class of organizations to which inference is intended, nor by inadequate description of the characteristics of the model. The investigator must enlist support for the credibility of his model, either by argument or demonstration, before attempting the presentation of substantive results. If the credibility of the model is allowed to

140

depend upon the intuitive acceptability of results one can prove only the obvious and the model is essentially useless.

In general, it is a very difficult task to *create knowledge* with a computer model. It is much easier, and much more common, to use a computer model to provide a cloak of pseudo-objectivity for the investigator's own assumptions and constructions. Perhaps the only circumstances under which information can really be created is when an investigator possesses at the outset a solid knowledge of the operation of individual elements of a system and seeks only to learn how they behave in concert. It is not clear that these conditions are satisfied in the investigation described by Bonini. His model for the transfer of, and response to "felt pressure", basic to the operation of the overall system, is more properly an hypothesis for study than an assertion of fact. If it were the principle purpose of the investigation to study this phenomenon, it could be more directly and effectively pursued if it were not embeded in a confounding larger system. As it is there are simply too many variables and too many areas of uncertain performance to allow meaningful conclusions to be drawn.

For example, it is concluded that a variable environment has a salutary effect on the firm's costs, sales and profits; but the overall response of the model to variability is heavily dependent upon the reaction of the individual elements of the system to variability. It seems likely that independent investigators might postulate widely different parameters or even different forms for this reaction mechanism, but some specific description had to be selected and programmed into the model by its author. Similarly, the author concludes that a tightening of performance standards in an organization does not have the desired effect. This effect is the resultant of the reaction of many individual elements of the model to a tightening of standards; again a highly debatable phenomenon for which the author had to make a specific and arbitrary specification.

To achieve credibility of results it would seem that a researcher must adopt one of three possible strategies in the choice of each of the elemental mechanisms in the simulation model:

1. Choose a mechanism which is not controversial, because it is trivially obvious, or because it is a general consensus
2. Offer a careful defense of a controversial choice, and make all conclusions explicitly conditional upon the choice
3. Offer a convincing demonstration that the conclusions are relatively insensitive to the particular mechanism employed

Data presented by Bonini at the Seminar, but not included in his paper, cast further doubt upon the validity of his conclusions. It was apparent from these data that the model was inherently unstable, even under "normal" conditions with a stable environment. The variability of each of the measures of performance appeared to be constantly increasing during the course of the experimental run, reaching rather dramatic proportions near the end of the run. While it is probably not impossible to obtain meaningful comparative results when the system is not in a steady-state condition it is certainly more difficult to ensure comparability. One should also inquire why this model should exhibit instability even in a stationary and stable environment.

While the present writer remains an exponent of simulation he is somewhat unconvinced that Bonini's paper does a great deal to "establish the value of the comprehensive model as a research tool."

Discussion

SIMULATION AND MANAGEMENT CONTROL

AUSTIN C. HOGGATT

University of California at Berkeley

In this section we are concerned with the application of computer and man-machine simulation to the study of management. To many students of Management Science, simulation is a new and powerful tool which holds out immediate promise for the mastery and control of organizations. We may forget that Student (first of the operations researchers) employed "model sampling" in his studies of the distribution of sample means and that ultimately simulation is but one instance of reasoning by analogy, a mechanism which has not improved noticeably in its reliability over its long history. Most of us at the conference share in the optimism concerning the promise of simulation—it may not be new but it is a powerful technique. Much of my time has been expended in working with simulation models and perhaps this has made me overly critical of the way in which the practice of simulation is carried out. I shall leave the apology for my following remarks to others, if one be required, and proceed in the hopes of bringing discussion to a critical level. I shall briefly comment on the three papers and conclude with a few general remarks.

Professor Charles Bonini in "The Simulation of Organizational Behavior" is presenting results extending beyond those of his thesis.[1] He sketches the bare outlines of an interesting model containing decision rules which for reasons of space are not given. In spite of care taken to keep the model simple it was still necessary to employ a large factorial analysis of variance in the study of the results. In the presentation Professor Bonini mentioned that he had employed computer programs to analyze the data. This is an important point. We must harness the computer for analysis even as we have done so for purposes of model construction. The results of this study appear to be perverse: "uncertainty", "loose engineering practice" and "contagion of pressure" all act in a positive way to increase measures of performance. We can only speculate as to the nature of the mechanism in the model which generated this unfortunate state of affairs.

Professor Edward B. Roberts provides us with an interesting view of the approach to management control which is taken by per-

[1] *Simulation of Information and Decision Systems in the Firm*, Englewood Cliffs, N. J.: Prentice-Hall, 1963.

sons working in industrial dynamics. A principle point is that firms are feedback mechanisms and that management models ought to be cast in terms of language taken from control system engineering. That this is a fruitful approach cannot be denied; this provocative and interesting article clearly demonstrates this. Why, however, must it follow that this is the only way to reach understanding. In fact, the discussions of the failing of PERT analysis may be correct but they are not substantiated either by references to errors in the literature or by refutation of the reported results obtained in application.

In Section IV (p. 123) we come to some principles of management control system design. We find that the key to effective control may lie outside the formal boundry of the firm, that we are concerned with complex man-machine systems, and that the problems of control are top management problems which cannot be solved by parts within the confines of the traditional departments of the organization. With this statement of the industrial dynamics approach we most assuredly agree. In fact, it is buttressed in earlier writings on organization theory, for example, the work of Barnard and Simon.

Professor Stanly Buchin is representative of the groups studying systems in which man-machine interactions are important and in which there is an attempt at experimental control of the situation. Here we have the problem at two levels; the subjects are revealing their heuristic control techniques in the behavior which they exhibit in trying to control the simulated company and the experimenters are trying to reveal to us the manner in which they are controlling the environment of the human subjects in their attempt to understand their behavior.

In view of the fact that this is a progress report on a continuing research effort it does not seem useful to attempt a critical review of the project or of the interesting, tentative results which are put forward. It is fortunate that considerable effort seems to have been expended in attempting experimental control, data recording, and analysis. Much, if not all, of the complex gaming sessions which have been run since Bellman, et.al., started it all, are a total loss to Management Science because no experimental control was achieved and the data have not been saved in accessible form. This is unfortunate. Consider the Harbret's "exercise" in which there is the investment of thousands of hours of top executive time together with a team research effort measured in man years. From this we will obtain a result based on only one experimental situation. But of course, it is high time that this effort be carried out, else we ought to abandon gaming as too expensive for the results obtained. We hopefully wish our colleagues onward to a first result.

In conclusion we turn to certain problems in the application of the simulation technique which are revealed in these three papers.

It would seem that there is little interchange between the practitioners of the art—there is no indication that the work of groups doing simulation studies has had much of an impact on others. One may
look in vain (but for one exception) for a cross reference in these
three papers.

Results are presented here which cannot be checked. Behind these
three papers are millions of computational steps performed by modern digital computers at great expense. Many hours of drudgery have
gone into the construction of computer programs which controlled
these computations and (hopefully) many hours of labor over listings
and dumps have gone into the attempt to assure that the results are
not *obviously* in error. Yet in no way is any of this accessible to the
reader. We don't even know what the models are because the programs (which indeed, are the models themselves) are too extensive
to be reproduced for publication and even if they were published no
one would take the time to read them.

We need a better methodology! Communication failure at this
level simply won't do for a discipline that calls itself a science. At
present we have no economical way to share or test our results.
Methodological contributions which overcome these difficulties will
be necessary before the promise of this exciting technique can be
fulfilled.

Discussion

SIMULATION AND MANAGEMENT CONTROL

CLAY SPROWLS

University of California at Los Angeles

In September, 1961, the Western Management Science Institute held a Simulation Conference to which a rather large number of people working in the field of simulation were invited to discuss their own work and that of others [1]. In their paper submitted to this conference, Fred Balderston and Austin Hoggatt wrote, "Our model of Market processes encompasses a variety of forces. By generating the time-path of the model on the computer, we observe how these forces interact. However, when this stage has been reached, it is not clear that we understand the model. We find that the problem of deriving implications from the model is difficult" [2, p.1]. Again, they wrote, "We now see that computer simulation permits us to 'solve' complex, dynamic models in the sense that we can trace and record the path of the system from any given initial conditions. We do not now have equal facility for deriving implications from these records of the simulation process" [2, p. 14]. At the same Conference, Richard Cyert and James March wrote in their contributed paper,". . . we outline a procedure for examining the properties of the model" [3, p.1]. "Our hope. . .is that additional thought will be generated on the problem of determining the implications of changes in the parameters and exogenous variables for a large scale model" [3, p. 28].

The two papers quoted from rather briefly raised, it seems to me, fundamental and disturbing problems in simulation methodology. I am rather disappointed that one and one-half years later at this Stanford Conference, the papers on simulation have practically nothing to say about these and other pressing problems. Bonini's paper first appeared in almost the same form in November of 1961 [4] and is abstracted from his published dissertation of May, 1962 [5]. Much of Roberts's paper is a discussion of the new famous (or infamous) Sprague Electric Case, reported in detail in book form in 1961 and based on work done as far back as 1957 [6]. Buchin's paper at least has the characteristic of being based on work so new that only preliminary results are available. It suffers, it seems to me, from lack of any reported awareness of the two problems mentioned above or of its relationship to other large laboratory models which have been in existence for some time and which involve people and computer programs for generating environments and substantial amounts of qualitative context.[1] I focus upon these aspects of simulation because I find myself in a dilemma in comparing Bonini's and Roberts' papers.

One of Bonini's major conclusions is "The firm, in a highly variable environment, had lower costs, higher sales, and greater profits than when the environment was relatively stable." Roberts's discussion of Industrial Dynamics points to a first example of the Sprague Electric Company in which the highly volatile or fluctuating incoming customer orders appeared to give sizeable fluctuations to inventory, order backlog, and employment, just the opposite of Bonini's conclusions. He then goes on to argue that is it not the customer order fluctuation that is the cause at all; rather, the company delivery policy is the key to the system's problem. Later on, in a simulation model of a quality control system, with production quality held constant, oscillations in reject rate and production appear. These are explained very plausibly in terms of responses to internally created rather than outside changes.

Now I have a hard time knowing what to believe. I see one simulation model taking a highly variable environment and from it, producing a "better" operating firm and a very reasonable explanation of why this could happen in terms of "keeping the firm on its toes", making it more likely to take advantage of cost and market opportunities, increasing pressure to cut costs and increase sales, etc. I see a second model with highly variable external forces damping these by internal policy changes and a third one with constant external forces generating oscillations from internal policies. I think that I can only conclude at this time that there is no question but that a computer simulation model can generate time paths of many variables from many kinds of initial conditions. There is still a very large question whether anyone understands the model, although reasonable sounding explanations can be given for almost any input-output phenomenon observed. Until some reasonably decent work is done on deriving implications from simulation studies, I am prepared only to look at each of them as an interesting isolated case which can be described to me but from which I shall draw no conclusions. If Buchin and his colleagues have not considered this fundamental problem in the design of their large and (probably expensive) exercises, drawing inferences from their executive decision-making behavioral studies will be just as difficult.

I do not wish to convey only a critical or negative attitude toward the papers in this seminar. I think they form the basis for a judgment about what may be meaningful research in the future. I like Bonini's approach which uses statistical experimental designs in testing his model. More research needs to be done on just this problem. I like Buchin's use of people in conjunction with a computer

[1] I am thinking here of the simulation laboratory at the Rand Corporation.

generated environment as an experimental procedure. My opinion is that the rewarding future research in this field will wed the computer, qualitative materials, and people in order to study the design of large-scale management control systems. The role of the computer is as a generator and processor of environmental conditions on a greatly reduced time-scale. The role of people is an experimental subjects operating and planning and deciding in simulated real-life situations. A laboratory of this kind should further meaningful research if we can learn how to understand our models from a study of their observable behavior.

BIBLIOGRAPHY

1. Simulation Conference, Western Management Science Institute, Los Angeles: Graduate School of Business Administration, University of California, Sept. 12-15, 1961.
2. ———: Paper presented by F. E. Balderston and A. A. Hoggatt, "Simulation Models: Analytic Variety and the Problem of Model Reduction," p. 1.
3. ———: Paper presented by K. J. Cohen, R. M. Cyert, J. G. March, and P. O. Selberg, "A General Behavior Model of Price and Output Determination and a Procedure for Examining its Properties, p. 1.
4. Bonini, Charles P.: "Simulation of Information and Decision System in the Firm: A Summary of Research," mimeographed, Nov. 10, 1961.
5. ———: "Simulation of Information and Decision Systems in the Firm," mimeographed dissertation, Graduate School of Business, Stanford University, May, 1962.
6. Forrester, Jay: *Industrial Dynamics*, New York: Wiley, 1961.

8

DIVISIONAL PERFORMANCE REVIEW:
AN EXTENSION OF BUDGETARY CONTROL

GORDON SHILLINGLAW
Columbia University

The prevalence in this seminar of papers relating to problems of corporate decentralization is a symptom of the rapid growth in interest in this phenomenon that has taken place within the last ten years. For my part, I shall try to look at the problems of internal profit measurement through the eyes of the corporate controller, in the hope that this will add perspective to the more exclusively economic point of view. I propose to discuss three topics, but with unequal emphasis:

1. Objectives of decentralization
2. The role of budgetary control
3. Application of budgetary control to decentralized divisions

OBJECTIVES OF DECENTRALIZATION

The underlying cause of corporate decentralization is complexity of operations. This complexity is reflected in longer lines of communication, more numerous decision variables, and greater heterogeneity of products, processes and contributory activities. Under these conditions, several problems tend to arise in centralized organizations:

1. The decision maker is removed from close contact with daily operations, leading to slower decisions and requiring heavy-traffic communications lines.
2. Top management lacks the time to evaluate the large quantities of relevant data and the numerous variables that must be considered when all important decisions are made centrally.
3. Lower-level executives lose contact with the ultimate profit objective of the firm, and this may lead to inappropriate decision rules at lower levels.
4. Subordinate management tends to become specialized in the various functional areas, which may hinder the development of replacements for top executive positions in which a comprehensive viewpoint is necessary.

5. The employee's vision of his own importance to the organization tends to become obscured and morale suffers.[1]

Many companies have turned in recent years to profit-center decentralization as a partial means of solving these problems. By delegating substantial decision-making authority to lower executives and by reshaping the organization structure to integrate the functional areas at lower levels, top management hopes to develop more adequately trained executives, improve the morale and motivation of subordinate executives and to shorten and simplify the channels through which information flows to the decision maker. It is an attempt to simulate small-company flexibility without sacrificing the economies of large-scale organization.

Delegation of authority of any kind carries with it an answerability for the use of that authority. Higher management controls the exercise of authority at lower levels by evaluating the performance of subordinate management. This evaluation is the means by which answerability is applied. The initial presumption in profit-center decentralization is that the performance of the profit-center manager is reflected in his reported profit. Authority can be delegated in the secure knowledge that misuse or inefficient use of authority will be reflected in lower profits. Furthermore, this visibility of the effects of his decisions will motivate the profit-center manager to make decisions on a profit basis, consonant with the overall profit objective of the firm.

Unfortunately, two main difficulties arise in the application of this concept. First, profit must be reported on an interim basis, before the full profit effects of current decisions can be measured. This problem is dealt with to a very limited extent later in this paper, but by and large it has been ignored in the literature. Second, the profit center is not truly independent and thus its profits reflect to some extent the operations of other company units. The reported income of a profit center would represent its true profit contribution only if each profit center were to purchase *all* its inputs and sell *all* its outputs in external markets, an impossible set of conditions. Any transfer of goods or services between a profit center and some other unit of the company represents a departure from this ideal. If the price at which a transfer is recorded does not equal the true economic sacrifice to the profit center supplying the item, then the internal decision rules will lead to an inappropriate allocation of resources. It is not surprising, therefore, that many writers, including Arrow [1], Dean [2], Hirshleifer [4, 5], and others, have devoted their attention to the problem of setting transfer prices that will not lead to suboptimization in conflict with overall company objectives.

---

[1]Worthy [13] reports this experience in the larger operating units of Sears, Roebuck and Company.

This attention to transfer pricing has been highly productive, but the quality of the inputs to decision making is only part of the problem raised by decentralization. The aspect with which I am concerned is the task of evaluating performance under any given set of transfer prices. In many companies the objectives of constructing a simulated profit environment have been less to improve the quality of immediate decisions through improved decision rules than to improve the motivation of middle management and to sharpen their managerial skills by forcing them to adopt a broader frame of reference.[2] In other words, even if all major resource allocation decisions were made centrally, there would still be a need for decentralization in some companies to overcome the problems of centralization that were mentioned earlier. This suggests that factors other than optimization deserve consideration in designing systems for internal profit measurement, and these are factors that occupy an important position in budgetary control.

CONTROL METHODS AND THE BUDGETARY PROCESS

Authorities differ in their conceptions of what budgetary control is or should be, and what follows is my own synthesis. This may or may not reflect a concensus, but it provides the premise on which the conclusions of this paper are based.

Organization Structure

Both budgetary planning and budgetary control work through the formal organization structure of the company. The budgetary process views the corporation as a network of organizational *modules*. These modules are of two types, primary and ancillary. Primary modules deal directly with customers outside the firm or with physical product flows (a machining department or a warehouse, for example). Ancillary modules exist to provide services to other modules within the company, either primary or ancillary or both.

It is through these modules and clusters of modules that control is exercised. The basic modules are grouped in a hierarchical network, generally pyramidal in shape, each major subpyramid being known as a division. For budgeting purposes, each module is regarded as a separate unit in which all control responsibility is assigned to a single supervisory position. The budgetary process deals with the obvious interdependencies of individual modules largely by exclusion—that is, effort is made to insulate the performance measurements of one module from the effects of performance of others.

---

[2] See Newman and Summer [9].

Control Methods

It is a truism that control is exercised only by positive action of some sort. A control *method,* however, encompasses the techniques used to identify the need for action and to review possible action alternatives as well as the ultimate control action itself. Using this definition, management has four basic methods or approaches to the control of internal operations:

1. Control by planning or decision making
2. Control by scheduling, direction and supervision
3. Control by follow-up response to feedback comparisons
4. Control by manipulation

Planning, in this view, serves to control initially by selecting the desired pattern of resource use, after a deliberate comparison of alternatives. The immediate end-product of planning, the established plan, is then used as a general set of instructions for carrying out planning decisions. Whether this is truly part of the *control* process is a problem in semantics; it is, however, part of the *budgetary* process and underlies all subsequent control.

Scheduling is a narrower concept. It too is based on selection among alternative ways of resource allocation but within a much narrower range. It works by establishing time tables for the performance of tasks and seeing to it that men, materials, facilities, and funds are available to carry out the plan.[3] Scheduling, direction and supervision all have a similar control objective—to prevent or minimize unfavorable deviations from the plan.[4] This is what might be called "concurrent control," and without it no control system can be expected to be effective.

The third control device, the follow-up response to feedback comparisons, may be the most prevalent control technique in human activity. It consists of measuring and analyzing deviations from previously determined norms of behavior or performance, reporting these deviations to the appropriate control center, and initiating a corrective response. The key to the success of this method is the analysis of the deviations. A rational response is possible only if the basic causal patterns can be identified or inferred. Thus the analytical emphasis is on assigning a causal explanation to as much of the deviation as possible.

Finally, we have control by manipulation. This approach is fundamentally different from the others, although it usually works through its influence on planning. It consists of varying the weights assigned

---

[3] These distinctions are discussed at greater length in [11 chap. 2].

[4] It may also be desirable to minimize favorable deviations in certain items if these are likely to produce greater unfavorable deviations elsewhere or at later times.

to each variable subject to subordinate management's control or influence, to induce behavior on this level that will direct company resources in directions that have been chosen by higher management. Manipulative control may be used consciously, or unconsciously, in that behavior tends to follow patterns that experience has indicated will lead to greater rewards in the existing environment.[5] Insofar as manipulation is an element of the budgetary process, it is conscious, purposive manipulation because control is always purposive.

Budgetary Control

Although Stedry [12] would introduce a greater degree of manipulative control into the budgetary process, its main elements relate primarily to planning and control by feedback response. The feedback in budgeting consists of deviations or variances from desired or expected performance, measured in monetary terms and classified insofar as possible by responsibility and causes. These variances are assigned initially to individual modules and then accumulated for each structured cluster of modules, e.g., factories, sales regions, or divisions. The response is the action taken by an executive to correct an unfavorable situation (control response) or to adjust his other activities to adapt to it (adaptive response or replanning).

In any feedback control system there is a need for analysis to translate the indicated deviations into corrective instructions. In automated production operations, for example, the linkage is often some kind of computer program which matches the pattern of deviations with the patterns identified in advance with specific causes and then selects the appropriate correcting instruction from those previously stored in the computer's memory. In budgetary control, however, the responses cannot be completely programmed in advance due to the multiplicity of causes. Thus the linkage between variance and response requires human intervention at some point after the variance has been identified.

Appraisal: An Instrument of Control

The linkage between variance and response may be characterized in another way, as a process of appraisal. Budget variances are useful inputs to at least three separate but interrelated types of appraisal:

1. *Self-appraisal*, by lower management to identify the need for action programs and to guide the response
2. *Subordinate appraisal*, by higher management to evaluate the performance of subordinate executives, and
3. *Activity appraisal*, by higher management to evaluate the performance of various company activities

[5] See March and Simon [7, chap. 6].

Taking the last of these first, feedback data are used in the evaluation of the performance of the activity, as something distinct and apart from the performance of the manager in charge of that activity. This aspect of performance evaluation is a part of control by planning because the response is adaptive rather than corrective. For this purpose, the variances ideally should be all those attributable to the activity, whether they arise within the module or outside it. Thus a variance resulting from a reduction in sales in one division that results from a complementary or competing activity elsewhere in the company should be assigned to the latter. Unfortunately, in the present state of the art this cannot be done on a routine basis. Therefore, variances for this purpose are assigned on the basis of traceability. Analysis of the causes of the variance then becomes part of the planning process, and is largely outside the scope of the present paper.[6]

Of the two types of control appraisal, self-appraisal is the more immediate. The need for delegating responsibility in an organization leads to the presumption that a good control system should rely heavily on self-correction. Thus in designing the accounting system the emphasis must be on providing variance information which can help the executive or supervisor at each level, particularly the lowest, exercise control in his area of responsibility without intervention by his immediate superior.

Accordingly, the variances reported to a foreman or supervisor should be limited to those over which he has some current degree of control and thus has some possibility of designing an action response. Noncontrollable variances are an essential element in activity appraisal, but there is no *a priori* reason why they should be relevant to appraisal for control purposes.

The assumptions implicit in this are that (1) budgetary standards are sufficiently demanding to require vigorous efforts by subordinate management, and (2) subordinate management is adequately motivated to meet or possible exceed the standard. These motivations are provided by the entire reward structure of the firm. What is not commonly understood is that the budget itself is not intended to act as a motivating force. The budget embodies an agreed plan and provides a basis for measuring variances. The reward structure may penalize unfavorable variances and reward favorable ones, but it should not do so without adequate analysis of the causes of the variances.

The emphasis on self-appraisal and self-correction does not imply an abdication of authority by higher management. Summary variances for each modules are also an input to the second of our three forms of appraisal, appraisal by a manager of his subordinates' perform-

---

[6] For an extended discussion of the accounting problems of providing this kind of variance information, see [11, chap. 21].

ance. On the surface, the notion of control as a process of self-correction might seem to contradict the use of variances in the appraisal
by higher management of the performance of their subordinates.
This apparent conflict results from a failure to distinguish between
appraisal and *intervention*. Appraisal examines effectiveness and the
expectation of appraisal probably contributes to effectiveness. Intervention, on the other hand, consists of an abrogration or transfer of
the authority of subordinate management to initiate corrective or
adaptive action. Appraisal does not imply immediate intervention by
the appraising body. Instead, intervention presumably is deferred
until a series of successive appraisals indicates a lack of effectiveness at the lower level.

BUDGETARY CONTROL IN DECENTRALIZED DIVISIONS

The typical profit center is a structured cluster of organization
modules, or division. Both centralized and decentralized companies,
of course, are divisionalized; as Shubik points out elsewhere in this
volume the distinction between centralization and decentralization is
a matter of degree rather than absolute. Decentralized divisions may
in fact be identical in structure and content to the centralized divisions that they supplant, but in the typical decentralized division the
modules within a division are less homogeneous than those in a division of a centralized organization. This being the case, budgetary
control should take the same form in both types of organizations, but
applied to different combinations of elements in each.

Profit Center Variances

Each module within the profit center has its own variance structure, depending on the nature of the activities carried on within the
module. The variances identified at any level may be cost variances,
revenue variances or profit variances, depending on the nature and
function of the organization segment. A variance, after all, is simply
the difference between an objective and a result and can be measured
in any unit in which objectives and results can be expressed.

In the typical functional department or division the variance is
essentially one of either cost or revenue, although there may be
variances in both categories. For example, a sales division manager
typically has some responsibility for selling costs as well as for
sales volume. Analogously, a production division might have variances in production volume, due to failures to meet schedules or to
revisions of schedule reflecting changes in plans, and these might be
regarded as equivalent to revenue variances. The profit center, however, *always* has both cost and revenue variances, and a net variance
that is regarded as a summary measure of the division manager's

profit performance for the period. The size and interpretation of this variance depends on the purpose of the performance review (activity appraisal or control appraisal) and on the type of standard selected.

Dimensions of Performance

The concern of budgetary control with those aspects of performance that can be measured in monetary terms does not imply in any way that these are the only important facets of the manager's job. The relative importance of financial measures in the overall appraisal of management depends heavily on the nature of the operation and the objectives of the company in committing resources to it.

In a decentralized operation, for example, there is always some degree of reliance on the quest for profit as a means of securing satisfactory decentralized results. The overall financial measure of performance, therefore, is reported profit. Unfortunately, this measure is incomplete as an index of the total performance of the manaager, and this leads to the use of supplementary measures, mostly qualitative. The weakness of current profit, however, is less a weakness of concept than a product of deficiencies in the available methods of measurement. Performance ultimately is and must be measured in financial terms. Evaluation of performance on the basis of observations of aspects of managerial activity that are not measured in financial terms stems from two factors: (1) a belief that good performance in these aspects will contribute to financial performance over a longer period of time; and (2) an inability to measure the present value of these future benefits. Thus employee welfare and recreation programs generally must be justified by their anticipated effects on morale or goodwill, rather than by increments in short-term profits. The implicit assumption, nevertheless, is that improved morale or enhanced goodwill engendered by such activities will pay off in the form of a positive present value of the incremental cash flows in a series of successive short-term periods.

The Selection of Standards

Probably the most important single step in the entire budgetary control process, and certainly the most crucial in its application to profit center divisions, is the selection of standards or benchmarks for variance computation. These benchmarks are essentially of three kinds:

1. Standards *externally derived* and independent of the current operating circumstances of the company
2. Standard created by the establishment of the initial plan for the current period, embodied in the plan and reflecting the *expected* environment

3. Standards based on *actual* conditions—those that would have
been incorporated in the plan if the actual conditions had been
known in advance

All three of these kinds of standards have a place in the performance review process. Thus a captive power plant may be subject to
an external standard of so much per kilowatt-hour because this is
the basis on which the power could be purchased from external
sources. This standard provides a basis for planning or for that aspect of planning which attempts to choose between alternative courses
of action. For example, in planning it might be projected that the
company's own power generating operation would produce power at a
cost in excess of the purchase cost. This can lead either to corrective action (that is, find means of cost reduction), or adaptive behavior (discontinue power generation and purchase it from the outside).
Or the production department may be told that it must produce a certain part at a cost of not more than five cents because otherwise the
product will not be competitive in the market. This constitutes a
planning standard to force consideration of ways and means of meeting the predetermined goal.

Most standards in budgetary control must be internally derived.
The reason for this is relatively simple. To be a valid basis for review of managerial performance, a standard must be regarded by the
manager himself as currently *attainable* in the period under review.
Although Stedry's work |12| questions the long-standing assumption
that unattainable standards are ineffective as devices for performance *improvement,* there has been no refutation of the *a priori* case
for the use of attainable standards in performance evaluation.

This kind of standard is one outcome of budgetary planning, a
standard represented by the established plan for the period. It is an
internal standard, adapted to management's own expectations as to
the external and internal environment. Unfortunately, deviations from
such a standard may reflect not only deficiencies in control, but also
failures of the environment to conform to expectations. The former
should lead to corrective action, the latter to adaptation and replanning. Management thus needs some device for separating the controllable and environmental portions of the overall variance. This is
accomplished by preparing a supplemental plan that has been adapted
to reflect the actual environment in which the operations took place.

Thus the appropriate standard for the review of the profit performance of decentralized division management is an *adjusted budgeted
profit,* not some specified profit ratio that is the same for all divisions at all times and under all conditions. Return on investment
standards, exemplified by those publicized by members of the duPont

organization,[7] suffer from this basic defect. They must be regarded as highly imperfect tools for use in control by planning, with little relevance to control by feedback response. They may serve as *effective pressure devices,* but if so they serve an objective apart from those of budgetary control.

These relationship between standards and the various forms of appraisal are summarized in Exhibit 8-1. Internal standards have some relevance to all three types of appraisal, although the decisions to which they relate in activity appraisal are more limited than those in which external standards are applied. It must be emphasized, however, that the immediate output of appraisal is a decision; appraisal that does not lead to a decision is not really appraisal but curiosity.

Analysis of Profit Variances

The emphasis on budgeted profit as a standard for internal profit evaluation lends considerably greater importance to the analysis of

Exhibit 8-1
Appraisal of Past Profit Performance

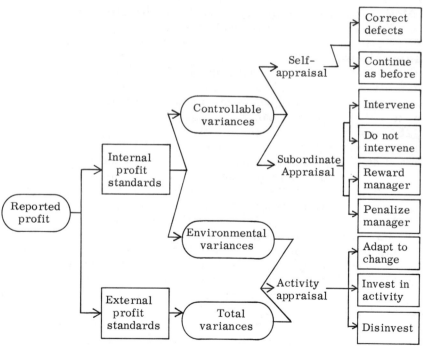

---

[7] See Kline and Hessler [6], for example.

profit variances. The objective of this analysis must be first to separate the controllable and non-controllable elements and second to indentify the causes of the variance insofar as possible.

Controllability, of course, must be interpreted in broad terms; seldom, if ever, is a profit determinant completely controllable. Thus, if a division manager is responsible for the sales of his division's product, it is readily apparent that his ability to increase sales depends not only on his ability to shift the demand curve (or to prevent negative shifts) but also on other external factors that act to cause exogenous shifts in the shape or level of demand. Nevertheless we quite rightly include this as a controllable element and use variance analysis to attempt to identify the effects of exogenous shifts in the demand curve.

Many tools are available for this kind of variance analysis. Some cost elements, for example, may be identified as wholly noncontrollable at the divisional level. Variances in any such items may simply be reported as noncontrollable, although some analysis of the reasons for any significant variance is usually desirable for planning purposes. Secondly, the flexible budget may be used to isolate the variances due to deviations from planned production volumes in goods or internal services. At a more aggregative level, standard selling prices applied to actual physical sales volumes permit derivation of selling price variances, while variances due to deviations in sales volume can be isolated by multiplying standard variable profit ratios by both actual and planned volumes. This latter analysis may be refined further to identify the effects of changes in product mix.[8]

All of these techniques except the flexible budget adjustment assume linear cost functions with price and volume as separate independent variables. The linearity assumption may not be too serious a limitation, but the independence assumption is highly vulnerable. The justification must be that our analysis has not yet reached down to causes but merely to symptoms. Thus a favorable selling price variance may be the cause of an unfavorable sales volume variance, or even *vice versa*. The point is, however, that this issue would never be raised in a manageable way without prior quantification of this sort.

Our techniques for identifying real causes apart from their surface manifestations are highly fragmented and depend to a great extent on personal judgment, but they are not to be rejected on these grounds alone. For example, a decline in sales volume may be due partly to environmental influences, partly to ineffective sales management, partly to other causes. Some effort must be made to separate these various influences. One crude adjustment device is the

---

[8] Evans [3] gives a good illustration of how this technique is used as an input to planning at Westinghouse.

market share ratio, on the assumption that a sales decline accompanied by a stable market share is evidence of satisfactory managerial performance. Oxenfeldt [10] points out, however, that market share maintenance is a valid index of performance only when market shares are stable and management is content to have them remain so. Oxenfeldt's solution is to move toward a more fragmented, judgmental evaluation of performance, which supports anew the case for detailed variance analysis rather than summary ratio comparisons.

A second technique to accomplish some of the results of variance analysis is to *eliminate* certain types of variance before they appear. This is not the time for an extended discussion of cost allocation principles, but such principles do exist [11, chap. 9]. For example, a noncontrollable but partly variable item such as centralized billing can be charged to each division at a predetermined rate, perhaps covering the variable cost component only. Thus variations from the predetermined rate never appear in the divisional reports but remain where they belong in the performance reports of the centralized billing department. Divisional variances will reflect volume deviations only. If a cost is neither variable nor currently controllable within the division, however, then the charge, if any, should take the form of a predetermined lump sum, equal to the budget provisions, so that no variance will appear in the divisional report.

Application of these simple rules should insure a set of allocations that will produce neither spurious variability nor noncontrollable cost variances in the divisional profit statements. The variances reported will represent classified deviations of costs and revenues from the predetermined plan. These variances should then be analyzed in detail to determine insofar as possible the causes of the variances, with particular emphasis on deviations in sales volume, product mix, and selling prices, as well as the usual variances from standard or budgeted cost.

A third approach is to adjust the standard by preliminary variance analysis to isolate the noncontrollable elements or influences. Thus if there is reason to change the internal transfer price from that determined at the start of the period, the change should be accompanied by a compensating adjustment of the standard or plan. This identifies the effect of this deviation from the initial plan and focuses attention on the variances that remain.

The Danger of Manipulation

One problem in internal profit measurement that has been given little attention in the literature is the susceptibility of periodic profit to managerial manipulation. The full effects of many decisions are not felt until some future period, but profit is measured currently. By curtailing current maintenance outlays, for example, division management may be able to improve its current profit showing at the expense of the future. Promotional outlays whose effects may be delayed for months or even years may be withheld in the interest of current profit. Or extra effort may be made to shift sales from a later to an earlier period for the same purpose. All these are forms of borrowing from the future, often at a cost greater than the current value of the cash flows thus shifted forward.

There is no simple solution to this problem. Many companies deal with it in part by establishing overall policies—as for example with respect to standards of adequate maintenance—and then auditing adherence to these policies. This represents a restriction on the autonomy of the division manager, of course, but it need not destroy the profit center system. What it does is place on the division manager the burden of justifying a maintenance policy in his area that differs from that applied elsewhere. Other techniques applicable to maintenance shifting are ratio and trend analysis, routine explanation of any substantial favorable variances, and interperiod cost equalization.

In one sense this problem arises due to an improper conception of the purpose of the budget. Wagner's paper elsewhere in this volume questions the compatibility of cost minimization rules with sound production scheduling decisions, and this same incompatibility may exist with respect to maintenance cost. The budget is a standard, not a target, and for some items it is the average *deviation* that is to be minimized rather than the average cost. This is consistent with the concept of the budget as presented in this paper, as an evaluation standard rather than a pressure device.

Less thought has been given to the problem of interperiod shifting of sales. On the one hand the manager ought to be discouraged from promotional policies,that reduce the present value of the income stream, but at the same time his motivation to press for profitable current sales volume should not be dulled. Considerable research is needed in this area, and one line of investigation ought to be on how sales variance analysis can be improved to isolate the effects of borrowing from the future to increase sales volume now. In the meantime a considerable amount of judgment will continue to be necessary in the interpretation of sales variances.

The Influence of the Transfer Price

No paper on divisional profit measurement would be complete without some reference to transfer pricing. Both Arrow [1] and Hirshleifer [4, 5] see the transfer price as an element to be adjusted until some form of economic equilibrium is reached. Most such schemes, unfortunately, would produce operating losses in any division in which marginal cost is constant and internal transfers are significantly large. Furthermore, such a scheme would require information on marginal revenue that in the present state of the art is unobtainable and is likely to remain so, even with the trial-and-error solution recommended by Hirshleifer and Arrow.

The proper approach to transfer pricing must be much less ambitious, it seems to me. As Menge [8] points out, the major automobile companies do not hesitate to use artificially constructed transfer prices when reliable market prices are unavailable. The objective is not equilibrium, however, but equity. Similarly, a medium-size steel fabricator establishes both transfer prices and ultimate selling prices centrally, but refers to the individual sales branches as profit centers on the grounds that they have authority over selling costs, inventory levels and product mix, three of the major determinants of profit. The motivational objectives of decentralization are achieved, despite the absence of any equilibrium model.

We know very little about the response of managers to variations in the transfer price. In theory, if budgeted and actual transfer prices are equal, the level selected should be motivationally neutral. Yet any observer of transfer price disputes in industry will agree that absolute profit levels are important to the managers. They will argue to get a price reduced (or raised, if they are on the selling side) with as much vigor as they exert in interfirm bargaining. This may be due to an unconscious bias in the reward structure, but whatever its source it militates against any administered transfer pricing scheme that results in prices that are widely regarded as unfair or biased. On these grounds the mixed system of market-based negotiation when markets exist and the average variable cost plus lump-sum subsidy recommended by Myron Gordon elsewhere in this volume deserves careful consideration.

CONCLUSION

To conclude, I should like to repeat my basic contention that control in decentralized operations is essentially no different from control of subsegments or homogeneous functional activities within either a centralized or decentralized division. The same principles of standards, variance identification and analysis, and action response are as applicable at the division level as at the departmental.

Budgets and standards, in this view, are benchmarks for evaluation or appraisal of performance rather than minimia or maxima. Budgeted profit provides a sounder basis for control appraisal than the economist's normal profit, not only because it allows for current environmental factors but also because it can be subdivided in great detail. Details of the profit variance are more significant in evaluation than its aggregate magnitude, and it is entirely possible that ostensibly favorable deviations from budgeted profit may in fact be undesirable because of their unfavorable effects on other items or other time periods.

This approach need not conflict with the approach that emphasizes planning and decision making, but it does need recognition. Concentration on the decision-making objectives of decentralization should not be allowed to obscure its control objective as well as other subordinate goals. Recognition of these other facets of the problem may well require the modification of measurement methods, particularly in transfer pricing, to facilitate progress toward all goals simultaneously.

BIBLIOGRAPHY

1. Arrow, Kenneth J., "Optimization, Decentralization, and Internal Pricing in Business Firms," in *Contributions to Scientific Research in Management, The Proceedings of the Scientific Program following the Dedication of the Western Data Processing Center*, Los Angeles: University of California, 1959.
2. Dean, Joel: "Decentralization and Intra-company Pricing," *Harvard Business Review*, vol. 33, 1955.
3. Evans, Marshall K.: "Profit Planning," *Harvard Business Review*, vol. 37, 1959.
4. Hirshleifer, Jack: "Economics of the Decentralized Firm," *The Journal of Business*, vol. 30, 1957.
5. ———: "On the Economics of Transfer Pricing," *The Journal of Business*, vol. 29, 1956.
6. Kline, Charles A., Jr., and Howard L. Hessler: "The duPont Chart System for Appraising Operating Performance," *N.A.(C.)A. Bulletin, 1950 Conference Proceedings*.
7. March, James G., and Herbert A. Simon: *Organizations*, New York: Wiley, 1958.
8. Menge, John A.: "The Backward Art of Interdivisional Transfer Pricing," *Journal of Industrial Economics*, vol. 9, 1961.
9. Newman, William H., and Charles E. Summer: *The Process of Management*, Englewood Cliffs, N. J.: Prentice-Hall, 1961.
10. Oxenfeldt, Alfred R.: "How to Use Market-Share Measurement," *Harvard Business Review*, vol. 37, 1959.
11. Shillinglaw, Gordon: *Cost Accounting: Analysis and Control*, Homewood, Ill.: Irwin, 1961.
12. Stedry, Andrew C.: *Budget Control and Cost Behavior*, Englewood Cliffs, N. J.: Prentice-Hall, 1960.
13. Worthy, James C.: "Factors Influencing Employee Morale," *Harvard Business Review*, vol. 28, 1950.

9

BUDGETARY CONTROL IN INVENTORY SYSTEMS

HARVEY M. WAGNER

Stanford University

1. INTRODUCTION

1.1 The Question of Management Control

To a large extent Operations Research literature focuses on problems and techniques of economic optimizing. A central assumption is that the principal elements of an actually functioning system can be mathematically modeled, and subsequently the system's decision mechanism can be optimized. We well may ask whether evolving a technique of solution is sufficient for a complete and successful application of an Operations Research model. Experience has amply shown that more than a method is essential for full implementation. Staying within the context of inventory control, this paper explores an important facet of the implementation phase, namely, to determine whether a decision mechanism predicated on a proposed Operations Research model is consistent within the milieu of an existent management control system, and to design control mechanisms for adequately supervising a new Operations Research oriented segment of the system. It is easiest to clarify these goals by rephrasing them as inquiries about a multi-item inventory complex:

Will a set of newly proposed stockage policies be able to operate under previously existent managerial controls, such as quarterly budgets? Is a previously operative management objective of a high inventory turnover consistent with the implied policy decisions of the suggested stockage rules? Under the proposed inventory model, how can control limits be placed on the dollar value of inventory on hand? Is the objective of staying within such limits in keeping with the aims of the stockage policies?

If there are reasons to believe that operating personnel might not fully observe the inventory policies, can a control scheme be devised which will adequately audit the degree of complicance, and yet will not require that the individual records be examined in detail? If the environmental conditions assumed within the Operations Research model do in fact change,[1] can a procedure be designed which will

---

[1] By environmental conditions, we mean the set of demand probability distributions.

detect the alteration, and which will not necessitate an individual review of each inventory component?

These are the kinds of inquiries studied in the present paper. Almost needless to say, in order to arrive at substantiated answers we necessarily confine our investigation to a particular class of managerial environments, inventory situations, and control devices. In brief, we deal with an organization in which some actions are to be taken on the basis of the over-all inventory system's behavior; the drains on inventory are probabilistic, and replenishment can be instituted only at fixed intervals of time; the control data aggregate and summarize the fluctuations in the detailed item-by-item behavior; and the system's operating characteristics are to be viewed according to their long-term properties. Although such a configuration obviously is not universal, nevertheless it represents the essence of an important class of situations and well approximates many others.

1.2 Organizational Setting

We focus our attention on large and complex organizations in which inventory management and operational responsibilities are partially divided and decentralized. Upon top management falls the task of guiding the organization so that its inventory operations meet the accompanying requirements in an economic fashion. In these complexes, it is reasonable that top management concentrates mainly on such indices as aggregate holding costs, depletion penalties, purchase expenditures, etc. To say so is really tautological, of course; if top management had the same interest in detail as the operating echelon has, then, from an inventory control point of view, there would be little distinction between the two echelons.[2] Another factor reinforcing top management's proclivity for index number evaluation is that top management may, in turn, be controlled by, say, supreme management through means of aggregate financial restrictions. In a business enterprise, for example, a vice-president responsible for company-wide inventory stockage may be given a total budgetary restriction on expenditures by the Board of Directors. Consequently, top management may find it essential to devise control schemes which, in their turn, reflect analogous restrictions on other echelons.

The assignment of attending to such detailed inventory operations as deciding when and how much of each item to reorder falls upon lower management. Although top management by its very function is not able to undertake detailed supervision, it is typically able to offer unequivocal policy recommendations with which lower management is expected to comply.

[2] In terms of modern statistical decision theory [1, 3, 9, 11], we are claiming that employing an aggregate ought to imply that top management's "utility function" has the probability distribution of the index number as its argument, rather than the underlying joint distribution of the individual components.

lag λ_i is given. In Section 3 we consider situations in which the $\varphi_i(\xi)$ are not known with certainty. We assume top management has devised a set of recommended (s,S) inventory policies for a lower echelon to follow.

A potentiality for control arises because lower management, without the imposition of a surveillance scheme, may be motivated to adopt stockage rules differing from those recommended. Reasons for this divergence of policy, of course, depend on the facts of a real situation, but a list of typical influences would include[7] a desire of the lower echelon (1) to meet any demand contingency, a motive leading to uneconomical surpluses of inventory, (2) to avoid surpluses of inventory, leading to uneconomical shortages of stock on hand, and (3) either to keep inventory on hand varying within a narrow range or to avoid handling small shipments, leading to an uneconomical frequency of ordering. Scientific approaches to the derivation of inventory rules seek to strike an economic balance between these cost factors, each being measured from the view of top management and not of the lower echelon. A natural question to pose in examining a particular control scheme is whether the control device encourages lower management to adopt the recommended policies; if it does, we call the control consistent.

2.2 Consistency Criterion for an Inventory Model

In Section 1.3 we stressed two important aspects of a control scheme: the ability of the device (1) to guarantee or encourage the fulfillment of certain standards, and (2) to ensure or make likely the detection of deviation from these standards. In our present context the standards are to be interpreted as lower management's observance of a set of (s,S) policies which are specified by top management for each item in the system.[8] We say a control scheme is strongly consistent if it positively encourages the exact fulfillment of these standards.

As we shall discover in Section 2.6.1, a control device may be strongly consistent in a single-item inventory system, but its analog in a multi-item system may be strongly inconsistent.

Our concentrating on the property of consistency is warranted because, whenever a control device is suggested, we are at once confronted with the question of whether the system possibly misdirects operating personnel. But determining whether a system is either con-

---

[7] The enumeration to follow is not to be interpreted as a set of internally consistent factors; on the contrary, the influences are opposing. The idea to be conveyed is that, in real situations, any one of these motivations may arise.

[8] The specification procedure, of course, may be a computing algorithm for the determination of (s,S) from data inputs such as average demand per review period, inventory cost, outage cost, purchase price, etc.

For a variety of reasons top management commonly desires control devices in order to ascertain the degree to which changes in inventory are being economically met and the extent to which lower management is acting in consonance with the recommended policies. We emphasize at the outset that the employment of such controls is not meant to imply a supersedure of item-by-item quantity controls; the need for the latter is usually conceded. Therefore, a primary objective of this paper is to discuss whether statistical aggregates can be beneficially employed by top management to supplement existing single-item control by lower management. In particular, we examine the aspects of

1. Exploring whether commonly used aggregate control devices, such as expenditure budgets and limitations on inventory on hand, are consistent with recommended inventory policies
2. Determining whether aggregate control schemes can be devised which are consistent with item-by-item stockage rules.

For large-scale inventory systems, in addition to the complexities due to the attendant institutional structure, there are the complications arising because of the multitude of different items stocked. If an inventory system were comprised of a single item, there would be little, if anything, to be gained by transforming physical quantity data, such as stock on hand, quantity backordered, amount purchased, number of orders, etc., into index data such as inventory holding charges, depletion penalties, purchase costs, ordering costs, etc. But if the system encompasses stocks of more than one item, a conversion from quantitative to, say, financial data allows top management to aggregate item-by-item detail into summary indices.[3]

This aggregation potentiality commonly leads top management to rely on statistical indices which presumably mirror the effectiveness of the current detailed operations with some degree of accuracy. The actual determination of the items aggregated in a single index may involve such criteria as

1. A common demand pattern
2. Identical stockage costs, such as holding charges, stockout penalties, purchasing and ordering costs
3. Utilization characteristics, such as stationery, tires, hardware
4. Personnel allocation
5. Geographical location

Indices of primary interest include

1. Value of inventory on hand
2. Value of inventory on order

---

[3] It is often convenient to refer to these aggregates as financial indices, even though they do not always involve actual cash-flow expenditures.

3. Value of inventory on hand and on order
4. Number of orders placed
5. Number of orders outstanding
6. Number or value of current purchases
7. Number or value of shortages
8. Number or value of backorders
9. Number of outages

Indices of this sort, in addition to giving information about the important system stockage costs, are intimately connected with the operation of the stockage policies. Since the drains on the inventory of a single item are conceived as occurring in a probabilistic fashion, in general, the level of such inventory, the number of lost customers or backorders, or other characteristics of the item's stockage, are then also envisaged in terms of random variables. A fortiori index numbers based on the operations of a multitude of items, or control policies founded on such index numbers must be described stochastically, and we usually can expect perturbations of the probability distributions of demand or of the stockage policies to have an effect on an index's pattern of fluctuations. In this paper we explore just how well devices based on these types of indices do fulfill the requirements of top management to maintain control.

1.3 Definition of Management Control

Throughout we shall be primarily concerned with two aspects of control:

1. Given a set of management standards, does the mechanism being examined guarantee or at least encourage the fulfillment of these standards? Figuratively, we may say this is management by rule.
2. Given a set of management standards, as before, does the mechanism ensure or at least make likely the detection of deviation from these standards? We may call this management by exception.

In Section 2 these standards are defined in terms of lower management's observance of recommended stockage policies. In such a context, management by rule is fostered insofar as the control schemes employed motivate lower management to follow the stated objectives; management by exception arises when the control devices signal top management that there is statistical evidence pointing to violations of the specified rules. One possible cause of failure to observe standards is that lower management is subject to strong pressures and commitments which are at variance with those imposed by top management; another reason is that, because of the decentralized structure of the organization, lower management may not be sufficiently well informed about top management's true objectives, a condition which might be alleviated by the imposition of a control scheme designed to indicate these objectives properly. In Section 3 standards are characterized in terms of the depletion of inventory. Lack of fulfillment of these standards may be due to factors leading to a change in customer demands, which are beyond the immediate control of the establishment. Succinctly, management by rule, when appropriate, is the encouragement of personnel to be economical in the replenishment of inventory; management by exception is the detection of depletion occuring at rates not anticipated by top management.

We do not discuss the derivation of recommended stockage policies. Our analysis might be viewed as beginning *after* top management has arrived at its stockage objectives. The justification for this approach is that, whatever the factors influencing the selection of an inventory policy for an item, the resultant rule implies a certain pattern of fluctuations in any operating characteristic of the inventory system; for control purposes, it is this implied pattern which is of principal interest.

1.4 A Framework for Evaluation of Control Systems

In examining a particular control system, six interrelated stages of analysis are essential. First, it is necessary to decide what operations potentially warrant control. This entails establishing operating standards that define the meaning of "in control", and ascertaining whether there is significant freedom of decision so that an "out of control" state is a real possibility. The standards for "normal" or "satisfactory" operations must not be so broadly defined as to encompass all eventualities (unless we desire to vitiate completely any potential for control).

Second, the action possibilities available to constrain such decisions must be ascertained, with a view toward encouraging certain decisions and discouraging or prohibiting others. Even if an "out of control" state frequently occurs, the notion of control is meaningless unless it can be either prevented or corrected by appropriate action.

A third important consideration is deciding to whom the various responsibilities associated with control are to be delegated. Since our intention is to offer only an economic and mathematical analysis of inventory control systems, we shall limit our discussion of this question, which is primarily oriented toward political and organizational issues. But, almost needless to say, the controversies stemming from this consideration may very well be crucial in determining the ultimate adoption of a control system.

The fourth stage is an economic evaluation of the worth of ensuring that the standards are met, of detecting when they are not, and of making mistakes in the process of controlling.[4] Although such evaluation is perhaps the most difficult task in the analysis, it is fundamental to the establishment of a beneficial control system. To some extent the task is aided by the very analysis which leads to the development of economic inventory stockage policies. In certain cases a precise evaluation of worth may not be necessary, since the criterion for selecting a control system may be insensitive to fairly large changes in the worth values assumed.

In our discussion so far, the stages of investigation have not depended on the specific control system being analyzed. In the fifth stage it is necessary to examine the operating characteristics of the system. These include the related aspects of the very feasibility[5] of the plan, of the rules to be followed for taking managerial actions depending on data emanating from the system, of the cost of maintaining the control system, and of the important concomitant benefits not directly attributable to control per se. The latter may contribute largely to the desirability of the system, but by definition are obtainable even if the control aspects are ineffective.[6]

The sixth stage is the synthesis of the previous information to yield an economic evaluation of the entire control system. Even if the evaluation provides a favorable indication, it is usually advantageous to compare the suggested system with other possible alternatives.

2. CONTROL OF INVENTORY POLICY DECISIONS

2.1 Assumptions

Throughout we postulate that the inventory system is comprised of a multitude of items, each of which is demanded and stocked according to an (s,S) model. The (s,S) inventory rule is to review periodically the amount of inventory on hand and on order, and to place an order whenever this amount falls below s, so that, after the order, the amount equals S; often s is called the reorder point and S the reorder or imprest level. Specifically, we assume that the demand distribution for each item i, $\varphi_i(\xi)$, is known and is independent of the demands for other items in the system, and that the delivery time

---

[4] The interdependence of the stages of analysis is clear here, for the worth of ensuring minimal standards is usually low as compared to that of ensuring comprehensive standards, whereas the costs of control in the latter case are usually high.

[5] For example, availability of personnel and other resources necessary for the scheme's operations, establishment of responsibilities within the plan in the framework of the organization, and internal consistency of the control device.

[6] These benefits may be referred to as external economies.

sistent or inconsistent is not sufficient to ascertain its full merit. For reasons which we elaborate below, we cannot say that a consistent system is to be preferred unequivocally to an inconsistent control.

2.3 Elementary Control Schemes

We focus attention on two generic types of control schemes.

Barometer control: lower management is rewarded or penalized according to the magnitude of deviation of a control index number from a preset target value.

Quota control: lower management is assumed to be meeting standards as long as the control index number remains under a preset quota limit.[9]

Most real control systems are a combination of several of these devices. In this section we analyze examples of each of the generic types; from these results, it is possible to draw conclusions in a straightforward manner concerning the consistency of composite schemes.[10] Because the number of potential control schemes is sizeable, we necessarily must forego any detailed taxonomic approach; we must be content to investigate those devices which are commonly employed or seem promising.

Throughout we postulate that the inventory records accurately indicate the status of the system. To assume otherwise is to admit for consideration the possibility of apparent fulfillment of standards by means of willful "adjusting" of such data which would otherwise indicate an out-of-control state. A study of this aspect goes beyond our intended scope.

2.4 Control Indices

A sufficient condition to establish that the aggregation process in computing any control index number is well defined, insofar as timing considerations are concerned, is that the inventory review periods assumed for each of the (s,S) policies coincide. Reflection on the matter shows that there are many other possible timing configurations for the composite of (s,S) policies which also permit an index aggregation. We shall not attempt to give a necessary condition regarding this timing consideration, and mainly for convenience of presentation, our

[9] If the index number can take negative as well as positive values, or if small values are possibly indicative of inconsistent actions, the quota restriction may be given in terms of an allowable range for the index.

[10] We caution that probability analyses of a combined system for example, determination of the over-all probability that any one of the quotas is exceeded during a period—can be genuinely difficult. Such complexity is not peculiar to inventory control; analogous problems exist in some statistical quality control procedures which simultaneously employ several control charts and rules for deciding out-of-control situations.

discussion in the remainder of this section and the next will proceed as if all the review intervals do coincide. But we note that more general configurations can be encompassed in a conceptually obvious way.

The control period and inventory review period may or may not coincide. For example, purchases may accumulate for several review periods before a quota is applied; or shortages may be averaged during a certain number of sampled periods and then compared to a target value.

From a formal point of view, we may derive the probability distribution for an index of the sort listed first by obtaining the appropriate probability distribution of the control number[11] for each item to be included in the index [13], and then by convoluting these distributions. If the index is to be an aggregate over a number of review periods so that a normal distribution approximation may be employed, the convolution process is considerably simplified; only the proper mean and variance contributions from each item are required. In the following sections we proceed beyond this formal prescription to a probability analysis of specific control schemes and, in particular, to a judgment concerning their consistency.

2.5   Barometer Control

2.5.1   Index Design and Random Behavior

We consider as indices the quantities cited in Section 1.2 weighted and summed over the various items in the system and perhaps over several consecutive or sampled inventory review periods. We postulate here that lower management's objective is to optimize[12] the expected value of the deviation between the index and the target value. Since the latter is preset, the problem focuses upon optimizing the expected value of the index number per se. Our analysis in [13] yields the stationary expectation of such a sum; since the demands for the items are independent, the variance of the index sum is the sum of the variances associated with each item. In most real situations, if the number of items comprising the index is large, the central limit theorem [4] may be applied on this account to yield the conclusion that the index number is approximately normally distributed with the aforementioned mean and variance.

Considerable difficulty is encountered in providing consistent control by means of fragmentary indices, that is, indices which focus on only one aspect of the system's operating behavior. For example, if the inventory model permits backlogging and the sole index is the

---

[11] We speak of a control number with reference to each item, and of an index number with reference to a system-wide summation of the control numbers.

[12] That is, to maximize or minimize, depending on the nature of the particular control scheme.

value of inventory on hand, we may conclude that lower management, being strongly motivated to reduce the index figure below a target value, would tend to diminish the value of s and D in the (s,S) rules, where D = S − s. Similarly for the same model, if the sole index is value of shortages or backlogs, there is a strong motivation to increase s and D; or, if the sole index is the number of orders placed, there is a tendency to increase D. Thus fragmentary control may lead to strong inconsistencies in an obvious way.

Assume that a normal distribution is an adequate representation of the probability distribution of the index number. Then it is simple to demonstrate that under fragmentary control the aggregation process may hide or confound violations which are offsetting. For example, it may occur that the reorder point s from one item is shifted upward, causing an increase in the mean and variance of the probability distribution of the item's control number; that for another item, the point is shifted downward, with a similar change in the mean and variance of the probability distribution of the control number; and that the result is no net change in the parameters of the normal distribution of the index number. A simple example of this situation is where two items both have the same demand distribution $\varphi(\xi)$ but differing (s,S) policies due to the composite of economic factors involved. If the index number weights each of these items equally, then an interchange of the two (s,S) policies has no effect on the distribution of the index; this conclusion follows irrespective of the form of the probability distribution of the index number.

We conclude by posing the following problem, to be discussed in the next section. Is it possible to devise a top management barometer control index[13] which is strongly consistent for the composite of the (s,S) policies?

2.5.2 Rationalizing (s,S) Policies

Barometer control involves rewarding or penalizing lower management by the amount[14]

(1) θ(index number − target)   where $\theta > 0$.

The target is set at the expected value of the index number and, therefore, is merely the sum of the expected value of each item's control

---

[13] If it is possible to make use of full item-by-item detail, then the design problem becomes trivial—ascertain the number of items for which the recommended (s,S) policies have been violated and penalize lower management proportional to this number. This suggested control, of course, is not in keeping with our notion of top management control.

[14] For example, suppose shortage costs are being controlled, the index number is 50, the target number is 100, and θ is .5. Then lower management is rewarded 25. If the values 50 and 100 are interchanged, lower management is penalized 25.

number in a single review period times the number of periods comprising the control interval.

For each item stocked, we seek a set of weighting or pricing factors to be assigned to the various states describing the status of the item at the end of an inventory review period, such that the expected value of the associated control number is a strict minimum whenever the specified (s,S) rule is being followed.[15] Thus, even after system aggregation, the index is strongly consistent, since the best course of action for lower management to follow is to obey, item by item, the prescribed stockage policies[16] which may differ.

Of course, prior to assigning weights, we must decide upon those characteristics of the inventory state which are to be priced. Let the variable x be the amount of inventory on hand (or backlogged) and on order, and a variable indicating the placing of an order. Then we let:

$$
(2) \quad
\begin{array}{ll}
\text{control number} = C_{in}x & s + 1 \leq x \leq S, \\
\qquad\qquad\quad = C_{fix} + C_{in}x & 0 \leq x \leq s, \\
\qquad\qquad\quad = C_{fix} - C_{out}x & x < 0,
\end{array}
$$

where C_{in}, C_{out}, and C_{fix} are positive constants to be determined, and (s,S) is the *actual* policy being employed.[17] This scheme has the advantage that the relevant probability distribution of x is independent of the presence of any time-lag [13]. This independence between λ and the rationalizing values of the economic parameters is to be sharply contrasted with the dependence we must usually observe in selecting a preferred (s,S) policy. Thus, when a significant delivery lag is present, in general we cannot expect an agreement between the rationalizing economic values and the economic parameters leading to the selection of the preferred (s,S) policy. Making use of the basic result in [10] and the continuity properties of s and S in terms of C_{in}, C_{out}, and C_{fix}, we can be assured of the existence of rationalizing values for these control constants.

If the index number chosen to rationalize each (s,S) policy does, in fact, represent top management's total utility of the situation, and, according to our postulate, top management is interested solely in the expected value of the index, then by setting $\theta = 1$, top management has obtained a control device which provides a complete hedge against inconsistent actions. In other words, if the index number can

---

[15] That is, the expected value of the control number with these weights strictly increases with any change from the prescribed (s,S) rule.

[16] Note that this conclusion follows irrespective of the value assigned to the target.

[17] In other words, at the end of a period each unit of inventory on hand (or backlogged) is costed at C_{in}, if the amount is positive, or at $-C_{out}$ if the amount is negative, and if an order is then placed, a further charge of C_{fix} is added.

be treated as a cardinal utility indicator, then management's total utility is the sum of the expected value of the index, and the reward or penalty on lower management is

$$E(index) - \theta E(index - target) = target \qquad for \ \theta = 1;$$

this constant is independent of the actual (s, S) policies being followed.

If lower management violates the rules despite the consistent situation, then top management will suffer a utility loss whenever it is not practicable to employ a complete hedge. It is plausible that after a number of periods top management would notice a persistent tendency to exceed, say, the target, and would institute corrective action; but this consideration carries us beyond our present realm of discussion of barometer control into that of quota control. We turn to this latter subject below. Thus, aside from any possible hedging operation, barometer control in its strict meaning does not admit considerations of "management by exception."

2.6 Quota Control

2.6.1 Assessment of Analytic Difficulties

The modus operandi of quota control is for top management at the beginning of a control period to set a limit (or limits) on the value of the index which is calculated at the end of the period;[18] if the actual index value exceeds the preset quota, top management presumes that the rules or standards have been violated[19] and investigates the situation in further detail. As in virtually every application of statistical techniques to problems of inference, in general there exists a chance that the index exceeds the quota when the standards are being followed. A consistent control scheme is one in which the probability of exceeding the index limit is greater when violations of standards are present than when they are not.

Whereas under barometer control schemes we needed only the first moment [4, 6] of the probability distribution of the control numbers for our analysis of consistency, we now require at least a second moment, namely, the variance and, in certain instances, the entire probability distribution. We investigate the consistency of a quota scheme by examining the procedure when only a single item is in the system; we impose as a necessary condition for consistency of a quota controlled index that an analogous limitation on a control number be consistent in a single-item system. Consequently, if a quota control is inconsistent when applied to a single-item system, we will not consider it for a multi-item system.

---

[18] The calculation may entail a summing or averaging of index values during several intervening inventory review periods.
[19] Recall throughout Section 2 we postulate that the $\varphi_i(\xi)$ are known.

Violations of specified (s,S) policies alter the stationary probability distribution of the control number in such a way that both the mean and variance change. As a consequence, lower management, faced with a quota controlled index which top management would like to assume small values, may find it beneficial to violate the prescribed rules in such a way that the variance of the index is decreased despite the fact that, contrary to top management's over-all intentions, the mean value is thereby increased. In general terms, this tradeoff between mean and variance is the fundamental difficulty to be faced in quota schemes.

Our discussion in Section 2.5.1 of the problems connected with establishing a consistent barometer scheme which utilizes fragmentary indices applies equally well here.

Finally we point out that the difficulties raised in Section 2.5.1 with respect to the aggregation process have direct parallels in a quota scheme. To cite a plausible quote control index scheme for which gross violations in the specified policies can occur with no corresponding change in the probability distribution of the index number, we consider a backlog model with $C_i x_i$, $C_i > 0$, as the control number for item i. The rationale of the scheme is that if s and D are increased for many items, many of the x will take on relatively high values; similarly, if s and D are decreased, many of the x will take on relatively low values.[20] Assuming that the number of items comprising the index is sufficiently large for the probability distribution of the index to be well approximated by a normal distribution, we may argue that considerable violations in the prescribed values of s can occur with a completely offsetting effect; as a result, the scheme is at best only weakly consistent. The underlying reason is that changing s merely shifts the distribution of x but does not change its shape, as is proved in [13]; consequently only $C_i E(x_i)$ changes, but not the variance of the control number $C_i x_i$. Thus, increasing s for some items and decreasing it for others in a way that leaves constant the sum of the expected values $C_i E(x_i)$ has no visible effect on the probability distribution of the index.

More sophisticated schemes encounter similar or more sophisticated difficulties. For example, control might be attempted in a backlog model by means of quotas on two separate indices: (1) stock on hand or backlogged, and (2) value of current orders. At first look this suggestion seems promising, since for a single-item inventory system a consistent control might be devised. But in a multi-item system, increasing some D values and decreasing others may have offsetting tendencies for both indices due to the effect on the variance of the control numbers. Further if the $\varphi_i(\xi)$ are different, lower man-

---

[20] As usual, x is the amount of inventory on hand (backlogged) plus on order before placing any order in the current period.

agement may be motivated positively to alter several (s,S) rules to obtain a mean-and-variance tradeoff among the various items.

We summarize our discussion by stating that quota control has at least all the hazards with respect to consistency as does barometer control. In addition the analytic complexity increases because more than the first moments of the constituent control number distributions are needed to determine the requisite probability information concerning the distribution of the index. In the next two sections we explore the extent to which it is possible to construct a consistent quota scheme.

2.6.2 Quota on Index of Rationalized Control Numbers

A plausible quota scheme to test for consistency is setting a limit on the index comprised of rationalized control numbers such as those suggested in Section 2.5.2. To investigate this suggestion we consider a one-item system under the backlog case and with control number (2) in Section 2.5.2. We want to determine whether, for a given (s,S) policy, the rationalized values C_{in}, C_{out}, and C_{fix}, and a properly set quota value L^*, the control scheme is consistent. It is convenient to refer to the amounts $C_{in}x$, $- C_{out}x$, and C_{fix}, whenever relevant, as inventory, backlog, and ordering costs, respectively.

We consider whether lower management's objective is better met if, period after period, upon facing the same quota, lower management adopts an (s,S) policy different from the prescribed (s,S) rule. In other words, is the stationary probability of remaining under the quota increased by violating the suggested inventory policy through the adoption of another (s,S) rule? The mathematical analysis required to answer these questions involves the probability distribution of the control number, given the stationary probability distribution for x. For this stationary analysis, we assume the control number is calculated by adding all the costs incurred in the current period.

We shall demonstrate that in general we cannot assume it is possible to set a quota yielding a consistent situation. We examine a numerical example; further analysis of this sort is contained in [13]. Suppose $\varphi(\xi) = 1/3$, for $\xi = 0, 1, 2$, and management has selected a (0,3) inventory policy. This policy is rationalized by $C_{in} - 1$, $C_{out} = 4$, and $C_{fix} = 4$, with E[control number | (0,3)] $- 77/27$. Using an algorithm to find the stationary probability distribution of x as found in [13], we can exhibit the corresponding cumulative probability distributions for the control numbers in Exhibit 9-1. In this table we demonstrate that for each possible quota value, there exists an alternative (s,S) policy[21] with a higher probability of remaining under the limiting value.

---

[21] A policy with a negative value for s merely implies that backlogs accumulate before a replenishment order is placed.

Exhibit 9-1

Backlog, (0,3)
Uniform, E(ξ) = 1

	$C_{in} = 1$	$C_{out} = 4$	$C_{fix} = 4$
L*	Prob(control number ≤ L*)		(s'S')
	(0,3)	(s'S')	
8	1.0000	1.0000	(0,2)
7-4	.8889	.9275	(0,4)
3	.7037	.7681	(-1,3)
2	.5555	.6522	(-1,3)
1	.3333	.4783	(-1,3)

We might ask whether the following weakened version of the consistency property holds: Suppose, for some value of L*, lower management's objective is better met by the recommended policy than by some alternative policy having E(control number) = E*. Does this consistent situation extend to the class of all alternative policies having E(control number) ≥ E*? The answer is no. A counter example is provided by the model in Exhibit 9-1. For L* = 3, the probability of not exceeding the quota is .7037 for (0,3) as compared to .5556 for (0,2), where under the latter policy E(control number) = 3. But as we show in Exhibit 9-1, under (-1,3) the probability of remaining under the quota L* = 3 is .7681 and for this alternative policy E(control number) = 3.10.

2.6.3 The Existence of a Consistent Quota Scheme

In this section we turn to the question of whether for a given inventory system a consistent top management quota scheme exists. In answering affirmatively, we emphasize that our argument mainly describes from a formal mathematical approach how it is possible to construct a consistent quota device. However, we do not argue that in real situations the scheme need be economically advantageous, nor do we attempt to be precise about quantifying the proposal; the latter task in any case seems to be essentially dependent upon the composition of the actual inventory system.

As in the previous section, we start by considering a single-item inventory system and assuming that a control number has been derived from a rationalization process of Section 2.5.2. The law of large numbers and the central limit theorem [5, 6] assert that, if we average the observed control number over T periods, as T grows large the distribution of the average tends to a normal distribution with a mean equal to the expectation of the control number and variance as given in [13].

Postulating that violations of the recommended (s,S) rule can only involve revising either s or S or both by integral amounts, there is an alternative policy (s',S') such that the associated expected value of the control number is closest to the expected value of the control number for the recommended policy. Because we have assumed the parameters of the control number are rationalized values, the two expected values are distinct. We then can view the problem of establishing a consistent control scheme as analogous to a problem of testing statistical hypotheses concerning the mean of a normal distribution [4, chap. 35]. If T is sufficiently large so that the normal approximation to the distribution of the index number fits well for any set of (s,S) policies being followed, a quota slightly larger[22] than the expected control number for the recommended rule produces a consistent control scheme; for any such quota limit, a further increasing of T reduces the probability that the sample average of the control numbers exceeds the quota when the recommended policy is being observed.

A similar line of reasoning may be followed to demonstrate the existence of a consistent quota control on an index number. That is, if the index is the sum of the control numbers for the various items in the system averaged over T periods, and if T is sufficiently large, then the index is approximately normally distributed, and it is possible to place a quota on this index to produce a consistent situation.

However, it is still an open question whether there are alternative (and hopefully simpler) approaches to the design of general quota controls that are consistent.[23]

3. CONTROL UNDER VARYING DEMAND DISTRIBUTIONS

We now extend the discussion for the situation where the φ_i (ξ) are not known with certainty. Specifically, in Section 2.5.2 we proposed a barometer scheme that rewards or penalizes lower management by the amount

$$(1) \qquad\qquad \theta \text{ (index number } - \text{ target)} \qquad\qquad \theta > 0,$$

where the target is set at the expected value of the index number com-

---

[22] Since the variance of the control number for the recommended policy may very well be larger than the variance for alternative policies, we cannot ensure that a consistent situation is present if the quota is relatively large. But this guarantee certainly holds if the control number is between the expected value of the control number for the recommended policy and that for (s',S').

[23] We remark that throughout we have approached the analysis from a probabilistic, as distinguished from a statistical, point of view. In the actual implementation of such schemes, it may be possible to adopt statistical techniques such as those employed in quality control [2, 7] to estimate the parameters of the probability distribution of the index number from time series data. In such applications, the role played by our analysis is to indicate the general form that the index number distribution may be expected to take and the dependence of its parameters on the random variables associated with the underlying (s,S) policies.

puted under the assumptions that the recommended policies are being observed and the demand distributions are known. When the latter assumptions are in fact true, that is, when the system is in-control, the scheme is "fair"[6, chap. 10] in that the expected payoff is zero. Two factors militate against a parallel target setting in the present situation: (1) The demand distributions are not known with certainty. (2) Top management most likely wants lower management to select (s,S) policies according to the current best estimates of the demand distributions in operation, rather than to follow a rigid set of stockage rules. The apparent differences between the situation in Section 2 and the present one seem significant, but recall that the factor in the previous barometer scheme leading to consistency is the beneficial effect of lower management's being motivated to minimize the index number, given that the target figure is a preset constant, Section 2.5.1. If we abandon the fairness property in a barometer control, we may be able to devise a consistent control mechanism, provided that we can construct such an index number that lower management, in minimizing the expected value of the index number, is in fact following top management's recommendations. Almost needless to say, the warnings in Section 2.5.1 against employing fragmentary indices are pertinent to the construction of the proper underlying control numbers.

An important example of such a suitable index arises when top management's stockage preferences are expressed in terms of a minimum expected cost criterion. Here top management specifies a set of economic parameters for each item and instructs lower management to adopt an (s,S) policy minimizing the expected value of the associated control number. In terms of stationary probability analysis, lower management in fact obtains a minimum expectation of the index number comprised of the various control numbers by adopting the recommended policies. Thus a barometer control scheme may operate as follows. Top management specifies a target figure; this may be fixed with reference to a likely set of distributions φ_i (ξ) and perhaps so as to make the expectation of (1) favorable to lower management if the assumed values of φ_i (ξ) occur and the corresponding preferred stockage rules are adopted. Whatever the setting of the target, lower management remains motivated to adopt policies which minimize the expectation of the index number. Since the demand distributions are not known with certainty, lower management faces a difficult statistical decision problem; as data emerge and the uncertainty about the demand distributions decreases, the consistency property strongly motivates lower management to follow the preferred policies.

In contrast to the foregoing results pertaining to a barometer control, the conclusion stemming from an examination of our previously considered quota control scheme, based on rationalized control numbers, is that its asymptotic consistency property is relinquished. Recall we found in Section 2.6.3 that if the demand distributions are known, it is possible to design a quota device that at least will be consistent if the number T of review periods of observation is sufficiently large. The idea underlying the analysis was that with sufficient data, the probability distributions of the control number for two different (s,S) policies could be distinguished, and with a quota upon the arithmetic average of an index comprised of rationalized control numbers, lower management's objective would be better met if the recommended policies were followed. One detail of the analysis is that, as T becomes large, it is possible to find a consistent quota despite the fact that the variance of the distribution of the index may be larger when the recommended policies are being followed than when the policies are being violated.

Consider as the index number the same one that we discussed above for a barometer scheme and impose a quota, say, on the average of this index value over T periods. Because of the difficulty created by variances being altered when changes in $E(\xi_i)$ occur, we cannot conclude the situation is consistent for an arbitrary value of the quota. In other words, the positive conclusion of Section 2.6.3 depends in an essential way on setting the quota with knowledge of the demand distribution and the associated index number distribution when the system is in-control.

The impediment to finding a consistent quota scheme in the present situation may be mitigated to the extent that the variance of the distribution of the index number averaged over T periods is insensitive to actual changes in the demand distributions and stockage policies observed, and insofar as we can use a normal distribution with a fixed variance as an adequate approximation. Given these assumptions about the probability distribution of the index number, lower management is encouraged to adopt recommended policies. This result follows in part from the preceding analysis of the motivation involved in a barometer scheme, namely, a desire to adopt minimum expected cost (s,S) policies, and in part from the observation that lowering the expected value of a normal distribution shifts the entire distribution toward lower values of the random variable, so that the probability of remaining under an arbitrarily set quota is a maximum when the expected value of the index is a minimum.

4. POLICY IMPLICATIONS

4.1 Consistency and Detection Probabilities

The consistency property affects the relative evaluation of control schemes in two ways, namely, in influencing the values of the a priori probabilities of system situations and in determining the ability to detect out-of-control situations. We discuss each of these factors in turn.

The property of consistency is an appealingly plausible require-ment,[24] for top management to adopt a control procedure which fails to meet this criterion appears to be at variance with top manage-ment's prescription of stockage policies. To the extent lower man-agement ascertains the possible benefits in terms of its own objec-tives to be derived from inconsistent actions, top management is able to foresee that the imposition of an inconsistent control will bring about violations in the recommended policies. This realization could very well lead to the rejection of the scheme for control purposes.[25] But if there is reason to believe that these violations are unlikely to occur, or if their occurrence entails little economic loss to top man-agement, then our predilection for this criterion is correspondingly weakened. Furthermore, in real situations, the imposition of a con-sistent control does not automatically ensure that the recommended policies will be followed.

An inconsistent system by its very nature may prove relatively ineffective in detecting the out-of-control situation whenever such occurs. In other words, the scheme may lack the power to detect violations as they occur. But it also must be realized that a consis-tent control scheme may be ineffective in discovering out-of-control situations.

An acceptance or rejection of a control scheme ought to be made on the basis of a full economic analysis. Despite the lack of consis-tency of a scheme it may be preferable to no control at all. In essence there are two economic losses to be compared: (1) the expected loss resulting from the imposition of a control which encourages certain violations in the recommended policies, and (2) the expected loss stemming from violations which might occur if the inconsistent con-trol is not imposed. The latter quantity may very well outweigh the former.

4.2 Concluding Remarks

Up to this point we have outlined the manner in which quantitative analysis of an index number control scheme may be undertaken. Here we offer a personal critique of the efficacy of index number con-

---

[24] The reader familiar with mathematical statistics will observe the pre-viously mentioned parallel between our view of consistency and the statistician's notion of an unbiased test of hypotheses [4, chap. 35; 8, chap. 27].

[25] Here is the crucial difference between our situation and the one usually encountered in the theory of statistical testing of hypotheses. In the latter in-stance, there is usually no reason to believe that the adoption of a biased test will in and of itself change the likelihood of any hypothesis being true.

trol for the purpose stated in Section 2.2. As usual, we emphasize
the two notions "management by rule" and "management by exception." By concentrating on these two ideas we do not intend to give
the impression that we are foresaking the approach in Section 1.4 or
in the preceding discussion; rather we are stating that within the
confines of our analysis these two elements play a crucial role in
the final economic evaluation.[26]

We stress that a sensible discussion of the merits of control
schemes must take cognizance of the fact that top management is
forced to choose among several broad alternatives: (1) to impose no
top management control over lower management's observance of
recommended policies; (2) to adopt an index scheme such as the one
presented in this paper; or (3) to devise another type of control
method. Because of the aggregation process and the nature of the
probability distributions thereby convoluted, it is not surprising if
choice (2) turns out to be ineffective for detecting a low or moderate
level of violation except when T is large. But choice (1) is trivially
ineffective in this respect, and choice (3), insofar as we have envisaged it, is also limited by the nature of the costs associated with
such a procedure. Thus in a large-scale inventory system it may be
inevitable that top management has no economically advantageous
way of maintaining close control over lower management's observance of the recommended rules.[27] Furthermore, in certain real situations it may be that the principal economic benefit derived from
taking an audit when it is in fact called for stems from the future
operations of the system; past losses suffered by top management
through violations of recommended policies may not be recoverable.
In addition, the employment of an aggregate type of control may be
necessitated by restrictions imposed by a Board of Directors. Consequently, we reaffirm the validity of top management's need to impose aggregate control.

We may ask whether a consistent barometer control is to be preferred to an inconsistent device, other factors such as control costs
being equal. In answering we begin by pointing out that in actuality
it is not a trivial matter to institute a pure barometer scheme. It is
unlikely that top management can ensure itself a barometer control
giving a complete hedge, because the index comprised of rationalized

----

[26] Another important factor in the design of a control scheme is the economic cost associated with its operations, e.g., charges for personnel, docu-
ment handling, and office equipment. We go no further in our theoretical analysis than to mention this factor, for at present, it appears that such considerations by and large are mainly dependent on whatever real situation is actually
involved.

[27] It must be realized that top management is unlikely to be very concerned
about a low level of violation. Indeed, it is an advantage that a small number of
infringements is obscured in an index, and thus does not tempt top management
to investigate in detail.

control numbers is not likely to represent top management's utility
function, and it is difficult in real situations to set θ at a sufficiently
high level.[28] Consequently, in real applications of barometer control
schemes top management is often justifiably motivated to take corrective action if it observes several consecutive periods in which
penalties occur; in effect it has thereby combined an element of
quota control with the barometer device. Furthermore, lower management, when faced with a nominal barometer device, may not view
its own objective as optimizing

$$\theta \text{ (index number } - \text{ target)}$$

but rather as minimizing the probability that a penalty exceeds a
given amount; once again, the resultant effect is a quota control.

This discussion means that imposing a nominally strongly consistent scheme does not guarantee the system operates according to
the prescribed management rules. Therefore, we cannot recommend
without qualification that consistent systems are to be preferred.
Lower management may quickly realize that aggregate control
schemes tend to be weak in their power to detect mild violations.
Whether in actual situations the consistency motivation will dominate
the realization of an ineffective power to detect mild violations is a
question which transcends an economic and statistical analysis and
falls into the scope of industrial psychology.[29]

Our analysis has led to the conclusions that almost all commonly
used aggregate control schemes are inconsistent, and that it may be
nearly impossible as well as undesirable to impose a strongly consistent control device. We must not infer from these conclusions
that aggregate controls should be rejected entirely. Rather we must
face the fact that inconsistency is a price which in most cases will
have to be paid whenever aggregate controls are instituted. The ultimate determination of the merit of imposing a control scheme can
only be provided by means of evaluating one device relative to another
in the fashion prescribed in Section 1.4.

BIBLIOGRAPHY

1. Blackwell, D., and M. A. Girshick: *Theory of Games and Statistical
    Decisions*, New York: Wiley, 1954.
2. Bowker, A. H., and G. J. Lieberman: *Engineering Statistics*, Englewood
    Cliffs, N. J.: Prentice-Hall, 1959.
3. Chernoff, H., and L. E. Moses: *Elementary Decision Theory*, New York:
    Wiley, 1959.

[28] In other words, it is unlikely that top management can enforce a penalty
that would fully compensate it for systemwide losses that are possibly incurred.
[29] Research in this area seems to have already begun [12].

4. Cramer, H.: *Mathematical Methods of Statistics*, Princeton, N. J.: Princeton University Press, 1954.
5. Doob, J. L.: *Stochastic Processes*, New York: Wiley, 1953.
6. Feller, W.: *An Introduction to Probability Theory and Its Applications*, New York: Wiley, 1957.
7. Grant, E. L.: *Statistical Quality Control*, New York: McGraw-Hill, 1952.
8. Kendall, M. G.: *Advanced Theory of Statistics*, vol. II, London: Griffin, 1951.
9. Savage, L. J.: *The Foundations of Statistics*, New York: Wiley, 1954.
10. Scarf, H.: "The Optimality of (*s*,*S*) Policies in the Dynamic Inventory Problem," *Mathematical Methods in the Social Sciences*, Stanford, Calif.: Stanford University Press, 1960.
11. Schlaifer, R.: *Probability and Statistics for Business Decisions*, New York: McGraw-Hill, 1959.
12. Stedry, A. C.: *Budget and Control and Cost Behavior*, Englewood Cliffs, N. J.: Prentice-Hall, 1960.
13. Wagner, H. M.: *Statistical Management of Inventory Systems*, New York: Wiley, 1962.

10

INVESTIGATIONS IN THE THEORY OF MULTIPLE BUDGETED GOALS

ABRAHAM CHARNES AND ANDREW STEDRY
Northwestern University

and

Massachusetts Institute of Technology

INTRODUCTION

Implicit recognition of the existence of multiple goal structures possessed by individuals in organizations and by organizations themselves is far from new. Even in the scientific management literature where employers' objectives are described as " ... to secure a maximum output of standard quality at a minimum cost per unit ..."[1] (which is in itself a dual goal) mention is made of "such obvious benefits to the employer as having a better-satisfied labor force; resulting in minimum turnover."[2] More recently, explicit recognition of the presence of multiple goal structures in an organizational setting has taken place. Cyert and March [12, 13] have specifically postulated a mechanism within the organization through which a "ruling coalition"—a group at the top of the organizational hierarchy which is "in control"—sets short and long range goals for several areas of organizational activity. Cyert, Dill, and March [11] have provided evidence in support of these hypothetical goal structures.

Such multiple goal structures may be considered in contradistinction to the "goal" of unconstrained profit maximization assumed in classical economic theory. As suggested by Cooper [10], the classical assumptions, however useful they may be for prediction of macroeconomic behavior, provide neither guidelines for nor descriptions of the behavior of an individual firm. Viewing the firm as a whole, it (or its ruling coalition) may simultaneously form goals for a percentage of share of the market, level of employee welfare (e.g., as manifested by a "no layoff" policy), level of total assets and so on. It may be tautological, but nevertheless interesting, that it is impossible to simultaneously optimize two functions; one can, at best, optimize one, placing a constraint on the other; or, one can construct a super-functional which is some function (perhaps a weighted sum) of the initial functions. While it is frequently suggested that short-run constraints can be derived from an (unconstrained) optimization of long-run profit the usefulness of such an approach either for descriptive or normative analyses of micro-economic phenomena is questionable; from the evidence

---

[1] Lowry, Maynard, and Stegmarten [34, p. 6].
[2] ibid., p. 7.

available[3] firms both can and do construct constraints in the short run (or over a foreseeable horizon) which do not appear to derive from any explicit long run profit function.

Thus, in constructing short-run models of organizational behavior, one may postulate a process of profit maximization subject to certain constraints. These constraints may be stated deterministically or probabilistically. For example, in a short-run profit maximization,[4] the optimal solution will drive ending inventory to zero (assuming positive selling proces) unless some lower bound is placed on it. This inventory constraint becomes the link between the correct short-run problem and that of the next period, such an extension being required to preserve the economic reality of the dynamic organization model without the necessity of constructing a (generally unavailable) long-run profit function.[5] In certain periods, this constraint may be extremely costly—e.g., if the price at which a portion of the ending inventory could be sold is high relative to prices obtainable in subsequent periods. It may not be possible to assess the cost, however, because of uncertainty in future prices.[6] Thus it becomes advisable to state the constraint on ending inventory probabilistically—e.g., the probability that ending inventory will fall below 100 units will not exceed .05. The ending inventory figure of 100 units thus becomes a goal. It is something which one will try to achieve. If several such chance constraints exist, the model may be considered a multiple goal model wherein a profit maximization goal is joined by these other goals which relate to the attainment of specific *performance levels*. The properties of several such models have been investigated.[7]

In this paper, however, our focus will be on the description of a new class of models whose properties relate specifically to the allocation of resources so as to satisfy goal attainment motivations. We assume that an individual (or an organization, or a ruling coalition within an organization) constructs a set of goals. These goals may be aspiration levels internally arrived at or may be goals imposed by superiors, the market or the social environment.

---

[3]See, for example Charnes and Cooper [5], and Cyert, Dill, and March [11].

[4]As, for example in a warehousing model. See Charnes, Cooper, and Miller [8].

[5]In fact, a process similar to this is utilized in partitioning virtually insoluble long(er) run models into soluble short-run problems. See Charnes and Cooper [6].

[6]The use of the term *uncertainty* here should be noted. If future prices are uncertain, it is impossible to construct even the expected cost function in terms of future prices. This should be distinguished from the frequently assumed, but rarely observed, case of *risk* where the distribution of future prices is known.

[7]See Charnes and Cooper [5]; and Charnes, Cooper and Symonds [9].

IMPOSED GOALS AND ASPIRATION LEVELS

It is indeed difficult to understand why a dichotomy has so often been assumed to exist between an "imposed" goal and an internally generated aspiration level. The latter may be defined as the level of performance whose attainment leads an individual to experience "success" and whose non-attainment leads him to experience "failure" (Becker and Siegel [3]). Frank [16] has defined the aspiration level as "that level which an individual, knowing his level of past performance, explicitly undertakes to reach." Lewin, Dembo, Festinger and Sears [21] have described construction of an aspiration level from the maximization of the expected utility (or valence) of success (diminished by the expected disutility (negative valence) of failure). Simon [26] has used a utility function with a discontinuity at the aspiration level—performance at or above the aspiration level possesses positive utility, below it, negative utility. There is nothing in any of these definitions in widespread use which would preclude the possibility of the incorporation of goals imposed by a superior as a factor in influencing aspiration levels. Particularly if one appeals to the notions which are related to utility theory, the contribution to utility of attaining a level which is associated with reward (promotion, prestige, salary, or bonus) as may well be the case with "imposed" goals, must certain establish that level as a lower bound on aspiration provided the reward is sufficiently large. The effects of various factors on aspiration level— need achievement (Rotter [24]), social norms (Chapman and Wolkmann [4]), reality-irreality (Diggory [14]), and previous success (Festinger [15], Becker and Siegel [2]) have been investigated, to cite only a sample. Although Siegel and Fouraker [25] showed that the experimenter's goal was accepted by subjects and translated into performance and Stedry [27] has investigated the frequency of acceptance of experimenter-presented goals as stated.aspiration levels, such examples are rare. In general, superior-initiated goals have received attention through having their existence deplored by many writers including McGregor [23], Argyris [1], and Becker and Green [3].

It is not clear that a goal set by a superior is any more "imposed" than a social norm or need be more abhorrent. An individual's need for achievement derives at least in part from his external environment; that the affectors may be circumstances of an earlier environment would not seem to make them any less imposed than a contemporary superior, but rather the opposite since they are less easy to change. Finally, it is difficult to imagine an environment more imposed than the random elements present in a game against an impersonal nature in an uncertain world which result in a pattern of success and failure; while the long-run effects of the effort devoted to a task may be observable, for any single period, increased effort may be almost as likely to lead to failure as success if the amount of random noise is great. To accept these environmental factors as determinants of "internally generated" aspiration levels but reject superior-initiated goals on the basis that they are "externally imposed" would seem to be highly artificial.

Therefore models with which we shall deal here do not distinguish between goals that are set by an individual (or organization) which are the presented goals of a superior and those which are set with reference to other external or (presently) internal forces. The goals which are accepted by an individual or organization, however arrived at, and the rewards perceived as being associated with them, whether tangible or intangible, are of interest. As will be revealed from analysis of the solutions to the goal problems posed, some areas of endeavor will not receive any effort toward goal attainment because a combination of too great difficulty of attainment in these areas and too small associated reward with them will render alternative areas more attractive. This withholding of effort is tantamount to goal rejection. Thus, if goals set by a superior fall into the category of effort allocation withdrawal because the reward associated with their attainment is inadequate these goals will appear to be rejected. Our models thus embrace both cases where superior-initiated goals are accepted and where they are rejected. We are thus constrained to accept neither the assumptions of the standard budgeting literature that (budgeted) goals are accepted without question nor the assumptions of more recent literature in budgeting and social psychology that only participatively set goals will be accepted. We readily accept the notion that the presence of participation in goal setting may, under certain conditions, increase the amount of personal satisfaction associated with goal attainment and thus raise the overall level of perceived reward. It is not clear from recent evidence,[8] however, that participation in goal setting is so advantageous as to preclude the inclusion of non-participatively set goals in behavioral models.

A STOCHASTIC REPRESENTATION OF GOAL ATTAINMENT AS A FUNCTION OF EFFORT

Let us assume that an individual (or organization) has a set of goals $\{g_j\}$ with whose attainment are associated a set of rewards $\{r_j\}$ for attainment and penalties $\{p_j\}$ for non-attainment. The index j designates the activity area for which a performance goal has been set. Finally, let $\{x_j\}$ represent the set of performances in the n activity areas and let performance behavior be stochastically described by the function:

$$P\{x_j \geq g_j\} = k_j(1 - e^{-\alpha_j \rho_j}) \qquad j = 1, \ldots, n$$

[8]See Vroom [33], French, Israel and Ås [17], French, Kay and Meyer [18], and Stedry [27].

where the left hand side represents probability of goal attainment in the jth area, ρ_j the search effort allocated to the jth area, and k_j and α_j are parameters dependent upon the difficulty of the selected goal g_j with $0 < k_j \leq 1$ and $\alpha_j > 0$.

This stochastic function, as shown in Exhibit 10-1, incorporates a limiting probability of goal attainment (k_j) as ρ_j grows large. This represents a formal recognition of the infeasibility of eliminating *all* random noise from the system which would enable the determination of success and failure by mere application of additional effort. The parameter α_j determines the rate of ascent to the limiting probability as effort increases—the effort required to obtain a probability of attainment equal to a specified proportion of k_j is inversely proportional to α_j.

This probability function would appear to possess several desirable properties. It reflects diminishing returns, has sufficient flexibility to describe a wide variety of hypothetical situations and, from the standpoint of solving problems, is both monotone increasing and strictly convex. Although other functions might both represent behav-

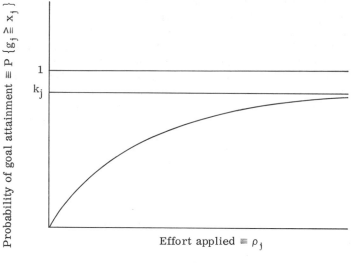

Exhibit 10-1

ior in specific situations it would appear that extensions to other probability functions are less interesting, at least in exploratory work, than observations of model behavior change under different motivational assumptions. At the level of allocation of individual or organizational search effort at a motivational level, the limitations on human ability to perceive subtle refinements in probability functions would seem to preclude the desirability of constructing models on an overly complex base. It would seem that a more precise specification or greater complexity in the function would be required for consideration of practical budgetary planning problems—e.g., problems of allocating funds to several competing projects or investment opportunities—but that even here, the difficulties inherent in estimating probability functions from real data in an organizational setting may render superfluous much greater complexity.

MODELS OF EFFORT ALLOCATION FOR OPTIMAL REWARD

The concept of effort used here is adapted from that of Simon [26], and March and Simon[22]. We refer not to physical effort, but rather to "search effort"—effort which results in problem solving, innovation and change. While actual time allocation to various areas of endeavor may be indicative of the search effort allocation (and, because of the difficulties of measurement inherent in the latter, may be required as an operational definition for observation) it is recognized that certain kinds of routine or stereotyped activity do not lead to goal attainment.

Moreover, it is worth noting that, whether or not search effort is an easily measurable quantity, mere measurement of the allocation of *time* to tasks of a non-repetitive nature is an unsolved problem.[9] Development of a theory of rational (or quasi-rational) effort allocation, may make it possible for the problems of measurement to be at least partially solved through imputations of effort from performance measures—in which case search effort (defined circularly as that effort which results in innovation) becomes the more likely operational measure.

Toward this theory, we postulate a set of models predicated on an assumption of expected reward maximization. It has been observed above that profit maximizing does not adequately describe organizational behavior. It is possible, however, that the maximization of reward associated with discrete goals may provide a step toward a better description of behavior.

SHORT TERM MAXIMIZATION OF EXPECTED REWARD SUBJECT TO AN EFFORT CONSTRAINT

We can define a reward function over the probability function given above by observing that reward, R, over the n goal areas may be expressed as:

$$R = \sum_{j=1}^{n} r_j z_j^+ - \sum_{j=1}^{n} p_j z_j^- \tag{2}$$

where

$$z_j^+ = \begin{cases} 1 & \text{for } x_j \geq g_j \\ 0 & \text{for } x_j < g_j \end{cases}$$

[9]See, e.g., Stogdill and Shartle [32].

and

$$z_j^- = \begin{cases} 0 & \text{for } x_j \geq g_j \\ 1 & \text{for } x_j < g_j \end{cases} \tag{3}$$

indicating that the contribution to reward of the jth performance area will be r_j if the goal; g_j, is attained and $-p_j$ otherwise. To formulate expected reward, we observe that:

$$E(z_j^+) = (1)\, P\{x_j \geq g_j\} + (0)\,[1-P\{x_j \geq g_j\}]$$

and

$$E(z_j^-) = (0)\, P\{x_j \geq g_j\} + (1)[1-P\{x_j \geq g_j\}]$$

$$= 1 - E(z_j^+) \tag{4}$$

Recalling that

$$P\{x \geq g\} = k_j\,(1 - e^{-\alpha_j\, \rho_j}) \tag{1}$$

we obtain for the expected reward,

$$E(R) = \sum_{j=1}^{n} (r_j + p_j)(k_j)(1 - e^{-\alpha_j \rho_j}) - \sum_{j=1}^{n} p_j \tag{5}$$

$$= -\sum_{j=1}^{n} (r_j + p_j)\, k_j\, e^{-\alpha_j \rho_j} + \sum_{j=1}^{n} [r_j k_j - (1-k_j)p_j]$$

The second term in the finally obtained expression for $E(R)$ may be viewed as a long-term factor relevant to considerations of the inducements to an individual's remaining in the industry. It may also affect the amount of effort, ρ, which is available for allocation among the competing areas but, as we will consider ρ to be constant in the short run, this facet will not be relevant to the problem posed. The second term, constant in the short run, may thus be ignored and our problem stated as:

Minimize $\displaystyle\sum_{j=1}^{n} \eta_j\, e^{-\alpha_j \rho_j}$ \hfill (6a)

Subject to:

$$\sum_{j=1}^{n} \rho_j = \rho \tag{6b}$$

$$\rho_j \geq 0 \quad j = 1, \ldots, n \tag{6c}$$

where $\eta_j = (r_j + p_j)k_j$ and the non-negativity conditions (6c) reflect the inability to "borrow" effort from one area beyond no effort at all to provide more capacity for another. We have given a formal derivation of the solution to this problem and a computational algorithm elsewhere [30]; the derivation is an extension of a solution of Charnes and Cooper [6] based on the Kuhn-Tucker conditions. The latter become:

$$\eta_j \, \alpha_j \, e^{-\alpha_j \rho_j^*} = \mu \qquad \text{for } j \epsilon J \tag{7a}$$

$$\eta_j \, \alpha_j \leq \mu \qquad \text{for } j \notin J \tag{7b}$$

where $J = \{j \,|\, \rho_j^* > 0\}$ —that is, the set of areas at optimum to which some effort is allocated. The process followed for computational solution begins by ordering the $\eta_j \, \alpha_j$ from the largest ($j = 1$) to the smallest ($j = n$). It will be observed that this quantity is a product of the reward for attainment[10] ($r_j + p_j$), the limiting value for possible probability gain (k_j) and the proportionality constant for return to effort (α_j) —basically an overall measure of potential gain from effort allocated to the jth area. It is intuitively clear that effort should be allocated first to those with the highest potential gain. The formal algorithm does this, first allocating all of the available effort to activity 1 and utilizing the conditions (7a) and the overall constraint on activity expressed in terms of those conditions, namely:

$$\left. \begin{array}{l} -\alpha_j \rho_j^* + \ln \eta_j \, \alpha_j = \ln \mu \\[2em] \rho_j^* = -\dfrac{1}{\alpha_j} \ln \mu + \dfrac{1}{\alpha_j} \ln \eta_j \, \alpha_j \end{array} \right\} \quad j \epsilon J \tag{8a}$$

which yields, on summing:

$$\rho = \sum_{j \epsilon J} \rho_j^* = -(\ln \mu) \left(\sum_{j \epsilon J} \frac{1}{\alpha_j} \right) + \sum_{j \epsilon J} \frac{1}{\alpha_j} \ln \eta_j \, \alpha_j \tag{8b}$$

$$\ln \mu = \left[\sum_{j \epsilon J} \frac{1}{\alpha_j} \ln \eta_j \, \alpha_j - \rho \right] \left[\sum_{j \epsilon J} \frac{1}{\alpha_j} \right]^{-1}$$

to obtain a possible value for μ. This value for μ is then tested against the constraint (7b) for the largest of the remaining areas (initially, activity 2). Observing (8b) it will be noted that μ will increase in size with each additional activity added to the set J of positive effort allocation activities. Thus μ will be small initially and unless $\eta_2 \alpha_2$ is much smaller than $\eta_1 \alpha_1$, the condition (7b) will be violated for at least $j = 2$. Then a new trial value for μ will be computed from (8b) with the set J now containing two elements. The process con-

[10]Including the evidence of a penalty.

tinues until a value of μ is found that is sufficiently large that it is larger than the maximum of the $\eta_j \alpha_j$ for $j \notin J$ (and hence all of the others). The conditions of (7b) are now fulfilled and the conditions of (7a) may be fulfilled by solving for the values of the individual ρ_j by (8a).

An heuristic interpretation of the procedure is possible. Certainly an ordering of activity areas according to potential gain is not infeasible. Then "data breaks"—natural divisions formed as a result of a difference between two consecutive values of the parameter being substantially greater than the differences between values in the groups formed between the decisions—are examined. Then the "top priority" group can be examined along with the next group in priority to determine whether all of the effort should be allocated to the former or whether allocating some to the latter will improve the overall goal attainment "picture." The process can be continued until the items of sufficiently low priority (either because of low reward attached or because of tremendous amount of effort required to attain a reasonable probability of success) are decided upon as worthy of ignoring (or postponing).

Within the groups of relatively similar potential, effort may be allocated as demanded to provide roughly equivalent probabilities of success, a simple and reasonable approximation to the relationship of (8a). Perhaps the most difficult problem to attack without recourse to the formal methodology is the distribution of effort between groups—i.e., how high is "high" priority. Returning to earlier terminology, the risk of failure to attain a goal, at optimum, may be expressed as:

$$1 - [k_j(1 - e^{-\alpha_j \rho_j})] \approx \frac{\mu}{(r_j + p_j)\alpha_j} \qquad \text{where } k \approx 1. \qquad (9)$$

To provide an appropriate guideline, the risk of failure should be inversely proportional both to the reward available and to the responsiveness of the activity to effort. Since k_j would not be expected to vary excessively—only values between, say, .8 and 1.0 making very much sense—the activities in the groups formed between the data breaks in $\eta_j \alpha_j$ should have similar $(r_j + p_j)\alpha_j$. Thus effort can be allocated between groups in such a way that the risks of failure to achieve goals in any group is approximately inversely proportional to a multiplicative measure of reward and difficulty.

It has been observed that tolerable probabilities of failure to attain goals are more easily arrived at by organization executives than the cost of failure. Charnes, Cooper, and Symonds [9] found this to be the case in scheduling heating oil where the goal was satisfying all customers. Stedry and Griswold [31] observe that supply control officers in a military organization could more easily establish risk categories than costs of stock out. In both cases the researchers observed a willingness to alter the acceptable risk level where it was pointed out that the cost (generally of inventory investment and storage) would be excessive in certain cases. Thus the groupings of risk were found *a priori* and the mathematical models were used to determine the operating procedures required to attain them, subject to inventory investment (that is, effort) constraints. We thus are able to provide evidence for the viability of the approximate solution to our reward maximization model[11] in one form—i.e., where the establishment of acceptable risks of goal attainment provide the missing data for approximate reward maximization even where the rewards attached to the individual goal attainments in the functional cannot be specifically stated.[12]

OPTIMAL REWARD SUBJECT TO RISK CONSTRAINTS

The evidence presented for explicit risk limitation in specific areas strongly suggests an extension to the expected reward maximization model. Risk constraints of the form:

$$P\{x_j < g_j\} \le \delta_j \qquad j \epsilon J' \tag{10}$$

may be placed on specific activity areas where J' is a subset of the n activity areas represented in the functional and δ_j, the acceptable risk of non-attainment in the jth area, is a constant such that $0 < \delta_j < 1.$[12] Defining these constraints over the probability function, we obtain:

$$1 - k_j(1 - e^{-\alpha_j \rho_j}) \le \delta_j$$

$$\frac{1 - \delta_j}{k_j} \le 1 - e^{-\alpha_j \rho_j} \tag{11}$$

$$\frac{1 - \delta_j - k_j}{k_j} \le -e^{-\alpha_j \rho_j}$$

which provides us with a minimum effort constraint:

$$\rho_j \ge \frac{1}{\alpha_j} \ln \left(\frac{k_j}{1 - k_j - \delta_j} \right) \text{ where } 1 - k_j - \delta_j > 0.$$

[11]Or a profit maximization model which, in [30], we have shown, under certain conditions to be equivalent.

[12]Some evidence from the study of children is also suggestive. Hoppe [19] found that the goal to "get dressed without help" received less effort (that is, more requests for help were observed) when a reward was offered for attainment of the goal to "get dressed." It should be noted that this interpretation is somewhat different from that offered by Lewin *et al.* [21], where a clear dissimilarity between these two competing goals has been ignored, resulting in the misleading conclusion that reward for attainment lowers aspiration levels.

[13]An alternative formulation would allow $\delta_j \pm 1$ and the constraints (10) could could apply for $j = 1, \ldots, n$ where $\delta_j = 1$ for $j \epsilon J'$.

If we now let:

$$\overline{p}_j = \frac{1}{\alpha_j} \ln \left(\frac{k_j}{1 - k_j - \delta_j} \right) \quad j \epsilon J' \tag{12}$$

and perform the transformation:

$$\rho'_j = \rho_j - \overline{\rho}_j \quad j \epsilon J'$$

$$\rho'_j = \rho_j \quad j \notin J' \tag{13}$$

$$\rho' = \rho - \sum_{j \epsilon J'} \overline{\rho}_j$$

we have the problem in a form which is identical to that of (6) above with ρ'_j substituted for ρ_j and ρ' for ρ. (Clearly if ρ' is negative the constrained problem is infeasible.)

The new set J will contain only those activity areas where effort is to be allocated in excess of the constraints for $j \epsilon J'$. If the parameters of the original problem are preserved, elements formerly in J but whose solution provided $\rho_j^* < \overline{\rho}_j$ will not now be in J. It is intuitively clear (and can be proved) that the amount of effort available for allocation to the unconstrained areas is thus diminished so that no additional elements will be added to J. Indeed, if ρ' is sufficiently small, the problem is effectively constraint-determined and the decisions as to which areas to allocate some (additional) effort may be made at the periphery. This distinction may be noted in the military terminology which distinguishes between "military-essential" and "nice-to-have" categories of endeavor and the observed avoidance of effort allocation to the latter.

A similar effect has been noted at an experimental level in the aspiration level determination of subjects in a goal-oriented situation.[14] In a series of time trials, subjects were given performance goals with monetary rewards attached. Two competing goals for effort could be discerned. The first was to "do a good job" or "solve many problems." The second was to obtain the monetary reward. Competition for effort expenditure may have existed among the several time trials as well. The perceived difficulty of attainment of the experimenter's goal (with monetary reward attached) in early trials would provide (as the experiment was designed) a good estimate for future goal difficulty. It was observed that as goal difficulty increases (across subjects) stated aspiration levels for individual trials diminished *relative* to the experimenter's goals.[15] A possible interpretation arises from the suppression of the goal to "do well" in a given time trial (short run) which would

---

[14]Stedry [27] and [28].

[15]Although not, as frequently assumed, in an absolute sense. Apparently the increasing goal difficulty had some beneficial effect in raising the overall ef-

require effort which could otherwise be allocated to reducing the risk of non-attainment of the monetary rewards in later periods. This interpretation is one of several possible explanations of the observed behavior but suggestive, nevertheless, of the possible application of multiple-goal models to the analysis of dynamic phenomena.

A CONSTRAINT ON THE RISK OF UNACCEPTABLE PERFORMANCE

Frequently of interest rather than (or in addition to) the risk of non-attainment of individual goals is the risk of unacceptable performance where acceptable (or satisfactory) performance is considered to be the simultaneous attainment of minimally acceptable performance levels in several activity areas. These levels, say h_j, would be lower than the corresponding g_j. They may be viewed as minimum standards rather than desirable levels, thus establishing a goal hierarchy defining different degrees of satisfactory performance.

Ordering the n areas so that the first m of them are represented in the acceptable performance criterion, the constraint may be expressed as:

$$\prod_{j=1}^{m} k_j' \, (1 - e^{-\alpha_j \rho_j}) \geq \delta \tag{14}$$

Noting that $\left(\prod_{j=1}^{m} k_j' \right)$ may be factored out of the expression and making the substitution

$$W = -\ln \left(\frac{\delta}{\pi_j k_j'} \right) \tag{15}$$

we obtain:

$$- \sum_{j=1}^{m} \ln (1 - e^{-\alpha_j \rho_j}) \leq W \tag{16}$$

A value of W for which the constraint is useful as a policy will be quite small. An acceptable risk of unacceptable performance would not seem sensible were δ less than, say, .8. Even if the k_j were close to 1, reasonable values of W would probably not exceed .2.

Clearly, a feasible solution requires that the maximum value attainable for the product of the probabilities under the effort constraint be equal to or greater than δ. This value can be obtained in the manner

fort expenditure for most subjects, at least as observed by performance, although an interaction effect was observed between goal difficulty and manner of presentation which was independently varied.

presented by us in [30] and if this value is equal to δ the solution to
the reward maximization is entirely constraint determined and may be
obtained by the methods of the earlier paper. If the maximum value is
greater than δ, the reward maximization may be stated as:[16]

Minimize $\displaystyle\sum_{j=1}^{n} \eta_j \, e^{-\alpha_j \rho_j}$

Subject to:

$$-\sum_{j=1}^{m} \ln (1 - e^{-\alpha_j \rho_j}) \leq W \tag{17}$$

$$\sum_{j=1}^{n} \rho_j = \rho$$

$$\rho_j \geq 0 \qquad j = m+1, \, ..., \, n$$

The constraint on ρ is stated as an equality inasmuch as it is monotone increasing, and the functional monotone decreasing, in ρ_j. The
explicit statement of non-negativity conditions is required only for the
ρ_j which are not included in the constraint on W, whose satisfaction
requires $\rho_j > 0$, $j = 1, \, ..., m$ for W finite. (Intuitively, if even one activity involved as a criterion of acceptable performance is ignored,
overall acceptable performance cannot be attained.) It can be shown
that the constraint on W may be replaced by equality unless the optimal solution to the problem without this constraint (but with the non-
negativity conditions on the first m of the ρ_j restored) overfulfills
it, in which case the problem solution is obtained by the methods used
above.

Provided the problem is feasible and the constraint on W is not
redundant, the conditions of solution (Kuhn-Tucker) become:

$$\eta_j \alpha_j \, e^{-\alpha_j \rho_j} = -\nu \left(\frac{\alpha_j \, e^{-\alpha_j \rho_j}}{1 - e^{-\alpha_j \rho_j}} \right) + \mu \qquad j \in M$$

$$\eta_j \alpha_j \, e^{-\alpha_j \rho_j} = \mu \qquad j \in K \tag{18}$$

$$\eta_j \alpha_j \leq \mu \qquad j \in K'$$

where $M = \{j \mid j = 1, \, ..., \, m\}$, $K = \{j \mid j = m+1, \, ..., \, n$ and $\rho_j^* > 0\}$ and
$K' = \{j \mid j = m+1, \, ..., \, n$ and $\rho_j^* = 0\}$. For simplicity, let:

$$x_j \equiv e^{-\alpha_j \rho_j} \tag{19a}$$

[16] A more formal treatment of this model will be made available elsewhere.

$$\mu_j \equiv \frac{\mu}{\alpha_j \eta_j} \tag{19b}$$

$$\nu_j = \frac{\nu}{\eta_j} \tag{19c}$$

for all j. It will be observed that $k_j x_j$ approximates the probability of non-attainment of h_j. Thus x_j must be quite small for $j\epsilon M$ in order that joint attainment of several goals will be meaningful, as suggested above. The Kuhn-Tucker conditions and the constraints restated in terms of (19) appear as:

$$x_j = -\nu_j \left(\frac{x_j}{1 - x_j} \right) + \mu_j \quad j\epsilon M \tag{20a}$$

$$x_j = \mu_j \quad j\epsilon K \tag{20b}$$

$$1 \le \mu_j \quad j\epsilon K' \tag{20c}$$

$$-\sum_{j\epsilon M} \ln (1 - x_j) = W \tag{20d}$$

$$-\sum_{j\epsilon M} \frac{1}{\alpha_j} \ln x_j - \sum_{j\epsilon K} \frac{1}{\alpha_j} \ln \mu_j = \rho \tag{20e}$$

where the last is obtained by substitution in (19a), (19b) and (20b).

The computation of an exact solution to this problem is sufficiently complex and tedious that it is unlikely that it is of much value in terms of explanations of behavior. An approximate solution is, however, readily available. Multiplying both sides of (20a) by $(1 - x_j)$ we obtain:

$$x_j - x_j^2 = -\nu_j x_j + \mu_j - \mu_j x_j \tag{21}$$

Clearly, for realistic cases W will be small—of the order of .2 or .1— for the constraint on it to be meaningful as a limitation of risk on unacceptable performance. If, for example, these minimum standards were a set of specifications set by a purchaser for acceptable product, traditional values of "producer's risk" would be even smaller—that is, of the order .05. Noting that:

$$W = -\sum_{j\epsilon M} \ln (1 - x_j) \ge \sum_{j\epsilon M} x_j \tag{22}$$

since the individual x_j's, particularly if numerous, must be extremely small.[17]

It is clear that:

[17]By definition they may only take on values $0 \le x_j < 1$ for $p_j > 0$.

$$0 \leq x_j - x_j^2 \leq x_j \tag{23}$$

so that, utilizing (21):

$$\frac{\mu_j}{1 + \mu_j + \nu_j} \leq x_j \leq \frac{\mu_j}{\mu_j + \nu_j} \leq \frac{\mu_j}{\nu_j} \tag{24}$$

which, for small x_j, requires that ν_j be very large relative to μ_j. By substituting the lesser upper bound in (20d) we obtain:

$$
\begin{aligned}
W &= - \sum_{j \in M} \ln (1 - x_j) \\
&\leq - \sum_{j \in M} \ln \left(1 - \frac{\mu_j}{\mu_j + \nu_j} \right) \\
&\leq - \sum_{j \in M} \ln \left(\frac{\nu_j}{\mu_j + \nu_j} \right) \\
&\leq \sum_{j \in M} \ln \left(1 + \frac{\mu_j}{\nu_j} \right) \\
&\leq \sum_{j \in M} \frac{\mu_j}{\nu_j}
\end{aligned}
\tag{25}
$$

Recalling the definitions of μ_j and ν_j from (19), (25) yields:

$$W \leq \sum_{j \in M} \frac{1}{\alpha_j} \left(\frac{\mu}{\nu} \right) \tag{26}$$

or:

$$\frac{\mu}{\nu} \geq \frac{W}{\left(\sum_{j \in M} \frac{1}{\alpha_j} \right)} \tag{27}$$

Approximations to x_j^* for $j \in M$ are readily obtained by substitution of the lower bound for μ/ν in the upper bound for x_j, or:

$$\hat{x}_j^* \cong \frac{\mu_j}{\mu_j + \nu_j} = \frac{1}{1 + \frac{\nu_j}{\mu_j}} \approx \frac{1}{1 + \frac{\alpha_j \sum_{j \in M} \frac{1}{\alpha_j}}{W}} \qquad j \in M \tag{28}$$

or:

$$\overset{\star}{x}_j^* \cong \frac{\mu_j}{\nu_j} \cong \frac{W}{\alpha_j \sum_{j \in M} \frac{1}{\alpha_j}} \qquad \text{as } W \to 0 \tag{29}$$

Either of the approximate solutions, which differ from the true value by second and higher order terms only, is clearly independent of the η_j. The approximate solution to the effort allocation problem among areas involved in a minimum standard thus appears to depend only on the relative ease of attainment, α_j, and the ratio of an overall measure of difficulty, $\sum_{j\in M} \frac{1}{\alpha_j}$, and the size of the risk, W. It will be noted that the risk taken in individual areas varies approximately inversely with the ease of attainment—i.e., the easiest things to attain are allocated sufficient effort to be "very safe." In the second solution, it will be noted that the sum of the estimates is equal to W.

The approximate solution for x_j^*, $j \in M$, readily yields a solution for $j \notin M$. If we denote the approximate amount of effort allocated to the m constrained areas by $\hat{\rho}$, we observe:

$$\hat{\rho} \equiv -\sum \frac{1}{\alpha_j} \ln \hat{x}_j^* \tag{30}$$

so that we may now solve the reduced problem:
Minimize

$$\sum_{j=m+1} \eta_j \, e^{-\alpha_j \rho_j}$$

subject to

$$\sum_{j=m+1} \rho_j = \rho - \hat{\rho}$$

$$\rho_j > 0 \quad j = m+1, \ldots, n$$

by the method given in a previous section.

The pattern of behavior described by the second of the approximate solutions might result in the following instructions:

1. Choose a trial value for one of the $\alpha_j x_j$
2. Set individual risks for all of the areas subject to the joint risk constraint so that the $\alpha_j x_j$ are constant across them
3. Add the risks so obtained
4. Multiply each of the trial x_j's by n and divide by the sum found in (3) to find the estimated risks $(\hat{\hat{x}}_j^*)$
5. Allocate the remaining effort so as to approximately maximize reward over the areas not involved in the joint risk constraint.[18]

The results are suggestive of a possible interpretation of the frequently observed tendency in organizations to "put out brushfires" rather than to work on areas where the effort would be of long-run

[18] As given in a section above.

benefit. The only solution which appears credible as an implicit behavior determinant where it is desired to hold the risk of unacceptable performance to some small value is one which allocates effort independent of the rewards attached to desirable goals. The relative risks of not attaining the minimum standard in individual areas are set approximately inversely proportional to α_j —i.e., the easiest thing to protect will be made the safest. Only where areas are not part of an overall acceptable performance criterion will effort be allocated in terms of desirability rather than safety. The computational difficulty inherent in taking into account both reward for a desired attainment and a joint risk constraint to obtain effort allocation for both purposes would seem to result in the elimination of one of the two criteria—and the obvious one to eliminate is the "nice-to-have" criterion.

SUMMARY AND CONCLUSIONS

We have presented three models of optimizing behavior in response to a set of presented goals. It is interesting to note how closely the optimal solution to these reward (or profit) maximization models resemble behavior which may be termed "satisficing." In general, the addition of constraints on risk of individual activity areas or a subset thereof tends to quite easily subordinate the importance of the coefficients in the form of profit function used. Furthermore, the need for use of approximate solutions because of the complexity of the exact solutions provide quasi-optimal behavior which, at least in the cases examined, depends even more heavily on the constraints at the expense of the influence of the coefficients in the reward function.

From the standpoint of capital budgeting models where the actual distributions are known and computational complexity is not limited by human computational shortcomings, the exact solutions on which we have concentrated elsewhere ([29] and [30]) are of interest. For predicting behavior patterns which would logically occur in response to desired ends when the effort allocation process is (more or less) implicit, the approximate solutions seem to be of greater interest. Systematic study of behavior in response to multiple budgets or goals is rare.[19] Observations at the non-systematic level, however, appear to lend credibility to the possibility that the approximate solutions do resemble behavior in response to the reward functions postulated.

[19]Data collected by one of the authors and E. Kay appear to approximate the behavior in response to the third model in an industrial budgeting system.

BIBLIOGRAPHY

1. Argyris, C.: *The Impact of Budgets on People,* Prepared for the Controllership Foundation, Inc., at Ithaca, New York: Cornell University, 1952.
2. Becker, S., and D. Green, Jr.: "Budgeting and Employee Behavior," *The Journal of Business,* vol. 35, no. 4, 1962.
3. Becker, S., and S. Siegel: "Utility of Grades: Level of Aspiration in a Decision Theory Context," *Journal of Experimental Psychology,* vol. 55, pp. 81-85, 1958.
4. Chapman, D. W., and J. Volkmann: "A Social Determinant of the Level of Aspiration," *Journal of Abnormal Psychology,* vol. 34, pp. 225-238, 1939.
5. Charnes, A., and W. W. Cooper: "Chance-Constrained Programming," *Management Science,* vol. 6, no. 1, 1959.
6. —— and ——: *Management Models and Industrial Applications of Linear Programming,* 2 vols., New York: Wiley, 1961.
7. —— and ——: "Management Models and Industrial Applications of Linear Programming," *Management Science,* vol. 4, no. 1, 1957.
8. ——, ——, and M. H. Miller: "Application of Linear Programming to Financial Budgeting and the Costing of Funds," *Journal of Business,* vol. 32, no. 1, 1959.
9. ——, ——, and G. H. Symonds: "Cost Horizons and Certainty Equivalents: An Approach to the Stochastic Programming of Heating Oil," *Management Science,* vol. 4, no. 3, pp. 235-263, 1958.
10. Cooper, W. W.: "A Proposal for Extending the Theory of the Firm," *Quarterly Journal of Economics,* February, 1951.
11. Cyert, R. M., W. R. Dill, and J. G. March: "The Role of Expectations in Business Decision Making," *Administrative Science Quarterly,* vol. 3, no. 3, 1958.
12. —— and J. G. March: "The Behavioral Theory of the Firm: A Behavioral Science-Economics Amalgam," Paper read at the Conference on Research in Organizations, Pittsburgh, Carnegie Institute of Technology, 1962.
13. —— and ——: "Organizational Factors in the Theory of Oligopoly," *Quarterly Journal of Economics,* vol. 70, 1956.
14. Diggory, J. C.: "Responses to Experimentally Induced Failure," *American Journal of Psychology,* vol. 62, 1949.
15. Festinger, L.: "A Theoretical Interpretation of Shifts in Level of Aspiration," *Psychological Review,* vol. 49, 1942.
16. Frank, J. D.: "Individual Differences in Certain Aspects of the Level of Aspiration," *American Journal of Psychology,* vol. 47, 1935.
17. French, J. R. P., Jr., J. Israel, and D. Ås: "An Experiment on Participation in a Norwegian Factory," *Human Relations,* vol. 13, no. 3, 1960.
18. ——, E. Kay, and H. H. Meyer: "A Study of Threat and Participation in an Industrial Performance Appraisal Situation," unpublished manuscript.
19. Hoppe, F.: "Erfolg and Misserfolg," *Psychologische Forschung,* vol. 14, pp. 1-62, 1930.
20. Kuhn, H. W., and A. W. Tucker: "Nonlinear Programming," *Proceedings of the Second Berkeley Symposium on Mathematical Statistics and Probability,* Berkeley: University of California Press, pp. 481-492, 1951.
21. Lewin, K., Temara Dembo, L. Festinger, and Pauline S. Sears: "Level of Aspiration" in J. McV. Hunt (ed.), *Personality and the Behavior Disorders,* New York: Ronald, 2 vols., 1954.
22. March, J. G., and H. A. Simon: *Organizations,* New York: Wiley, 1958.
23. McGregor, D.: "An Uneasy Look at Performance Appraisal," *Harvard Business Review,* vol. 35, no. 3, 1957.
24. Rotter, J. B.: *Social Learning and Clinical Psychology,* Englewood Cliffs, N. J.: Prentice-Hall, 1954.

25. Siegel, S., and L. E. Fouraker: *Bargaining and Group Decision Making: Experiments in Bilateral Monopoly*, New York: McGraw-Hill, 1960.
26. Simon, H. A.: *Models of Man*, New York: Wiley, 1957.
27. Stedry, A.: "Aspiration Levels, Attitudes and Performance in a Goal-Oriented Situation," *Industrial Management Review*, vol. 3, no. 2, 1962.
28. ———: *Budget Control and Cost Behavior*, Englewood Cliffs, N. J.: Prentice-Hall, 1960.
29. ——— and A. Charnes: "Exploratory Models in the Theory of Budget Control," Evanston: Northwestern University, The Technological Institute, Office of Naval Research Project on Temporal Planning and Management Decision under Risk and Uncertainty, ONR Memorandum No. 43, March, 1962.
30. ——— and ———: "Some Models of Organization Response to Budgeted Multiple Goals," Organization Research Report No. 1, Cambridge, Mass. Massachusetts Institute of Technology, School of Industrial Management, 1962.
31. ——— and J. Griswold: "The Development of Supply Control Procedures for the Defense General Supply Agency," *Proceedings of the United States Army Operations Research Symposium, Part I*, Durham: Army Research Office (Durham) at Duke University, 1962.
32. Stogdill, Ralph M., and Carroll L. Shartle: "Methods in the Study of Administrative Leadership," Research Monograph No. 80, Columbus, Ohio: The Ohio State University Bureau of Business Research, 1955.
33. Vroom, V. H.: *Some Personality Determinants of the Effects of Participation*, Englewood Cliffs, N. J.: Prentice-Hall, 1960.
34. Lowry, S. M., H. B. Maynard, and G. J. Stegmerten: *Time and Motion Study and Formulas for Wage Incentives*, New York: McGraw-Hill, 1940.

11

INCENTIVES, DECENTRALIZED CONTROL, THE ASSIGNMENT OF JOINT COSTS AND INTERNAL PRICING[1]

MARTIN SHUBIK
Yale University

1. THE PROBLEMS OF CONTROL AND COST ACCOUNTING

Cost accounting in the modern corporate economy is recognized as a tool with many purposes. It must serve, to a greater or lesser extent, financial and legal requirements, the technical needs of branch managers of industrial plants, and at the same time is used by top management as a basis for policy decisions. The growing recognition of the importance of cost accounting control [1, chaps. 3, 27; 2] has high-lighted several problems which belong jointly to the fields of concern of managers, engineers, cost accountants, and economists.

Information which is portrayed and set out with one purpose in mind may be worse than useless when used for another purpose. The detailed reports and statistics which are of the utmost necessity to a branch manager concerned with technical problems may confuse and mislead a controller interested in investment policy and other areas where finance and tax structure come to the fore and technical, physical details are of secondary importance. The boiled down aggregate information used by a board of directors may seem to be a travesty of the facts to an operating engineer, but in a world where information is expensive, time dear and decisions cannot be postponed, abbreviations and condensations must be made.

A goal of good management should be to design a reward system for those who take risks in making decisions in such a manner that the rewards to the individual correlate positively with the worth of the decision to the organization (taking into account the attitude of the top management to variance as well as to expected gain). In many organizations cost accounting supplies much of the information used for control at several levels. In this paper we examine some of the control problems that arise if joint costs are assigned by various cost accounting and some internal pricing conventions.

A method for assignment of costs which has desirable incentive

---

[1] A slightly revised version of the paper in *Management Science*, vol. 8, no. 3, April, 1962.

and organization properties is then discussed. This method is based upon a result in the theory of games obtained by L. S. Shapley [3]. A self-contained exposition of the features of game theory required for this paper is given in Section 2 following [4].

2. BASIC CONCEPTS RELEVANT TO THE STUDY OF THE ASSIGNMENT OF JOINT COSTS

The theory of cooperative games, as developed by von Neumann and Morgenstern depends upon a measure of the interrelatedness and increase in joint rewards obtained by a group of individuals who are willing to act together, as compared to acting individually. The profitability of a corporation may be viewed as depending upon the sum of the joint rewards which can be obtained by the optimum co-ordination of all branches. This analogy will be specified even more closely in Section 3. The *players* in a von Neumann and Morgenstern game may be regarded as the branches or departments of a corporation or the sections in a factory.

The measure of the complementarity in a game (that is, the worth of jointly coordinated action) is given by its *characteristic function* [4, pp. 238 ff.]. This function is a *super-additive set function*, and although its technical name may at first frighten the non-mathematician, the meaning of it is relatively easy to explain. It is called a set function as it is defined, that is, it takes on values for a set of entities. In this case the entities consist of every possible combination of departments in a corporation. For example, suppose that a corporation consisted of a central office and two departments; if each of these were regarded as an independent entity denoted by 1, 2, and 3 then the characteristic function would be defined for seven values. These are values for 1, 2, and 3 individually; the pairs (1, 2) (1,3) and (2, 3); and the firm as a whole (1, 2, 3). For completeness we assign a value of zero to a coalition consisting of no one. This gives eight values to the characteristic function of a firm considered as three entities.

The characteristic function is called *super-additive* because the value of the amount obtained by any grouping of participants is always as much or more than they can obtain by individual action. For instance, a coat may be worth more than two halves of the same coat. The characteristic function provides a handy way in which complementarity can be described between different objects or groups.

Consider a firm with several branches, say different plants. They share the common overheads of the firm, and the actions of one branch may affect the direct profits of another (vertical integration might cause this, or there may even be competition in the market

between differentiated products of the same corporation; for instance
the different automobiles produced by General Motors). One way in
which an index of the importance of any branch can be measured is
by calculating the effect upon profits if it is closed down, and the optimum alternative use were made of the resources it relinquished. In
a similar way we can evaluate the importance of any set of branches
to the corporation as a whole. Let $v[i, j]$ stand for the profit that
branches i and j of a firm can make on the assumption that the remaining branches have closed down.[2] In general, $v(S)$, the characteristic function, describes the profit made by the set S, of departments
or other separate components of the firm which are to be considered
as acting in unison.

As a simple example consider a factory consisting of two departments, 1 and 2. The only cost that they share in common is a joint
overhead for the factory. Furthermore, suppose that if either department closes down, there is no alternative use that can be made of the
excess plant facilities. Assume that the net receipts for Department 1,
leaving out the joint cost assessment, are x, and for Department 2,
are y. Let the joint cost be c. The set consisting of the two departments is denoted by $\{1, 2\}$. The value of the profits they can obtain
together is:

$$v(\{1, 2\}) = x + y - c$$

The amount that the firm obtains if the second department is closed
is:

$$v(\{1\}) = x - c$$

with the first department closed it can obtain

$$v(\{2\}) = y - c$$

We note that:

$$v(\{1\}) + v(\{2\}) = x + y - 2c$$

hence:

$$v(\{1, 2\}) > v(\{1\}) + v(\{2\})$$

---

[2] We are implicitly assuming that the strategy space of a top manager is
limited to such a manner that he has the choice of closing down or producing
optimally with those branches which do not close down. This assumption is
discussed further in the text.

Although formally the inequality above can be defined, in this example care must be taken in interpreting the meaning of $v(\{1\}) + v(\{2\})$. Both departments cannot simultaneously realize their own survivor's value. If instead of two departments, the example had been that of a husband and wife deciding to file a joint tax return or to both "go it alone" then the above sum would have a direct physical counterpart.

In order to avoid difficulties such as the one above, it is necessary to divide the firm into separate decision-making entities and to specify the powers of the various decision makers to close down a plant, to go out of business or to "secede from the union." This is discussed in more detail in Section 3.

By utilizing the characteristic function, the von Neumann and Morgenstern theory of games leads to a concept of solution in which all players act in a manner to jointly maximize profits and then use their bargaining power as represented in the possible coalitions to arrive at an imputation of the proceeds. The method suggested for splitting the profits [4, p. 264] is somewhat complicated and does not concern us here. No unique imputation is given, although certain bounds are placed upon the shares received by each individual.

The method for assigning a portion of joint proceeds to each player which has been advanced by Lloyd Shapley does provide for a unique division. Furthermore, it will be shown that this method satisfies a certain set of properties which an accounting system should have if decentralized decisions are to be based upon the internal imputation of profits to semi-autonomous sections of an organization.

3. INCENTIVES, CONTROL AND COST ACCOUNTING

Broadly speaking it is often deemed desirable to be able to delegate as many decisions as possible to the branches of a firm. In many organizations of large size the exponential growth of messages and red tape cause diseconomies in centralized decision-making for those decisions which depend heavily upon on-the-spot knowledge. If decision-making power is to be delegated it is preferable to have an organization which is designed to encourage initiative. One way of doing this is to have the reward structure designed so that the selection of choices which are best for the individual decision-maker will always coincide with those which are best for the organization. For instance, a branch manager may be aware of a change which may have the effect of increasing corporate profits, but decreases the size of his own department and may even reduce the profits assigned to it by the accounting system. If his success and income are measured and determined by the accounting profits assigned to his department then it may not be in his interest to select the decision optimal for the firm.

Of course there are many sociological and psychological aspects to an incentive structure in a corporation, church, university or commissariat. Thus gold medals, memberships in golf clubs, prestige, pride in workmanship and so forth all play an important role[5]. Furthermore, in even the most impersonal and mechanized systems single number measures of the performance of an individual are rarely used. For purposes of this paper, however, the sociological, psychological and psychiatric aspects of the individuals are taken as given. As bonuses and "incentive compensation" to executives in many corporations are based upon the profits imputed to their operations the economic and accounting problem may be of interest by itself.

There are many technical and conceptual difficulties to be faced in the accounting treatments of fixed costs, variable costs and joint costs. There is a wide variety of practice in accounting methods, Lee Brummet notes five for example:

(1) Complete absorption costing
(2) Expected or average activity standard costing
(3) Practical capacity standard costing
(4) Direct standard costing
(5) Prime standard costing [2, p. 32].

Joint costs have been assigned as a percentage related to the direct labor costs of each operation; charged as a rate per direct labor hour; a rate per unit of product; a percentage of direct material cost or a percentage of prime cost (direct labor + direct material cost)[1, chap. 13]. No exegesis of accounting methods is to be presented here. Many important and vexatious accounting problems are ignored. However, viewing one of the roles of accounting as helping: "to provide management with cost information necessary to business decisions and related policy,"[6] it is observed that under several of the methods above it is possible that a department be assigned costs which make its "paper profits" negative even though it may be a vital and efficient part of the firm. It is also possible that an improvement in the efficiency of a department may damage its individual profit statement even though it increases the overall profitability of a firm.

There should always be an incentive for a manager to implement an efficiency or report a new idea if it benefits the firm as a whole no matter what changes it may cause to take place in his own operation. Under some methods of cost assignment, for example, if the decision to discontinue a product line rests with individual department heads it is possible that individual rational action based upon the cost assignment may add up to corporate idiocy. A simple example of this is given in Section 5.

Ideally, the assignment of joint costs to individual products or departments is not necessary from a purely economic point of view if the decision to maximize for the company as a whole is made in a single office. This is usually impossible in practice, hence a cost accounting and internal pricing scheme can serve as an administrative device in the design of a viable and economic decision-making system.

4. DECENTRALIZATION, DECISIONS AND INFORMATION

The concept of decentralization deals with the possibility of delegating decision making to more than one location in an organization. An optimally decentralized system will have the property that the net effect of all individual actions will be more favorable to the firm than the actions selected by any other array of decision centers. This must take into account costs of messages and organization and the possibilities of committing errors when decisions which appear to be locally optimal are not of benefit to the organization as a whole.

The limiting case for the possibilities for decentralization comes when all decision centers or units are independent. This is merely another way of saying that an action by anyone or any group has no effect on any other unit or combination of units. This is true for small numbers in a purely competitive market which may be viewed as a decentralized organization. It is not completely true as can be seen by problems in agriculture and other "chronically competitive markets." If the characteristic function of an organization is *flat*, that is, if the sum of the amounts which can be obtained by any two coalitions acting together is precisely the same as the amounts that they can obtain by acting independently, then obviously there is no need whatsoever to coordinate their actions as each unit is an autarky and neither gains from nor adds to any joint venture sufficiently to merit other than individual action.

Interesting and important cases for decentralization arise when the joint welfare is influenced by individual action, or the action of coalitions. The degree of influence is reflected in the characteristic function, which, if its values are appropriately defined, display both the technological and decision structure of the firm.

In a game, a player is characterized as an individual decision-maker with some degree of free choice. By analogy we may consider a general manager in a corporation as a player in a position to choose among a set of actions pertaining to his department or part of the corporation. He is a "dummy player" if, in fact, his actions are irrelevant to the functioning of the organization. This happens when some other individual is in a position to overrule and change any of his decisions. This is so in a completely centralized organization; or is apparently so until we consider the information conditions. In theory as well as in practice the selection of what type of message to send up to the decision-maker is a decision in itself and gives the individual a degree of power which varies as the difference between his knowledge and the knowledge of his superior, and the importance of this to the decision.

Effective complete centralization requires either that the central office is completely informed and merely uses the remainder of the organization as an instrument for execution and not for information gathering; or that all individuals are assumed to be unbiased gatherers of data. In other words the central office, if it is not totally informed, must assume that individuals within the organization will not be motivated to distort the information they send or to take actions based on goals which do not correlate with those of the central office. This calls for a concept of an organization as a *team* [7] rather than a series of arrangements between individuals with possibly differing goals.[3] The former can be regarded as a limiting case of the latter. Our interests here are concerned with simple problems arising from the latter concept.

The specification of a characteristic function as a model of the potentials of sectors of a firm contains within it both considerations of the decision structure of the firm and the potential worth of the resources. This can be seen when an attempt is made to assign a worth to what can be achieved by a subset of departments. In order to do this several questions must be posed concerning the location of responsibility for key decisions. A partial list of relevant decisions is given below:

1. The decision on major investment
2. The liquidation of a department
3. The abolition of a product line
4. The introduction of a new product
5. The introduction of other innovations (such as a change in distribution)
6. The merger of several departments
7. The splitting of a department into several independent entities
8. Pricing, purchase of raw materials and sales of final product

If, for example, the managers of each department had decision responsibility for all of the above (which might be the case if the organization being described were a weak cartel rather than a corporation) then the meaning of the value attached to any subset would be the value that a subgroup of participants in the cartel agreement could obtain by acting together by themselves outside of the cartel agreement.

If only some of the decisions are to be delegated while others remain under the control of an executive or central office, then it may be desirable to introduce the office as a player. Returning to and re-

---

[3] An organization may be regarded as a game with restraints on the players and the sending of messages as one of the major weapons of control.

working the example of a factory with two departments given in section 2, it can be regarded as an organization with three participants.
Suppose that there is a president and executive office which has delegated decisions 2, 3, 4, 5 and 8 above to the two managers of the departments, but maintains his decision-making power on the others.
Furthermore, suppose that each manager is instructed to maximize
the profit assigned to its department under the accounting system used
by the firm. We assume that the central office has dictated a method
of accounting which calls for all costs and revenues to be imputed. As
the managers are in a position to liquidate their departments unilater-
ally and to discontinue product lines, they can guarantee themselves
individually a profit of not less than zero. Let the central office be
player 1 and the departments be 2 and 3. The characteristic function
for this firm with structure shown in Exhibit 11-1 is:

$$v(\{0\}) = 0 \qquad v(\{1, 2\}) = x - c$$

$$v(\{1\}) = 0 \qquad v(\{1, 3\}) = y - c$$

$$v(\{2\}) = 0 \qquad v(\{2, 3\}) = 0$$

$$v(\{3\}) = 0 \qquad v(\{1, 2, 3\}) = x + y - c$$

We assume that the central office can obtain a value of zero by liq-
uidating and employing the proceeds elsewhere, hence $v(\{1\}) = 0$.

A good decentralized system should have the property that each decision center will make a decision which is optimal for the whole with
a minimum of cost for coordination and information and message
costs. In the example above, the role of the executive or central office

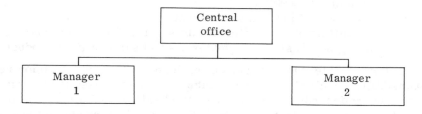

Exhibit 11-1

is to assign joint costs. It must do so in a manner that will guarantee
that if a department should exist for the good of the firm as a whole,
then it will not get an assessment that makes its net revenue negative.
For example, suppose $c = 10$, $x = 4$ and $y = 7$, then an assignment of
costs of 5 each to the two operating departments will motivate player

2 to shut down even though his operation is of value to the business, hence this is not a good assignment.

If $c = 10$ and $x = y = 4$, then the assignment of costs should be such that the firm should be motivated to liquidate (or otherwise change drastically).

Looking at this firm as an administrative system, the only information needed by the central office from the departments is their individual net revenues, and the only information that it will send them is the size of their assessments (it is presumed that the executive office has some other economic, financial or service function which it renders to the firm as a whole).

For another example we consider a firm without overheads or other joint costs, but with two departments producing the same item at costs $C_1(x)$ and $C_2(y)$ which is then sold by the central office which acts as a marketing agency for the firm as a whole. Here the problem is to assign shadow prices to be paid by the central office to the departments and to impute the remaining profit. We assume that the only decisions which are decentralized are production levels and individual technology. The characteristic function will be:

$$v(\{\theta\}) = 0 \qquad v(\{1\}) = 0 \qquad v(\{2\}) = 0 \qquad v(\{3\}) = 0$$

$$v(\{1,\ 2\}) = \underset{x}{\text{Max}} \left[x\phi(x) - C_1(x) \right]$$

$$v(\{1,\ 3\}) = \underset{y}{\text{Max}} \left[y\phi(y) - C_2(y) \right]$$

$$v(\{2,\ 3\}) = 0$$

$$v(\{1,\ 2,\ 3\}) = \underset{x}{\text{Max}} \ \underset{y}{\text{Max}} \left[(x + y) \phi (x + y) + C_1(x) - C_2(y) \right]$$

where $p = \phi(q)$ is the final demand schedule for the product. It has been shown by Dantzig and Wolfe that for certain appropriate limitations on technology, a firm decentralized in the manner above need only send messages concerning shadow prices and outputs in order to reach a joint optimum. This is the "decomposition" principle for solving a linear program, and although it is primarily a computational device it may be viewed as an administrative arrangement[8].

The two examples given above are treated in Section 6. We turn in Section 5 to the development of the general method for imputing costs and assigning prices to satisfy incentive criteria.

Although the topic is only pursued briefly in Section 7, it should be noted that the problem to which this paper is addressed is closely related to the more general problems of organization and stability in an economy[9, 10]. This in turn is related to the role and effectiveness of group action in administrative systems[11].

5. AN INCENTIVE SYSTEM FOR DECENTRALIZED CONTROL

A corporation is characterized as a set of n decision centers. The characteristic function of a corporation reflects not only the technological features of complementarities between products, common overheads, joint costs and other technological interrelationships, but also the decision structure of the various centers.

We limit ourselves to considering only firms which should not completely liquidate. A firm should not liquidate if there is at least one subset of decision centers S which can earn as much or more than the income obtained from investing the proceeds of liquidation.

Let the set of decisions of the ith center be denoted by D_i. An individual decision is $d_i \in D_i$. In general the characteristic function is calculated for all values as follows. We define $\psi s_j(d_i, d_j, \ldots, d_m)$ as a function of s variables which represents the payoff to the firm as a whole on the assumption that a particular set of s centers denoted by S_j are active and the remainder have been dissolved.

$$v(S_j) = \max_{d_i \in D_i} , \max_{d_j \in D_j} , \ldots, \max_{d_m \in D_m} \psi s_j(d_i, d_j, \ldots, d_m)$$

In particular,

$$v(I) = \max_{d_1 \in D_1} , \max_{d_2 \in D_2} , \ldots, \max_{d_n \in D_n} \psi_I(d_1, d_2, \ldots, d_n)$$

For many large corporations with diversified businesses some of the structure of the functions ψs_j can be specified simply. For instance, if a firm sells two products which share no joint variable costs, incur no joint economies in marketing and have negligible influence on each other's markets, the function $v(S_j)$ where S_j consists of department 1 and department 2 can be written as:

$$v(S) = \max_{d_1 \in D_1} \max_{d_2 \in D_2} [\psi_1(d_1) + \psi_2(d_2) - c]$$

The only connection between the departments is a joint fixed cost.

The more obvious forms of interconnection also serve to enable us to specify the calculation for the characteristic functions without great difficulty. These include vertical integration, aspects of horizontal integration, joint variable costs, such as transportation or the use of a commonly owned computing machine. Interconnectivity in the market is also reflected in the characteristic function. For example, many consumer durables may compete with each other in the market.

The ascribing of a value to the one decision unit acting by itself, $v(\{i\})$ depends upon whether the decision system allows the manager to close his plant or production.

We assume that it is desirable not to assign negative profits to any decision center whose existence is of value to the firm as a whole. This can be achieved by using a characteristic function where for any i

$$v(\{i\}) = \max[0, \max \psi_{1_i}(d_i)]$$

This is tantamount to allowing a manager to close production or dissolve his unit if he is assigned a negative profit. If the system only assigns him a negative profit when in fact, the liquidation of his activity is for the good of the firm, this has a desirable property for a well decentralized system.

We present the five properties or *axioms* for a good assignment of the proceeds of a joint profit (and hence, implicitly the imputation of joint costs, internal prices and revenues) to different decision centers of a firm. A verbal statement of each axiom is given first, this is followed with the precise mathematical formulation.

AXIOM 1: The profit assigned to a given center depends at most upon the various revenues which can be earned by all alternative uses of all centers or combinations of centers.

Symbolically, if we use the notation ϕ_i to stand for the profit assigned to the ith center, we can write;

$$\phi_i = F(v(\theta), \ldots, v(S), \ldots, v(I))$$

where $v(S)$ is the characteristic function which portrays all complementarities inherent in the optimal use of any combination of the facilities of the firm.

AXIOM 2: The profit assigned to a center depends symmetrically upon all centers in a firm. In other words, if two firms are identical except that their departments or decision centers are called by different names, then the accounting system will assign the same profit to the centers which are physically the same despite the difference in names.

Symbolically if we let Γ stand for the game characterized by $v(S)$ and Γ' the game such that

$$v'(S) = v(S*)$$

where $S*$ is like S but with i replacing j and j replacing i, then

$$\phi_i' = \phi_j \qquad \phi_j' = \phi_i$$

AXIOM 3: The accounting system imputes all the profits earned by the firm.

$$\sum_{i \in I} \phi_i = v(I)$$

where I is the set of all decision centers.

AXIOM 4: A homogeneous expansion of fixed costs, variable costs and profits will result in a homogeneous rise in the accounting profits imputed to all processes.

$$\text{If } \Gamma' = \beta\Gamma \qquad \beta > 0 \qquad \text{then } \phi' = \beta\phi$$

For example, if the currency unit were changed so that one new franc is worth one hundred old, the new profit assignment ϕ' if measured in francs is such that $\phi' = \frac{1}{100}\phi$.

The fifth axiom envisions a strange situation which might arise if two independent firms jointly share a facility. For instance suppose that each rents a certain plant and each have managers to run it, one for the day shift and the other for a night shift! Furthermore, let us imagine that neither firm has any use for more than one shift from the facility they both rent. If we were confronted with the strange arrangement then:

AXIOM 5: If two independent firms are considered as a unit, the profit imputed to the operations utilizing this facility will be the sum of the profits that each firm imputes to its own operation which utilizes the facility separately. The profits imputed to any department or decision center which is not jointly used by each of the firms will not be changed by the consideration of both firms as a unit.

If Γ consists of the game obtained by considering the games Γ' and Γ'' together, then:

$$\phi_i = \begin{cases} \phi_i' + \phi_i'' & \text{for } i \epsilon I'\Omega I'' \\ \phi_i' & \text{for } i \epsilon I - I'' \\ \phi_i'' & \text{for } i \epsilon I - I' \end{cases}$$

The proof that these five axioms lead to a unique formula based on the characteristic function is given by L. S. Shapley.[4] We will not be concerned with this mathematical problem here, but rather with the interpretation of the result. The formula is:

$$\phi_i = \frac{1}{n!} \sum_s (s-1)!\,(n-s)!\,[v(S) - v(S - \{i\})] \tag{1}$$

where $i \epsilon S$. It assigns a share of the joint profits to each center (and hence automatically imputes joint costs). The rationale behind the

[4] The axioms used in this paper are an earlier formation by Shapley in a RAND paper RM-670 which are equivalent to those used in his latter publication. See R. D. Luce and H. Raiffa, *Games and Decisions*, New York: Wiley, pp. 246-250, 1957, for a lucid mathematical description.

formula can be seen in terms of addition to productivity. The addition
to profits caused by a center acting jointly under all possible conditions with the other centers (i.e., every possible arrangement with
some shut down and other operating) is evaluated and an average is
taken.

The economist will recognize that this amounts to assigning a profit
to each center according to its expected marginal or incremental
value productivity. This can be seen immediately by examining the
terms in (1). First,

$$[v(S) - v(S - \{i\})]$$

is simply the contribution which department i makes to a coalition S
if it is a member of S. Second, the term

$$(s - 1)! \ (n - s)!$$

is the number of orderings of the remaining departments of S and
$I - S$, where the latter is the set of all departments of the firm excluding S. n! is the total number of permutations of all members of I.

We now show that the method of imputation obtained by using the
Shapley Value defined in (1) upon the characteristic function of the firm
has desirable incentive properties.

THEOREM 1: The profit assigned to a Department which should be
in operation if resources are efficiently allocated by the firm will
never be less than $v(\{i\})$ for the ith Department.

This is trivially proved. In the formula given in (1) the sign of θ_i
depends upon the terms $[v(S) - v(S - \{i\})]$, but as the characteristic
function is super-additive all terms are at least as large as
$[v(\{i\}) - v(\theta)] = v(\{i\})$. This completes the proof.

THEOREM 2: An increase in efficiency or flexibility (see example
3, section 6 for a definition of flexibility) or any action taken by a center which is of value to the firm as a whole will never cause the profits assigned to that center to fall.

This is easily demonstrated. If the game Γ is defined by $v(S)$ and
the new game is defined by $v'(S)$ where $v(S) = v'(S)$ for all S not containing i, $v(S) \leq v'(S)$ for all S containing i, then for all S:

$$[v'(S) - v'(S - \{i\})] = [v'(S) - v(S - \{i\})] \geq [v(S) - v(S - \{i\})]$$

This completes the proof.

6. SOME EXAMPLES CALCULATED AND INTERPRETED

Example 1. Common Fixed Overhead

As a first example we take the first case presented in Section 4; consider a factory that produces two products which use all the same facilities with the same intensity. Each product is under an independent manager. Each process takes up one half of the factory floor space, railyard, etc. The same number of man hours are used on each production method. An apparently natural way to assign joint fixed and variable costs between the two decision centers is to charge one half of the costs to each as they all utilize one half of the resources of the factory. If we assume that the costs of the raw materials are the same for the products, then all the cost accounting methods noted would assign overhead equally. The characteristic function for this example is given below:

$$v(\{\theta\}) = 0$$

$$v(\{1\}) = v(\{2\}) = v(\{3\}) = 0$$

$$v(\{1, 2\}) = \text{Max}\,((x - c, 0)) \qquad v(\{1, 3\}) = \text{Max}\,((y - c, 0))$$

$$v(\{2, 3\}) = 0 \qquad v(\{1, 2, 3\}) = x + y - c$$

If $x + y > c$ then the firm runs at a profit. Suppose, however, that $x < c/2$. Standard accounting in this instance would compute the overhead evenly, giving $\theta_2 = x - c/2 < 0$, $\phi_3 = y - c/2$.

The first manager would be motivated to close down. To be fanciful let us suppose that this firm were highly decentralized in communication, that $c/2 < y < c$ and that there is no alternative use for the closed plant. On the next assignment, all the costs will be put on the second manager (who, after all, is using the plant himself). This gives $\phi_3 = y - c < 0$, hence he is motivated to close down even though the plant as a whole with the two products could make a profit.

Applying the Shapley value we obtain:

$$\phi_i = \frac{1}{3!}\left[(2!)(1!)(v(\{i\}) - v(\theta)) + (v(\{i, j\}) - v(\{j\})) + (v(\{i, k\}) \right.$$

$$\left. - v(\{k\})) + (1!)(2!)(v(\{i, j, k\}) - v(\{j, k\}))\right]$$

which gives

$$\phi_1 = \tfrac{1}{6}\left[2(0) + 2(x + y - c)\right]$$

$$= \tfrac{1}{3}(x + y - c)$$

$$\phi_2 = \tfrac{1}{6}[2(0) + 2(x + y - c)]$$

$$= \tfrac{1}{3}(x + y - c)$$

$$\phi_3 = \tfrac{1}{3}(x + y - c)$$

Suppose $c = 10$, $x = 4$, $y = 7$. This gives $\phi_1 = \phi_2 = \phi_3 = \tfrac{1}{3}$ thus the assessments are $3\tfrac{2}{3}$ and $6\tfrac{2}{3}$ respectively.

If the values had been $y > x > c$ then we would have had

$$\phi_1 = \frac{3x + 3y - 4c}{6} \qquad \phi_2 = \frac{3x - c}{6} \qquad \text{and} \qquad \phi_3 = \frac{3y - c}{6}$$

For $c = 10$, $x = 16$, $y = 17$ this gives $\phi_1 = \tfrac{59}{6}$, $\phi_2 = \tfrac{38}{6}$, $\phi_3 = \tfrac{41}{6}$ giving assessments of $\tfrac{58}{6}$ and $\tfrac{61}{6}$. In both instances the two operating departments are assessed more than the total overhead. They pay a levy to the central office, but their net revenues are always positive. The central office requires only one number from each of them, their net profit before assessment.

Example 2. Common Marketing and Technological Improvement

In the second example in Section 4 we considered a centralized sales operation with two decentralized factories. We will modify the example to a trivially simple linear program which will nevertheless be useful in demonstrating the appropriate decentralization properties.

Suppose the sales operation handles two products, 1 and 2, and the market will buy up to 10 units of each at prices π_1 and π_2. Both factories produce both items. Factory 1 has technology coefficients α_1 and α_2 (both less than π_1 and π_2 respectively). Factory 2 has technology coefficients β_1, $\pi_1 > \beta_1 > \alpha_1$ and $\beta_2 < \alpha_2$. There is some limit larger than 10 on their productions.

$$v(\{\theta\}) = 0$$

$$v(\{1\}) = v(\{2\}) = v(\{3\}) = 0$$

$$v(\{1, 2\}) = 10\pi_1 + 10\pi_2 - 10\alpha_1 - 10\alpha_2$$

$$v(\{1, 3\}) = 10(\pi_1 + \pi_2 - \beta_1 - \beta_2)$$

$$v(\{2, 3\}) = 0$$

$$v(\{1, 2, 3\}) = 10(\pi_1 + \pi_2 - \alpha_1 - \beta_2)$$

Suppose that the marketing board sends out shadow prices p_1 and p_2 and gets back information on production possibilities. By merely solving three local linear programs production will be optimally allocated. In particular the prices $p_1 = \alpha_1$ and $p_2 = \beta_2$ will satisfy. They cause the correct specialization and give the market operation a profit of $10(\pi_1 + \pi_2 - \alpha_1 - \beta_2)$ and the others obtain profits of zero.

Suppose there is a potential shift in technology which can be installed by the manager of the first plant. It replaces α_1 by $\alpha'_1 \ll \alpha_1$. If he puts this in, then in the optimum production search via shadow-pricing, the prices $p_1 = \alpha'_1$ and $p_2 = \beta_2$ will serve to allocate production. The accounting profits of the first plant are still zero. Is there a measure which will more or less automatically reflect the worth of the action of the first manager? Calculating the set of values we obtain:

$$\phi_1 = \tfrac{10}{6}\left[(\pi_1 + \pi_2 - \alpha_1 - \alpha_2) + (\pi_1 + \pi_2 - \beta_1 - \beta_2) + 2(\pi_1 + \pi_2 - \alpha_1 - \beta_2)\right]$$

$$= \tfrac{10}{6}\left[4\pi_1 + 4\pi_2 - 3\alpha_1 - 3\beta_2 - \alpha_2 - \beta_1\right]$$

$$\phi_2 = \tfrac{10}{6}\left[(\pi_1 + \pi_2 - \alpha_1 - \alpha_2) + 2(\beta_1 + \beta_2 - \alpha_1 - \beta_2)\right]$$

$$= \tfrac{10}{6}\left[\pi_1 + \pi_2 - 3\alpha_1 + 2\beta_1 - \alpha_2\right]$$

$$\phi_3 = \tfrac{10}{6}\left[(\pi_1 + \pi_2 - \beta_1 - \beta_2) + 2(\alpha_1 + \alpha_2 - \alpha_1 - \beta_2)\right]$$

$$= \tfrac{10}{6}\left[\pi_1 + \pi_2 - 3\beta_2 + 2\alpha_2 - \beta_1\right]$$

We observe that if α_1 is replaced by $\alpha'_1 \ll \alpha_1$, both ϕ_1 and ϕ_2 rise in value. There is an extra information cost implicit in this method however, inasmuch as extra computations were needed to obtain the value of subsets such as $v(\{1, 2\})$.

The ϕ_i can be used to calculate shadow prices or awards which are both consistent with the optimal production under current technology and provide an incentive for improvement. It should be noted that throughout this paper the discussion switches from costs to prices and profit allocations. If information and computation were free and all men had the same goal there would be no need to allocate many joint costs or revenues. It is suggested here that allocation, whether involving costs or revenues, is part of the same problem which is the utilization of these imputations for the appropriate incentives in a decentralized decision system.

Example 3. Incentives for Flexibility

Suppose a firm has two identical departments. One say, produces pink refrigerators, the other white ones. Let us furthermore suppose that they each have the same costs and face identical inelastic markets and each can more than cover total overheads. Thus:

$$v(\{\theta\}) = v(\{1\}) = v(\{2\}) = v(\{3\}) = 0$$

$$v(\{1, 2\}) = v(\{1, 3\}) = x - c$$

$$v(\{2, 3\}) = 0$$

$$v(\{1, 2, 3\}) = 2x - c$$

As everything is symmetric for the two departments we expect and find that the imputation to both centers is the same. Suppose that there were a probability p that demand for both products would decrease, leaving both with excess capacity. Thus expected revenues are down symmetrically. Suppose, however, that new product entry has been decentralized; if one of the departments has a business plan ready to utilize the expected excess capacity while the other does not, the general managers know that the imputation scheme will acknowledge this immediately any change in state occurs.

Example 4. Cost-Plus Internal Pricing

Under some methods of dividing joint profit an improvement instigated by one operation may not only improve its own profit imputation but can actually have an adverse effect. An example is provided by "cost plus" pricing in a vertically integrated organization. Suppose there is a sales office and a factory. The factory produces a product not produced elsewhere, hence there is no "lowest priced alternative supply" method for establishing a price. A common practice is to use

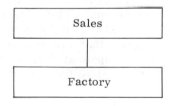

Exhibit 11-3

a cost plus formula. Suppose the sales office faces an inelastic demand for its product, hence at any (sufficiently low price) it will buy the same number from the factory. Say its selling price is π and that it has a fabricating, packaging or selling cost of k per unit. The cost at the factory is c per unit. The markup is $(1 + \theta)$. Then if q units are sold

$$P_1 = (\pi - k - c(1 + \theta))q$$
$$P_2 = c\theta q.$$

Now suppose that the factory has a technological breakthrough which halves costs $c' = c/2$, the new imputation is:

$$P_1 = \left(\pi - k - \frac{c}{2}(1 + \theta)\right) q$$

$$P_2 = \frac{c\theta q}{2}.$$

The innovator is penalized for his action. A manager whose bonus depends on the ''profits'' of his department might think twice before acting here.

$$v(\{\theta\}) = v(\{1\}) = v(\{2\}) = 0$$

$$v(\{1, 2\}) = (\pi - k - c)q$$

$$\theta_1 = \theta_2 = \frac{(\pi - k - c)_q}{2}$$

Any improvement by either is shared in this scheme.

Example 5. Inferior Goods

The next two examples envisage relatively complex relations between the components of the firm. If such relations exist they have to be known and their effects on profits coordinated for optimum behavior of the firm.

Consider a firm with three centers which produce and market, and with a headquarters whose expenses vary directly as the volume of business. Suppose that the first two sell products to the third, say potatoes, rice and meat. Suppose that a drop in the price of either of the first two will be more than compensated by the rise in revenues from the third. The initial characteristic function could be as follows:

$$v(\{\theta\}) = v(\{i\}) = 0 \qquad i = 1, \ldots, 4$$

$$v(\{1, 2\}) = R_2 - C(q_2),$$

$$v(\{1, 3\}) = R_3 - C(q_3) \qquad v(\{1, 4\}) = R_4 - C(q_4)$$

$$v(\{1, 2, 3\}) = R_2 + R_3 - C(q_2 + q_3)$$

$$v(\{1, 2, 4\}) = R_2 + R_4 - C(q_2 + q_4)$$

$$v(\{1, 3, 4\}) = R_3 + R_4 - C(q_3 + q_4)$$

$$v(\{1, 2, 3, 4\}) = R_2 + R_3 + R_4 - C(q_2 + q_3 + q_4)$$

All other coalitions not noted have a value of zero.

Suppose that there is an important improvement in the technology for producing potatoes. If the manager of the potato board is in control of both technology and pricing he has a choice. He can introduce the efficiency and maintain his price. This replaces R_2 by $\tilde{R}_2$ where $\tilde{R}_2 > R_2$ and all other costs, levels of production and revenues remain the same. We can see from the calculation of the ϕ_i below that this is of benefit to the manager. He also can reduce the price of his product. This will reduce his individual net revenue vis-a-vis the market, however, *if* the executive office is able to gauge the overall effect of his action his assessment will be such that this will constitute his most profitable course. In a decentralized system we can imagine that, at least as a first approximation, he can send a message stating that unless his minimal estimates of his effect on the values of the characteristic function are regarded as reasonable, he will merely maintain his price.

If there are strange complementarities or complex relationships between departments which are present, then it is reasonable to suspect that at least those most concerned will attempt to evaluate them. In general, such an attempt is not going to call for the reevaluation of $2^n - 1$ values for coalitions, but for observations on a very limited number.

$$\phi_i = \frac{1}{4!}[(0)!(3)!(v(4) - v(4 - \{2\})) + (1)!(2)!(v(\{i, j, k\}) - v(\{j, k\}))$$
$$+ (1)!(2)!(v(\{i, j, \ell\}) - v(\{j, \ell\})) + (1)!(2)!(v(\{i, k, \ell\} - v(\{k, \ell\}))$$
$$+ (2)!(1)!(v(\{i, j\}) - v(\{j\})) + (2)!(1)!(v(\{i, k\}) - v(\{k\})$$
$$+ (2)!(1)!(v(\{i, \ell\}) - v(\{\ell\})) + (0)!(3)!(v(\{i\}) - v(\{\theta\}))]$$

$$\phi_1 = \frac{1}{24}[6(R_2 + R_3 + R_4) - C(q_2 + q_3 + q_4)) + 2(R_2 + R_3 - C(q_2 + q_3))$$
$$+ 2(R_2 + R_4 - C(q_2 + q_4)) + 2(R_3 + R_4 - C(q_3 + q_4))$$
$$+ 2(R_2 - C(q_2)) + 2(R_3 - C(q_3)) + 2(R_4 - C(q_4))]$$

In this example we will assume that $C(\sum_i q_i) = \sum_i q_i$, hence:

$$\phi_1 = \tfrac{1}{2}(R_2 + R_3 + R_4 - (q_2 + q_3 + q_4))$$

$$\phi_2 = \tfrac{1}{2}(R_2 - q_2), \qquad \phi_3 = \tfrac{1}{2}(R_3 - q_3), \qquad \phi_4 = \tfrac{1}{2}(R_4 - q_4)$$

Suppose the manager does not change price, then the values become:

$$\phi_1 = \tfrac{1}{2}(\tilde{R}_2 + R_3 + R_4 - (q_2 + q_3 + q_4))$$

$$\phi_2 = \tfrac{1}{2}(\tilde{R}_2 - q_2), \qquad \phi_3 = \tfrac{1}{2}(R_3 - q_3), \qquad \phi_4 = \tfrac{1}{2}(R_4 - q_4)$$

Now we consider the case where he cuts price. This changes his revenue by ΔR_2. Suppose it has no effect on player 3 but sends up the revenue of 4 by ΔR_4 (where $|\Delta R_4| > |\Delta R_2|$). Furthermore we assume that the output of player 2 is reduced by Δq_2 and the output of player 4 is raised by Δq_4; these affect costs. The new value for ϕ_2 is given by:

$$\phi_2 = \tfrac{1}{2}(R_2 - q_2) + \tfrac{1}{24}[8(\Delta R_4 - \Delta R_2) + 8(\Delta q_2 - \Delta q_4) + 4(\tilde{R}_2 - R_2)]$$

The first term in the square bracket represents the effect of the overall changes in revenue upon the imputation to the second manager. The second term (which is negative here) measures the change in the structure of joint costs; and the third term takes account of the value of improvement even under conditions of absence of the fourth player (in which case price should not be cut and the second player would take in a revenue of $\tilde{R}_2$).

An example for which a price cut is marginally better is given. Suppose:

$$R_2 = 10 \qquad q_2 = 4 \qquad R_2 = 15 \qquad \Delta R_2 = 5$$

$$\Delta q_2 = 1 \qquad \Delta q_4 = 2 \qquad \Delta R_4 = 12$$

Initially $\phi_2 = \tfrac{1}{2}(10 - 4) = 3$.
If he puts in his improvement but does not cut price

$$\phi_2 = \tfrac{1}{2}(15 - 4) = 5\tfrac{1}{2}$$

If he cuts price:

$$\phi_2 = 3 + \tfrac{1}{24}[8(7) + 8(-1) + 4(5)] = 5\tfrac{5}{6}$$

In the three instances the overall profits to the firm are respectively $v(\{1, 2, 3, 4\})$, $v(\{1, 2, 3, 4\}) + 5$ and $v(\{1, 2, 3, 4\}) + 6$.

The ϕ_i represent the final allotments, hence the actual assessments are obtained by subtracting the net revenues collected by each decision center from the ϕ_i.

6. FURTHER COMMENTS AND CONCLUSIONS

Although the properties of this method for the imputation of revenues have been discussed, no examination of problems of enforcement or calculation has been made. Unfortunately, it is not fool proof against distortions of information. It may pay individuals to lie about the values of the characteristic function unless there is some method to check their estimates and a penalty for falsification.

In general, 2^n values must be calculated for the characteristic function of an organization with n separate decision centers. Usually there are considerable simplifications. Thus, for example, if the only joint cost or revenue is a common overhead, only n + 1 numbers are needed, the net revenue of each center and the overhead.

This paper has stressed the role of the allocation of joint costs within the firm. However, the basic general problem is that of methods for decentralized control. There are three solution concepts to n-person games viewed as economic processes which are relevant to different levels of this problem. They are (1) the competitive equilibrium, (2) the core, and (3) the Shapley value. If the structure of the economy is sufficiently regular, all three types of solution exist. Furthermore, dynamic schemes involving only the changes in prices and individual adjustments of excess demand and supply may be sufficient to bring about the appropriate allocation of resources. It is not necessary to examine the fine structure of all coalitions.

When features such as external economies or diseconomies appear, the competitive equilibrium may no longer exist, although both the core and the Shapley value continue to do so. The core makes use of some, but, in general, not all of the fine structure of the coalitions; roughly speaking, its existence and size depends upon the "fatness" of a subset of the coalitions, that is, how much more on the average members of certain coalitions can obtain than their average share when acting as members of a coalition of the whole.

Both the competitive equilibrium (which always lies in the core) and the core have a "fairness" property inasmuch as any division of proceeds within the core cannot be effectively challenged by any group.

There exist many games which possess neither competitive equilibria nor a core, but all will have a Shapley value. This solution makes use of all of the fine structure of the coalitions. All power blocks, potential and actual, are weighted in the computation. Special use is made of symmetry and "fairness" to do this. However, the result no longer necessarily has the property that groups could not obtain more than their assigned share by the independent pursuit of their own profit. In particular, this means that independent uncoordinated optimization schemes may be inconsistent.

BIBLIOGRAPHY

1. Lang, T., W. B. McFarland, and M. Schiff: *Cost Accounting*, New York: Ronald, 1953.
2. Brummet, R. L.: *Overhead Costing*, Ann Arbor, Mich.: The University of Michigan Press, 1957.
3. Shapley, L. S.: "The Value of an N-Person Game," in H. W. Kuhn and A. W. Tucker (eds.), *Contributions to the Theory of Games*; vol. 2, Princeton: Princeton University Press, pp. 307-317, 1953.

4. von Neumann, J., and O. Morgenstern: *Theory of Games and Economic Behavior*, 3d ed, Princeton: Princeton University Press, 1953.
5. Argyris, C.: "The Individual and Organization; Some Problems of Mutual Adjustment," *Administrative Science Quarterly*, June, 1957.
6. "Report of the Committee on Cost Concepts and Standards," *The Accounting Review*, p. 175, April, 1952.
7. Marschak, J., and R. Radner: "Economic Theory of Teams," Cowles Foundation Discussion Paper No. 59, 1958.
8. Dantzig, G. B., and P. Wolfe; "Decomposition Principle for Linear Programs," *Operations Research*, vol. 8, no. 1, pp. 101–111, 1960.
9. Arrow, K. J., and Gerard Debreu: "Existence of an Equilibrium for a Competitive Economy," *Econometrica*, vol. 22, pp. 265–290, 1954.
10. ——— and L. Hurwicz: "On the Stability of Competitive Equilibrium," *Econometrica*, vol. 26, pp. 522–552, 1958
11. Shubik, M.: "Extended Edgeworth Bargaining Games and Competitive Equilibrium," Cowles Foundation Discussion Paper No. 107, 1961.

Discussion

THE BUDGETARY PROCESS AND MANAGEMENT CONTROL

HECTOR R. ANTON

University of California at Berkeley

In a large sense the four papers included in this section of the seminar are representative of the acute dilemma faced by researchers in the area of management control. The dilemma is posed by the need to construct *general* systems of control which are rich enough to offer "practical" extensions and applications, but these in turn are imprecise and indeterminate as testable models. On the other hand there is a plethora of pieces of systems that are formulated as simple models (these often also suffer from interdependencies or indeterminacies) which at best offer rigorous tests of an insufficient or trivial nature. Nonetheless, these simpler models, both of abstract general systems and of parts of general systems, need to be formulated with the hope of eventually being able to form rich and rigorous general systems. A synthesis of the former is required, but unfortunately, even when the parts are undertaken as parts of "coordinated" group research, too often they are non-compatible or non-consistent with each other. Compatability, if not consistency, is the required base for adaptability of partial systems into more general ones.

Gordon Shillinglaw's paper, "Divisional Performance Review: An Extension of Budgetary Control" is, within the confines of the assigned section the closest approach to an over-all systemic view. As such he poses the problems at large: The objectives of decentralization, the role of budgetary control, and the application of such control to decentralized divisions. The very reasons he sets forth as underlying the *cause* of corporate decentralization (complexity of operations) and the problems engendered in centralized organizations support the need for generality, as indeed does the purported strength of decentralization—that the profit center will refocus the problems within narrower (and presumably easier to control) confines. Unfortunately, as he well points out, this device raises another set of problems which on their own restore complex decision problems, namely, how to grant divisional authority without sacrificing top-management control. (Shubik addresses himself to this problem in part.) Shillinglaw's solutions, admirable as they are, are but general guide-lines resulting, ultimately, in a "need for personal unprogrammed intervention to translate the identified deviations into effective action". The point is, to be redundant, that not much is offered except another list telling us what has to be done without giving criteria for selection and implementation. For example, "2. Decide what index will best measure each critical aspect of performance." is a perfectly good dictum, but it begs the question of which index to use or whether an "index" or some other measure is pertinent (Wagner concerns himself with the validity of index control); "best measure" assumes some *a priori* value consideration of "best", and at the same time permits manipulation (unspecified) by assignments of weight to the index; "critical aspect" assumes that the problem of determing (both quantitatively and qualitatively) what the aspects *are* has been resolved, which are critical, and so forth.

Nevertheless, this type of exposition, and the one being discussed here in particular is a relatively good one, seems to have the better carryover into practice in almost all situations except those with relatively narrow constraints. Perhaps with the present tools we should not be overly ambitious—but this is a seminar on basic research.

Of course, Shillinglaw offers pertinent and incisive observations, and he suggests many areas that need to be researched. For example, he directs attention to other aspects and objectives beyond the simple concentration on inputs for decision-making in the decentralization process. That major attention has been focused on the problem of sub-optimization consistent with over-all company goals is apparent even by a cursory inspection of the literature. Major research in other areas has been sparse.

His parenthetic remark on the *follow-up* of feedback comparisons, which even according to Shillinglaw, "needs no elaboration" suggests an entire near-virgin area of control research. Albert Danielsson of the Stockholm School of Economics is working precisely on models of budgetary planning, adaption, replanning and the continuing cycle. This process, itself, is little understood.

The point of differentiating between activity performance and the performance of its executives or supervisors is certainly well taken. As is amply illustrated in the last section, this problem is by no means solved. The dilemma is further posed by Shillinglaw's attempt to overcome this through "internal standards, adapted to management's own expectations as to the external and internal environment". The internal standard apparently is an attempt to have the supervisors suggest reasonable activity levels for which they can be held accountable. (As Charnes and Stedry point out this may also increase perceived reward due to personal satisfaction with goal attainment.) But as Shillinglaw points out, deviations from such standards may be due to deficiencies in control (for which presumably supervisors may be held accountable), but also to failures in the environment. A *review* of performance, may be aided by an adjusted profit (as suggested to

take care of environment changes), but certainly this is no aid to
control, and further, it shifts the problem of performance evaluation
to another plane—the determination of the "adjustments" for the adjusted budgeted profit—which in their turn have "little relevance to
control by feedback response".

Shillinglaw's comments on transfer prices properly belong in the
first session of this seminar, but serve to strengthen the underlying
assumption that the present state of the accounting art is incapable
of handling sophisticated data requirements for transfer pricing
models. His examples of the use of "artificially constructed" transfer prices when market prices are not available again raises the
question as to who constructs the prices, and the value criteria for
their construction and use. Similarly, his remarks on the response
of managers to variations in transfer price are quite well-taken.
Managers do seem to argue diligently on absolute levels (as even
college administrators know), and undoubtedly there are unconscious
biases in the reward structure. It is a fiction, however, to assume
or theorize that if budgeted and actual transfer prices are equal that
a motivationally neutral level will result.

Concluding, Shillinglaw repeats his basic contention that control
in decentralized operations is essentially no different from control
of subsegments within either a centralized or decentralized division.
This contention appears to have universal validity as most recently
expressed for ever supra-central "firms" such as the Russian economy. (See for example, R. W. Campbell, *Accounting in Soviet Planning and Management*, especially chap. 2.)

The other three papers in this section are more explicitly concerned with the implementation of control by some top-management
(or centralized) level over lower management operations. All three
use the notion of achieving company-wide objectives by means of encouraging or rewarding subordinates through furthering the subordinates' objectives although all three differ in their assumptions as to
how subordinate objectives are to be set or their achievement rewarded.

Harvey Wagner in his paper, "Budgetary Control in Inventory
Systems" attacks the basic problems of implementation directly. In
a sense, he raises the same general issues raised above, but attempts
to give more precise and unique answers. Namely, he questions
"whether a decision mechanism predicated on proposed OR model is
consistent within the millieu of an existent management control system". Wagner attacks the problem within the confines of inventory
control. His model, essentially, has top-management setting goals and
relying for control on indicies, such as aggregate holding costs, to
supplement single-item control by lower management. In a real sense,
Wagner is asking whether policies formulated on a different basis—or
with essentially dissimilar objectives—can be superimposed on lower

management, and be effectively controlled by lower management with a sub-control system predicated on differing objectives. Then *if* operating personnel do not observe the inventory policies fully, can a control scheme be devised that will test compliance without detailed examination of individual records. Intuitively one would have to say no to the former and perhaps to the latter, and essentially Wagner's findings substantiate this. The former is predicated on the concept of management by rule, the latter by the well-known management by exception concept.

Wagner lays out a concise framework for evaluating control systems (Sec. 1.4, p. 169) that poses the significant problems to be considered in the choice of a control system and its implementation. Again, most of the implementation dicta here rely on external (to the list) value judgments. Since he specifically disclaims any discourse on the normative issues involved, suffice it to say that he has shown an acute awareness of the problems involved.

Wagner has developed criteria for testing his inventory model (or similar models) in terms of consistency between the standards set and lower managements' observance of the rules. Thus, a strongly consistent control scheme is one which positively encourages the exact fulfilment of the standards (Cf. Shubik's incentives discussion), and weakly consistent if it does not encourage a violation of the standard. Deviations from the rules are inconsistent actions and may result at only some periods, or period after period. If of the latter type the action may be due for a variety of reasons including the special case where lower management adheres to a rule, but the rule is not the same as that set forth from top management. These schemes are used to determine whether the system possibly misdirects operating personnel.

In the main, his analysis leads him to the conclusion that all commonly used aggregate control schemes are inconsistent, and that it may be impossible as well as undesirable to impose a strongly consistent control device due to costs, sensitivity, and other factors. However, Wagner stresses the practical validity of using index or aggregate controls due to predictive requirements, board of directors' restrictions on management control, and so forth.

Attention is focused on two generic types of control schemes, barometer control and quota control, and while the distinction is valid, it must be noted that most real control systems are a combination of both. Barometer control by which process lower management is rewarded (positively or negatively) for deviations from a preset index are typical of most sophisticated incentive systems. Quota control can be considered a special constraint on the barometer. In the barometer control situation lower management's objective within the reward system is assumed to optimize the expected value of the deviation between the index and the target value, or actually the ex-

pected value of the index number itself. Barometer control implies
that a sharing of the savings due to deviation control will result in
achievement of the desired objective. This means for control purposes a real ability to distinguish between the operator and the operation (Cf. Shillinglaw), or else a further assumption as to the *a
priori* distribution of the predicted index. It also implies that the
generality of the index be such as to preclude attempts "to beat the
system" by using inconsistent (type 3) rules. This last point again
shows how critical is the *choice* of any index as the sole measure of
control.

With respect to quota control, the key to management by exception,
Wagner uses the consistency scheme to pose anew the questions
raised above. Again he concludes that inconsistency is a price that
must be paid whenever aggregate controls are instituted, but that this
must be matched against the price of having no control—and that ultimately the merit of approving one control scheme versus another
(including no control) can only be provided by evaluating one device
relative to the other. Perhaps then Wagner's evaluation system is
the more important contribution.

Specific points of interest that seem relevant for extensive study
include the "chain" of similar control schemes from upper echelons
to lower. If control is exercised as in Wagner's example (p. 165) by
aggregate indices from the Board of Directors on a vice-president
(top-management), who then may find it essential to devise control
schemes to reflect analogous restriction on other echelons, a com-
pounding effect of the limitations discovered above will result. It is
not intuitively clear what such a chain would mean for the control
system in general. In addition, the necessary and sufficient conditions for the aggregative process in computing any control index are
considerably complicated.

Wagner's admonitions relative to fragmentary indices, of course,
reinforce the difficulties in using indices for multiple goal purposes
(Cf. Balderston's "Optimal and Feasible Choice in Organizations
Having Multiple Goals", U. C. Center for Management Science, Work
Paper #12). In the example cited, Wagner's lower management is
taking advantage of *dominant* goals where apparently an optimal multiple-goal situation is not feasible. This may, in fact, be more generally consistent (in the technical sense) with top-management's objectives that is reflected by Wagnerian inconsistency.

Charnes and Stedry in their paper take up the problem of multiple
goals in contradistinction to a single goal—say for example, "unconstrained profit maximization". While conceding that short-run
models may be able to use a single goal subject to certain constraints
they indicate that due to uncertainty (or sometimes cost) even in these
models the constraints lead to other goals which relate to performance levels, and thus to short-run multiple goal situations.

However, they are more interested in a new class of models whose properties relate specifically to the allocation of resources so as to satisfy goal attainment motivations. In these models they take as given that the ruling coalition (peak coordinator) constructs a set of goals that may be internal aspiration levels, or imposed by superiors, the market, or the social environment. In passing they make a forceful argument against treating these classes of goals essentially differently in behavioral models. They do admit that goal setting participation *may* increase personal satisfaction in goal attainment, and thus raise the level of perceived rewards. However, research in this area has given conflicting results in the past, and they are on sound ground in ignoring its effects.

Charnes and Stedry depict a stochastic representation of goal attainment as a function of *search* effort which incorporates a limiting probability of goal attainment as effort gets large. This explicit recognition of random noise in the system is consistent with search effort criteria. The assumed probability function has obvious advantages and the authors make a good case for not introducing greater complexity due to human inability to perceive subtle refinements (Cf. Wagner on the lack of necessity for controlling "mild violations"), and even when greater complexity is required for practical budgetary problems the difficulties in estimating probability functions from real data would seem to render greater complexity superfluous. The simple model given assumes independence of goals which is difficult. In the case given there seems to be a strong dependency.

In the set of models that the authors postulate they postulate search effort allocation for optimal reward. While recognizing that search effort may be difficult to measure they point out that the measurement of time allocation to non-repetitive tasks is an unsolved problem, while it may be possible in developing a theory of rational effort allocation to partially solve this problem through imputations from the performance (Cf. Shubik).

Charnes and Stedry's three models are based on short-run maximization of expected reward subject to an effort constraint, on optimal reward subject to risk constraint, and the last on a constraint on the risk of unacceptable performance. The first model (with search effort being limited) gives a quantity which is a product of the reward for attainment, the proportionality constant for return to effort (diminishing returns), and the limiting value for possible probability gain—basically an overall measure of potential gain for effort allocated to the 'jth' area. If the maxima criteria is to govern, it is intuitively clear than an ordering system is required—and once so ordered the activities will be used until some margin is achieved. At this "margin", either due to low reward or to its requiring a tremendous amount of effort for a reasonable probability of attainment, it is decided either to ignore or postpone the activity. If we equate either of these with some notion of cost, it is apparently the same as the economic solution. A *path* for accomplishing the dynamics, however, is provided here. It must be pointed out that ordering systems or systems of absolute priorities are difficult to set up on an *a priori* basis.

Further, we are still (accounting-wise) unable to account satisfactorily for such things as cost of failure, cost of loss of sales, stocks out, etc. In these cases working back from levels of permissible risks gives added advantages to these models, since optimal rewards can thus be derived. Charnes and Stedry suggest several examples as well as indicate a proof of this. Finally, they discuss the case where risk of unacceptable performance is a constraint, "acceptable performance being defined as the simultaneous attainment in several areas of a minimal performance". These minimal performances may be considered as standards. (Cf. Wagner's quota control.)

The three models, and the general framework in which the models are postulated lend interesting hypothesis for systematic empirical testing. Simulations or games may also be appropriate devices for these purposes. The Churchill-Cooper auditing study reported in another section of this volume appears to be amenable as a testing device also.

Martin Shubik has tackled a problem which is age-old in accounting circles. He is quite right in stating that, "Information which is portrayed and set out with one purpose in mind may be worse than useless when used for another purpose." He should follow his own advice! Shubik's presentation relies heavily on the theory of cooperative games and thus in a measure to interrelations between cooperative segments of a company and to the increase in joint rewards obtained by the cooperators. The profitability (used as an index measure of control) is then viewed as depending upon the sum of the joint rewards which can be obtained by the optimum coordination of all branches. All players (branches, segments, etc.) thus act in a manner to jointly maximize profits, and then use their bargaining power as represented by possible coalition to arrive at imputations of the proceeds. Shubik then proceeds to use the Shapley method for the unique division. In this way he attempts to show the properties that an accounting system should have "if decentralized decisions are to be based upon the internal imputations of profit to semi-autonomous sections of an organization".

It should be noted that he has explicitly set forth an ethical premise on the reward system to attain the players' own aims in the organization, and implicitly assumes that individuals will then act on the reward system to attain their own ends—and the organizations'. Without further belaboring the point here, this is not necessarily so (see the example of college professors, and Mason Haire's comments below). Although Shubik takes refuge in other incentives "being given", he does talk about the reward system in the general discussion of joint cost, and points out quite correctly that one of the roles of accounting is to help management with cost information necessary to business decisions *and related policy*. While admittedly ignoring "many important and vexations accounting problems", Shubik then proceeds to state that joint costs are often assigned in such a way that it makes "paper profits" negative even though a department or branch may be a vital and efficient part of the firm.

Later he sets up a straw man to prove this point (see his section 6) postulating a firm with two departments using the same facilities with equal intensity, and equal work forces, etc. If joint overhead costs are less than total revenues ($x + y > c$), then the firm runs at a profit. However, reasons Shubik, if $x < c/2$ (since *"all* cost accounting methods noted would assign overhead equally") then manager #1 would be motivated to close down; and manager #2 on the next assignment of cost, even though $y > c/2$, would close down since $y < c$, and *all* costs would be assigned to y. Shubik then applies the Shapley value and "proves" that both departments would continue to operate using this method of cost assignment.

Before proceeding to a discussion of his remarks and his example, a short digression on Shubik's use of joint cost is in order. In an economic sense a joint cost would be defined such that given an input (c) with any given facility (K) two or more products (outputs) would result, say b_1 and b_2; the conditions being such that an increment in c would result in an increment in both b_1 and b_2, and a decrease in c would result in a decrease in both outputs. We may define this as true joint cost. A joint cost may or may not be fixed, in and of itself, and the product output may be in fixed or variable proportions for any given unit of c. Further, these should be distinguished from *common-costs* which are incurred in joint production although it is not physically imperative to do so. Accounting-wise careful distinction must also be made between costs to be allocated to products (presumably within one branch here), and costs allocable to departments or branches since bases of allocation and the reasons for their allocation are quite different. Shubik makes no such distinctions. Instead he appears to be using joint cost, overhead, etc., as an economic fixed cost in limbo.

Let us now analyze his argument carefully. First, unless the "overhead" were not a true joint cost, it would not, even under traditional cost accounting, be handled as an equal distribution. By far the most common method of *imputing* joint costs in a similar situation is the relative-sales method (or net realizable value to the split-off point for products) (See the *Accountants' Cost Handbook*, New York: Ronald, 1959, Sec. 13). Thus in Shubik's first example pp. 219 the allocations would be made on a basis of c = 10, x = 4, y = 7. This gives cost assessments of 10 (4/11) and 10 (7/11), respectively, or 3 7/11 and 6 4/11, respectively, as compared to Shubik's 3 2/3 and 6 2/3. In the second example, c = 10, x = 16, y = 17, the relative sales method give $\varphi2$ = x−(c16/33), φ_3 = y−(c17/33), or joint cost assignments of 4.85 and 5.15, respectively, compared with 9.67 (or 58/6), and 10.17 (or 61/6) as per the example. The relative proportions charged to each being approximately the same as per Shapley. No allocation, of course, is given to the central office. "Their net revenues are always positive and the central office requires only one number from them, their profit before assessment."!

Further, the profit is in accordance with their individual contribution to joint overhead (contribution to profit). In fact, statements are frequently prepared on a contribution to overhead basis—and these are especially pertinent in the case of true joint costs where all allocations are arbitrary and imputations must be made to *achieve a desired result.* This is quite pertinent because if the Shapley value takes into account the second allocation of all cost, c, to manager #2, then some further assumptions must be made about the nature of the costs, and there are obvious interdependencies between c and x + y! If the costs are truly unavoidable (fixed costs in the theory of the firm), if either manager can shut down then there are joint conditions on cost such that c_x = 0 if either x + y, or y are existent (both operating or manager #2 operating); and c_y − 0 if cither x + y, or x, are existent (both operating or manager #1 operating) where $c_x + c_y$ = c; and c = 0 only if *both* branches shut down. There are in the case posed by Shubik "cooperative" cost coalitions as well, and an "enlightened" manager would have to assume (with no information) either full joint costs (c = 10) or no joint costs (c = 0) in any one period. The managers would thus either be given an allocation as above or make an assumption about the existence of the other department. Even *if* a misallocation is made of assigned costs, if the manager of either branch knows that the other one is operating, any contribution toward covering joint cost is a justification to keep operating, that is, he may assume his relevant joint cost as zero. If, on the other hand, some of these costs are avoidable by shutting down either department, they are no longer joint costs *for these purposes,* and may be assigned directly to the department in question.

In the case of cost-plus pricing (example 4) the problem of the reward structure is well-known; that an inefficient operator would get a larger profit than an efficient one. For that reason either extensive auditing of such contracts (as in renegotiation) has always been made, or where it is inadvisable, cost-plus has been abandoned in favor of cost-plus-fixed-fee. The latter has the advantage of giving a higher net return to investment (or to sales) figure for the efficient units without sharing the "profit" for improvements with other branches. In fact under that system it is possible to give bonuses for cost reductions. All this naturally abstracts from the situation given. What incentive is there for innovation if it's known that others will get as many "brownie points" as we for *our* breakthroughs? The best that can be said is that it is motivationally neutral.

Refutation of the main points in the joint cost case (and by inference the joint revenue case) should not obscure the fact that where the situation is truly a series of coalitions that the Shapley method offers clear-cut advantages. This means, however, that the information be derived and set forth for *this purpose* within the organization else it may be worse than useless. Normally information of this sort (value of various coalitions) is not available in corporate accounting, is not easily obtainable, and should not be obtained (since it is expensive) if easier alternatives are found, as in the case of joint costs above.

In concluding, Shubik's remarks about the danger of distortion of information sent from within the organization to the central office brings forth two observations: (1) When lower level information is widely used to measure rewards (without a recourse to a market) distortion is quite high (Cf. Campbell, pp 175, ff.), (2) *Unbiased* gatherers of information are nonexistent. The very act of gathering (choice of data) and measuring (choice of standards) implies subjectivity on the part of the data-gatherer. Distortion really may then be unintentional. (Cf. Churchman, *Prediction and Optimal Decisons;* esp. Ch. 3).

In spite of the objections raised above, Shubik's paper has presented much food for thought and possible areas of research for enlightened bookkeepers.

Discussion

THE BUDGETARY PROCESS AND MANAGEMENT CONTROL

SIDNEY DAVIDSON
University of Chicago

To a non-mathematician, Shillinglaw's paper on "Divisional Performance Review" is a welcome oasis in a desert of formulae and algebraic notation. Unfortunately, I can not agree with the major conclusion reached in his paper. The major processes and conclusions of the three other papers in the session on the Budgetary Process and Management Controls are, in varying degrees, easier to accept.

Shillinglaw presents a thoughtful and thorough summary of the role of budgetary control in facilitating decentralized divisional operations. He focuses primary attention on the feedback response aspects of budgetary control—(1) the selection of the significant aspects of performance, (2) the establishment of a criterion of satisfactory performance for each aspect, (3) the measurement of performance and its deviation from the predetermined criterion, (4) the search for causes of deviation, and (5) the report to remedy-seeking, action-taking executives. Emphasis on these internal control features of the budgetary process is well deserved. Too much reliance is placed on the budget, however, when comparison of actual profit with budgeted profit is described as "the appropriate standard" for evaluating overall divisional performance. Rate of return on investment, even recognizing its many shortcomings, is a superior standard for evaluating overall performance of autonomous divisions.

In selecting between rate of return on investment and deviation from budgeted profit as a measure of successful operations for a division, the absolute rate of return approach seems substantially preferable. Budgets and standards are subjective estimates of what the world will, or should, be like. In setting standards for individual tasks or assemblies, subjectivity is limited by the data of the stop watch, the camera, and the bill of materials. Even with these objective benchmarks, the first defense by supervisors when deviations from job standards or department budgets occur is usually the claim that the standard or budget is unfair or unrealistic. In these areas, however, it is difficult to find any other satisfactory measure of effectiveness of performance. Partly by virtue of the availability of objective evidence for standards and partly by default, budgetary controls hold an undisputed place in evaluating effectiveness of task performance.

In appraising management of a decentralized division (or of the firm as a whole), the situation is quite different. Comparison of over-all division performance with a predetermined budget involves sum-ming all of the uncertainties of the individual department operating budgets and combining them with the even more subjective estimate of divisional sales. In place of these projections, rate of return analysis offers the coldly impersonal, ruthless testing ground of the market place. The division's ability to gauge the market and produce effectively for it is summed up in the rate of return. Despite years of budgetary indoctrination, managers still seem motivated to seek absolute dollar results; comparisons with budget do not have the same psychological force. Despite the conceptual and computational problems in rate of return analysis,[1] despite the fact it does not take into account differences in profit potentials among divisions, rate of return on investment is the single most satisfactory standard for divisional performance review.

It is disappointing, in a way, that comparison with budgeted profit is not a satisfactory test, for if it were the transfer pricing problem would be largely eliminated. If actual transfer prices were set equal to their budgeted level, no manager—either on the buying or selling end—should complain since he would be meeting his budgeted cost or revenue figure. Shillinglaw expresses his skepticism about this solu-tion in a passage that serves as an indictment of his entire budgetary comparison system for divisions. He says, "Yet from my observa-tions of a number of transfer price disputes in industry, it is appar-ent that absolute profit levels are important to the managers. They will argue to get a price reduced (or raised, if they are on the selling side) with as much vigor as they exert in interfirm bargaining." It is hard to find a more telling argument against his suggested standard.

The papers by Shubik and Charnes and Stedry are pioneering ef-forts in dealing with vexing management problems in areas where traditional budgeting processes have offered little help. Shubik con-centrates on the problem of allocating joint costs in a multi-division enterprise. This task, impossible on logical grounds, must be per-formed if some degree of local autonomy is to be permitted in deci-sion making. The allocation system should have the property that "the selection of choices which are best for the individual decision-maker will always coincide with those which are best for the organi-zation."' Shubik proposes an allocation method, based upon sugges-tions of Lloyd Shapley, that requires developing a "characteristic function" for each division of the organization. The system seems logically satisfactory, but the problems of developing and measuring values of the characteristic function seem immense. Practical im-

[1] See William J. Vatter, "Does the Rate of Return Measure Business Effi-ciency?", *N.A.A. Bulletin*, January, 1959.

plementation of the system is not likely to be immediately forthcoming, but it does offer hope for the future.

Charnes and Stedry are concerned with studying and predicting
individual and organizational behavior patterns, where the individual
or organization has a set of goals rather than the single goal of profit
maximization. In grappling with this problem, economic theory has
traditionally relied on efforts to measure utility functions of individuals and groups. Charnes and Stedry, instead, seek to construct a
series of models incorporating the entire set of goals, in order to
predict behavior patterns. Their complete models are difficult to
implement, but they present substantial evidence to indicate that approximate solutions may yield satisfactory predictive results in
some problem areas.

Wagner is on more familiar ground when he considers budgetary
control in inventory systems, although he is primarily concerned
with a special aspect of the problem—monitoring of lower echelon
adherence to inventory policy established by top management. The
problem, of course, has cost aspects; it would be possible to use
standard audit procedures continuously but they are ruled out as being too expensive. Instead, management must choose between an index system (a "barometer system" in Wagner's terms) and some
other type of control system, usually a control limit or quota system.
Wagner develops systems of both types and concludes that a barometer system which measures the extent of deviation from desired
performance and provides for rewards as well as penalties is preferable if it can be made effective. He concludes on a pessimistic
note by expressing his doubts on the likely effectiveness of a barometer system.

Wagner may be too modest in predicting the efficacy of the barometer system he has devised. If the (s,S) inventory system successfully takes into account all significant financial factors, it is likely
that a suitable system of rewards and penalties can be devised that
will limit continuing departure from the plan. If only personal convenience and response to local pressures motivate lower echelon departures from the inventory control system, a suitable reward and
penalty system could probably exert sufficient pull to insure general
compliance with the plan. Continued departure from plan probably
indicates a lack of confidence in the inventory model rather than a
weakness in the barometric system.

Discussion

THE BUDGETARY PROCESS AND MANAGEMENT CONTROL

GERALD L. THOMPSON
Carnegie Institute of Technology

I INTRODUCTION

The point of view that I shall take in my comments on the papers presented in this part of the seminar is that a business organization, considered in its environment, is a player in a general n-person game. The word "game" does not imply anything frivolous about my approach, as a perusal of [20] will confirm, but rather the fact that possible actions that a firm can take are limited by various factors, including the actions of its "opponent" firms, and involve payoffs from time to time. In order to have a finite scope to the game. I assume that either there is a finite horizon (say of 100 years) or else that future payoffs are discounted so that the far distant future can effectively be ignored.

The "player" or firm is, in fact, made up of many different persons such as directors, managers, foremen, workers, etc. The rules of the game are partly formal and partly informal, and are determined in the following (and other) ways:

1. Historical development of the firm and the industry
2. The formal organization of the firm
3. Physical limitations on moves, e.g., speed of communication, speed of delivery, technological capability, technological capacity, etc.
4. Governmental, moral, and legal restrictions on moves
5. The way that various persons in the firm structure their own situation. Note that not only directors and managers have the capability of structuring moves, but also so do workers, secretaries, etc. What these persons choose to do depends in part on what the operating rules of the firm permit them to do and, in part, on what their own psychological make-ups permit them to do.

If it could be spelled out in all detail, the above game would be fantastically complicated. But as constructors of business games

---

[1]I am greatly indebtedly to H. A. Simon for comments and ideas which he gave me during the preparation of this paper.

have found, it is literally impossible to write down all the possible
legal moves or actions that even a small firm can make. Even a relatively complex business game, such as the Carnegie Tech business
game [5], is far from approximating the reality of the detergent industry, which was used as a model in its construction. Yet that business
game (as well as many simpler games) is sufficiently complicated
that we have but fragmentary ideas of what are good (much less, optimal) strategies for it, even though it has been observed over a number of years of simulated play.

To make this point even clearer, consider the problem of assemb-
ling a simple kitchen appliance such as a toaster or dishwasher.
Given the parts that go into such an appliance there are thousands
upon thousands of ways that they can be assembled into the completed
product. For a complicated piece of equipment such as a battleship
or a large electronic computer, there are an astronomical number of
ways of assembly. Theoretically each of these ways should be considered, if an optimal assembly plan is to be designed.

The problem is still further complicated if some of the parts are
made by subcontractors at various locations, the completed product
is to be shipped via several different conveyances to various warehouses and dealers, and eventually to the customers. So far we have
considered only production difficulties. We can add the problems of
advertising, distribution and marketing, service policies, etc. But
we still aren't done because we must also consider financial problems
(both long and short run) such as investments, dividend payments, etc.
Still further, there is the interaction of the firm with other firms in
the industry, and also with the customers that make up its market.
To enumerate the strategic possibilities open to a firm is an impossible task. Yet business organizations do exist and work. Later I shall
try to give an explanation of how this is possible.

The payoffs of the game are also determined by a host of different
factors of which we mention only a few:

1. Interaction of the firm with other firms and the market
2. "Sociological, psychological, and psychiatric factors of the
   persons in the firm" (Shubik's phrase in [20])
3. Accounting procedures
4. Reward and penalty factors imposed on the game by players
   (particularly management)
5. Legal and governmental payoffs such as taxes, fines, sub-
   sidies, etc.

Each person in the firm has his own payoff vector which has a number
of components such as salary, status, power, job satisfaction, fringe
benefits, physical location, etc. Again, the complete description of all
these factors is impossible, but some gross approximations can be
made.

In terms of the above concepts we can make some useful definitions. First, a *control device* is a rule of the game that is imposed
by a group of the players (typically, but not always, management)
that affects one or more of the payoff entries of the players. Second,
the *management control problem* is to choose control devices so that
the resulting behavior of the persons in the firm will be to the "best
interest" of the firm. The definition of "best interest" is rather
difficult, but I shall assume, for purpose of argument, that the objective of the firm is to maximize the expected discounted future stream
of stockholders dividends.

II SOME GENERAL PRINCIPLES OF CONTROL

From the game-theoretic discussion of the previous section we
can draw some principles that can be used in the evaluation of different proposals for control devices. The first one is quite obvious:

(A) To evaluate the *effect* of a proposed or actual control device
on a given person in the firm, it is necessary to look at the
game from his point of view, that is, to see how the control
device affects his possibilities for choice of action and how
it affects the components of his payoff vector.

Control devices that do not elicit the kind of behavior that is desired
from the person being controlled probably fail because they do not
change the persons view of the game in a way that produces the desired behavior. This is the point of view taken in the "motivational"
or "human relations" approach to Industrial Psychology. If (A) is
not used to evaluate control devices, it may be found that decisions
made by management are not implemented. On the other hand, entirely new ways of controlling humans may be discovered by referring to this rule. I would not be surprised to see such results come
out of the work by Churchill and Cooper [3, 4] on the effects of an
audit, or out of the budgeting studies of Stedry [26], or out of the goal
oriented accounting studies of Ijiri [11]. Innovation of control methods
should be a fruitful area for future research.

The second principle is not quite as obvious, but must clearly also
be taken into account when considering control problems.

(B) To evaluate the *worth* of a proposed or actual control device,
it is necessary to look at it as a *strategy* in the game theory
sense, and to see how it affects the firm's position (both long
and short run) in its environment.

To give an example, one should pose the question of the effect on the
market position of the firm of changing the rules by which an inventory clerk supplies customers and orders replacement parts. Other

examples include the question of information flow in the firm, problems of signalling [27,28], ruin aspects [22], strategic questions such as those considered in the theory of teams [16], etc.

Most control devices depend upon using an index number to measure the performance of the humans being controlled. Let us assume that the rule for assigning the index number to a given performance is entirely deterministic in nature, i.e., is such that the person being controlled can readily compute his own index number. Then the following empirical observation has been made [6]: if the rules for determining index numbers are known exactly, then the persons being controlled will develop ways by which their performance relative to the index number will appear to be good, i.e., they will anticipate the evaluation technique. One way of appearing good is to behave in the way that management wants. However, as an application of (A), we must consider any method that will produce good index numbers since it may actually be employed. The recurrent purges in the Soviet Union and China to eliminate record falsifiers are instances where the records but not the performance were good. As a specialization of (A) we now state:

(C) In the evaluation of a proposed index number control device it is necessary to consider not only the desired kinds of performance, but also any behavior possible within the rules of the "game", whether desirable or not, that will similarly produce good index numbers.

One obvious proposal that one could make to get around the above problem, is that part of the rules for determining index numbers should be kept secret. But if this is done, it they pays the players to conduct "espionage" activities to find out these rules. A game-theoretic solution to the problem of secrecy that is "espionage proof" is to make part of the index number be determined by a random device, corresponding to a mixed strategy in the game-theoretic sense. However this proposal can lead to undesirable random phenomena governed by the so-called "arc-sine" law. To explain this I refer to the example treated on page 447 of [12]. There the experiment of two players matching pennies is considered, the problem being to determine the fraction of times that one player will be ahead of the other, that is, have his fortune larger than the other. Here the rather paradoxical result occurs that, even though the game is fair, the least likely event is that the two players should be ahead an equal number of times! In the case of 12 matchings, the probability that each player should be ahead 6 times (one-half) is about .1, while the probability that one of them should be ahead *all* of the time is about .23. The distribution this gives rise to is the arc sine law [8]. This leads to:

(D) If an index number has a random component then it is more likely than not that two kinds of performance which are in fact equally good, will be rated unequally purely by chance alone.

Since none of the papers being considered proposes such control devices, the criticism just ennunciated applies only to some conceivably new methods. It may be possible that bonus payments to employees may be subject to this criticism.

I would now like to return to the question posed earlier of how a business executive can make decisions in the face of the bewildering complexity of his environment. The "Babbitt" image of a business executive is that of a person who talks and thinks in platitudes. Whereas this is a commentary on his social behavior, there is also the inference that it is this kind of thinking that makes him a success in his profession. I find this most surprising in view of the already observed complexity of the environment in which he must make decisions. There is considerable evidence [6, 18, 19, 24, 25] that the way in which humans can successfully operate in large "unstructured" situations is by using *heuristics,* that is, rules of thumb, or *decision rules* to simplify their environment. Examples of such heuristics are:

1. The "first in first out" rule in inventory control
2. The "shortest immanent operation" rule in job shop scheduling
3. Modular construction rules in the design and construction of electronic (and other) equipment
4. "Market percentage" and "volume" goals in setting sales quotas
5. Seniority rules in personnel management
6. Bargaining rules for labor negotiations, e.g., "offer fringe benefits before wage raise"

The advantage to be gained by the use of such rules is not that they necessarily give good decisions—some times they do and some times not. But rather that they serve to limit search by reducing the number of alternatives to a manageable number and permit action in cases where a complete enumeration of all alternatives is impossible. The department store pricing model and the general price model in Cyert and March's behavioral theory of the firm [6] illustrate this very well. Also, it seems to me that a businessman's or shop foreman's "experience" consists of the accumulation of a large number of heuristics that are applicable to a variety of situations. And a good businessman or shop foreman is one who can use, and if necessary, invent "good" heuristics.

This point of view has been reinforced for me by my experience with the Carnegie Tech. Business Game [5]. While serving on boards of directors of the game I have regularly asked students playing the game to formulate, whenever possible, the decision rules that they develop for making moves in the game. One of the teams was able to formulate essentially all their strategic decisions that way. In 1962, all the players were required to make decisions in advance concerning the next three months of play. They were permitted to write simple decision programs if they wished, and these were incorporated in the game program. The game was run for three months without their further intervention. The advantage of good decision rules measured in net profit terms showed up very quickly.

It is my contention that the way the management of a real life firm is able to operate in its highly complex environment is by viewing it in an anecdotal, heuristic, decision rule way. Essentially the same point of view was stated earlier by H. A. Simon in [24] in which he develops the concept of "bounded rationality" to describe the fact that a decision maker has to limit his area of search. Similar points of view occur in March and Simon [15]. Also, the same concept seems to me to be an implicit assumption in the background of the behavioral theory of the firm of Cyert and March [5]. This opens the possibility [25] of replacing (as we did in the business game) many of the routine decisions of management by computer decision rules. When applied to rules for control, we have the following principle:

(E) One method of achieving *perfect* control of a managerial decision is to take it out of the realm of human management, and program a computer to make and enforce the decision.

I hasten to add that there are rather considerable costs incurred in the implementation of this rule. But there are also a number of unexpected side benefits.

To give an illustration, let me briefly describe the operation of the retail paint division of the Pittsburgh Plate Glass Company. When a retail sale is made at one of the sales outlets, a copy of the order is sent into the main office where it is punched on a card. Once a month a computer reads all of the sales made in the month, and on the basis of this data, plus data from past years, decides (1) what new inventory of paint is to be shipped to each outlet, including color of paint, can size, and quantities; (2) what new kinds of paint are to be manufactured by the company's plants during the coming month to meet expected future demands. Of course, the computer also updates inventories at the factory, warehouse, and retail outlets. It even prints up the shipping invoices for truck loads of paint to be delivered to branch outlets. Thus, the inventory and ordering functions of the branch manager have been taken over by a computer. Clearly in this case, the company can enforce with certainty any inventory policy it wishes—the control problem has been obviated entirely by means of a computer program. It is true that new problems have arisen in the process, but that is beside the point.

A second point concerning the impact of the computer on business decision making is that the computer can be used to make choices among alternatives in a much greater degree of complexity than humans can. This is possible in part because a computer can enumerate and evaluate alternatives much faster than can humans, and in part because precise mathematical models have been developed for solving some kinds of optimization problems. For instance, linear programming (particularly transportation) models have been used successfully to choose minimum cost or maximum profit sets of alternatives in realistic large scale situations. A second example, is that of the use of a computer employing heuristic ideas to smooth workload requirements in a large multi-project, multi-shop problem [14,30]. We thus have the principle:

(F) By formulating mathematical optimization models and solving them on the computer, it is possible to make optimal or good decisions in environments too complex for a human decision maker to analyze.

Here again, we by-pass the human decision maker and let a computer make the decision without simplifying (at all, or as much) the environment. After the decision is made, there may still be a control problem of enforcing the decision, but this can, in turn, be handled by the use of (E).

As an example of the use of this principle, General Mills has a large scale transportation model involving thousands of variables and constraints, which describes the flow of materials from flour mills to food processing and packaging factories, to warehouses, and then to retailers. Complicated rules hold on freight rates, mixed car loadings, etc. The model is translated into a non-linear model involving a few hundred variables, and solved on a computer to obtain decisions concerning where the products are to be manufactured, from which flour mills they are to get their materials and to which customer they are to be shipped. These decisions are given to management for further implementation, and at that level a control problem arises which could be handled by principle (E). The latter will probably be done as soon as the management obtains sufficient experience with and confidence in the decisions. Fairly substantial savings are obtained by use of the model. In addition, unexpected uses have been found for the model in planning new warehouse locations and in formulating other long range plans.

I have given these examples from actual industrial practice because I feel that one of the lacunae of this part of the conference (and indeed, of the whole conference) is the lack of emphasis on actual control practices being used by management today. These are highly sophisticated, in many ways more sophisticated than most of the methods we are presently discussing. Even more important, they completely bypass some of the academic problems we are discussing. Here, as in some accounting procedures, actual practice is considerably ahead of academic knowledge. I could imagine another very interesting and informative senimar, as long as the present one, that considered the present control practices of industry, and emphasized the effect of the electronic computer on control procedures.

Returning to (E) above, a second conclusion from the observation of management's use of heuristic rules to simplify environment can be stated in the behavioral theory of the firm framework of Cyert and March as follows: Assume that we have a behavioral description of the behavior of the management of a firm and we wish to predict the effect on the firm of adding a control rule. To do this we add the control rule to the list of behavioral rules, predict its effect on the existing rules, predict what new behavioral rules will develop as a consequence of the introduction of the control rule, and then simulate the new behavior on a computer (or by other means). This leads to:

(G) One way of evaluating the effect of a control rule on an existing organization is to make a behavioristic analysis of its effect on existing and possible new decision rules in the firm and then to simulate the operation of the resulting set of decision rules.

I do not know of any instance where this has actually been done but I would be interested to see an attempt made in this direction. The work of the Bonini in this volume represents a similar application to a hypothetical firm.

III DISCUSSION OF PAPERS ON THE BUDGETARY PROCESS AND MANAGEMENT CONTROL

After this somewhat lengthy introduction I shall give a rather brief discussion of each of the papers.

Wagner's paper [29] deals with the problem of top management trying to control lower management, and considers two kinds of devices—barometer control and quota control. His discussion in Section 1.3 concerning the necessity for and evaluation of control procedures covers, in part, the ideas I have embodied in (A) and (B) above. Also his definition of inconsistency in 2.2 embodies, in part, principle (C). It does not include such behavior as that of falsification of records as he points out in 2.3. It is also true that the (s,S) policies such as Wagner discusses can be enforced with complete control by a computer as suggested in (E) above. Of course, most of his discussion is applicable to a wide variety of management situations besides (s,S) inventory policies. Hence, let us assume that principle (E) is not adopted. If then a description of the behavior of the firm is available, it would be possible to apply (G) in evaluating the effect of such control devices on the firm. In such a manner it might be possible to study the effect of consistency—or lack of it—in a given control device. This, in turn, may make it possible to get around the very discouraging result of Wagner, that consistent control devices are very difficult to find. The latter result reminds me of similar impossibility results in the theory of welfare functions [1] and in games against nature [17]. As a measure of the amount of inconsistency, one could take the ratio of the amount of behavior encouraged by the control device that is beneficial to the goals of the firm to the amount of behavior not beneficial that is similarly encouraged, and try to select or devise rules that have the smallest amount of inconsistency relative to this index.

Charnes and Stedry [2] start with the assumption that a game-theoretic analysis, ala (A) and (B) above, has been made and a list of suitable goals plus their payoffs is available. Then they analyze the problem of the allocation of effort to achieve the maximum payoff, when the probability of goal attainment depends upon the amount of effort expended toward it. This is an instance of the application of (F) above. In the normative sense they do not have a control problem, for even if their model tells how the effort is to be expended, they do not have a scheme for management to control the actions of the firm so that the desired allocation of effort is achieved. However, for simple goals such as (s,S) policies, principle (E) can be used to implement the theoretical results. For more complicated goals such as market share, sales, or profit goals, a computer may be able to give only indications of how human effort should be expended. Ijiri's thesis [11] has some interesting ideas in this direction. Thus principle (C) and perhaps (G) must be invoked to see in what ways, other than the desired way, humans can behave in meeting goals. Charnes and Stedry indicate how their model can also be used in a descriptive sense to explain behavior in experimental situations involving multiple goals. Goals thus become control devices of the "carrot" variety, whereas barometer or feedback control devices are of the "stick" variety. It seems to me that it might be possible to devise control devices that are combinations of these two kinds.

An interesting generalization of the Charnes-Stedry work can be posed in the following way: Suppose that goals are interdependent, e.g., if we cannot reach our market share goal then we create the new goal of improving our product or of increasing advertising percentages or of entering new markets, etc. A model that would capture this idea would be of interest.

I turn now to Shillinglaw's paper and note that initially we agree as to the complexity of the environment of an industrial firm. However, although in the past this has caused an increase in decentralization of firms, in the still more recent past a counter tendency has been observed largely due to the existence of the electronic computer. One example of this is the Pittsburgh Plate Glass retail paint operation that I described earlier. Another is the Westinghouse Company that is now building a central computer installation in Pittsburgh that can communicate with other computers in other parts of the country via ordinary telephone lines using some recently developed equipment. Thus, if an order for a transformer is received in Texas, it is immediately flashed to Pittsburgh where the central computer searches its inventory records to find the nearest warehouse, say it is St. Louis, with a suitable transformer in stock, then communicates directly with the St. Louis computer at that site to order it sent to Texas. The time of this communication is perhaps 10 to 20 seconds. The transformer can be placed on a railroad car for shipment to Texas within hours or even minutes from receipt of the order. Of course, the central computer will update all inventory records and also, when necessary, initiate production orders to a factory to replenish stock. As far as I am concerned, the most important problem with decentralized operations is that of information flow. Such problems can be given game-theoretic treatment [7,13, 27,28] or that of the theory of teams [16]. These problems are rather subtle, but now that computers can dial each other via long distance, their complexion is radically changed.

In Shillinglaw's discussion of control processes I think that he omitted one of the most important—namely goal setting. Also in his discussion of transfer pricing, I do not believe that the most important thing about transfer prices is *equity* (whatever that is) but rather that the transfer prices should produce the desired kind of behavior. Also, transfer prices can be anticipated, and hence principle (C) has to be considered in their evaluation. Nevertheless, Shillinglaw gives a good description of a number of salient points in the decentralization problem.

Shubik's paper [20], and the approach I take here agree quite well. I do feel that his method of assigning transfer prices does get at the principle reason for such prices, namely to coordinate the company strategy. His examples bring that point out very well. I would only add that his transfer prices are also subject to anticipation on the part of branch managers, and hence to the criticism of (C). The mention of the "distortion of information" that he makes in Section 7 is, of course, exactly to this point. I think that additional work along the line he has initiated in his paper would lead to additional fruitful results.

IV CONCLUDING REMARKS

I would like to conclude by making a few remarks on other possible control systems.

The first remark is that a modification should be made of the goal system to permit the goal to be changed depending upon the environment of the organization. Such a variable goal could permit the organization to adapt to a changing environment. Further modifications could be devised to permit the organization to anticipate future changes in the goal and to "roll with the punch" when goals become hard to reach or to take maximum advantage of easily attainable goals.

It might also be possible, although it is less obvious, to adapt barometer control ideas to a changing environment. Actually, some indications of how this can be done are given in Ijiri's work [11].

As I have indicated earlier, one of the important areas for further study is that indicated in (C) above, namely the kinds of undesirable behavior that can be rewarded by a given control system. To give an extreme example from contemporary industrial life, the control indicator of "maximize profit" provided rewards to the behavior of certain executives in Westinghouse and General Electric whose activities were directed to operating a price-rigging system in the electrical generator industry. The result was catastrophic for the companies and more particularly for the individuals involved, but the controlling indicator reinforced rather than prohibited their behavior.

A final remark on the impact of computers on the control area is in order. One of the newer kinds of hardware under development by computer companies are input devices which are very easy for management to use. For instance, suppose a console is installed in a president's office or board of director's room with buttons on it marked PROFIT AND LOSS, BALANCE SHEET, EXCEPTION REPORT, etc. Pushing one of these buttons will cause the printer in the console to print out an instantaneous report of the kind named. It should also eventually be possible to write statements in English that request certain specific pieces of managerial information from the computer. At worst, some simple programming language might have to be used to communicate with the computer. In this way, reports on the status of the business could be generated whenever they are wanted. Any executive could request daily or weekly status reports of a control nature, etc. The possibility of such reports being available should give new dimensions to the control problem, and the impact of these should be studied carefully. Here again, I expect the main innovation in the uses of these devices to take place in industry, and we in academic circles will have to take steps to find out what is going on. Presently, academic contributions are being made to the theory of programming languages which are obviously important in connection with this problem, but direct contributions to the overall problem are also needed.

BIBLIOGRAPHY

1. Arrow, K. J.: *Social Choice and Individual Values,* New York: Wiley, 1951.
2. Charnes, A., and A. Stedry: "Further Explorations in the Theory of Multiple Budgeted Goals," this volume, pp. 186-204.
3. Churchill, N. C.: *Behavioral Effects of an Audit: An Experimental Study,* Ph.D. Dissertation, Ann Arbor: University of Michigan, School of Business Administration, 1962.
4. ———, W. W. Cooper, and Trevor Sainsbury: "Laboratory and Field Studies of the Behavorial Effects of Audits," this volume, pp. 253-267.
5. Cohen, K. J., W. R. Dill, A. A. Kuehn, and P. R. Winters: *The Carnegie Tech. Management Game: An Experiment in Business Education,* to be published in 1963 by Richard D. Irwin and Co.
6. Cyert, R. M., and J. G. March: *A Behavioral Theory of the Firm,* Englewood Cliffs, N. J.: Prentice-Hall, 1963.
7. Dantzig, G. B., and P. Wolfe; "Decomposition Principle for Linear Programs," *Operations Research,* volume 8, pp. 101-111, 1960.
8. Feller, W.: *An Introduction to Probability Theory and Its Applications,* vol. I, 2nd ed., New York: Wiley, 1960.
9. Forrester, J. W.: *Industrial Dynamics,* New York: Wiley, 1961.
10. Holt, C. C., F. Modigliani, J. F. Muth, and H. A. Simon: *Planning Production, Inventories and Work Force,* Englewood Cliffs, N. J.: Prentice-Hall, 1960.
11. Ijiri, Y.: *Studies of Linear Models for Planning and Control; An Accounting Consideration,* Ph.D. Thesis, Carnegie Institute of Technology, 1963.
12. Kemeny, J. G., A. Schleifer, J. L. Snell, and G. L. Thompson: *Finite Mathematical Structures,* Englewood Cliffs, N. J.: Prentice-Hall, 1959.
13. Kuhn, H. W.: "Extensive games and the Problem of Information," in H. W. Kuhn and A. W. Tucker: *Contributions to the Theory of Games,* II, (eds.), Princeton, N. J.: Princeton University Press, 1953.
14. Levy, F. K., G. L. Thompson, and J. D. Wiest: "Multiship, Multishop, Workload-Smoothing Program," *Naval Logistics Research Quarterly,* volume 9, pp. 37-44, 1962.
15. March, J. G., and H. A. Simon: *Organizations,* New York: Wiley, 1958.
16. Marschak, J., and R. Radner: "Economic Theory of Teams," Cowles Foundation Discussion Paper No. 59, 1958.
17. Milnor, J.: "Games Against Nature," in R. M. Thrall, C. Coombs, and R. L. Davis, (eds.), *Decision Processes,* New York: Wiley, 1954.
18. Muth, J. F., and G. L. Thompson: *Industrial Scheduling,* Englewood Cliffs, N. J.: Prentice-Hall, 1963.
19. Newell, A., and H. A. Simon: "Computer Simulation of Human Thinking and Problem Solving," Reprint No. 103, Graduate School of Industrial Administration, Carnegie Institute of Technology.
20. Shubik, M.: "Incentives, Decentralized Control, the Assignment of Joint Costs and Internal Pricing," this volume, pp. 205-226.
21. von Neumann, J., and O. Morgenstern: *Theory of Games and Economic Behavior,* Princeton, N. J.: Princeton University Press, 1944, 1947, 1954.
22. Shubik, M., and G. L. Thompson: "Games of Economic Survival," *Naval Logistics Research Quarterly,* volume 6, pp. 111-123, 1959.
23. Shillinglaw, G.: "Divisional Performance Review: An Extension of Budgetary Control," this volume, pp. 149-163.
24. Simon, H. A.: *Administrative Behavior,* 2d ed., New York: Macmillan, 1957.

25. ———: "The Corporation: Will It Be Managed by Machines?", in M. Anshen and G. L. Bach (eds.), *Management and Corporations*, 1985, New York: McGraw-Hill, 1960.

26. Stedry, A.: *Budget Control and Cost Behavior*, Englewood Cliffs, N. J.: Prentice-Hall, 1960.

27. Thompson, G. L.: "Bridge and Signaling," in H. W. Kuhn and A. W. Tucker (eds.), *Contributions to the Theory of Games*, II, Princeton University Press, pp. 279-289, 1953.

28. ———: "Signaling Strategies in N-person Games," in H. W. Kuhn and A. W. Tucker (eds.), Contributions to the Theory of Games, II, ed. by Princeton N. J.: Princeton University Press, pp. 267-277, 1953.

29. Wagner, H.: "Budgetary Control in Inventory Systems," this volume, pp. 164-185.

30. Wiest, J. D.: *The Scheduling of Large Projects with Limited Resources*, Ph.D. Thesis, Graduate School of Industrial Administration, Carnegie Institute of Technology, 1963.

12

LABORATORY AND FIELD STUDIES OF THE BEHAVIORAL EFFECTS OF AUDITS[1]

NEIL C. CHURCHILL
WILLIAM W. COOPER
TREVOR SAINSBURY
Carnegie Institute of Technology

I INTRODUCTION:

The growth of modern industry has generated interest in ways of organizing supervisor-subordinate relations, allocating authority, fixing responsibility, etc. Especially in large and decentralized organizations, attention has also been devoted to ways for developing better "controls" over the actions of subordinates. The use of various kinds of audits is a case in point. Many business firms, government agencies, etc., now employ permanent staffs of "internal auditors" and hence apparently feel that they can no longer rely exclusively on the itermittent use of "external auditors" supplied from, say, the staffs of independent CPA firms.

From one standpoint, the control problems of management can be viewed as one of ensuring that the actions of subordinates will conform to the plans or wishes of their superiors. From this standpoint a control instrument such as auditing, say, would then be evaluated in terms of whether it serves to strengthen supervisory direction of subordinates.

It is at least conceivable, however, that the use and possible further evolution of these kinds of control instruments may also open ways to new methods of managing. Thus, from this point of view it may be proper to inquire whether all aspects of the techniques of auditing are now being fully exploited or whether further extensions might be devised and used as alternatives to current modes of managing—e.g., such extensions might even be used as ways of securing more "self management" in order to bypass or supplant some aspects of the supervision-direction procedures that are now deemed to be a necessary part of managing.

[1]This paper was written as part of the contract "Planning and Control of Industrial Operations," with the Office of Naval Research and the Bureau of Ships, at the Graduate School of Industrial Administration, Carnegie Institute of Technology.

Acknowledgment should be made to Vincent J. Freund, Jr. for his assistance in the content analyses of the field inquiries which are reported herein. Professor Cooper wishes to note also an indebtedness to the Ford Foundation for the award of a faculty fellowship that made time available for this work.

253

This topic has formed the focus of a series of research efforts, with special reference to auditing and related controls, which are reported in subsequent parts of this paper where particular reference will be made to (1) field studies that have been directed to studying the effects of actual (past) audits on the personnel of various kinds of firms as well as to (2) studies that were designed to ascertain the behavioral effects of various kinds of audits on persons dealing with certain tasks under controlled laboratory conditions.

II AUDITS PER SE:

A fairly common view specializes auditing only to its accounting aspects and we, too, shall find it convenient to emphasize this aspect of auditing. Hence to avoid possible misunderstanding we should state, at the outset, that we are concerned with the use of audits as an instrument of management. We are not particularly concerned with issues like the proper role of an accountant in his advisory and auditing capacities. Neither are we concerned with obtaining a balanced view of all aspects of an accounting audit. Our main concern is rather with the effects that an audit, or even its anticipation, might have on persons engaged in various kinds of managerial endeavor.

For example, in the studies that are of interest here, we may, in fact, consider a supervisor to be using one kind of audit when he observes his subordinates in the performance of a certain task. We also consider an audit to be underway, of course, when an accountant examines a record of past performance. And we are also interested in the effects of various mixtures of these two types of audit even when they are curtailed or extended in various ways, or when they are used with differing frequencies and different kinds of personnel etc.

We may use the term "audit per se" to indicate that it is the fact of auditing which is of interest, itself, rather than the fact of whether the procedures utilized conform to accepted canons of accounting practice.[2] Then we can, in this context, consider various facets of an audit—or audit mixtures—such as the procedures of examination employed, the kinds of reports that are filed, the nature of the recommendations that are made (as well as to whom they are made), and the penalty-reward structure in which audits are embedded. We can thus study possible behavioral effects that audits produce without reference to whether the situation confronted by the auditor and the evidence he has uncovered really justifies his methods, findings, etc.

---

[2]For extended discussions of the history and philosophy of accounting audits see, e.g., [3] and [8]. See also [6] *passim*.

III AN AUDIT EXPERIMENT:

We can best secure further perspective and insight if we now try to summarize aspects of some audit experiments that we have discussed elsewhere in greater detail.[3] Perhaps the easiest way to enter this topic is first to view these audit experiments in terms of the "observer effects" that are commonly encountered in other kinds of social studies. Here, however, the problem is to design a variety of observer effects into an experiment so that each can be identified and assessed for its effects on different parts of a total task.

We have already mentioned, for example, the possible use of direct observation by a supervisor as well as the record-examination procedures that might be employed by an accountant. We might also add the further possibility of a record examination by the supervisor; conducted perhaps after the fact (e.g., after the experiment was concluded) and in a different manner than would be expected from an accountant, and finally we should add further possibilities such as a subject's anticipation of an audit since this, too, might have behavioral consequences even though the anticipated audit is never performed.[4]

The above characterizations suggest that the idea of observer effects is not really an adequate guide for these sorts of studies and this idea had best give way to more general ones such as the "ideas-influence functions," etc., which have been examined in the literatures of sociology and political science.[5] Even here, however, some further care is needed since we wish to identify various kinds of audits (and auditors) with different parts of the task assignment. The attempt was made to associate the accounting audit with "methods" rather than results and with the goals of a (removed) "overall" organization; i.e., the accountant was to appear as the agent of "third party" interest and to focus on whether the methods utilized in task solution and record keeping conformed to the methods and procedures that had been prescribed. It was also desirable to construct an experiment in which the accounting auditor would appear to be independent of the task and not involved in its penalty-reward structure. The auditor was to evidence little or no concern with actual task accomplishments. His examinations were to be confined to "the record" of the way in which the task was performed and the examination was to be done by means of an "objective comparison" in accordance with specified "criteria."

The supervisor on the other hand was highly task oriented. In contrast to accounting audits of the record for instance, the supervisor was to use, in part, direct observation of the task and also to

[3]See [1] and [2] as well as the references cited therein.
[4]Subject of course, to memory decay, diminution of expectation, etc.
[5]See for example, [7].

conduct what we called an "output check." Noticing that the experimenter would himself have to recruit subjects, train them, answer their questions, serve as custodian of the experimental records, etc., it was decided to carry these "supervisory attributes" a stage further and also have the experimenter conduct the output checks, etc., and thereby cast him even more completely in the role of "supervisor." The auditor role was assigned to a third individual who, as already noted, was to represent an hypothetical organization. More precisely, the impression was conveyed that the experiment itself was being done for this hypothetical organization and the auditor was to serve as its representative in evaluating the way in which the experiment was conducted.

Although one method was prescribed for performing the task there were also other ways that were available—some better, some worse, as judged by task performance. The prescribed method, on the other hand, could be used as an objective basis of comparison by the auditor.[6] Provision was made for having an "audit trail" for use by the auditor and a record was also to be maintained which was in part a hindrance and in part an aid to task accomplishment. The measure of task performance was characterized very simply in terms of an output variable and was scored accordingly. The overall organizational criteria and objectives were also simply characterized in terms of adherence to prescribed procedures and the practice of record keeping was merely the number of errors made in the record department.

The experimental task involved a "trouble shooting assignment" which was in reality an extension of a certain type of binary response device previously tested in other psychological experiments.[7] Briefly, the subjects were to press "buttons" in order to locate a "trouble-causing" block from one of a large number of possibilities. This was to be achieved, if possible, within a given period of time and was to be accomplished by pressing the minimum number of buttons. By this minimization, the subject would optimize his score.[8] Subjects were also instructed to follow organization procedures when executing the task and to maintain a "daily" record in proper manner on prescribed forms called "a data log." The experimental apparatus was activated in a way that caused the response information to disappear whenever a button was released from pressure but otherwise no scoring incentives were provided either for maintaining the record properly or for conforming to "organization procedures" in other

[6]This prescribed method was a good way to attack the problem task although it was not completely optimal.

[7]See [1] as well as [4] and [5] for further discussion and other references.

[8]Each subject was awarded 25 points for a correct solution achieved within the indicated time and he was penalized 2 points for each button that he pressed. He was also explicitly told to "maximize his score."

ways. Thus, the incentives were designed with a task orientation that was also further reenforced by the possible use of a supervisory audit (output check) with the further fact of a rather clear-cut and easily perceived relation between the task and the scores received. The organization objectives, on the other hand, were vaguer in character and an incentive was also provided by prescribing procedures which could be discovered to be non-optimal for task performance. The organization controls were then represented (1) by the initial instructions and (2) by the fact of anticipated or actual accounting audits. There was provision made also, of course, for the case of no observation—i.e., cases in which neither accounting nor supervisory audits were to be performed or even mentioned—since it was desired to measure this case, too,[9] for its possible behavioral implications.

Measurements were obtained and evaluated for (1) the number of problems solved correctly, (2) the number of steps omitted in the procedures that were actually employed and (3) the manner in which the record was kept including the record keeping errors that were made by the subjects. Various combinations of audit "dosages" were studied and the experiments were conducted on subjects whose backgrounds ranged from college students with no industrial experience to industrial subjects with no college training.

IV SOME EXPERIMENTAL RESULTS:

In general, the experiment indicated that the actual occurence of an *audit per se* exerts an effect on the behavior of those audited, even where there is no direct connection between the auditor's findings and the penalty-reward structure. The main direction of this effect appeared to be toward conformance patterns in which the behavior of those who were audited tended to move toward the auditor's criteria. The results of the experiment indicate that the subjects who were audited consider the auditor as being concerned with comparing their actions against some "organizationally desirable" standard. Even without exact knowledge of the overall organization or the desiderata, the subjects tended to respond as though the criteria that the auditor was employing were in conformance with certain methods or procedures characterized as "organizational goals."

We should note that the subjects were not given any explicit information on how the audit would be performed or the kinds of criteria that the auditor would use. Moreover, his actions were not directly

[9]From a more sophisticated standpoint, of course, an observer (influence) effect is probably present in any experiment and it thus seems better, as here, to attempt to measure its intensity rather than to assume that it can be reduced to zero amount by properly designed experimental controls.

connected with any penalty reward structure on record keeping aspects of the experiment. In short, we relied on the audit—or its anticipation —to provide its own "informational effects."

It cannot be assumed, of course, that even an actual auditor's true criteria are accurately perceived by those audited or even, in fact, that the auditor can always articulate these criteria when asked. It is the perception of his criteria that is the cause for action regardless of the correspondence of this perception to the true basis of evaluation.[10] Notice, then, that the experiment suggests that audits may conceivably be employed as managerial control instruments, when certain kinds of actions are desired, even in the absence of an expert well-trained auditor.[11] This is brought into view most prominently by the audit anticipation variable when its effects are exhibited even in the absence of a previous actual audit where the quality or expertise cannot be known in any concrete sense.[12]

Some qualifications should be entered here. While all aspects of the evidence concerning the effect of the anticipation of the audit were not definitive, two conclusions emerged. The first is obvious: to be effective, an audit of historical actions should have, or at least be perceived as having, the power to go beneath the apparent evidence to determine what in fact did happen. The second is that the anticipation of an audit as studied in this experiment, did produce behavioral effects, but the direction of these effects was unexpectedly sensitive to the characterization of the impending audit and to the type of organizational personnel involved.

The difference between the types of subjects—industrial and academic—in their reactions to audit anticipation was, perhaps, somewhat surprising. The industrial subjects significantly decreased the errors they made in the record while the student subjects reacted significantly in the opposite direction and increased the number of record errors. While this may be attributable to anxiety and confusion resulting from knowledge of an impending examination, it may also be indicative of a class of people or of backgrounds that would behave perversely to the knowledge of an audit. In either case additional study is certainly needed before we can seriously entertain

[10] Since audits cross organizational structures and move up and down the chain of command—examining some actions in one group and supposedly related actions or events in another—the perception of the people in any one part of the organization may easily be based on partial evidence and the auditor's actions consequently misperceived.

[11] We are, of course, not referring to the actions of an auditor as an expert in evaluating or designing business control systems.

[12] Of course allowance must be made for halo effects carried over by the industrial subjects who were previously exposed to commercial audits. However this tends to reenforce the point especially since the auditor used in their experiments was not a trained accountant but rather a behavioral scientist— with the added qualification of a mustache and a general auditor's "mien."

the hypothesis that knowledge of an audit causes certain individuals to behave to the detriment of themselves or of the organization. The point to be made here, however, is that, conceivably, various kinds of audits may have perverse effects if applied uniformly without respect to persons and organization structure.

The supervisor's output evaluation had no noticeable effect on the student subjects but caused the industrial subjects not only to significantly increase the number of problems solved correctly but to increase the errors made in the record. These results suggest the pervasiveness of the supervisor's influence not only on the output but on the method of task performance and on the information produced by his subordinates.[13]

Finally, the interactions should be noted. For the student subjects, the audit occurrence and the supervisory output check each tended to increase (but not significantly) the care with which the problems were solved and the records maintained. Moreover, no significant additions were achieved when the two were applied jointly on these subjects. For the industrial subjects, the combination of audit anticipation and supervisory check increased significantly the number of problems solved correctly. However, the combination of audit anticipation, supervisory check and audit occurrence significantly decreased the number of problems solved correctly.

These results suggest that various kinds of audit mixes may have countervailing tendencies so that nothing is really added and, furthermore, that an "excessive" amount (or combination) of examinations may even be detrimental. Of course, the results of this experiment are only indicative. But they do bear on possible managerial strategies which are worthy of further examination in terms of possible mix combinations of audits and supervision, especially as these are reflected in a structure of organization relations, spans of control and related considerations. The possibility must be at least entertained that an injudicious use of control devices may, of itself, give rise to a need for further controls, and so on.

V DESIGN OF A FIELD STUDY:

The preceding study did include certain kinds of industrial personnel as experimental subjects. However, this cannot be used really to justify any claim for validating the kinds of behavioral effects that

---

[13] Where a manager of, say, a decentralized branch is evaluated unidirectionally—e.g., on profits made or on units produced—the influence of his concern with this "output" may permeate the organization and result in unconscious or even well-intentioned bias in the actions or reports of his subordinates. This may be true even when their rewards or penalties are less involved than his in the performance attained.

are likely to attend the conduct of an actual commercial audit. For one thing, the experiment was confined, as already noted, so that only certain aspects of an *audit per se* were actually examined. For another thing, no attempt was made to extend the experiment in order to trace the effects of an audit conducted more or less simultaneously at different levels of an organization hierarchy.

There is, of course, an extensive literature on auditing that has been developed in connection with the practices of accountants for both external and internal audit purposes. Unfortunately, however, almost all of this literature is preoccupied with topics like procedural propriety, conditions of disclosure and certification, and the assistance that managements might secure from accounting reports. There does not appear to be any part of this literature which deals with the behavioral consequences that an audit per se might produce in an organization.

Under these circumstances it appeared to be prudent—e.g., for purposes of designing the preceding experiment—to assess the kinds of behavior that might be expected when an actual audit was anticipated or executed. For this reason a field inquiry was initiated and conducted in depth on two business firms in the Pittsburgh area.[14] This produced some of the needed experimental guides. It also produced a variety of additional insights that were deemed to be valuable enough to warrant continuation of this inquiry. Thus, we proceeded to extend this inquiry so that it now includes eight enterprises with differing characteristics—e.g., size, type of business or industry, etc. The results are, even now, not all in and completely analyzed. Some of the preliminary findings, however, appear to be of sufficient interest to warrant at least a brief discussion in the present paper. This can, in fact, best be done by weaving some of these findings together with the results of our laboratory experiments in order to achieve better perspective and insight on both of these aspects of the total study.

The nature and objectives of this inquiry were not such as to lend themselves easily to the use of highly structured procedures such as scientific samples, pre-arranged questionnaires, etc. Eight organizations were chosen on a basis which, it was hoped, would produce considerable diversity in size, type of industry, even though all of the designated firms were conveniently located in or near Pittsburgh. One way of classifying the number and kinds of executives who were interviewed is given in Exhibit 12-1. In each case a so-called open ended interview technique was utilized which entailed a considerable expenditure of time by each interviewee as well as the interviewer. Although the interviews were of open-end type and exploratory in

[14] We are indebted to conversations with H. J. Leavitt which suggested this course of inquiry to us.

EXHIBIT 12-1

Positions of respondents in their organizations

Function and position		Description	Number of respondents
Accounting	Upper level	Vice presidents in finance	5
		Controllers	5
		Accounting supervisors of over 200 subordinates	4
	Middle level	Accounting supervisors of from 50 to 200 subordinates	7
		Accounting supervisors of from 10 to 50 subordinates	8
	Lower level	Accounting supervisors of less than 10 subordinates	7
		Accounting personnel with no subordinates	9
Non—accounting		Upper-level executives	6
		Middle-level executives	8
		Lower-level personnel—with supervisory responsibility	2
Special and technical		Internal auditors	3
		General "corporation" accountant supervisors	2
		Total	66

character some general direction was necessary in order to ensure that the interviewee would focus on the somewhat subtle and complex processes that are involved when an audit is being examined for its behavioral consequences. Detailed records were compiled and maintained for each interview so that, subsequently, they could all be submitted to a "content analysis" of the kind which is now under way.

Details of the study methodology will be reported elsewhere and so here we need only note the kinds of variables that are being examined. Thus, referring to Exhibit 12-2, we see that the content analysis is restricted to perceptions, as reported, on internal audits only. Seventeen of the variables being studied in accordance with the classification system are given in Exhibit 12-2. For instance, variable number 1 (contacts with internal audits) is to be placed in one of four categories, ranging through 0 (= not available) and 1 (= none, or no contact) through 2 (= limited or few contacts) and 3 (= extensive).

As is usual in content analysis, different coders will sometimes differ with respect to how a particular item should be classified even when they are employing the same code. This has occurred in the present study, too, and these "classification differences" are now being submitted to further check and analysis. Barring complete upsets or reversals from this quarter, however, the following kinds of conclusions appear to be emerging from this study.

The contact ranges (variable number 1) depended on the respondent's level in his organization. In general, the contacts with internal audit tended to be more extensive at middle management levels and more limited or even non-existent at the top or bottom of the company hierarchy. It is possible, of course, that external and internal auditors have developed some degree of specialization in their labors by reference to executive level contacts. If so, then this might well have been accompanied by other specializations as well. For instance 73% of the respondents (though all levels) characterized internal audit as being predominantly a "procedural check.[15] Furthermore, the respondents who characterized internal audit either as an "accuracy check" or a "systems evaluation" were all in the lower accounting group.

The material on the audit report (variables 11 through 14) is of interest especially since this report is considered to be one of the primary objectives of an audit control in the writings of accountants. As we noted earlier in our discussion of *audit per se,* this view of the audit is a rather natural concomitant of the classical view of supervisor-to-subordinate direction controls. Hence it is interesting to

---

[15] This, of course, is consistent with the way the experiment was designed and, in fact, this procedural check aspect of an audit was suggested in part by these field inquiries.

EXHIBIT 12-2. Content analysis variables used for examination of perceptions of internal audits.

Variable number	Variable name	Classification used				
		0	1	2	3	4
1	Contacts with internal audits	Not available	None	Limited	Extensive	---
2	Purpose of internal audit	Not available	Procedural check	System evaluation	Accuracy	Other
3	Attitude toward internal audit	Not available	Negative	Neutral	Positive	Mixed
4	Attitude toward internal auditor	Not available	Negative	Neutral	Positive	Mixed
5	Education required for auditing work	Not available	High school graduate	College graduate	---	---
6	Stereotype of auditor	Not available	Teacher	Policeman	Attorney	Mixed
7	Changes in the internal audits in the past 3 to 5 years	Not available	Little	None	Substantial	---
8	Changes in the internal audits in the next 3 to 5 years	Not available	Little	None	Substantial	---
9	Respondent's knowledge of the internal auditor's report	Not available	Yes	No	Don't know	---
10	Does the auditor review the report with respondent	Not available	Yes	No	---	---
11	Does the supervisor review the report with respondent	Not available	Yes	No	---	---
12	The most important part of the audit report	Not available	Findings	Recommendations	---	---
13	Is it desirable for respondent to see the report	Not available	Yes	No	Don't know	---
14	The internal audit as an information flow	Not available	One-way	Two-way	---	---
15	The effect of audit on respondent	Not available	None	Little	Substantial	---
16	The use of internal auditors for consultants	Not available	None	Little	Substantial	---
17	Who are the auditors perceived as checking on	Not available	Self	Boss	Other than self or boss	No individual

observe that 82% of the respondents view auditing in terms of a one-way information flow, upwards, via the audit report. Since our experiment showed that audit per se involved a two-way flow, we need to note here that these more subtle aspects of an audit are not easily brought out by the techniques of non-directed interviews.

We shall shortly return to the latter topic. For the moment, however, we want to notice that the effects of an audit report are more complex than they may appear on a first interpretation. For instance, we may note that 89% of the respondents at least knew of the existence of audit reports and, in fact, all those who did not know this were in non-supervisory posts. Our classifications for variables 10 and 11 suggest that these questions are not pertinent at top executive levels.[16] The data clearly indicate also that these auditors did not review their reports with persons in the two lower accounting levels but, on the whole, such reviews were conducted fairly frequently at middle management levels. It is apparently also a common practice for supervisors to review their audit reports, when available, with their subordinates at all except the very lowest company levels.

As might be expected, a respondent's perceptions of the most important part of an audit report was influenced by whether or not his supervisor had reviewed the report with him. It is common practice to distinguish, for instance, between audit "findings" and audit "recommendations." All respondents who reported that their supervisor had reviewed audit reports with them also regarded the "findings" as the most important part of the report. Those who did not report such a supervisory review tended to be evenly divided when classified according to whether they regarded the "findings" or the "recommendations" as being more important.

In this latter context it is of interest to compare what the data reveal on variable 10 as well as 11. An auditor's review—as contrasted with a supervisor's review—does not appear to effect the even division reported with respect to the relative importance of "findings" vs. "recommendations." The main effect of such a review seems to occur in the respondents' perceptions of the internal auditor. For persons who reported that internal audits do not have any effect on their behavior, approximately 70% had not had the experience of an auditor reviewing his report with them. Among those who had experienced such a review, however, all but one reported some effect—little or substantial.[17]

---

[16] Or else that these questions are interpreted differently at these levels.
[17] On the other hand, the number of such respondents is also relatively small.

Another interesting result which emerges from these data is that people nearer the bottom of the managerial hierarchy—both in the accounting and non-accounting tiers—tended to see the auditor as a useful consultant more often than was the case for executives nearer to the top. Any tendency to use the auditor as consultant would presumably be related to the view held with respect to his duties as a control agent and especially so in a system of supervisor-to-subordinate controls and checks. Here our evidence is only partially satisfactory. Only 14 of the responses contain information on variable 17 - who are the auditors perceived as checking on. Half of those who said "no individual" were in the lowest level accounting group. The rest were all non-accounting managers. Only accountants saw auditors as checking on them (= self). But now referring to variable 2, we can say that half of the people who saw the audit as a procedural check also saw the auditor serving as a check on "self" in variable 17.[18] Finally, of the persons who indicated "self", approximately 2/3 of them stated that they would not use an internal auditor as a consultant. On the other hand, nearly 3/4 who indicated that they perceived the auditor as checking on "no individual" also indicated that they never used internal auditors as consultants.[19] From the evidence at hand, however, no case was reported in which an individual regarded "self" as being subject to check when either a supervisor or an auditor reviewed the report with him.

The auditor's review of the audit report influenced the respondent's perception of the degree of audit contact—variable 1. It appeared to have little effect on respondents' attitudes as reported in 3 and 4 except, possibly, indirectly via variable 1. In particular it did appear to influence respondent perceptions with respect to the amount of education an auditor should have. Over 85% of those experiencing an auditor's review of his report indicated that they thought a high-school education was sufficient for an internal auditor. On the other hand, 80% of those who did not have such a discussion indicated that a college degree was necessary.

It was not expected that a field interview such as this one could turn up very much direct evidence on the behavioral issues which are of interest for *audit per se*. In 28 out of 66 interview reports,

[18] This is more than 80% of those responding by "self" for variable 17.

[19] In one company, every one at the top appeared to believe that the audit was not a check on their actions but was, instead, a check on the actions of subordinates. They then went on to indicate that it was a "real help" to them in their own control evaluations. People in the lowest ranges, however, felt that the auditors were checking on the "system" and in so far as individuals were concerned the auditor was perceived as mainly serving to check their supervisors. (It is interesting to observe in this case, anyway, that many of the experimental subjects also perceived the auditor as checking on their "boss."

no information could be uncovered on this variable. Among the remaining 38 a total of 23, or some 60%, indicated that the internal audit produced "no effect" on their behavior and an additional 12 indicated that it had only "little effect." This left a total of only 3 interviews which admitted to the classification "substantial effect" but these three were all accountants and the reasons for their responding in this manner were not wholly clear.

These results are difficult to reconcile with the flavor of the interviews and the character of the resulting reports viewed en toto. Higher order analyses may help to reveal further details that may be relevant but even here the promise is not very great.

The kinds of problems involved here are perhaps illustrated very well by the interview reported with one high level officer who felt that auditors (here external auditors) had little effect and that he would question their value except for fulfilling certain requirements of law, banking and finance, etc. This was subsequently followed by an interview with a subordinate who jokingly remarked that his superior (this same person) would probably evidence a negative attitude towards auditors if only because in the past they had not "gone along with some of his pet ideas."

A variety of approaches will be needed. Field interviews alone will apparently not suffice if we are ever to assess the potentials of audits and other (like) control instruments with respect to their full range of possible managerial uses. In the approaches to date, we have been using laboratory experimentation as well as field interviews in a complementary fashion. It is not contended, however, that these two approaches will alone exhaust the possibilities for research. Thus, we expect to utilize still other approaches such as machine simulations, etc., not only to model the audit processes but also to test the power of currently employed auditing methods.

BIBLIOGRAPHY

1. Churchill, N.C.: *Behavioral Effects of an Audit: An Experimental Study*, Ph.D. Thesis, Ann Arbor: University of Michigan School of Business Administration, 1962.
2. _____and W. W. Cooper: "Effects of Auditing Records: Organization Objectives," ONR Research Memo No. 98, Pittsburgh: Carnegie Institute of Technology Graduate School of Industrial Administration, June, 1962.
3. Edward, James Dow: *History of Public Accounting in the United States*, MSU Business Studies, East Lansing: Bureau of Business and Economic Research, Graduate School of Business Administration, 1960.
4. Folley, John D., Jr.: *A Study of Strategies in Procedural Task Performance*, Ph.D. Thesis, Pittsburgh: Carnegie Institute of Technology, Department of Psychology, 1961.
5. Goldbeck, Robert A., et al.: "Application of Half-Split Techniques to Problem-Solving Tasks," *Journal of Experimental Psychology*, vol. 53, pp. 330-338, 1957.

6. Littleton, A. C., and B. S. Yamey: *Studies in the History of Accounting*, Homewood, Ill.: Irwin, 1956.
7. March, James G.: "An Introduction to the Theory and Measurement of Influence," *The American Political Science Review*, vol. 49, pp. 431-451, 1955.
8. Mautz, R. K., and H. A. Sharaf: *The Philosophy of Auditing*, American Accounting Association Monograph, Menasha, Wis.: Banta, 1961.

13

GOALS, PROGRAMS AND THE TRAINING FUNCTION

CHADWICK J. HABERSTROH
University of Denver

The objective of this section is to relate research in behavioral science to the basic problem of managerial control. The specific parts of behavioral science that will be touched upon in this paper are germane to my own continuing research interest in exploring purposive behavior, both of the organizational aggregate and the disaggregated components. The relation between purpose and control is adequately presented in the cybernetics literature, and there is no need to repeat it except to indicate its relevance to the subject matter of this paper.

There is a distinction that has become progressively sharper in recent years between the control properties of a first-order closed-loop servo-mechanism and the notion of *adaptive control* which may be defined briefly as second-order closed-loop servos with complex information input and processing and information output serving only to regulate the parameters of first-order servo systems [22, 23]. The pertinence of this paper is to adaptive control. The *goals* to be referred to occupy the position of standards read into a servo loop for comparison with output. The *programs* are the detailed recipes by which information input including that on goal attainment is transformed into output. Some parameters of first-order programs that could be the outputs of adaptive control systems are resource availability, transfer prices, delay time in information transmission, inventory reorder points, etc. Training activity is also one possible output of an adaptive control system that would serve to alter a certain class of first-order parameters, the perceptions of individuals or groups. In non-automated activities, at least, the programs and parameters that count are those in people's heads.

Thus, one process of adaptive control in organizations involves directed change induced in personnel. Two aspects of this process stand out. First, the specific changes are dominated by the task goals toward which control is oriented. Second, the change is induced in the perception and behavior of a human individual or group acting in a social context. There is a basic tension between these aspects of the process, in that a change functional for the aggregate (the organization) is induced only if it serves the purposes of the component (individual, group, or department). The resulting dynamics, including the integration of purpose necessary for success, the resistance and conflict observed before integration is achieved, and the determinants of these phenomena, are within the special province of behavioral science. Bennis, et al. [1] have collected together much of the work that is relevant to these questions. The following remarks are directed only toward the organizational variables that might condition the process. They will be divided into three sections: Methodology, Some Research Results, Discussion.

METHODOLOGY

The problem in this area is to get definitions of theoretical variables such as *goals* and *purposes* that are behaviorally meaningful. Stated negatively, this implies the avoidance of definitions that turn on a priori design (i.e. what the boss thinks the organization is doing or ought to be doing) and constructive definitions (e.g. profit maximization, chosen because economists think it theoretically important). This is one place where study of managerial control can draw heavily from behavioral science. Organization purpose is one kind of human purpose, and techniques for the measurement of human purposes by content analysis and attitude survey are well developed.

I have participated directly in the design of three different techniques for measuring organization goals. The first of these is reported in [9] and will be discussed in some detail below. The second was an attempt by a thesis student, [5] to list and categorize objectives by means of depth interviews with high ranking executives. The third was a pre-coded questionnaire that was given to the faculties of two different business schools, partly for administrative purposes and partly as a methodological investigation.

This third technique consisted of a list of five possible objectives for business education which the respondents were asked to rank by order of their preference, giving separate rankings of the five objectives for the graduate and undergraduate programs of their respective colleges. The major purpose of the investigation was to measure the degree to which educational objectives were shared. See Exhibit 13-1. As might be expected, overall concordance was low. A comparison of the two schools, however, shows substantially higher concordance among Faculty A than among Faculty B. From examination of the questionnaires, it appears that this is due partly to lesser applicability of the instrument to College B and partly to the greater degree of departmentalization within College B. College A had essentially one program at each level; College B had about a dozen. The questionnaire was designed specifically for College A and later applied with almost no change to College B. Unfortunately, it was not possible to make a rigorous test of the effect of depart-

mentalization; not all questionnaires were identifiable as to departmental affiliation of respondent.

Exhibit 13-1. Concordance* on educational
objectives

	Graduate program	Undergraduate program
Faculty A	.417	.338
Faculty B	.174	.156

*Coefficient W, [13, pp. 410-20] .

A secondary objective of the investigation was to measure the
similarity between individual faculty members' conceptions of their
graduate and undergraduate programs. Exhibit 13-2 gives the distribution of a coefficient of rank correlation, Kendall's tau, calculated
from the two rankings on each questionnaire. As can be seen, the
results for Faculty B did not differ from randomized rankings. The
results for Faculty A, however, show a significant polarization of
opinion between those who perceived the programs as essentially
similar and those who perceived them as different. This investigation is presented here only to illustrate how an attitude instrument
can be applied to a question about organizational goals.

Exhibit 13-2. Perceived similarity of graduate and
undergraduate objectives.

τ *	Faculty A		Faculty B	
	Random rankings	Observed rankings	Random rankings	Observed rankings
1.0	.31	9	.39	.5
.8	1.23	4	1.57	2.5
.6	2.77	5	3.53	4.0
.4	4.62	5	5.88	7.0
.2	6.17	4	7.83	5.0
0.0	6.78	5	8.62	8.0
- .2	6.17	1	7.83	7.5
- .4	4.62	1	5.88	8.0
- .6	2.77	2	3.53	.5
- .8	1.23	1	1.57	3.5
- 1.0	.31	0	.39	.5
Total	37	37	47	47

*[13, pp. 391-407] .

Now I wish to return to the first technique mentioned above, which
involved a content analysis of administrative communications in a

steel plant. Unlike the other two techniques, this one did not use responses elicited in interview as a surrogate for actual organizational behavior. The stream of administrative communication is itself an important part of organizational behavior and is, in fact, the main coordinative mechanism. A measurement applied to this stream has the same face validity for studies of organization as an implanted microelectrode has for studies of animal nervous communication. Some anthropological work applying much the same methodological approach (i.e., measurement and analysis of the logic implicit in certain types of in-group communication) has been reported by Wallace [20]. A recent survey of content-analytic technique is given by Pool [15].

This technique is much more elaborate than the simple pre-coded questionnaire used on the business school faculties. It retains the generality of impressionistic methods, yet permits meaningful treatment of the question of reliability. The content-analysis procedure sub-divides into three different operations. The first two are the well-known steps of unitizing a stream of communication and categorizing the units. There were essentially three categories needed, irrelevant, goal relevant, means-end relation. A reliability check on this categorization yielded a percent agreement score of 71%. This is adequate for the purpose but should be improved. The third step in the procedure has elements of novelty. It involves essentially a sorting of all goal-relevant units by the semantic referent of the unit in question. A rigorous definition of reliability can be established for this operation, so that a check is feasible for the whole procedure. This was not done, however, in the investigation cited, and the sort was handled impressionistically.

Once the content analysis is completed, the semantic units can be arranged by means of the coded means-end relations into a hierarchy of goals, subgoals and means activities. The result is an operational definition of an organization's *task model.*

Postponing the question of what a "task model" might be used for, the technique just described appears to be capable of being completely automated. Techniques for handling natural languages on large-scale digital computers have advanced to the point where the problem outlined above should be a relatively easy one [2]. Thus, the question of reliability would be eliminated as would the relatively large amount of labor needed for this sort of content analysis. Similar undertakings have been reported by Stone et al. [19] and Jaffe [12]. Let us pass on to the substantive questions that could be investigated by means of such a tool.

SOME RESEARCH RESULTS

In my steel-plant study, the objective was to test a number of general hypotheses about organization structure that collectively established the anatomy of an organizational control mechanism. The first of these was that in any stable organization a relatively small number of mutually independent supergoals would be found. This hypothesis was tested directly by the "task model." Four such goals were found. They related to production, safety, costs, and in-plant medical service. They each appeared in the task model as the goal of a number of means activities, but were never mentioned as means to other ends. In a sentence, the plant objective was to make steel as ordered, keep injury rates down, incur low costs in terms of resources susceptible to accounting valuation, and maintain the health of the work force.

Another hypothesis was that goals that survive in an organization will be operative. A necessary condition for operativeness is that means be perceived to attain goals. The task model included means activities relating to each goal, thus verifying this part of the hypothesis.

Another hypothesis is that main goals in large organizations are achieved, at least in part, through independent control over subgoals in the task model. The safety goals were factored into departmental goals, and departments were assigned responsibility for their achievement. At least one intermediate goal, housekeeping, was also controlled. Information was reported by several inspection procedures and this resulted in clean-up activity.

The most ambitious use of the task model related to the last hypothesis: The most central or highest executive centers react to a failure to achieve goals by making changes in the executive organization or in the means activities of the program. It was hoped that measurement of the task model in successive years would yield a direct measure of the rate of innovation which could be correlated with performance relative to goals. The measure did not work out. This probably was due to insufficient sensitivity, because a more direct rating of amount of innovation based on annual reports did indicate a close correlation with performance relative to goals.

A full discussion of the control system found in this study was reported in [10]. Here I wish only to make a few points relevant to the present topic. Adaptive control was clearly seen in the steel plant. The innovations made, however, mostly involved provision for more intensive application of known techniques. Some of these changes involved training programs, but these were compromised by resistance of those affected in the same ways shown in many behavioral science studies. The input side of this adaptive control process was also relatively simple. The cue for its evocation appeared to be an increasing gap between target figures for injury frequencies and the actual performance. The program changes considered were limited to ideas immediately available in the environment of the executive group, mainly practices in use in other plants to which they were directed by company staff personnel.

For a contrast in style of adaptive control we can refer to the work of Burns and Stalker [3]. The above example fits quite well into their category of "mechanistic organization". They take the position that this organizational type can function adequately when not exposed to extreme change, i.e. when a low rate of innovation is required. Burns and Stalker describe several organizations which, like the steel plant mentioned above, did maintain control with this rather crude style of adaptation. There is a great contrast, however, between these firms and others discussed by Burns and Stalker which were able to maintain control successfully in a rapidly changing environment by means of a much higher rate of innovation carried on through a vastly different organizational system, an "organic" organizational type.

There were two properties in which the "organic" type differed from the more usual "mechanistic" type. It had a network structure of communication and influence emphasizing lateral rather than vertical channels and information or advice rather than instruction or command. It also evoked a higher degree of commitment from personnel to the overall tasks of the organization based on a broadly shared conception of the task model.

These properties permitted prompt and effective use of specialized abilities where needed, e.g. technically qualified laboratory people in close touch with new developments communicating directly with machine operators to work out production routines for new designs, or production managers scheduling parts availability according to informal status reports from design departments rather than waiting for a formal handover of responsibility. The implication is, of course, that the lateral communication channels brought information directly from the locations where it occurs in most accurate and complete form to other locations where it could be used to reprogram operating phases. The shared task model provided a basis for cooperation between source and receiver and permitted the reprogramming to be carried out locally yet be relevant to the over-all task.

DISCUSSION

What are the determinants of adaptive activity in organizations? Burns and Stalker suggest three requirements for use of the "organic" form. These are (1) a high rate of environmental change, (2) de-emphasis of the political and status system, and (3) competent management. I am not satisfied with this formulation nor with their dictum that "mechanistic" forms are perfectly adequate "for conditions of stability". First, conditions of stability are increasingly hard to find, and often undesirable anyway from a social point of view (for example, a protected monopoly position). Second, they seem to ignore entirely the high human cost of conventional "mechanistic" organization in terms of alienation of the majority of people from their work [16]. Third, incompetence and excessive selfishness are much too convenient grounds for explanation of organizational failure to adapt "organically" to conditions of change. The human component of organizations has to be accepted for just such competence and selfishness as it in fact possesses. The interesting questions relate to the role of alternative institutional patterns in mobilizing both competence and purpose.

The two patterns discussed by Burns and Stalker seem to be a perfectly adequate beginning. A widely shared task model and a non-hierarchial communications network would appear to be directly functional to adaptation as well as to cooperation itself. There seem to be many possibilities for worthwhile research on these questions, the means of securing these patterns, and possible side effects.

A communication network, like a task model, is as much a property of the social system as it is of the task system. The notion that lateral communication produces more effective adaptation than vertical communication should come as no surprise. Psychological studies have shown that status differences between people tend to reduce the amount and validity of communication between them. If vertical communication is imposed anyway, is it any wonder that the prevailing atmosphere is one of threat, mutual punishment, defensiveness and bargaining? Or is it strange to find that, even in mechanistically run bureaucracies, much of the work gets done by informal lateral communications?

Elsewhere [14], I have developed the idea of a lateral specialization of managerial functions as a possible design feature in organizations. Training, development and research (TDR) activities are one such basis for specialization. All require a high order of competence in a limited range of subject matter. All require an ability to communicate ideas in this subject matter to other people. If personnel possessing a specialized competence are to utilize it in the interests of organization goals, the managerial nature of their contribution must be recognized. Nothing is easier than to alienate the expert from the central work interests of an organization, so that he becomes a curiosity occasionally called upon to produce an idea to the order of his managerial keepers. Actually, many of the demands upon an organization for adaptation first become sensible in the specialized studies of technical experts, e.g. new developments in technology, changes in markets, law, or employee morale. This information and the competence to deal with it need to be linked directly to the organization component where adaptation would be functional. This means that one responsibility of the TDR specialist should be to initiate a communication channel to the affected component for training purposes and for such further developmental work as may be required.

This design feature is, of course, consistent with the findings of Burns and Stalker and with a number of other research studies, especially of the Tavistock group. Its feasibility and desirability can be established only by further research on the underlying determinants of organizational behavior, preferably deliberate experimentation under competent scientific observation. Fortunately, more and more such research is being reported. Some of the Tavistock work is of this type. The findings of these studies and some of the classic research on the dynamics of organization purpose [7, 17, 18] have, however, carried us to a plateau in understanding that can be superceded only by methodological developments placing less reliance on an informed impressionism.

The combination of well-designed field research with more rigorous techniques of measurement and analysis holds great promise. The measurement of goal structure has already been discussed. Techniques for study of communication structure have also been reported [4, 11, 21]. Simulation techniques like those used in industrial dynamics [8] and behavioral theory of the firm [6] provide a means of linking these data and others so as to yield meaningful statements about organizational wholes. Adaptation is a property that can be studied in this manner.

BIBLIOGRAPHY

1. Bennis, Warren G., Kenneth D. Benne, and Robert Chin (eds.), *The Planning of Change*, New York: Holt, 1961.
2. Borko, Harold: *Computer Applications in the Behavioral Sciences*, Englewood Cliffs, N. J.: Prentice-Hall, Chaps. 16, 17, 1962.
3. Burns, Tom, and G. M. Stalker: *The Management of Innovation*, Chicago: Quadrangle Books, 1961.
4. Chapple, E. D., and L. R. Sayles: *The Measure of Management*, New York: Macmillan, 1961.
5. Clarke, Robert D.: *A Method of Measuring the Objective Thinking* in a Company, Unpublished M.S. Thesis, 1961, Massachusetts Institute of Technology.
6. Cyert, Richard M., and James G. March: *Behavioral Theory of the Firm*, Englewood Cliffs, N. J.: Prentice-Hall, 1963.
7. Dalton, Melville: *Men Who Manage*, New York: Wiley, 1959.
8. Forrester, Jay W.: *Industrial Dynamics*, New York: M. I. T. and Wiley, 1961.
9. Haberstroh, Chadwick J.: *Processes of Internal Control in Firms*, Ann Arbor: University Microfilms, 1958.

10. ———: "Control as an Organizational Process", *Management Science*, vol. 6, no. 2, pp. 165-171, 1960.
11. Jacobson, E., and S. Seashore: "Communication Practices in Complex Organizations," *Journal of Social Issues*, vol. 8, no. 3, 1951.
12. Jaffe, Joseph: "Toward the Automation of Discourse Analysis", Unpublished Paper, William Alanson White Institute of Psychiatry, Psychoanalysis, and Psychology, 1961.
13. Kendall, Maurice G.: *The Advanced Theory of Statistics*, 5th ed., vol. I, New York: Hafner, 1952.
14. March, James G. (ed.): *Handbook of Administration and Organization Theory*, Chicago: Rand McNally, 1964.
15. Pool, Ithiel, (ed.): *Trends in Content Analysis*, Urbana, Ill.: University of Illinois Press, 1959.
16. Presthus, R.: *The Organizational Society*, New York: Knopf, 1962.
17. Selznick, Philip: *TVA and the Grass Roots*, Berkeley: University of California Press, 1953.
18. Simon, Herbert A.: "Birth of an organization—the Economic Cooperation Administration", *Public Administration Review*, vol. 13, no. 4, 1953.
19. Stone, Philip J., Robert F. Bales, J. Zvi Namenwirth, and Daniel M. Oglivie: "The General Inquirer: A Computer System for Content Analysis and Retrieval Based on the Sentence as a Unit of Information", *Behavioral Science*, vol. 7, no. 4, p. 484, 1962.
20. Wallace, Anthony F. C.: "Culture and Cognition", *Science*, vol. 135, pp. 351-357, 1962.
21. Weiss, R. S.: *Processes of Organization*, Ann Arbor, Michigan: University Press, 1956.
22. Wiener, Norbert: *Cybernetics*, 2d ed., New York: M.I.T. and Wiley, chap. 9, 1961.
23. Yovits, Marshall C., George T. Jacobi, and Gordon D. Goldstein: *Self-Organizing Systems* - 1962. Washington, D. C.: Spartan Books, 1962, especially pp. 1-7.

14

PSYCHOLOGICAL RESEARCH ON PAY

MASON HAIRE

University of California at Berkeley

INTRODUCTION

Oddly enough, there is relatively little empirical work on psychological problems underlying pay. It has been a tired cliche for the psychologist to rail at economists' naive and unsophisticated assumptions about motivation in the concept of the economic man. However, railing at the concept is about all that's been done. In spite of the fact that most of the assumptions underlying compensation are psychological, very little research has gone on. This paper reports a series of studies which are part of a first step toward correcting this state of affairs.[1]

It might help, first, to identify a group of what seem to be properly psychological problems lying behind pay. First, there is the most basic assumption that pay is an incentive. It may seem to be an *a priori* given that this is so, but the very fact, and the manner in which it is true is subject to test. Second, the structure of wages and salaries opens psychological questions. By structure I mean, for example, the slope of the line of pay plotted against merit, time, productivity, or other desirable commodities. At what rate should we pay, or, restated, what structural pattern buys in most of the criterion good per dollar invested? From this flow three subsidiary questions: the perception of pay, satisfaction with pay, and the interaction between organizational structure and pay. By perception I mean both such questions as "How big a difference is perceived?" and "How does a given step look to me?" and, on the other hand, "How does my boss's (or subordinates') pay look?" It also includes the determination of indifference points—i.e. "What pension plan is worth x cents per hour?" and "How does this figure differ with individual variables such as age, marital status, etc.?" The satisfaction area raises all the questions of structure again—with satisfaction as a dependent variable. "What pay-slope (or step-size) leads to satisfaction?" Finally, variables such as level in the organization, flat

---

[1] The studies referred to here were done by the Industrial Psychology Group in the Institute of Industrial Relations, University of California, The Behavioral Research Service, General Electric Company, and The University of North Carolina. They appeared in more detail in the journal *Industrial Relations*, October 1963.

versus tall organizations, large versus small, and the like are all related to the leverage of form and rate of pay.

One of the studies mentioned here belongs in a third class of problems—the psychodynamics of pay. By this I mean the interaction of pay with other psychological activities within the person. Here it deals with the problem of equity—one of the most important problems in pay today. Equity here refers to the experienced balance (or discrepancy) between one's own estimate of worth and the rate of payment. It includes, for example, the question of the comparison groups one uses in estimating equity, ego evaluation, and the like. The internal character of these variables is the justification for calling them psychodynamic.

Finally there are a group of over-riding attitudinal variables to which we need answers. Without further data it is by no means easy to answer such questions as "What do you think you get paid for?" "What do you think you should be paid for?" "What (asked of management) do you pay people for?" A set of answers to these questions is assumed in dealing with logical analyses of pay. A psychological analysis must be grounded in more realistic data.

One final issue: What is the purpose of such psychological data on pay? With respect to the conflict between labor and management, two extreme positions may be taken. One extreme—mistaken, I believe—is that if we understood perfectly all conflict would disappear. This is a variant of the *tout comprendre c'est tout pardonner* view and seems to assume a pre-established harmony which is approached through a miasma of human fallibility. I will only say at this point, "I doubt it." The other extreme—equally misleading—is the notion of wages as a market item and labor as a contract. This view assumes an irreconcilable conflict between labor and management with each bargaining with the other for an advantage which must ultimately be to the disadvantage of the other. This view has been politically useful in organizing unions, and many managers have been seduced by it, but I think it is neither correct nor in the public interest.

The view of wages (or salaries) as the best bargain in the market place assumes the employer-employee relationship to be of the form of a two-person zero-sum game where what one wins is necessarily the other's loss. In such a game information about the other is of value to a player only that he may better anticipate the other's strategy and choose his own to the further disadvantage of his opponent. In two-person non-zero-sum games, on the other hand, information takes on a quite different role. The defining difference between the two is that one's gain is not necessarily the other's loss. It is not necessarily true that information can only help one and hurt the other. It is exactly in the non-zero-sum game that each party, knowing the other's objectives and possibilities can find joint solutions,

less good perhaps than his maximum but less bad than his (or the other's) minimum. This kind of coalition-solution can create productive solutions where only either-or conflict seemed to exist.
What kind of evidence have we that labor-management conflict over pay is truly a zero-sum process? Only an oversimplified bookkeeping approach and a traditional theory. If we set these aside, the provision of more information about each side's desiderata in pay may lead to more fruitful solutions for both.

It should be mentioned that this kind of coalition has, of course, the danger of combining against a third party—in this case the public. Labor and management can, in principle, agree on a division of spoils and increase the amount to be divided by exploiting the other partner. Again, widespread information on the effects of pay can make it possible to maximize the returns to all three partners simultaneously.

RESULTS

The five studies mentioned here consist of two on hourly paid workers, two on salaried managers and one laboratory study with paid subjects. I won't go into methodological detail because that is available in the papers referred to on the first page. Instead, I will confine myself to illustrative results reported in very abbreviated form. First, the labor studies:

1. Both studies were attempts to work out equivalences of parts of the pay package—i.e., e.g., how much pay would one trade for a shorter work week, a union shop, a pension, or a hospital plan. The first datum to report is that, granted the usual methodological difficulties, it is quite possible to get accurate answers to these questions.
2. One quasi-methodological finding: One is bound to ask "How transitive are the preference choices?" and "How uni-dimensional is the scale on which exchanges are made?" In a sense these collapse into one question. In one study, 96.97% of 33,990 choices were transitive. With this much transitivity, uni-dimensionality seems a necessary condition. In spite of this, the data fit poorly Thurstone's tests for uni-dimensionality. However, where N is large his requirements become unusually stringent.
3. There are wide variations in the value of non-pay benefits (pension, hospital insurance, etc.) to hourly paid workers as a function of biographical characteristics. For example, younger workers choose pay over pension more than older workers do; women do so more than men, and the like. In general, preference varies with the stage in the family cycle. The results suggest a real benefit to be obtained from a cafeteria-style pay-plan.

4. In addition to the demographic data—which are not surprising—morale turns out to be importantly related to preference for alternative forms of pay. In general, the lower the morale the higher the preference for pay as opposed to benefits. This may be interpreted as one of the unaccounted costs of morale, since the preference for immediate pay implies a lack of long-term commitment to the company, or pay-preference may be seen as an alternative operational measure of morale.

5. In a unionized plant a merit-based bonus system was less valued than in an unorganized plant. For unorganized workers such a bonus system, depending on the foreman's evaluation, had a positive value; unionized workers were willing to give up 8.3 cents per hour to keep it out. Again, this can be seen as an effect of or an operational definition of attitudes connected with unionization.

Among the management studies:

1. At a given level in the organization all managers—across many companies—were remarkably similar about what the pay for their level *should be*—even though there was wide variation in what it actually was.

2. Satisfaction with pay varied inversely with educational level. Further, the higher education, holding managerial level constant, the more managers tended to compare their pay with reference groups outside the company. Professionalism, education, and dissatisfaction seem associated.

3. Managers anticipating a large step in pay in the next five years were more dissatisfied with present pay than those anticipating small steps.

4. Higher level managers were more satisfied with pay than lower level managers. Of course, they get more. On the other hand, they expect more. Equal deficits bring more dissatisfaction at lower levels than at high.

5. Holding level constant, higher paid managers were more satisfied in some other motivational areas. They felt more security and esteem. They were no more satisfied in social needs or in self-actualization.

Finally, in the laboratory studies:

1. It is possible to engender feelings of inequity by making a person feel that he is overpaid.

2. Those who were made to feel overpaid tried to retrieve their feeling of equity by increasing their input—i.e. doing more work.

3. Some subjects felt the work was easy; some felt it was hard. Those who felt it was easy and that they were overpaid made extra efforts to return to an equitable state by doing more work.

If they felt it was hard and they were overpaid, they did no more work than those who were not made to feel overpaid. In the group who felt they were paid equitably there was no influence on productivity of the feeling that the work was easy or hard.

Here, in brief, are a group of illustrative results of psychological research on compensation. It is clear that it can be done—both methodologically and practically. It seems equally clear that it should be done. We're beginning to do some of it. I hope lots of other people will, too.

Discussion

BEHAVIORAL SCIENCE AND MANAGEMENT CONTROL

JOHN L. KENNEDY
Princeton University

The plight of the commentator at a seminar such as this one is much like that of the unhappy after-dinner speaker who is expected to say something interesting after everyone is replete with the excellent food-for-thought provided by the actual participants. One way to begin is to say a grace--oh Graduate School of Business, we thank thee for that which was provided!

Chadwick J. Haberstroh, Professor of Management, University of Denver, began the assault on common assumptions about management control in the first paper, "Goals, Programs and the Training Function." He, like other participants, leans heavily on the servo-mechanism analogy to the control process to distinguish two types of control, (1) "mechanistic," that follows the thermostat model very closely, and (2) "organic" or adaptive control. In the mechanistic type of control, achievement of goals is obtained by a ponderous process of correcting error signals generated by a compartmentalized and vertically-organized network of communication, illustrated by the author's studies in a steel plant. The organic control system differs from the mechanistic in that the communication network emphasizes lateral rather than vertical channels and the messages carried in the network are more likely to be "information and advice rather than instruction or command." Organic control is illustrated by studies on certain companies in the electronics industry. Query, what is the effect of different levels of capital investment on the willingness of management to take the "risk" of organic control? Does the size of capital investment correlate with type of management? Haberstroh points out the advantages of organic control in terms of greater survival potential in a changing environment but his main argument is based upon "the high human cost of conventional 'mechanistic' organization in terms of alienation of the majority of people from their work."

After review of related evidence from the behavioral science literature on the effects of lateral communication in work groups, he makes a plea for scientific investigation in the field of the consequences of the mechanistic and the organic design principles for large organizations.

Haberstroh's paper raises an important and intricate question, namely, how do we measure the "high human cost of conventional mechanistic organization"? Possibly research on this value-laden issue will need to precede an organized empirical assault on the problems raised in his most interesting contribution.

Mason Haire, Professor of Psychology at the University of California, Berkeley, reviews some recent psychological studies on "the perception of pay, satisfaction with pay and the interaction between organizational structure and pay." These studies, in general, open a Pandora's box of troubles for the unsophisticated notion that pay is a simple incentive. It turns out that pay is a communication mechanism, an attitude and, in the case of college students who were made to feel overpaid, an embarrassment! Haire views these studies as a mere beginning on the knotty problem of the psychodynamics of pay and invites us all to dive into this "rewarding" area of research.

N. C. Churchill, W. W. Cooper, and Trevor Sainsbury, from the Graduate School of Industrial Administration, Carnegie Institute of Technology, reported field and laboratory studies on the effect of auditing on the attitudes and behavior of the audited. Auditing is a time-honored method of exercising control in the business community. Although much has been written about technique, this paper seems to be the first attempt to understand the consequences of a number of auditing procedures on those who are audited. Their results in a laboratory study "suggest that various kinds of audit mixes may have countervailing tendencies so that nothing is really added and, furthermore, that an 'excessive' amount (or combination) of examinations may even be detrimental." Preliminary results from a field interview study of a number of actual firms are reported but they are difficult to summarize.

These three papers reveal a healthy interest on the part of skilled professionals in re-evaluating some of the most sacred cows of traditional business management and control. If these papers are a representative sample of basic research in management controls, we can look forward to important modifications to the practice of management in the future.

Discussion

BEHAVIORAL SCIENCE AND MANAGEMENT CONTROL

PHILBURN RATOOSH

San Francisco State College

and

University of California at Berkeley

HABERSTROH

Any organization whose structure is not trivially simple has multiple goals. Any organization with more than a minimum of complexity has some goals that conflict with others. This seems to me so obvious that I wonder what Haberstroh has in mind when he states a general hypothesis that "in any stable organization a relatively small number of *mutually independent* (my italics) supergoals would be found." In a steel-plant study he found four such goals that were related to production, safety, costs, and in-plant medical service. Are safety and production independent? Do not safety devices have an (at least short-run) adverse effect on production? Are safety and costs independent? Don't safety devices increase production costs? Does the in-plant medical service contribute more to production than the cost of maintaining it?

Sometimes oversimplification leads to fruitful consequences. In this case it is not clear to me what is gained by treating as independent what can be so treated only by definition.

Another hypothesis Haberstroh tested is that the executive branch of an organization reacts "to a failure to achieve goals by making changes in the executive organization or in the means activities of the program." This hypothesis was not verified. How any group, executive or otherwise, behaves when its goals are not attained is of course a complex question. But let us suppose that we observe not an organization but an individual human being about to enter a complicated, realistic, problem-solving situation. Would we not expect this individual to display some resistance to new ideas and behaviors we might call irrational as a function of his past experience and personality? Yet curiously we expect organizations to be free of such peculiarities. One is tempted to speculate that the resistance on the part of most organization theorists and organization members to this idea is attributable to the anxiety that might be generated by the notion that organizations are human too.

HAIRE

Haire is certainly correct in decrying the paucity of research results on the psychology of pay, and studies of this kind should be welcomed. Is this dearth a consequence of the reluctance of economically-oriented scholars to look at the psychological aspects of their subject matter?

I shall comment on only one laboratory finding. Those subjects who were made to feel overpaid did more work if they felt the work was easy. Elliott Jaques reports, from findings in industry, anxiety and guilt on the part of those who feel overpaid. It may be that real situations seldom provide tasks so easy that the compensation displayed in the laboratory study would be seen.

CHURCHILL, COOPER, AND SAINSBURY

The paper of Churchill, Cooper, and Sainsbury is exciting because it is the first paper of which I am aware to describe an experimental study of auditing. Of all the areas of management, accounting is perhaps the one that is most oriented toward tradition and thus the one most antagonistic to new approaches. It is refreshing therefore to learn about an experimental work whose results can be applied to this field.

A significant result of this study is that one group—the industrial subjects—decreased errors in anticipation of an audit, while the student subjects increased errors. I feel that the writers are overly modest when they declare that "additional study is certainly needed before we can seriously entertain the hypothesis that knowledge of an audit causes certain individuals to behave to the detriment of themselves or of the organization." That such individuals exist no clinical psychologist would doubt, and the experimenters found them among their subjects. One must now ask: Where are such persons found in organizations? How can they be discovered and given positions such that their personal characteristics do not adversely affect their organization? Do these individuals tend to possess other characteristics that would make them valuable members of an organization?

Churchill, Cooper and Sainsbury have demonstrated that experimental work in this area is feasible. It is unfortunate that there remain individuals who doubt it.

15

CONTROLS, CONTROL AND MANAGEMENT

PETER F. DRUCKER
New York University

SECTION I

In the grammar of social institutions the word *"controls"* is not
the plural of the word "control." Not only do more "controls" not
necessarily give more "control"—the two words, in the context of
social institutions have different meanings altogether. The synonyms
for "controls" are measurement and information. The synonym for
"control" is direction. "Controls" pertain to means, "control" to
an end. "Controls" deal with facts, that is with events of the past.
"Control" deals with expectations, that is with the future. "Controls"
are analytical and operational, concerned with what was and is.
"Control" is normative, concerned with what ought to be, with significance rather than with meaning.

We are rapidly acquiring great capacity to design "controls" in
social institutions, based on a great improvement in techniques, especially in the application of logical and mathematical tools to events
of this social universe, and in the ability to process and analyze
large masses of data very fast. What does this mean for "control?"
Specifically what are the requirements for these greatly improved
"controls" to give better "control" to management? For, in the task
of a manager, "controls" are purely a means to an end; the end is
"control."

That here is a problem, ordinary language and its use makes
abundantly clear. The man in a business who is charged with producing the "controls" is the "controller." But most, if not all executives, including most controllers themselves, would consider it gross
misuse and abuse of controllership were this "controller" to use his
"controls" to exercise "control" in the business. This, they would
argue would actually make the business be "out of control" altogether.

The reasons for this apparent paradox lie in the complexity, both
of human beings and of the social task. I do not intend to go into meta-
physics, nor is this necessary. I am willing to grant that both, the
human being and society are actually completely determined. But
there are so many determinants, and their form and impact are so
varied, that, at least on the microcosmic level on which we operate—
and on which even the basic policy decisions of great powers are

286

being made—there is so much complexity as to result in a genuine "uncertainty principle" insofar as the relationship between "controls" and "control" is concerned. A genuine feed-back is not possible.

If we deal with a human being in a social institution, "controls" must become personal motivation to lead to "control." Instead of a mechanical system, the control system in a human-social situation is a volitional system. That we know very little about the will is not even the central point. A translation is required before the information by the "controls" can become ground of action—the translation of one kind of information into another which we call *perception*.

In the social institution itself there is a second complexity, a second "uncertainty principle." It is almost impossible to pre-figure the responses appropriate to a certain event in a social situation. We can, and do, build a control into a machine which slows down the turning speed whenever it exceeds a certain figure. And we can do this either by mechanical means or by instrumentation which shows a human operator what the turning speed is, and which gives him the specific, unambiguous instruction to turn the speed down when the indicator reaches a certain point. But a control reading "profits are falling" does not indicate, with any degree of probability, the response "raise prices" let alone by how much; the control—reading "sales are falling" does not indicate the response "cut prices," and so on. There is not only a large—a very large—number of other equally probable responses—so large that it is usually not even possible to identify them in advance. There is no indication in the event itself which of these responses is even possible, let alone appropriate, not to mention its being right. The event itself may not even be meaningful. But even if it is, it is by no means certain what it means. And the probability of its being meaningful is a much more important datum than the event itself—and one which is almost never to be discerned by analyzing the event.

In other words what is needed in the social situation is a decision based on assumptions—and essentially assumptions not in respect to the recorded event but in respect to the future, that is expectations which know no probability but can only be judged according to plausibility. For there are no "facts" in the future in a social universe in which periodicity—at least on our minuscule scale—cannot be assumed, must indeed rather be considered quite unlikely.

There are at least parts of such a situation which resemble the phenomena of the physical universe. We can in other words "simulate," that is, pretend that we deal with physical events rather than with social events. And such "simulation" is indeed highly fruitful as we have learned these last ten years or so. But we should never forget the fact that this is "simulation"—and therefore something completely different from the symbolic representation of reality which the physicist's formula represents. It is always based on assumptions regarding volition, perception and expectations which need constant re-appraisal.

SECTION II

Does this mean that "controls" are unimportant? Does it mean that they are misleading? The opposite actually follows. Precisely because we deal with such a complex subject, we need control very badly. And precisely because we find ourselves in constant uncertainty as managers in such a situation, "controls" tend to have tremendous impact. In fact both the need and the impact are so great that the wrong "controls" can be exceedingly misleading and dangerous. It is, therefore, important today when our capacity to design and to manipulate controls is increasing so fast, to think through what controls in a social institution and in particular in the business enterprise have to be and have to do, and also what they cannot be and must not attempt to do.

There are four major characteristics of "controls" in business enterprise—two pertain to all social institutions and reflect the fact that business enterprise is a social institution. One of these characteristics pertains to institutions within a society of which business enterprise is one. And the fourth and last one is specifically a characteristic of business enterprise as an economic institution.

1. When we measure the rate of fall of a stone, we are totally outside the event itself. By measuring we do not change the event; and measuring the event does not change us, the observers.

Measuring is both objective and neutral.

In a wide range of natural phenomena, however, especially on the microcosmic level, the act of measuring interferes with the event measured—whether the events are nuclear, microbiological or psychological. The observer in these events becomes a part of the situation. Measurement is still objective but no longer neutral.

In a perceptual situation of complexity, that is in any social situation of the kind we deal with in business enterprise, the act of measurement is, however, neither objective nor neutral. It is subjective and of necessity biased. It changes both the event and the observer. For it changes the perception of the observer—if it does not altogether create his perception. Events in the social situation acquire value by the fact that they are being singled out for the attention of being measured. No matter how "scientific" we are, the fact that this or that set of phenomena is singled out for being "controlled," signals that it is being considered to be important. Everybody who ever watched the introduction of a budget system has seen this happen. For a long time—in many companies forever—realizing the budget figures becomes more important than what the budget is supposed to measure, namely economic performance. This goes often so far that managers, upon their first exposure to a budget system, deliberately hold back sales and cut back profits rather than be guilty of "not making the budget." It takes years of experience and a very intelligent budget director to restore the balance. And there is any number of otherwise perfectly normal research directors who act on the conviction that it is a greater crime to get research results for less than the budgeted amount than not getting any research results at all while spending all the "proper" budget money.

"Controls" in a social institution, in other words, are goal-setting and value-setting. They are not "objective." They are of necessity moral. The only way to avoid this is to flood the executive with so many "controls" that the entire system becomes meaningless, becomes mere "noise." From that point of view maybe the gross abuse of our new data processing capacity, namely as a tool for grinding out huge quantities of totally meaningless data—the abuse of which every early computer user is guilty—is a blessing after all. But it is hardly the right way to use our capacity to provide "controls." This must start out with the realization that "controls" create vision. That is they both affect the events measured and the observer. They endow events not only with meaning but with value.

And this means that the basic question is not "How do we control?" But "What do we measure in our control system." That we can quantify something is no reason at all for measuring it. The question is: "Is this what a manager should consider important?" "Is this what a manager's attention should be focused on?" "Is this a true statement of the basic realities of the enterprise?" "Is this the proper focus for "control," that is for effective direction with maximum economy of effort?"

If these questions are not being asked in designing "controls," we will end up by making business essentially uncontrolled—for then we will simply have no remedy except to proliferate control information to the point where it does not register at all.

2. Because "controls" have such an impact it is not only important that we select the right ones. To enable controls to give right vision and to become the ground for effective action, the measurement must also be appropriate. That is it must present the events measured in structurally true form. Formal validity is not enough.

Grievances coming out of a work force are commonly reported as "five grievances per thousand employees per month." This is formally valid. But is it structurally valid? Or is it misdirection?

The impression this report conveys is first that grievances are distributed throughout the work force in a random matter. They follow, the report seems to say, a U-shaped Gaussian distribution. And secondly—a conclusion from the first impression—they are a minor problem especially if we deal with five grievances per thousand employees per month.

It is almost certain, however, that this, while formally valid, completely mis-represents and mis-informs, let alone mis-directs. Grievances are a social event. Physical nature knows no such phenomena. And social events are almost never distributed in the "normal distribution" we find in the physical world. The "normal distribution" of social events is almost always exponential—with the hyperbola the typical curve. In other words, the great majority of departments in the plant, employing ninety-five per cent of the work force, normally does not even have a single grievance during one year. But in one department, employing only a handful of men, we have a heavy incidence of grievances—so that the "five per thousand" may well mean (and in the actual example from which I took these figures, did mean) a major grievance per man per year. If this department is then the final assembly through which all the production has to pass, and if the workers in this department go out on strike when their grievances are being neglected by a management which has been misled by its own "controls," the impact can be shattering. In the case I quoted it bankrupted the company which is no longer in existence.

Similarly 90 per cent of the volume of a business is usually represented by 2 to 5 per cent of the number of its products. But 90 per cent of the orders by number cover, typically, only 4 or 5 per cent of the volume—but account for 90 per cent and more of the costs. And so it goes. A modern strategic bomber may have a million parts. But 90 per cent of its cost is represented by a very small number of parts, maybe fifty or so—and so is 90 per cent of the upkeep it need though, unfortunately, the 90 per cent of the dollars and the 90 per cent of the upkeep-needs rarely comprise the same parts.

Practically all the innovations in a research laboratory, no matter how large, come out of the work of a very small percentage of the research people. And invariably, 80 per cent of a company's distributors move, at best, 20 per cent of its output, while 10 per cent or fewer of the distributors move two-thirds to three quarters of total sales.

This, unfortunately, very few managers know. The traditional information systems, especially accounting, conceal rather than highlight this fact. (In particular the allocation of overhead tends to obscure the "normal distribution" of economic and social phenonema).

At the same time knowledge of this fact and understanding of it are pre-requisites for effective control. For control is above all a principle of economy. It means allocation of efforts where they can produce the most results with the minimum of energy. This means allocation of efforts to the small number of phenomena which in any social situation account for the great bulk of results.

Without controls that bring out sharply what the real structure of events is, the manager not only lacks knowledge. He cannot, normally expect to do the right thing. On the contrary, all the weight of the daily work pushes him towards allocating energies and resources in proportion to the *number* of events. There is a constant drift towards putting energies and resources where they can have the least results, that is on the vast number of phenomena which, together, account for practically no effects.

Any sales organization I have ever seen, has the bulk of its sales-men—and especially the good men—working on the 90 per cent of the customers who, together, buy 10 per cent of the output, or on the 90 per cent of products by number which, together produce 10 per cent of the company's revenue and markets, and so on. Any technical ser-vice force—one of the most expensive and most valuable resources of a company—in the absence of the right information regarding mar-ket structure and customers, will put its best men on the smallest and least valuable accounts, if only because these are the people who have the least technical competence themselves and therefore seem to need technical help the most. In fact this constant drift towards the irrelevant and unproductive is so great, and the weight behind it so heavy, that a "controls" system which did nothing but focus atten-tion on the central events—the events which under normal probability statistics are not seen at all—would give any manager a great deal more control and very much better performance and results than the most elaborate simulation and quantification can possibly produce.

To bring out the structure of economic and social events should be a major contribution of our new approaches to "controls." We now have the logical and mathematic tools available for the job. In-deed it is in this area that the new methods have been most produc-tive. Of course not everything there is to be measured, conforms to the "normal distribution" of social events. After all we also deal with physical events in business enterprise. And one of the most im-portant and least understood areas of operation are those where events following the "normal distribution" of the physical universe have to be coupled with events following the "normal distribution" of the social universe, for instance, where we have to bring together the physical flow of materials through a plant with an order pattern.

Here in other words is an area of very great contribution. But the new tools and methods will not make this contribution, will indeed miss their greatest opportunity, unless it is realized that how we measure is as important as what we measure—and that the question: "What is the proper measurement and the proper scale" is infinitely more important in social events than it is in the physical universe—precisely because perception is an integral part of the events them-selves.

3. The third characteristic important for the design and use of controls in business enterprise is that business is an institution of society. It exists to contribute to economy, society and individual.

In consequence *results* in business exist only on the outside—in economy, in society and with the customer. It is the customer only who creates a "profit". Everything inside a business, manufacturing, marketing, research and so on, creates only costs, is only a "cost center."

In other words the "managerial" area is concerned with costs alone. *Results are always entrepreneurial.*

Yet we do not have adequate, let alone reliable information regarding the "outside." They are not only by far the hardest to get—to the point where no organization for the acquisition and collection of meaningful outside information could really be set up—the job is much too big. Above all we simply lack the necessary entrepreneurial concepts. The job itself has never been thought through—at least not so far. And the century of patient analysis of managerial, inside phenomena, events and data, the century of patient, skillful work on the individual operations and tasks within the business, has no counterpart in respect to the entrepreneurial job.

To put it differently, we can easily record and therefore quantify efficiency, that is, efforts. We have very few instruments to record and quantify effects, that is, the outside. But even the most efficient buggy whip manufacturer would no longer be in business. It is of little value to have the most efficient engineering department if it designs the wrong product. The Cuban subsidiaries of U.S. companies were by far the best run and, apparently, the most profitable— let alone the least "troublesome"—of all U.S. operations in Latin America. And it mattered little, I daresay, during the period of IBM's great expansion in the last ten or fifteen years how "efficient" its operations were; it's basic entrepreneurial idea was the right, the effective one.

It is not only that the outside, the area of results, is much less accessible than the inside. It is at the same time much more remote as well. The central problem of the executive in the large organization is his—necessary—insulation from the outside. This applies to the President of the United States as well as to the President of United States Steel. What today's organization therefore needs, above all, are synthetic sense organs for the outside. If modern "controls" are to make a contribution, it would be above all here.

Yet this is exactly the area where we do not put to work the new technology of control. We tend—as people with a new tool kit always do—to go to work where it is easy. These are the inside, the managerial events. We should, however, go to work where we can make the greatest contribution. On the outside, we cannot indeed hope to come up with anything of such beautiful precision as a Queuing Theory inventory system. But we may come up with something which (unlike some fancy inventory systems I have seen) is actually useful and may even be used. In other words a new approach, a new technology, a new set of tools should always be put to work on the difficult rather than the easy, on the things the old tools could not do at all rather than on the things they did passably well. It should give new power rather than be frittered away on improvements. And unless we use the new approaches for an understanding and ordering of the outside, the entrepreneurial world of business enterprise— even though all we can produce there for the time being are insights rather than quantitative statements—we are not going to make the new technology truly useful. We are going to abuse it for the gratification of the technician's virtuosity rather than for the satisfaction of an urgent need of business and society.

4. Finally, in terms of specifications for effective quantitative controls, we should look at business enterprise as something separate, that is as business as a meaningful sphere of human action by itself. As such it presents a unique appearance to people interested in controls and control. Business, unlike all natural and mechanical systems, exhibits a wide range of events and results that are of profound importance and yet cannot easily be quantified within any meaningful system of measurement. But business, also, unlike any other social system, has a wide range of events and results which can be quantified. Business is the only system we know which has both quantifiable and non-quantifiable results and events, both equally important.

This gives business a unique opportunity for controls, but also a unique problem.

Any experienced executive knows companies or industries which are bound for extinction because they cannot attract or hold able people. This, every experienced executive also knows, is a more important fact about a company or an industry than last year's profit statement. Any logical positivist who were to tell an executive that this statement, being incapable of unambiguous definition is a "non-statement" dealing with a "non-problem," would be quickly—and correctly—dismissed as an ass. Yet the statement cannot be defined clearly let alone "quantified." It is anything but "intangible;" it is very "tangible" indeed (as anyone ever having to do with such a business quickly finds out.) It is just "non measurable." And the results, while exceedingly measurable, will not show up for a decade.

But business also has measurable and quantifiable results of true meaning and significance. These are all those that have to do with past economic performance. For these can be expressed in terms of the very peculiar measurement of the economic sphere, money.

This does not mean that these are "tangibles." Indeed most of the things we can measure by money are so totally "intangible"—take depreciation for instance—that they outdo any Platonic Idea in that nothing corresponds to them in any reality whatever. But they are measurable.

That they are abstractions the "management scientist" with his
background in physics or engineering often has to learn the hard way.
Far too few management scientists for instance realize that practically every single definition of accounting is based on assumptions
of high metaphysical content—and that any accountant worth his salt,
can convert any profit figure into a loss figure, or vice versa, if
given control of the accounting definitions, all unquestionably, "within the limits of proper accounting practice."

This does not alter the fact that there are important measurable
events. And then, to say it again, there are equally important events
that cannot be measured.

To this comes the fact that the measurable results are things that
happened, they are in the past. There are no "facts" about the future.
To this comes secondly that the measurable events are primarily inside events rather than outside events. The important developments
on the outside, the things which determine that the buggy whip industry disappears and that IBM becomes a big business—let alone that
Cuban subsidiaries of American companies are confiscated—are not
measurable until it is too late to have "control."

A balance between the measurable and the non-measurable is
therefore a central and constant problem of management. In many
ways it is *the problem* of management and the true decision area.

Measurements which do not spell out the assumptions in respect
to the non-measurable that are being made—as parameters if you
please or in any other form—misdirect therefore. They actually mis-
inform. Yet the more we can quantify the truly measurable areas, the
greater the temptation to put all out emphasis on those—the greater,
therefore, the danger that what looks like better "controls" will actually mean less "control" if not a business out of control altogether.

SECTION III

There is one more important thing to be said. There is a fundamental, incurable, basic limitation to "controls" in a "social institution." This lies in the fact that a "social institution" is both a
true entity and a complete fiction. As an entity it has purposes of its
own, a performance of its own, results of its own—and a survival of
its own. These are the areas of which we have been speaking so far.
But a social institution is comprised of persons, each with his own
purpose, his own ambitions, his own ideas, his own needs. No matter
how "totalitarian" the institution, it has to satisfy the ambitions and
needs of its members, and do so in their capacity as individuals but
through institutional rewards and punishments, incentives and deter-
rents. The expression of this may be quantifiable—such as a raise
in salary. But the system itself is not quantitative in character and
cannot be quantified.

Yet here is the real "control" of the institution, that is the ground of behavior and the cause of action. People act as they are being rewarded or punished. For this, to them, rightly, is the true expression of the values of the institution and of its true, as against its professed, purpose and role. Employment selection and promotion decisions are the real "controls." In the employment selection an institution decides what kind of people it wants altogether. In the promotion decisions it makes operational its true and actual values and its real performance standards. A company that tells its foremen that the job is human relations but which then promotes the foreman who best does his paper work, makes it very clear to even the dumbest man in the shop that it wants paper work rather than human relations. And it will get paper work.

A system of "controls" which is not in conformity with this true, this only effective, this ultimate "control" of the organization which lies in its people-decisions, will therefore at best be ineffectual—as most are. At worst it will cause never-ending conflict and will push the organization out of control. Unfortunately this is only too often the situation where economically focused controls are imposed upon a research organization which professes dedication to "scientific values." Either promotions are then being made according to economic criteria—which violates the profession of the research group. Or promotions are being made according to scientific criteria—which destroys the credibility and acceptance of the economic "controls."

In designing "controls" for a business one therefore has to understand and analyze the actual "control" of the business, its personnel decisions especially in respect to promotion. Otherwise one designs a system of "controls" which does not lead to "control." One secondly has to think through the actual "control" system, the personnel decisions, to see whether it really is in agreement with the true needs of the business. Otherwise there is no economic performance.

But finally one has to realize that even the most powerful "instrument board" complete with Computers, Operations Research, and Simulations is secondary to the invisible, qualitative control of any human organization, its systems of rewards and punishments, of values and taboos—as it expresses itself in the ultimate decision, the personnel decision.

The new controls technology has tremendous scope and power. There is tremendous need for new and better controls, and especially for controls that are quantitative and therefore not just matters of "opinion." But the new "controls" have this power and satisfy this need, precisely because they are not "objective," are not "neutral," precisely because they change both the events they record and observe and the men to whom they report and whom they inform. What is needed therefore for those who are the designers of these "controls'' is an attitude very different from that of the physical scientist or the instrument maker. Theirs is much greater power- but also much greater limitation. They have to know that they can do much less—and have to know what they cannot do. But they also have to know that what they can do means much more- and have to impose on themselves the responsibility appropriate to this power.

16

CONTROL IN ORGANIZATIONS: INDIVIDUAL ADJUSTMENT AND ORGANIZATIONAL PERFORMANCE

ARNOLD S. TANNENBAUM[1]
University of Michigan

Man's life in contemporary society can be characterized largely as one of organizational memberships. Man commits a major portion of his waking hours to participation in at least one—and more often several—social organizations. His motivation, aspirations, his general way of life, are tied inextricably to the organizations of which he is part—and even to some of which he is not.

Organizations are of vital interest to the sociologist and the psychologist because one finds within them an important juncture between the individual and the collectivity. Out of this juncture comes much in our pattern of living that has been the subject of both eulogy and derogation. That man derives a great deal from organizational membership leaves little to be argued; that he often pays heavily for the benefits of organizational membership seems an argument equally compelling. At the heart of this exchange lies the process of control.

Characterizing an organization in terms of its patterns of control, is to describe an essential and universal aspect of organization, an aspect of organizational environment which every member must face and to which he must adjust. Organization implies control. A social organization is an orderly arrangement of individual human interactions. Control processes help circumscribe idiosyncratic behaviors and keep them conformant with the rational plan of the organization. Organizations require a certain amount of conformity as well as the integration of diverse processes. It is the function of control to see that organizational requirements are properly met, and the ultimate goals of the organization achieved. The coordination and order created out of the diverse interests and potentially diffuse behaviors of members is largely a function of control. And it is at this point that many of the problems of organizational functioning and of individual adjustment arise.

Control is an inevitable correlate of organization. But it is more than this. It is concerned with aspects of social life that are of the

[1]Written under a grant from the Carnegie Corporation of New York to the Survey Research Center, Institute for Social Research, The University of Michigan. I would like to thank Robert Kahn, Rensis Likert, Stanley Seashore, and Clagett Smith for their helpful suggestions.

utmost importance to all persons. It is concerned with the questions of choice and freedom, with individual expression, with problems of the common will and the common weal. It is related not only to what goes on within the organization in question, but with what the organization does in its external relations as well. It touches on the questions of "democracy" and "autocracy", "centralization-decentralization," "flat and tall" organizational structures, "close" versus "general" supervision, "workers' councils" and "joint management."

The problems of control and conformity in organizations contribute to a serious dilemma. Organization provides order—a condition necessary for man to produce abundantly and live securely. Abundance and security in turn create opportunities and choice—conditions which form the basis for human freedom. Yet social order itself requires conformity and imposes limitations. Furthermore, the responsibility for creating and sustaining order tends to be distributed unevenly within organizations. Often, it is the few who decide about the kind of order to which the many must conform. But regardless of how order is created, it requires the conformity of all or nearly all to organizational norms.

The magnitude of this problem as it applies to our economic institutions has been indicated by Berle and Means [1]:

> To the dozen or so men who are in control there is room for. . . [individual] initiative. For the tens of thousands and even hundreds of thousands of workers and of owners in a single enterprise, [individual] initiative no longer exists. Their activity is group activity on a scale so large that the individual, except he be in a position of control, has dropped into relative insignificance.

And the *trend*, according to Barnard, is in the direction of greater concentration of control in the hands of fewer persons [2]:

> There has been a greater and greater acceleration of centralization in this country, not merely in government, and not merely in the organization of great corporations, but also a great concentration on the part of labor unions and other organizations. There has been a social disintegration going along with this material development, and this formulation of organized activities implies payment of a price, the amount of which we are not yet able to assess.

This, perhaps, is one of the most crucial problems of social morality which we face in the age of massive organization—although the problem is not an entirely new one. We see it in Rousseau's *Social Contract*, Freud's *Civilization and Its Discontents*, Huxley's *Brave New World*, Whyte's *Organization Man*. And social and administrative scientists have become increasingly interested in this question as illustrated by the work by F. Allport, Argyris, Likert, McGregor, and Worthy. As a result of this stimulation, social researchers have applied themselves to the study of the problems of control, individual adjustment, and organizational performance, and a body of facts and hypotheses is growing. We would like to review some of these, drawing heavily upon the work done at the Institute for Social Research, The University of Michigan.

SOME DEFINITIONS

Control has been variously defined, and different terms (e.g., power, authority, influence) are sometimes used synonymously with it. Its original application in business organizations derives from the French usage meaning to check. It is now sometimes used in a broader and perhaps looser sense synonymously with the notions of influence, authority, and power. We shall use it here in this broader way to refer to any process in which a person (or group of persons or organization of persons) determines or intentionally affects what another person or group or organization will do.

Control, of course, may operate very specifically, as, for example, a foreman's specifying how a subordinate will do a particular job. Or it may operate more generally, as, for example, in the determination of organizational policies or actions. Control may be mutual, individuals in a group each having something to say about what others will do; or it may be unilateral, one individual controlling and the other one controlled. We ascribe power to an individual to the extent that he is in a position to exercise control. Authority refers to the right to exercise control. If by freedom we mean the extent to which an individual determines his own behavior, being controlled can be seen in general to relate inversely to freedom. The more an individual's behavior is purposely determined by others (i.e., is controlled), the less an individual is free to determine his own course of action.

IMPLICATIONS FOR INDIVIDUAL ADJUSTMENT

The elementary importance of control to people can be seen in the fact that every act of control has two implications: pragmatic and symbolic. Pragmatically, control implies something about *what* an individual must or must not do, the restriction to which he is subject, and the areas of choice or freedom which he has—whether, for example, a worker is transferred to a new machine or stays on the old, whether he is classified into a $1.75 or a $2.00 wage category, whether he is free to talk, smoke, rest, slow down or speed up while on the job. These pragmatic implications are often of vital importance to the controlled individual as well as to the individual exercising power.

Control also has a special psychological meaning or significance to the individuals involved. It may imply superiority, inferiority, dominance, submission, guidance, help, criticism, reprimand. It may imply (as some students of control argue) something about the manliness and virility of the individuals involved. The exercise of control, in other words, is charged emotionally.[2]

Emotional reactions to control may be explained, in part, by the predispositions which individuals develop early in life to types of authority relations. The infant's behavior is controlled by persons upon whom he is highly dependent, and the process of socialization involves the imposition of controls by parents, teachers, and other "authority figures." In this growing-up process, a pattern of responses to control is developed and control takes on emotional meaning.

A great deal of research has been done regarding predisposition to varying patterns of control. Tests have been devised, for example, to measure "authoritarianism," "egalitarianism," "need for independence," "need for power." Research employing some of these measures suggests that individuals' reactions to patterns of organizational control may differ according to personality.

This is illustrated by an experiment in a large clerical organization in which about 200 female clerks were given greater responsibility to make decisions about some of the things that affected their work groups. They were able to make decisions concerning some of the rules governing work assignments, vacation schedules, length of recess, overtime, and other matters. These decisions had been made previously by persons at higher levels. Most of the clerks reacted favorably to this experimental program. A small number, however, did not. Among these were a relatively high proportion of clerks whose personalities were not suited to the type of authority relations represented in this experimental program. These were clerks who preferred to be submissive, depend on others, obey rules, and follow directions [4, 5]. Similar results were found among male workers in an industrial service type organization. Supervisors who were judged to use participative methods (to ask workers' advice, to try bringing them into some decisions) were less likely to elicit favorable reactions

[2]The criticism which labor groups have sometimes hurled at human relations research in industry is in large measure a criticism concerning the emphasis which this research has placed on the "psychological" or "symbolic" rather than the pragmatic aspect of control. The human relations approach, the argument goes, is not so much concerned with *what* decisions are made by management, nor with the implications of these decisions for the welfare workers, but rather with *how* these decisions might be conveyed to workers so as to facilitate their acceptance. See, for example, [3].

from workers who received high scores on measures of authoritarianism than those who received low scores. Workers who judged their supervisors to employ participative methods were generally higher in productivity than those whose supervisors were judged not to employ participative methods *providing* subordinates had low scores on measures of authoritarianism [6].

Preferences for kinds of authority relations may develop out of early childhood experiences. They may also represent reactions to certain contemporaneous circumstances. Research on the "authoritarian personality," for example, suggests that individuals who suffer anxiety because of a failure in their work may be led to prefer more structured authority relations. A study of high producing and low producing insurance salesmen suggests the tenability of this idea. Productivity varies widely for these agents. An agent may be high during one period and low during another. Those who are low tend to suffer some anxiety. They also indicate "a desire for interpersonal interaction where the status of a man's position was the basis for communication, where orders were to go through 'the chain of command,' where decisions 'must be made by the District Manager,' and where 'those in control' of the situation were to act 'aloof,' and/or 'be friendly but not too intimate'. . ."[7]. The more successful, less threatened salesmen preferred more permissive, informal authority relations—no communication barriers because of status and no "reporting through the chain of command" [7].

Emotional reactions to authority relations may develop because authority, control or power represents, as we have pointed out, an important social symbol. Power, for example, is often understood as synonymous with prestige, status, social eminence or superiority. Indeed, it is often correlated with these criteria of success. Persons obviously are perceived and treated differently according to their power. The man with power is often looked up to and treated with respect. Equally important, individuals can be expected to evaluate themselves in this way. An individual's self concept is very likely affected by his power in the organizations and other social situations in which he takes part. The emotional effects of authority, as they bear on the way organization members may perceive authority and non-authority figures, is illustrated by an experiment in which Navy recruits described the physical appearances of men, some of whom wore first class petty officer's uniforms and others of whom wore recruit uniforms. The men being judged as petty officers and those being judged as recruits were well matched in physical appearance. Differences existed, however, in their uniforms—the kind and number of stripes on their arms and whether or not they wore canvas leggings. The recruits viewed these persons through a series of lenses which distorted their appearance in varying degrees. However, a greater tendency to resist this distortion occurred in the perception of the "petty officer." The existence of rank may create an emotional set which affects how the men holding this rank appear to those who do not [8].

While individual differences may exist in preferences for types of authority relations, organization members generally prefer to be in a position of exercising influence rather than being powerless. Studies repeatedly show that workers and supervisors are much more likely to feel that they have too little authority in their work than too much. It is the rare individual indeed who thinks he has too much. Several thousands of workers in a large number of organizations (including one Norwegian factory) were asked to describe how much control various groups in their work places exercise and how much they *should* exercise. In all the organizations studied the "average" worker reported the not unsurprising fact that managerial personnel exercise more control than do the workers as a group. In response to the second question, workers also report that managerial groups *should* exercise more control than the workers. However, in 98% of these organizations workers feel that they do not have as much control as they should.[3] It is interesting to contrast these results with responses to the same questions addressed to supervisory personnel. None of the supervisory groups questioned feel that *workers* should exercise more control than they do.

For whatever reasons, power is desired. This desirability may be attributed to the gratification which individuals may derive simply by knowing that they are "in control"—from the psychological satisfactions which come from exercising control. Or it may derive from the pragmatic implications of power—being able to affect the work situation in ways favorable to one's personal interests, as the individual sees them.

However, a concern for the rewards which accompany power will represent a serious oversimplification unless one considers also some of the correlates of power which are sources of serious tension and frustration. Among these are the added feelings of responsibility for, commitment to, and effort on behalf of the organization. Power can be an important stimulant, pushing the individual toward a greater and greater share of the work load of the organization. Furthermore, insofar as control may imply weighty decisions, decisions affecting the welfare of people as well as the destiny of the organization itself, exercising control can be burdensome.

Individuals who are not able to exercise control are, in general, less satisfied with their work situations than those who have some power. But their dissatisfaction often has the quality of apathy and

[3]In the Norwegian plant the question was phrased in terms of control over the setting of piece rate standards. Not only do the workers indicate that they should exercise more control than they do, but that they should exercise more control than managerial groups.

disinvolvement. For the individual in control, added dimensions of personality come into play contributing to the energies which the individual puts into his work, and to the problems he may encounter. The man who exercises control gives more of himself to the organization. He is likely to be more identified, more loyal, more active on behalf of the organization. A recent national survey suggests that individuals in positions of control and responsibility in industrial and business organizations are more "ego involved" in their work. Managerial personnel, for example, not only derive greater ego satisfactions from their jobs, but also greater ego frustrations [9]. The responsibility which devolves upon persons in control creates a sense of personal involvement and concern over the success or failure of the decisions made. These individuals have a personal stake in the outcome of decisions taken. This can be a satisfying, even an exhilarating experience, but it can also lead to sleepless nights.

This mixed blessing which power sometimes represents is illustrated by the experiment in a large clerical organization described above in which about 200 clerks were given greater responsibility to make decisions about some of the things that affected their work groups. In general, morale increased in these divisions as a result of the change in control. Clerks felt more satisfied with the company, with supervision, with their work in general. They were, in large measure, favorable toward the increased control which they were able to exercise. However, despite the general increase in satisfaction, the clerks felt less of a sense of accomplishment at the end of the work day. They were also less satisfied with their present level in the organization. (See Exhibit 16-1) In acquiring an increased feeling of responsibility for the work through the added control which they were able to exercise, the clerks no doubt developed standards of achievement which are harder to satisfy.

A similar result is found in a study by Mann and Hoffman comparing a newly automated electrical power plant with a less highly automated one [10]. Workers in the new plant exercise more control, and experience greater responsibility than those in the older plant—according to the responses of the workers in the respective plants. The men in the new plant make important decisions about the work and have significant influence on their supervisors concerning what goes on in their work place. They also report greater satisfaction with their immediate supervisor, with the amount of information they receive about plant operations and with plant management in general. However, despite this generally heightened state of morale, workers in the newly automated plant more often report that their work makes them feel "jumpy" or nervous; that they are tense and on edge when equipment is being started up or shut down. (Workers in the *old* plant report slightly more danger in their work.) These may be some of the costs to the workers of their increased power and responsibility.

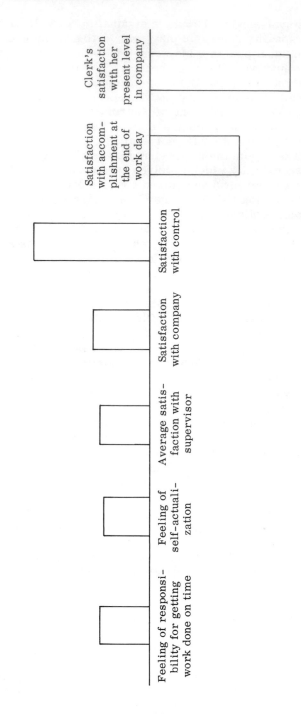

Exhibit 16-1. Changes in clerk's attitudes following delegation of control to clerks in work groups. (All the differences are statistically at the .05 level or better.)

Certain kinds of psychosomatic ailments are known to be relatively frequent among individuals in positions of control and responsibility in organizations. Research in this country and abroad provides added documentation for this generally recognized fact. French reports a greater prevalence of psychosomatic disorders of varying kinds among supervisors than among workers in a large Midwest plant [11]. Verlin found that the frequency of ulcers increased as he investigated incidence of ulcer at ascending levels of the hierarchy in a large Dutch company.[4] The old adage, "Uneasy lies the head that wears the crown," always seemed to make good sense. To the extent that power and responsibility are distributed widely among organization members, however, a number of heads may lie uneasy.

CONTROL AND PERFORMANCE

Variations in control patterns within organizations have important— and in some cases quite predictable—effects on members' reactions, on their satisfactions and frustrations, feelings and tension, self-actualization, or well-being. They also have implications for the performance of the work group and of the organization as a whole.

This can be seen in the plight of the first line supervisor who sometimes finds himself in the anomalous position of being a "leader" without power. The first line supervisor is often referred to as the man in the middle. He is often caught, as an innocent bystander, in a serious crossfire. In effect he may be a messenger transmitting orders from above. On the one hand, he must bear the brunt of resistance and expressed grievances from below and, on the other, he must suffer criticism from above for the failure of his subordinates to conform to expectations. The seriousness of this situation is compounded by the fact that orders coming from above are often formed without the advantage of adequate knowledge of conditions at lower levels. The powerless supervisor lacks effective means of gaining the confidence of his men, of understanding their views, and of transmitting this important intelligence up the hierarchy. The orders which he is responsible for relaying, then, are often the least likely to gain full acceptance, thus making his position all the more untenable and that of his subordinates all the more difficult. The power-less leader can do little in the hierarchy on behalf of his subordinates or himself, and is relatively helpless in the face of many serious problems which confront him and his work group. This is illustrated by the research of Pelz, who shows that unless the supervisor is influential with his own superiors, "good" supervisory practice on his part is not likely to make much difference to subordinates. Sub-

4Reported by French in [11].

ordinates are more likely to react favorably to "good" and adversely to "bad" supervisory practices *if* the supervisor is influential in the company [12].

THE TOTAL AMOUNT OF CONTROL IN AN ORGANIZATION

Many administrators seem to face a serious problem in their understanding of supervisory-subordinate relations. They often assume that the amount of control exercised by members of a group or organization is a fixed quantity and that increasing the power which one individual has automatically decreases that of others. There is good reason, however, for questioning this assumption; the total amount of control which is exercised in a group or organization can increase, and the various participants can each acquire a share of this augmented power. Conversely, the total amount of control may go down, and all may share the loss. This fact is illustrated in everyday social situations—friendships, marital relations, as well as supervisory-subordinate interactions. One can easily picture the *laissez faire* leader who exercises little control over his subordinates and who may at the same time be indifferent to their wishes. He neither influences nor is influenced by his men. A second supervisor interacts and communicates often, welcomes opinions, and elicits influence attempts. Suggestions which subordinates offer make a difference to him and his subordinates are responsive, in turn, to his requests. To the extent that this may contribute to effective performance—and we have good reason to believe that it does if the supervisor also has influence with his manager—the group itself will be more powerful or influential as a group. The manager under these circumstances is more likely to delegate additional areas of decision-making to the group, and he, in turn, will respect and be responsive to the group's decisions. To the extent that the organizational hierarchy, from top to bottom, is characterized in these terms, we have a more highly integrated, tightly knit social system. We have, in the terms of Rensis Likert, a more substantial "interaction-influence system" [13].

The importance of the notion of "total amount of control" and of the "interaction-influence system" is illustrated in an analysis by Likert of data collected in 31 geographically separated departments of a large industrial service organization [14]. Each of the departments does essentially the same work and careful records of department productivity are kept by the company. Non-supervisory employees were asked the following question in a paper and pencil questionnaire: "In general, how much say or influence do you feel each of the following groups has on what goes on in your department?" Answers were checked on a five point scale from "Little or no influence" to "A very great deal of influence." Employees answered this question relative to the following groups within their departments: the department manager, the supervisors, the men. Likert then divided the 31 departments into three groups according to their level of productivity. Exhibit 16-2 shows the average responses to the above question for the one-third of departments highest in productivity and for the third lowest in productivity. (See Exhibit 16-2)

According to these employees, not only do they have more influence as a group within the high producing departments, but so do the supervisors and managers. Likert's analysis of these departments suggests that the social systems differ in the high and low producing departments. The former is characterized by a higher total amount of

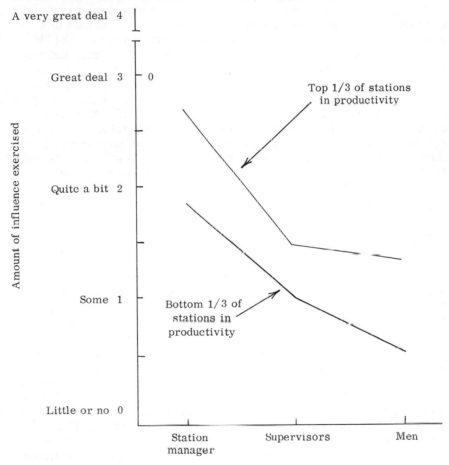

Exhibit 16-2. Relation of department productivity to average amount of influence exercised by various hierarchical levels

control, by a greater degree of mutual influence. "The high-performing managers have actually increased the size of the 'influence pie' by means of the leadership processes which they use. They listen more to their men, are more interested in their men's ideas, and have more confidence and trust in their men" [14]. There is a greater give-and-take and supportiveness by superiors; a higher level of effective communication upward, downward, and sideward. This all contributes to a greater sensitivity and receptivity on the part of each organization member to the influence of others—superiors relative to subordinates and subordinates relative to superiors. There is in all cases a higher level of mutual influence and control. Under these circumstances, the high level of influence among workers is not a threat to managerial personnel. On the contrary, it is part of a process leading to more effective organizational performance [14].

It is interesting to see that these results are not isolated and that similar findings occur in several other types of organizations. In a study of four labor unions, for example, we found that the two more effective, active, and powerful unions were highest in the total amount of control exercised by members and officers [15, 16]. The most powerful of the four unions had a relatively influential membership—but the leaders (the president, executive board and bargaining committee) were by no means uninfluential. In this union, members and leaders are relatively more active. They attend more meetings, speak up at meetings, communicate informally about union affairs, hear and consider the feelings and ideas of others. Members and leaders influence and are influenced and they create in the process effective concerted action. This union "keeps management on its toes" as the personnel manager at the plant philosophically points out. Or as an officer in another union puts it, this union "carries a hell of a lot of weight." In the least effective union, however, the members are relatively uninfluential in union affairs, and so are the leaders. A kind of *laissez-faire* anarchic atmosphere prevails. No one runs the show. Members are not integrated, tied together by bonds of interaction and influence. They are not really part of an organized system. The ineffectiveness of this union is illustrated by the comments of a union field representative: "If the company wanted to take advantage, they could make the people live hard here." An old timer of the local expressed his disillusionment: "We feel that it is not what it used to be. . . Nothing happens to grievances. You can't find out what happens to them—they get lost. . . .The [bargaining] committee doesn't fight anymore." The differences between the most powerful and least powerful union in their distributions of control as reported by members is shown in Exhibit 16-3. Although question wording is somewhat different between this study

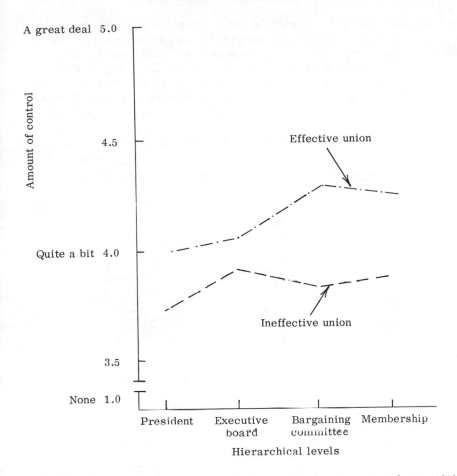

Exhibit 16-3. Control curves of effective and ineffective unions [15, p. 162]

and that of the industrial service organization shown above, the implications are very similar.[5]

Mann and Hoffman have applied a similar methodology in studying some of the effects of automation in a power plant. They illustrate, through a comparison of a new, highly automated plant and an older, less automated one, how changes in technology may affect the social structure of a plant including its patterns of control, worker

[5]Question in union study: "In general, how much do you think the president [membership, plant bargaining committee, executive board] has to say about how things are decided in this local?" Responses ranged on a five point scale from "a great deal of say" to "no say at all."

responsibility and level of morale [10]. Fewer employees operate the
new plant although the ratio of non-supervisory to supervisory personnel is about the same. The jobs in the new plant require more
knowledge and responsibility on the part of workers, and, as Exhibit
16-4 illustrates, the patterns of control in the two plants differ too.
According to the workers (and the supervisors are in essential agreement), the new plant is characterized by more control than the old.

Exhibit 16-4. Distribution of Perceived Influence[6]

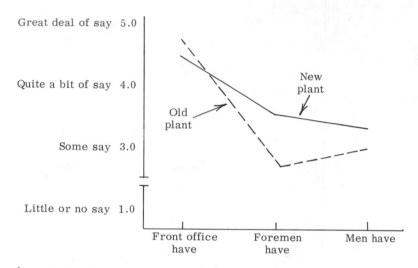

[10], p. 57. The following questions were employed:
"In general, how much do you and the other men of your work group have
to say about how things are done?"
   5 Our foreman gives us a great deal of say in how things are done
    .
    .
    .
   1 Our foreman gives us hardly any say at all in how things are done
"In general, how much do you think the foremen have to say about how
things are done in this plant?"
   5 They have a great deal of say
    .
    .
    .
   1 They have very little or no say at all
"In general, how much say do you think the men in the front office of this
plant have in how things are done in this plant?"
   5 They have a great deal of say in how things are done in this plant
    .
    .
    .
   1 They have very little or no say at all in how things are done in this plant

The difference between the plants at the foreman level is particularly interesting. In the new plant, foremen are judged to have more influence than the men; in the old, less. Nor is the more powerful supervisor considered a threat to the workers in the new plant. Despite—or should we say, because of—the greater influence of foremen together with that of the men here, the men report less often that their foremen treat them like inferiors, that he is a "driver" of men, that he is "bossy," or that he says one thing and does another. They report more often that the foreman tries to get ideas from the work group, that he is a warm and friendly person, that he will go to bat for the men and that he is a "leader" of men. Taking all things into consideration, 66 per cent of the men in the new plant and 36 per cent in the old report that they are quite or very satisfied with their immediate supervisor. The new plant is a more tightly integrated social (as well as physical) system. Workers feel more a part of a work group and feel free to call on others in the work group for help with job problems. There is a higher degree of interdependence between foremen and men and to some extent among the men themselves. The foremen in the plant have more influence than their counterparts in the old—and so do the men.

A study of forty insurance agencies shows the same direction of results. D. Bowers and S. Seashore compared twenty insurance agencies high in sales volume with twenty agencies low in volume. In the high producing agencies, the general agents, the district agents, and the sales agents as a group are all reported to have more influence in their agencies than are their counterparts in the low producing agencies.

The clerical experiment discussed above also yields similar results. The increased control which the clerks report is not accompanied by a corresponding decrease in the control attributed to supervisory and managerial personnel. The *total amount of control* reported by clerks increased, accompanied by a more effective social system. Not only did morale increase in this group, but so did motivation and productivity.[7]

Interestingly, the kinds of relationships suggested by these data apply in a voluntary organization too as indicated by research in over 100 geographically separate local Leagues of the League of Women Voters of the United States [18]. The effectiveness of each local League was rated by a group of judges in the national office and

---

[7]Productivity also increased in a contrasting experimental group within the company, under conditions of lowering the amount of control exercised by clerks. However, clerk morale, loyalty and motivation decreased here. Considerable tension was felt in this group and it gave the appearance of high instability. There is serious doubt that this type of system could sustain itself as well as the other for an extended period under conditions which prevail in American society. See [17; 13, chaps. 5, 6].

a sample of the members and leaders in each of these Leagues was then asked several questions relating to control within their Leagues. The results indicate that members in effective Leagues exercise more control than do their counterparts in ineffective Leagues, but leaders do not exercise less. A greater total amount of control is ascribed to effective than to ineffective Leagues.

While the above results from a variety of organizations seem to suggest an important hypothesis connecting the total amount of control and organizational performance, our research findings are not completely consistent on this point. A recent study in 30 automobile dealerships, for example, does not reveal any relationship between criteria of effectiveness (including growth in sales during the past year) and the total amount of control within the dealership as reported by salesmen. The automobile sales agency may present a somewhat different social structure in which "individual enterprise" and competitive behavior among salesmen is more at a premium. We do not know what the effect would be if agencies were structured more like the typical business organization with greater emphasis on coordination and cooperative effort. The total amount of control might be greater under these conditions, and this variable might prove, under these circumstances, to have important implications for effective performance.

A CONCLUSION

American management is dollar cost conscious—and rightly so. Many managers are also conscious of the costs of organized productive effort which cannot be calculated immediately in terms of dollars and cents. These are the human costs of organization, costs paid by members and ultimately by society as a whole. Nor are they to be calculated simply in terms of the dissatisfactions which industrial man faces. They may be paid in terms of the shaping of his very personality. The evidence on this is not very clear, but we have reason to believe that adult personality may change as a result of persistent conditions in the environment. The nature of man's experiences in an organization can affect his general mentality and outlook on life. In the clerical experiment described above, we saw evidence of slight changes in personality after a year's exposure of clerks to different patterns of control. These changes were in the direction of increasing the "fit" between the worker's personality and the nature of the control structure [19]. Notorious "brain washing" methods represent the ultimate in the process of institutionalized personality change and we see illustrated in the fiction of Orwell and Huxley the psychological bludgeoning of individual personality into a perfect fit to the institutions of a "hypothetical" society of the future. As Huxley puts it, "Round pegs in square holes tend to have dangerous thoughts about the social system and to infect others with their discontent" [20]. Organizations cannot often tolerate "odd balls," and there are pressures, sometimes subtle, on deviants to change.

Organizations in a democratic society present a seeming dilemma. "We are forever oscillating," as Geoffry Vickers puts it, "between two alternatives which seem mutually exclusive—on the one hand, collective efficiency won at the price of individual freedom; on the other, individual freedom equally frustrated by collective anarchy. Those who believe in a middle way which is more than a compromise do so in the faith that human beings are capable or can become capable of social organization which is both individually satisfying and collectively effective; and they have plenty of evidence for their faith. On the other hand, our knowledge of the laws involved is still rudimentary" [21].

"Middle ways" are sprouting up around the globe today. The work council systems in Yugoslavia, Germany, France, Belgium, and England, though differing radically in character and effectiveness are, within their respective cultures, experiments in the "middle way." We have our Scanlon plans, profit sharing and suggestion schemes, as well as varying degrees of participative management. However, our knowledge of the effects of these systems is, as Vickers says, rudimentary.

"The middle way," if the clues provided by our research so far are substantiated, will have to take into account the important facts about control: how control is distributed within an organization, and how much it all amounts to. Patterns of control—as they are perceived by organization members, at least—are tied significantly to the performance of the organization and to the adjustments and satisfactions of members. If our research leads are correct, the more significant improvements in the "human side of enterprise" are going to come through changes in the way our organizations are controlled, and particularly through changes in the size of the "influence pie." This "middle way" leans on the assumption that influential workers do not imply uninfluential supervisors or managers. This is a relatively novel assumption for many managers who have been weaned on the all or none law of power: one either leads or is led, is strong or is weak, controls or is controlled. Disraeli was no less influential a leader, however, for having questioned this when he said, "I follow the people. Am I not their leader?" And managers, who in their behavior question the all or none principle, do not seem less influential for it—quite the contrary.

Our "middle way" assumes further that the worker, or supervisor, or manager, who exercises some influence over matters of interest to him in the work situation, acquires a sense of self respect which the powerless individual may lack. And, what is more, he can elicit the respect and high regard of others. This is the key to good human relations practice. Supervisory training alone cannot achieve this any more than good intentions in bad organization will achieve it, or words alone will achieve it. The pattern of control in an organization, however, has a direct and profound effect on the organization's human relations climate. Workers who have some sense of control in the organizations we have studied, are, in general, more positive, not less, toward their supervisors and managers. And their managers are more positively disposed toward them.

We assume further, with some research justification, that increasing and distributing the exercise of control more broadly in an organization helps to distribute an important sense of involvement in the organization. Members become more "ego involved." Aspects of personality which ordinarily do not find expression now contribute to members' motivation. The organization provides members with a fuller ranger of experiences. In doing this, however, it creates its own dilemnas, similar in some respects yet different from the one described by Vickers.

A first dilemma concerns the increased control to which the influential organization member may become subject. While he controls more, he is not controlled less. The loyalty and identification which he feels for the organization lead him to accept organizational requirements, and to conform to organizational norms which he might not otherwise do. We find evidence of this in the behaviors of members of our effective, high total control union. Their behaviors are more uniform than are those of members in the ineffective laissez-faire union [15, 22]. Norms and pressures toward conformity exist in the former organization which are lacking in the latter. Members in the effective union pay for the increased control which they exercise (and for the effectiveness of their organization) not only in terms of the greater effort which they put into union activities, but also in terms of their greater sensitivity and accession to controls within the union. An analysis in the 31 departments of the industrial service organization described above reveals a similar phenomenon. Norms, measured in terms of uniformity in the behavior of workers, are more apparent in the high total control departments than in the low. In these "better" departments, influence by the men as a group is greater, morale is more favorable, productive effort is higher, and so is uniformity [23]. The exercise of control does not spare the controller from being controlled. The contrary may be true in our effective, high total control organizations, where influence tends to be reciprocal.

A second dilemma arises out of the increased involvement and motivation which are likely to accompany the exercise of control. While we see greater opportunity for human satisfaction in the "middle way," the result is not simple felicity. Whenever man is highly motivated he may experience the joys of success as well as the pangs of failure. He will know some of the satisfactions which come from a challenge met and a responsibility fulfilled. He may also feel frustration from the development of goals which are not easily reached.

BIBLIOGRAPHY

1. Berle, A. A., Jr., and G. C. Means; "The Control of the Modern Corporation," in R. Merton et al. (eds.), *Reader in Bureaucracy*, Glencoe, New York: Free Press, 1952.
2. Bernard, C. I.: "Organization and Management," as quoted in *Harvard Business Review*, vol. 29, no. 4, p. 70, 1951.
3. "Deep Therapy on the Assembly Line," *Ammunition*, vol. 7, no. 4, pp. 47-51, 1949.
4. Tannenbaum, A. S.: "One Man's Meat," *Adult Leadership*, vol. 3, no. 8, pp. 22-23, 1955.
5. —— and F. H. Allport: "Personality and Group Structure: An Interpretive Study of Their Relationships Through an Event-structure Hypothesis," *Journal of Abnormal and Social Psychology*, vol. 58, no. 3, pp. 272-280, 1956.
6. Vroom, V: *Some Personality Determinants of the Effects of Participation*, Englewood Cliffs, N. J.: Prentice-Hall, 1960.
7. Wispe, L. G. and K. E. Lloyd: "Some Situational and Psychological Determinants of the Desire for Structured Interpersonal Relations," *Journal of Abnormal and Social Psychology* vol. 51, no. 1, pp. 57-60, 1955.
8. Wittreich, W. J., and K. B. Radcliffe, Jr.: "Differences in the Perception of an Authority Figure and a Non-authority Figure by Navy Recruits, *Journal of Abnormal and Social Psychology*, vol. 53, no. 3., pp. 383-384, 1956.
9. Gurin, G., J. Veroff, and Sheila Feld: *Americans View Their Mental Health: A Nationwide Interview Study*, New York: Basic Books, 1960.
10. Mann, F. C., and L. R. Hoffman: *Automation and the Worker: A Study of Social Change in Power Plants*, New York: Holt, 1960.
11. French, J. R. P., Jr.: "The Effects of the Industrial Environment on Mental Health: A Theoretical Approach," paper presented at the meetings of the American Psychological Association, 1960.
12. Pelz, D. C: "Influence: A Key to Effective Leadership in the First-line Supervisor," *Personnel*, vol. 29, no. 3, pp. 3-11, 1952.
13. Likert, R.: *New Patterns of Management*, New York: McGraw-Hill, 1961.
14. ——: "Influence and National Sovereignty," in J. G. Peatman and E. L. Hartly (eds.), *Festshrift for Gardner Murphy*, New York: Harper & Row, 1960.
15. Tannenbaum, A. S., and R. L. Kahn: *Participation in Union Locals*, New York: Harpor & Row, 1958.
16. Tannenbaum, A. S.. "Control Structure and Union Functions," *American Journal of Sociology*, vol. 61, no. 6, pp. 536-545, 1956.
17. Likert, R.: "Measuring Organizational Performance," *Harvard Business Review*, pp. 41-50, March-April, 1958.
18. Tannenbaum, A. S.: "Control and Effectiveness in a Voluntary Organization," *American Journal of Sociology*, vol. 67, no. 1, pp. 33-47, 1961.

19. ———: "Personality Change as a Result of an Experimental Change of Environmental Conditions," *Journal of Abnormal and Social Psychology*, vol. 55, no. 3, pp. 404–406, 1957.

20. Huxley, A.: *Brave New World*, New York: Bantam, 1953, p. xvi.

21. Vickers, G.: "Control Stability and Choice," reprinted in *General Systems, Yearbook of the Society for General Systems*, vol. 2, pp. 1–8, 1957.

22. Tannenbaum, A. S.: "Control and Effectiveness in a Voluntary Organization," *American Journal of Sociology*, vol. 67, no. 1, pp. 33–47, 1956.

23. Smith, C. G., O. Ari, and A. S. Tannenbaum: "The Relationship of Control Patterns and Uniformity; Their Implications for Organizational Effectiveness," unpublished report, 1962.

17

RESEARCH IN MANAGEMENT CONTROLS: A CRITICAL SYNTHESIS

KENNETH J. ARROW

Stanford University

As empirical evidence on the present state of research in management controls, I will take the papers presented at this conference. I shall, of course, have to be somewhat arbitrary and selective as you may suppose; I will approach the problem with all the prejudices and biases of my particular background. For this reason I want to begin by using as my texts the first two papers of the conference, a starting place which shall not restrict the terminus. The papers of Professors Marschak and Hirshleifer both come from the discipline of economics and speak in terms of calculation of benefits and costs and maximization of expected profits, and yet it is fair to say that there is virtually no intersection between them at all. No criticism is intended; the fact itself is a very valuable piece of information, which guides us in understanding some of the problems that have confronted the later speakers and have been dealt with by them so ably.

It is clear in any discussion of organizations that controls are necessary to keep an organization viable and efficient in performing the purposes for which it was designed. To understand controls, the existence of uncertainty is one of the key factors—perhaps the key factor. Uncertainty arises for two reasons. One, the more essential in the sense that it must inevitably occur in any sizeable organization, is that the different parts cannot be perfectly acquainted with each other. All the discussion about centralization and decentralization has to do with precisely that fact. A given part in an organization may know what it is doing, and it may know a certain set of facts which come up in a natural way as a result of engaging in its activities. The transmission of this information is always costly, in greater or lesser degree. The result is that it does not by any standards pay other parts of the organization and particularly top management to know everything. It would not pay to have everything transmitted, and in any case the channel capacity of the human brain is limited, so that no matter how much information is available in the system, it would not be assimilated. Some of these distinctions were brought out more clearly in the discussion following Professor Marschak's paper. There is a fundamental area of uncertainty of different parts of management in respect to each other—of top management with respect to lower levels, of different departments with respect to each

other, of management, however defined, with respect to the performance of the work force in all its different forms.

A second uncertainty, which is not basic from a definitional point
of view but which is important from a practical point of view, is the
uncertainty about the external environment. Emphasis has been
placed on this by a number of our speakers; Roberts, for example,
was discussing a case in which a greater control over the external
environment achieved certain gains, and Drucker also placed great
emphasis on adaptability to a changing and uncertain environment as
the key to survival and efficiency. The presence of this uncertainty
is one force for creating organizations, for creating the kinds of
relationships—the hierarchical, authoritative relationships—that
characterize an organization, that separate it, as Professor Hirshleifer mentioned, from the outside world where market relationships
are usually thought of as predominating. I say, "usually thought of,"
because it is a matter of common observation that many relationships
among firms or between firms and their customers or suppliers are
not purely market relationships, as that term is used in economics
textbooks. The firm frequently does not just offer a commodity for
sale at a fixed price and have each buyer take as much as he wishes.
On the contrary, the specifications, for example, the delivery dates,
might be modified by individual bargaining. There are many qualitative terms to a transaction, even one involving what ordinarily is
thought to be more than one organization, which go beyond the usual
model of market relations. In a sense the organizations that we are
thinking of here are in fact parts of a larger organization, the whole
economy. It is no accident that people who have discussed the theory
of socialist economics are concerned with problems which are, as
has repeatedly been pointed out, quite similar in form to those in the
internal organization of a firm. Presumably, the problems related
to co-ordination and transmission of information become more and
more predominant relative to other kinds of transactions as we get
down to the units of the kind we call natural business organizations.

With this and with some other characteristics in mind that we will
come to in a minute, it is not totally surprising that transfer pricing
cannot be a thoroughly satisfactory solution to the organization of a
firm. Some writers, including some represented here, do not really
understand why there should be any attention paid to it at all, while
others place almost exclusive emphasis on it. It is easy to say, of
course, that the answer lies somewhere in between. Unfortunately it
happens to be also the correct statement in this case, as trite as it
is. The difficulties in using the price mechanism obscure the fact
that prices can play significant signalling roles, and if more attention
were given to them—to prices, standard costs or any other phrases
you might want to use—they can be an invaluable kind of control mechanism because they do transmit a good deal of information and exert
a good deal of pressure for efficiency in an inexpensive way.

Let me sketch very briefly what the limits of the price system are. What would prevent us from having universal adoption of prices? Every transaction between any two parts of the organization could be mediated through some transfer price. Why not? This problem has also been raised in regard to the whole economy, and there has been a long discussion. Prices are supposed, on one hand, to have the advantage of economizing on the transmission of information, and therefore they are to some extent a solution to the first problem of uncertainty, but we are aware and have been for a long time that there are certain limits. The most usual comment is that if you priced at marginal cost, departments would be losing money. What this, of course, means is that there are increasing returns to scale—e.g. a fixed overhead cost item. Anybody acquainted with the literature on economic development knows that increasing returns are used as an argument for coordination of plans. This is particularly true when the consequences of decisions extend into the future, and any decision about investments has this property. There has to be some coordination of future activities—some idea that it is worthwhile building a plant, which, once built, will be an overhead item, because it is expected that the demand necessary to justify the plant will in fact exist. If you write down the specifications carefully for an ideal price system, they become quite formidable, and the system is not quite as cheap as it might look at first. What is really needed is a series of forward contracts, where prices have to be attached not only to current activities now but also to plans for the future. Of course, a number of objections arise. Obviously, one problem is simply that there are going to be a lot of prices to consider. The planner no longer looks at a few things but he may have to decide in light of a great deal of information.

A second problem is that, if the external world is changing and particularly if it is changing uncertainly, prices as ordinarily conceived are not going to be adequate. You don't really want to set prices rigidly into the future because in fact the future brings surprises which will show that your price ratios are wrong. An invention may take place which will cheapen one of your factors of production, for example. Rigidity, as I imagine you hear remarked many times and quite correctly so, is the biggest enemy to be fought.

Development literature and economic theory and their counterpart in economic organization theory allude to another difficulty, that of externalities. The profitability of one part of the firm may depend upon what another part of the firm is doing. Now to summarize the long literature briefly, the usual argument is that if all the relationships between the different parts of the economic organization were listed and a price put on every possible such relationship, there would be no more externalities. Externalities are really influences which are commodities not immediate to the market. To be fanciful, suppose there are two departments, one next door to the other, and one is a very noisy process which interferes with the efficiency of the second. That could be taken care of by transfer pricing if you only charged for the noise. If the department making noise is required to pay a fee per decibel, or whatever the natural unit might be, to the other department whose efficiency is being impaired, then, by bargaining, a price would be found by which the two would come to agreement as to just what amount of noise was being transmitted from one to the other, just as they might come to an agreement on the amount of product that one department is to shift to another. You can see that it wouldn't take very long for this to become impractical simply because of the sheer number of prices. The pricing of externalities is more practical, by the way, in the context of an intra-organization allocation than it is in the context of inter-firm transactions. The reason is that members of an organization can be ordered to abide by accounting prices, where it may be extremely difficult to enforce the price system in an inter-personal context. Let me clarify this point by an example of a somewhat trivial nature; it can be generalized. Suppose what I do with my front lawn affects the welfare of my neighbors. This externality is made very vocal in a suburban community; its existence may not be economically very important but is not unrealistic, and the problem dealt with by zoning regulations constitutes a more significant version. This externality can be eliminated by agreeing that I have the right to maintain my front yard in any condition that I please, but my neighbors can pay me to improve my lawn for their benefit. Because of the small scale aspects of the matter there are very few people involved; also if I put up a lawn which will please one person, it will automatically please everybody else who isn't paying for it but getting the benefit. Unless I had a very elaborate system of fencing, there is no real way of keeping the non-paying customers out. For these reasons, payment by neighbors is an ineffective system of eliminating one externality. A corresponding use of accounting prices could be enforced in some measure within a firm. Nevertheless, one would hardly hope to apply prices to the relations of the material handling unit and the unit which it is supplying. It wouldn't be felt satisfactory to set and reset prices in situations which reflect minor fluctuations. The problem, of course, is dynamic. In a steady state, where the same amount were used hour by hour, minute by minute, there would be no real problem. But the trouble is that not only are materials wanted but they are wanted at certain moments, so that prices would have to depend on just when the materials were needed. The process of setting prices and of calculating optimal responses to them become so complex that it is preferable to have the externality settled by authoritative relationship. This is a limit of the price system.

Uncertainty, with which we started, further creates complication. Hypothetically, one can solve uncertainty problems by an extended

price system, and a few authors have indicated models of this type.
Consider an external uncertainty. I am engaged in a business, and I
don't know whether a rival of mine is going to have an innovation
which would upset my situation. I have to plan in my policies for two
contingencies and what I would really like to do is to have my departments make their plans in a flexible way to meet this contingency.
Theoretically what I should do is to fix one set of prices if the innovation of my rival is successful and a different set of prices if the
innovation does not work. With just two possible states of the world
(to use the language that writers on foundations of probability are
accustomed to using), I must double the number of prices that I have
to consider. If I have some firm estimate of what the probability of
this innovation is and this is made known to all my branches, I instruct each one of them to act on the basis of prices, but since there
are two possible sets of prices, they are supposed to maximize expected profit in the sense of probability theory. A price mechanism
elaborated to take account of uncertainties needs information about
probability. Thus we see how a detailed consideration of transfer
pricing leads to the economics of information.

If instead of just two states of the world, you consider all the uncertainties that a business, even the simplest, is confronted with it
is clear that calculations would begin to break down from sheer complexity. This remark does not mean that it isn't worthwhile making
some stab at price mechanisms. It does mean that you're going to
have a lot of problems left over when you use transfer prices all
you can.

There is another and more subtle problem connected with uncertainty, perhaps even closer to the heart of organization problems.
There are two reasons why things may not work out as expected.
One is the mere fact that the external world is uncertain and can be
in one of several possible states. Another is that a department manager may be simply not performing very well. He may not be doing
well—this point has been brought up a number of times here in discussion—simply because he is inadequate or improperly motivated,
or he may not be doing well because he is in an unfortunate situation.
This point has been made both by Balderston and Drucker. Then the
scheme just discussed, of assigning prices which can depend on un
certainties, logically simple though complex in practice, doesn't
really have the full incentive characteristics that it ought to have. It
runs against the difficulty that it is very hard to differentiate between
the two sources of error. If it is always assumed that the variation
from expected performance was due to objective uncertainty, one
would never in any way ascertain whether a manager is doing a good
or bad job. Variations in his performance would be attributed to the
fact that the world has changed. To take the other tack and say that
there is no uncertainty in the external world would be to blame

branch managers for matters which are out of their control, and the prices would not be providing the proper set of instructions. This dilemma arises clearly in insurance, where the literature refers to moral hazard—I think this is a key concept—and shows that in the presence of uncertainty there must be responsibility, a direct control not mediated strictly through the market. Suppose I want to buy fire insurance, but I don't even own any property. I want to bet that my neighbor's house is going to catch on fire. Why shouldn't the insurance company take this bet? If the occurrence of fires was strictly a matter of the external world, they would calculate their odds so as to make themselves a profit. They would be very happy to take my bet or anybody else's. But they believe that incentives to certain kinds of action may be influenced by the existence of insurance. They cannot differentiate completely between the external world and decisions of individuals whose incentives might be affected, and so they insist on an insurable interest. Further, fire insurance companies inspect the premises of the insured. They are not satisfied to offer insurance to any taker. They want to make sure that sprinkler systems are installed and whatever other precautions taken that they deem necessary. At the least their rates will vary with the precautions taken. There is a non-market relationship here between buyer and seller. The analogous relation within organizations is, in good part, what is meant by management. The uncertainties with which a subordinate is confronted mean there has to be a direct responsibility to central management and a control mechanism to enforce the responsibility.

The limitations on the possibilities of transfer pricing raise questions which have been examined by many of the writers here. There are other forms of controls. Let me cite an analogy. We have a lot of discussions on the question of disarmament control. It is assumed that there is a deal which, if it could be executed, would be mutually beneficial. This is the axiom on which negotiations take place; if one party can only gain at the expense of the other, there could be no possible deal between the Soviet Union and the United States on reducing the level of arms. But the basis of negotiations is that there is some mutual reduction of armaments such that we would both feel happier with this threat removed because the protective values cancel out and there obviously is some gain in having less destructive power around. The question is how do we insure that the deal is being carried out? We say that we have to inspect. We put more emphasis on this than the Russians. At least most Americans feel that somehow or other there has to be some guarantee that the arms reduction will in fact be carried out. Here, of course, the deals are between equals rather than between subordinates and superiors, and therefore the handling has to be more symmetrical than within an organization. But the problems are basically the same. A 100% inspection in this particular context is perhaps not so much impossible as rejected for other reasons which we needn't examine here. Therefore there has been quite a variety of schemes suggested for creating incentives and controls to assure the carrying out of this agreement.

One interesting point is an emphasis on sampling. Sampling is an old idea; it has been used in quality control for a long time. Indeed it is clear that any control relationship involving different parts is in one way or another always a question of sampling, whether this is understood consciously or not. Instead of depending upon the objective criteria of performance weighted by prices, direct controls check to see that the performance is being carried out according to some standards. But everything can't be checked; if management were literally capable of ordering every step and checking compliance completely, there would be nothing left of the organization problem. There must be an intermediate level of partial control–a sample or probe of performance. The problem emerges most clearly in the question of allocating the Government's resources. The Defense Department budget process particularly has attracted a great deal of attention. The problem formally is that the knowledge about military technologies is in one place and the budget is in another. The Budget Bureau and the military have in theory no other relationship than some exchange of memoranda, where the military request so much money and the Budget Bureau says yes or no or does some pruning. This process can lead to one of two possibilities—either the military simply decide whatever they want, in which case the overall resource allocations constraining the Government are not enforced, or the Budget Bureau in effect sets military policy on the basis of an arbitrary allocation without, however, having the technical knowledge to really know whether this particular level is wise or not. Obviously in practice what must happen is that more information is exchanged. The Budget Bureau to some extent does take upon itself either directly or through civilian organs in the Defense Department the job of finding out something about military technology. The Bureau cannot simply defer to the experts. On the other hand, of course, the Defense Department or the military branches have to know something about the over-all budget constraints. The demands can't be arbitrarily large, but within certain limits so that the negotiations can take place. In other words, there have to be other channels for direct exchange of information in order for coordination to take place. It is inconceivable to think of a pricing system that would completely accomplish the job, although again quantification by pricing can play a very important role in making it easier for these negotiations to take place.

At this seminar, Wagner has raised the idea of over-all control, based on watching the control characteristics of the probability or distribution of the sum of a number of individual items. This analysis

calls for searching hard for the inefficiencies when there is a strong
signal, but not monitoring everything in sight. This is a way of economizing on scarce information and management resources and at the
same time achieving a certain measure of control. It does depend,
however, upon knowing to begin with a good deal about what the optimum structure is, because in effect it is required to know really
what the over-all characteristics ought to be. Another over-all criterion that has emerged in Roberts' paper and the discussion after,
although I think perhaps he wouldn't entirely agree with this emphasis, is stability or instability. Time is of the essence here. If a system shows symptoms of instability, then there is reason to feel dissatisfied. To be sure, instability is a signal which frequently can be
seen rather easily, and that's why it is a good one to look at. But is
it a signal of error? One possibility is that instability may itself be
costly. Cost may attach not only to output, but also to the rate of
change of output. Similarly the changing level of the labor force has
certain well-known costs attached to it. Such costs can be put into a
price context, though not without difficulty. In Roberts' case, if the
delivery to its customer had been valued in some way in accordance
with the speed of delivery, some of the needed signaling for change
would have taken place automatically.

But there is another reason why stability is an important matter.
It has turned out in a number of analyses of quite different situations
that over a long period of time the outcome tends to be of an all-or-
none nature. A policy which is a little bit bad, if applied repeatedly,
is disastrous. In gambling, a policy of taking mildly unfair bets leads
to ruin with certainty. In many contexts, there may be only one policy
which permits survival so that the policy differences which may be
very small on single occasions become intensified with repetition. A
destabilizing policy has explosive characteristics which will, in most
contexts, eventually become intolerable. If a policy which is good
ought to be good forever, then the stability criterion can be used to
rule out bad policies.

In the discussion of Bonini's paper, it was, in effect, observed,
that there is a trade-off between these dynamic properties, which can
be thought of as variance or dispersion, and the average characteristics of the process. The basic criteria for maximization should be
long-run expected profits or expected discounted profits or something of this type. Dispersion is not bad in itself; it's only bad because it may and usually does indicate a policy which will also lead
to intolerable low average characteristics. But we must not overlook
the more fundamental importance of the average characteristic.

Let me briefly mention a distinction that has been drawn, I think
very interestingly, by a number of authors here (Shillinglaw, particularly, and Bonini and Haberstroh more incidentally) between two
kinds of control. (Perhaps this is also Drucker's distinction between

"control" and "controls.") In the achievement of the over-all goals
of the organization we are trying to set sub-goals for individual parts.
Two problems arise here. One is setting the sub-goals, and the other
is seeing that they're achieved. These aren't necessarily the same
thing. The first one is what is sometimes called adaptive or second-
order control. Information flows from the individual parts are needed
to accomplish both functions. On the one hand, information is needed
to make sure that people are in fact following out sub-goals set for
them, but information is also needed to detect the fact that maybe the
sub-goals aren't really the right one either. In the discussions of
transfer prices, such as Hirshleifer and I have engaged in, the second
aspect of the matter is stressed. The sub-goals are in this case maximization of profits at transfer prices. We have been concerned with
the idea that the initial set of prices may have been wrong. Some
mechanism is needed to tell us to change the prices. That's an example of changing the sub-goals, or what Bonini called "control-in-
the-large." But also we want to make sure that the individual units
are in fact maximizing profits at the given transfer prices or meeting set quotas or satisfying stability characteristics or living up to
whatever sub-goals have been set. The two types of control need different mechanisms for achievement.

"Control-in-the-small" is a question of incentives. The question
has appeared repeatedly in the writing on socialist economics. What
are the incentives to the individual manager to maximize profits? In
a capitalist system we ordinarily assume that the firm has the incentive because it keeps the profits, and we assume people have a goal
to maximize profits. At the seminar, there was some discussion of
Wagner's barometer scheme, in which, in effect, the branch manager
receives a share of the profits—possibly in money, possibly in the
form of a score which determines, over the long run, promotion or
bonuses or perhaps non-monetary awards. Do these rewards, in fact,
suffice to elicit the desired performance? The usual formulation of
the price system requires that an individual be paid his marginal
profitability, which means, in effect, that if he manages to save the
company money by proper decisions, the whole saving should go to
him. It was repeatedly pointed out during the seminar that this
doesn't seem to be the way the companies run their business. The
same problem came up a number of times in connection with the role
of marginal cost pricing as an allocative device in the national economy. The outcome of the discussion was that in order to allocate
correctly a resource in fixed supply, it is not necessary really to
pay it its full marginal profits. All that's necessary is that it receive
the same fraction of its marginal profits in every use. To apply this
result to the present problem of incentives for a manager to optimize, assume that he is going to put forth the same total effort regardless of reward. Then it is only necessary to pay him some frac-

tion of his value to the company in making good decisions. His incentive to do his best is exactly the same as it would be if he received his entire marginal contribution. Obviously, however, the initial assumption that supply of effort is given is not completely valid, and indeed the relation of effort to reward is the object of a great deal of empirical work on incentive schemes. If you are going to pay a man $2 for saving the company $100,000, you're not going to be very sure of getting the saving. On the other hand, a reasonable conjecture as to the supply of effort is that the response of effort to increased award may cease at a level which may be fairly low compared to the rewards involved. Thus, barometer control—or, in other words, a profit-sharing arrangement—make a great deal of sense because what is very important to the company may be exceedingly large by the standards of the individual, so that even a small fraction may be worth a great deal to him, perhaps enough to create adequate incentive. Furthermore, the reward may not be strictly in the form of an actual proportional payment; increased possibilities of promotion or pay raises are rewards even though deferred. It is important, though, that the rewards be determined by the amount of gain to the company and nothing else; otherwise there will be incentive for distortion. So the incentive problem, although it is one that most careful writers on socialist economics have always pointed out, is not necessarily an insuperable one.

At this seminar, there has been an exceedingly interesting group of papers on psychological and socio-psychological questions associated with the performance of management in the operation of different control systems, particularly the papers of Haire, Haberstroh and Tannenbaum. They raise a number of interesting questions about individual reactions to organizational and economic actions, which I do not feel qualified to discuss. We must, however, ask the question, "Does this have anything to do with the efficiency of the organization?" This point has been raised by several of the writers, and I gather that the evidence is rather obscure. Evidently there is some reason to believe in the existence of a connection between psychological states and efficiency although the words "morale" and "happiness" have to be interpreted carefully. It is not surprising to one who has read the world's great literature that happiness in the sense of contentment is not apt to be associated with high productivity. The great heroes of literature tend to be tragic heroes. Blaise Pascal, inventor of the theory of probability and of computing machines, may well be thought of as the patron saint of scientific management; yet who has written more movingly of the essentially tragic nature of the human condition? Dissatisfaction and striving are not surprising accompaniments of success, education and breadth of horizon, though the cause-effect-relations will take some sorting out.

The papers presented here point to the need for finer distinctions. Morale is found to have several dimensions—feeling of contentment with the job may be negative and yet feelings of participation may be very positive. While the relation of any type of morale to productivity and efficiency is not clear, it has also been brought out that the efficiency, productivity and profitability are not in fact the exclusive goals of an organization or of society as a whole, and that morale or feelings of participation may themselves be of value for their own sake.

Tannebaum's observation that it is possible to increase control in all dimensions points to a link between questionnaire responses on feelings and economic efficiency. After all, an economist would argue that an organization breeds economic interchange leading to an increase in total product, which might be thought of as increased control over the environment. It is easy to fall, as Aldous Huxley does, into the fallacy of supposing that more power, for example, ability to change biolgoical make-up, necessarily means more power over people. It may mean more power over yourself, and generally it increases the control of all individuals if properly handled.

The psychological studies are invaluable to economists in stressing new modes of thought. They certainly show, as has been repeatedly emphasized, that, at least in the short run, fluctuations in reward structures are of a kind that economics doesn't ordinarily take into consideration. This is bad because it complicates our analysis, but it's good because it means that there are more possibilities for achieving efficiency without necessarily sacrificing other goals. The simple payment of wages has trade-offs with respect to other dimensions of the labor bargain, and, these may be more important the higher the level of management. Hopefully, the future will show us more clearly how the incentive problems of management control can be understood better in terms of a multi-dimensional reward structure.

Discussion

RESEARCH DIRECTIONS IN MANAGEMENT CONTROL

WILLIAM W. COOPER
Carnegie Institute of Technology

I SOME COMMENTS ON DRUCKER'S "CONTROLS, AND MANAGEMENT":

In his Caesar and Cleopatra "Notes", G. B. Shaw refers to Oliver Cromwell and Julius Caesar as military "Johnny-come-latelies" in order to suggest that "the capacity of any conqueror is . . . more likely than not to be an illusion produced by the incapacity of his adversary" [1]. If this be true, then subsequent history might have changed if a management science had been able to make these adversaries only a little bit better.

I preface my comments to Drucker's paper in this way because I think some perspective may be needed when considering Drucker's call for immediate "scientific" attention to the things which he believes are important for contemporary management and society. Drucker, like Shaw, is a demanding idealist as well as a penetrating social commentator. Hence, though it may be impossible really to disagree with them, in general, one must also remember that persons such as they are likely to be impatient with great progress on many small things or small progress on a few great things. Thus, for one part of our perspective, I might say tht it is not immediately clear, at least to me, that one can always discriminate with any degree of validity between the important and the unimportant by comparing one issue against another—one (or a few) at a time!—in order to conclude that even small progress in one area will outweigh the advantages that might be secured from more progress sustained over a wider range of less important problems.

Drucker is impatient on other matters as well. This is perhaps most evident in the prescription that is provided by the following quotation drawn from his paper: "a new set of tools should always be put to work on the difficult rather than the easy, on things the old tools could not do at all rather than on the things they did passably well." This brings up issues concerning the nature of scientific progress in methodology, as well as in substance, which appear to be moot if only because a great deal of the postwar progress in science appears to be largely in the form of improved methodologies—lasers and masers, new mathematics and statistics, electronic computers, devices for

328

exploring space, etc.—as contrasted, say, with a previous period which witnessed such substantive progress as relativity, quantum theory, Freudianism, Keynsianism, etc. Without implying that a clear separation is possible, or desirable, I am concerned to emphasize the importance of improving methodology as a scientific activity (see, for example, [2]). For purposes of better understanding, as well as for maintaining scientific continuity, it is often the case that "first tries" are made by applying new methods to old problems and even very well solved old problems. And I am not at all certain of the virtue of the rather hard boiled Texas prescription—"match a rider who doesn't know how to ride with a horse that has never been ridden and let them both learn together."

As the present conference suggests, we are already at a point where work and sustained interest on management problems is in evidence in many different scientific disciplines. Although I am concerned that this work should maintain contact with and contribute to the body of scientific knowledge (and methodology) generally, I am also concerned with its bearing on the development of a management science. This means, of course, that I am concerned with relations between management science and the problems that management is— or ought to be—facing. Hence, from the latter standpoint, at least, I should like to use this opportunity to gage our direction by reference to Drucker's penetrating social commentary after making allowance for his idealistic impatience.

Concerning his law of "skew distributions" one should note, first, that there has been work in this area both by theoreticians as well as practitioners. Thus, in this connection, one might mention the work of George Kingsley Zipf, for instance, which contains numerous data on a wide variety of "social" phenomena as well as a report of his efforts to subsume their "skewness" patterns under a single unifying principle [3]. More recently, Zipf's work—along with that of Yule, Willis, Pareto, Lorenz, and others—has been given analytic form and generalized by H. A. Simon in "A Class of Skew Distributions" (Biometrika, vol. 42, 1955, pp. 425-440). To be sure, certain parts of the development are still in dispute but this may be taken as a sign of active interest in the topic and we are, in any event, now in a position to make greater use of these kinds of statistical distributions.[1]

Turning next to the topic of "control vs. controls" one must, I think, admit the general force of Drucker's criticisms in that our "scientific" knowledge and attention to these topics is in a very unsatisfactory state. This is true even though management practitioners, including accountants, have now been struggling with important

[1]See the exchanges between H. A. Simon and Benoit Mandelbrot in Information and Control, vol. 3, 1960.

aspects of these problems for many years. On the other hand, as this conference shows, we can at least report the beginnings of scientific interest in the topic of management controls *per se* even while we admit that our approach may have been delayed perhaps longer than necessary because of a prior preoccupation with problems in such areas as "planning," "testing and selection," "morale measurement," "opinion formation," etc.

Continuing in this same "control vs. controls" vein, but on a more detailed level, I should like to turn to certain studies that are directed in particular to control (as distinguished from planning) aspects of accounting, budgeting and auditing. In this manner I shall again be able to utilize Drucker's commentary as a gage for current directions of work and, at the same time, secure an opportunity for exploiting some of the remarks he has made on accounting, controllership, etc.

I begin by now turning to portions of some work by N. C. Churchill which may help to illustrate some of the control-vs-controls distinction that are emphasized in Drucker's paper. I refer to a series of experiments which Churchill conducted to study the effects of audits on both industrial and college student subjects and, of course, I can at best only do justice to a small portion of this work.[2]

Treating audits as a managerial control device, Churchill went one step further and distinguished between "supervisory audits" and "accounting audits."[3] A further distinction was made between task results, including method of task accomplishment, and record maintenance including the accuracy of the records maintained. Implicit in this is a distinction between "control" as a class concept[4] and the "controls"—e.g., combinations of control devices or procedures—which are members of this class. Using variables such as "audit anticipation" as well as "actual audit", Churchill found in his experiments on industrial subjects that when a supervisory audit only was applied, the subjects (a) improved their performance, as measured by correct task output but (b) tended systematically to introduce record keeping errors that showed even greater improvements in their performance.[5] When the variable "anticipate that an audit

---

[2] See [4]. I am using this and other examples in part to achieve some degree of balance with respect to the discussion by Kenneth J. Arrow and in part because I happen to be more familiar with this work by Churchill and others that I shall soon mention.

[3] See the paper in this Conference by N. C. Churchill, W. W. Cooper and T. Sainsbury for further details on the way these distinctions were made.

[4] The term "class" is used here in its logical rather than its sociological sense.

[5] The latter is perhaps of interest as an indirect way of measuring the effect of a managerial device on character, as an "intangible" especially since the erroneous records, when taken literally, would redound to the supervisor's rather than the subjects' benefit.

will occur" was introduced, the record keeping accuracy improved[6]
while actual task results were somewhat worsened. Finally, all three
variables when applied simultaneously—i.e., supervisory audit, anticipation of accounting audit and actual occurrence of an accounting
audit—produced adverse (higher order interaction) effects on both
record maintenance and actual task accomplishments. This suggests
the presence of "over control" already and as we learn more about
such phenomena it is possible that we may be able to forestall the
natural managerial tendency to impose even more controls in such
situations and, ultimately, even to devise optimal control schemes
[4].

Accounting in the U.S. is less arbitrary than Drucker in his ideal-
ism would have us believe. It is also subject to criticism, however,
on different—possibly more important—grounds than those which
Drucker suggests. In much of the accounting literature, as well as
accounting practice, there is evidenced a preoccupation with "accurate and timely" cost reports with the result that accounting has
failed to be sufficiently inventive or even exploratory of other approaches.

I can perhaps explain what I mean by this last remark by turning
next to some of the work by A. Stedry which is now being elaborated
in cooperation with A. Charnes via the evolution of models and
methods such as those which they report on in their conference paper
here. In contrast to the old, well-established, categories of costing—
e.g., historical vs alternative (opportunity) costs—Stedry introduced
[5] and experimented with a new category that might well be called
"motivational costs" because of its heavy psychological-behavioral
science content. By means of experimentation, as well as by models
and suitable interpretations, Stedry attempted to assess the behavi
oral consequences of varying the content and timeliness of his accounting and budgetary reporting mechanisms. The results have, I
think, called into question some of the supposedly universal efficacy
of many budgetary-accounting precepts as well as the recommendations of various psychologists who (mistakenly, I think) took existing
practices as the only possibilities of budgetary management.

Stedry's findings suggest the possibility of making even more extensive use of the cost "fictions" that are possible in accounting. In
particular, his work suggests the possible use of accounting reports
as information theoretic devices which can be matched to persons
and not merely to things (or functions) in various rings of an organization. By matching these reports to motivational and information
requirements we may be able to allow even for the supposed incompe-

[6] The effect on college students was in an opposite direction, however,
which suggests that the same controls may have differing effects when applied
to persons with different training or backgrounds in different organization
contexts.

tence or bias of particular individuals and thereby at least begin to consider alternatives to the kinds of shuffling involved in promotion-demotion schemes, etc., which are now regarded as managerial necessities [6].

Lest I now be hoisted all alone on a petard of "measurement immorality,"[7] I immediately note that biased reporting is not an unknown and untried part of management practice. It has been used in statistical quality control, for example, when it is necessary to allow for operator or machine bias in cutting tools, etc. I have also personally witnessed its use in other areas as well. For instance a student team from one of my courses at Carnegie Tech made a statistical analysis relevant to the waste resulting from over pouring and under pouring ingots in a steel mill. They discovered that the mill crews tended to overpour on orders for very small ingots and to underpour on very large ones. Utilizing these findings, then, these students recommended the utilization of "bogus" customer order sizes in order to compensate for this known mill crew bias relative to small and large ingot size orders. This was motivated, of course, by the thought that the mill crews would then, on the average, pour correctly for the sizes actually ordered by the customers.

Drucker, as I have already suggested, is a demanding idealist and so it is possible that he would disagree even with my doubts about the moral issues here. On the other hand, the contributions of management—and management science—to morality may be deficient in other quarters than those now being considered. From Aristotle and Plato onward, it has been traditional to consider morality in terms of fixed norms of either individual or social behavior. It may well be the case, however, that a more dynamic process is involved. Indeed we may be currently suffering from an unduly restricted range of choices and something might be gained if management and management science, together, were able significantly to increase the range of operable choices in ways that would permit new values to come into existence.[8]

I am aware, of course, that any great acceleration in this process may produce contradictions and stresses far worse than any that are now present. Here I can only observe that contradiction and resulting stress are themselves phenomena of managerial interest which might well find a place for more detailed study in the sciences. Some of this has already been done on the level of multiple goal seeking as well as on the level of means-end relations. At the empirical-societal level one may cite the discussion of moral strain in G. Myrdal's now classic *An American Dilemma* (New York: Harper & Row, 1944).

---

[7] See, for example, the discussion in [7].

[8] For further discussion of this aspect of management as a creative activity, see [8].

On the logical-managerial level it is of interest to note that some of the models developed by Charnes and Stedry have incorporated aspiration levels which are "impossible of attainment" in order that they might thereby study their relevance for improving performance that is actually capable of attainment [9]. Presumably, this could later be extended to analyses of the effects of contradictions generally on employee morale and like factors that affect employee and societal welfare. I should like, in any event, to see much more research on such phenomena as contradiction, biased reporting, etc., not only because of the possibility that this offers for improving management practice but also for the possibility it offers for contributing to our understanding of behavior in the face of conflict.[9]

Here it is of interest also to consider the topic of conflict as well as superabundance of the controls, decision machinery, and information processing devices utilized by business firms. Until recently we have been able to use only field and laboratory studies limited to a few, often highly aggregated,[10] variables since this was really about all that our available methodology enabled us to do. Hence, I find particular interest in attempts to exploit computer methodology— as reported in the papers by Bonini and Roberts—insofar as this permits us to study multiple interactions when variables such as decision and information centers in a firm are altered along with the content or timing of reports, positioning of personnel, etc.

It is from this latter standpoint that I perfer to judge Bonini's[11] simulation models and, provided one is aware of it, I am not much bothered by the issue of time-constant variations which were raised during the discussions in the conference. There is, after all, more than one kind of interest to be served by scientific inquiry. Thus, in his discussion of regression and identification analysis (in statistical estimation), J. Marschak distinguishes between measurements for purposes of "prediction" and measurements for purposes of "policy" [12]. I prefer to carry this somewhat further, however, and distin-

---

[9] Including the uses of rationalization as witness, for instance, the discussion of magic and rationalization as it occurs in the "production organizations" of primitive societies discussed in [10], "wherein technologically essential activities are institutionally prohibited [the mechanism of negation is often supplied by a rationalization] . . . . For example, the killing of fish is supposedly prohibited by the Buddhist religion, yet fishing is fairly widespread in many Buddhist societies . . . . Fishermen, consequently either take great pains to keep their fish alive until it is sold, or else make certain the fish is alive when it is removed from the hook. The latter precaution enables them to claim that they are not responsible; the fish, when left on land, simply died of its own accord."

[10] See the papers by Wagner and Marschak, for further discussion of the kinds of issues associated with aggregating information from many into a few variables.

[11] See Bonini's report in this volume. See also [11].

guish between "understanding," "prediction" and "control" as objects of scientific inquiry. Bonini's study is directed rather, I think, towards the second of these three objectives and I have little doubt that yet another run of his model would produce results which he could predict at satisfactory levels of confidence. Thus, even though Bonini may not have provided all "understanding" that might be desired—e.g., with respect to precise causal connections between his variables—his study has nevertheless suggested new issues and, equally important, it has suggested that there might be a need for reexamining old issues which we thought had already been settled. For instance, as Bonini's study shows, it is not at all clear that more current information on costs is conducive to better performance when accounting reports are used to evaluate the performance of others (e.g., subordinates) as well as to make decisions on input-output variables.

Although Bonini's study reflects reality in a very general way I would suppose that something more—much more—would be needed in the way of detailed study before it could be addressed to the control issues that are necessarily involved when actual installation studies are at issues—e.g., of the kind that Roberts and Forrester are concerned with.[12] Concerning the related issues of statistical and simulation testing and verification, which were also discussed in the conference, some of my own reservations relative to the Roberts-Forrester position could probably be dispelled if only they rephrased their remarks to indicate that the current state of statistical methodology is not, at present, really up to the task of entirely analyzing and validating the numerous interacting aspects of large-scale systems design. Further methodological developments in statistics are certainly in order here to obtain suitable measures of "system fits" if guides are to be provided thereby for analyzing and improving the results of previous simulations.[13] This does not mean, of course, that all simulations of complex systems must be held in

---

[12] Jay W. Forrester, *Industrial Dynamics* [13]. In reading Roberts "Industrial Dynamics and the Design of Management Control Systems" (this volume) one cannot help being struck by the difference in his "R and D model" which incorporates psychological-behavioral variables (e.g., engineering attitudes and motivations) and his production model which uses only functional-mechanistic variables. I would suppose that this would not always be the case and that in some production organizations, anyway, there might be a place on the flow chart to depict say union-management interactions and related psychological variables.

[13] An instance of the needed guidance may be found in K. J. Cohen, *Computer Models of the Shoe, Leather, Hide Sequence* (Englewood Cliffs, N. J.: Prentice-Hall, 1960) where it is not clear whether one does better by worsening (or improving) an already bad fit or a very good one in the underlying equations when the objective is an improvement in specified "overall" prediction measures.

abeyance until an improved statistical methodology is available.
Neither does it mean, as Roberts and Forrester[14] suggest, that one
cannot secure any help from available statistical methodology—as
witness, for instance, the effective use that Bonini makes of these
tools.

I should now like to conclude this portion of my discussion by
turning to a deep and very subtle issue that is raised by Drucker. I
refer to his "uncertainty principle" and the related distinctions he
makes between machines and men as objects of control. The issue
he raises here is very fundamental and at bottom it questions whether
any social or management science is possible. These kinds of issues
are already confronted in psychology and elsewhere. When dealing
with subjects who have become "experiment wise", for example, it
may be necessary to change experimental subjects. The same phenomenon is met in the field via "observer effects" or the "spoilage
bias" that may accompany the use of panels subject to repeated interviews in consumer surveys, etc. At present there are numerous
expedients that can be adopted such as replacing panel members at
random, etc., but in the end the issue must be confronted on logical
grounds in its own terms.

Frank Knight, when I was a student at the University of Chicago,
was fond of adding to Drucker's "uncertainty principle" the further
complication that science must, of necessity, be public knowledge.
To see the force that this adds to the uncertainty principle, let it be
supposed, for instance, that some economist has developed a scientifically valid method of forecasting the stock market. *Qua* scientist,
he must make this knowledge publicly available. But then the investing public will use this knowledge and thereby alter the behavior of
the stock market.

This does not, however, forestall the possibility of further scientific progress by means of which the "investor forecasts" are ac-
commodated so that, once again, scientific prediction is achieved.
But again, as a matter of science, this new method of prediction
must also be made available publicly. The possibility of a non-term-
inating infinite regress is thereby opened. It is therefore possibly of
interest to report here that a logical answer has been devised by
E. Grunberg and F. Modigliani[15] which shows that under a reasonably
wide set of assumptions, no infinite regress of this kind need be involved—i.e., there exists a prediction which will accommodate all
predictions (including the last one) which will yield a valid forecast.

Whether such refinements to our prediction machinery will actually become available is still an open question, of course, but if they

---

[14] See, e.g., [13] and Roberts' paper in this volume.
[15] See [14]. The argument is developed by reference to the so-called "fixed
point" considerations of mathematical analysis and hence involves assumptions
of continuity that may not always be valid.

do then the distinction between "events" of the future and "facts" of the past may also lose some of the significance that Drucker assigns it. Alternatively, we may proceed along the route of improved ability to control in such a way that our interest in "prediction" or even in "understanding" may become attenuated from the standpoint of management if not from the standpoint of science. Thus, as occurs in engineering and medicine, we may then say something like the following:[16]

> Research has not yet discovered the cause of either high blood pressure (hypoertension) or hardening of the arteries (arteriosclerosis). But enough has been learned about treatment and management [sic] to make changes that are almost revolutionary. Patients who would have been condemned twenty years ago to a useless life in bed are now advised to live normally, taking sensible precautions.

This, too, might be counted as scientific progress even though it does not wholly satisfy our esthetic needs for "understanding."

II SELECTED COMMENTS ON KENNETH J. ARROW: "RESEARCH IN MANAGEMENT CONTROL: A CRITICAL SYNTHESIS"

Because Arrow's paper is itself a commentary which includes implicit and explicit comments on Tannenbaum's presentation, it seemed better to focus my own discussion on the issues and insights provided by Peter Drucker. Personally, however, I am strongly attracted by some of the overtones and new ideas that Arrow's commentary has injected into these proceedings and I would now like to take the opportunity to examine some of them here.

First I turn to Arrow's emphasis on the phenomena of uncertainty and then I observe that traditional organization theorists are not represented in the conference papers.[17] I proceed in this manner because, in part, I share Arrow's interest in uncertainty, but then I think it is only fair to remark that these traditional theorists would not necessarily share in the view that uncertainty is "perhaps the key factor" in understanding organization, "[it] . . . is what creates

[16] Quoted from the popular pamphlet "Your Blood Pressure and Your Arteries" by Alexander L. Crosby, *Public Affairs Pamphlet No. 168*, rev. ed., 1957.

[17] Other groups, too, are not represented (e.g., those interested in Weberian "bureaucracy" phenomena, etc.) but, of course, this cannot be taken as a criticism, since it was the purpose of the conference to explore relatively new approaches to the topic of control. Besides, a fairly well balanced and exhaustive treatment is also already available in the relatively recent Simon March, *Organizations*, New York: Wiley, 1958.

organizations," etc. There is, for instance, the stock example of
men rolling a large rock up a hill which is often used as an organization illustration in books on administration and organization and, in
fact, Luther Gulick in *Papers on the Science of Administration*[18]—
something of a classic in the traditional literature—asserts, flatly,
at the outset

> "Work division is the foundation of organization; indeed the
> reason for organization."

(Gulick then goes on to describe a shoe factory in terms that are re-
miniscent of Adam Smith's famous pin factory discussion so that
things now seen to be turned around in the approaches to organization analysis that are being used by economists and others.)[19]

It may help to supply some perspective on the current state of
economics, too, if we recall that it was customary for economics
texts—at least until recently—to include lengthy discussions of character, population, creativity and intelligence as necessary material
before plunging into price theory, market exchange, etc. A good
illustration, perhaps, is Alfred Marshall's famous *Principles of
Economics*[20] wherein most of the material (some 300 pages) preceding the Book V discussion of "price theory" is occupied with this
kind of discussion. Alternatively, for those who may have some dis-
taste for Marshall's rather Victorian style we can refer to the pithy
statement of the American economist, Wesley Mitchell: Factories
produce goods but they also produce men.[21]

Of course one could probably devise better institutions for producing men if this were the main objective. On the other hand it
seems reasonable to suppose that much more can be done to improve
the forms of organization and modes of management with respect to
producing additional values such as status, power, contentment and
character—which are no less important because they are "intangible"—and here again I should like to underscore the importance of
pushing ahead with this work, as is done by Tannenbaum, Haire, *et.*

---

[18] L. Gulick and L. Urwick (eds.), New York: Columbia University, 1937.
See also the more recent small group, or social psychology, literature as
evidenced by, say, M. Sherif and C. W. Sherif, *An Outline of Social Psychology*,
New York: Harper & Row, 1956—"An important condition of group formation
is the awareness of common motives shared but incapable of separate attainment . . . ."

[19] I should perhaps also cite Udy [10] again for its interesting use of ethno-
graphic (anthropological) data to distinguish between the technological and
social requirements of production organizations in various pre-literate societies—many of whom know neither uncertainty nor market price phenomena in
the sense that Arrow is using these terms.

[20] 8th ed., London: MacMillan, 1936.

[21] *The Back Art of Spending Money and Other Essays*, New York: McGraw-
Hill, 1937, p. 372.

al., even while I admit the pressing need of a better methodology for studying complex phenomena like these.[22]

Turning now to the use of prices I should like to underscore Arrow's reference to "natural business units" since the formation of these units, too, must be assumed as a function of the price system—along with appropriate choices of technology—if the use of price guides and incentives is to have the virtues that are claimed for them by economists. One component entering into such "natural business units" is concerned with the absorption of externalities and the related uncertainties as shown, for instance, by A. Whinston in his *Price Coordination in Decentralized Systems.* [15] Indeed, from this standpoint it is useful even to consider business firms as being formed by internalizing a certain collection of externalities. In this way one may suppose that the theory of markets may be preserved from the limitations to pricing that such externalities impose, but one cannot then also blandly assume that the problem of externalities is also absent when one attempts to apply the theory of pricing inside the firm.

In order to bring into sharper focus some of the ways in which the presence of externalities is related to the issue of uncertainty, it may be helpful to turn to the literature of linear and nonlinear programming where, following some of the initial work of Koopmans, [16], a great deal is being done to study the use of prices as information devices to guide the operations of decentralized organizations. Here we may note, first, that Koopmans accords a very fundamental place to the assumption of convexity—with respect to supply, production possibilities, etc—in order to ensure the proper operation of a system of prices in achieving the efficient production of goods and services [17]. The idea of separability, as defined by A. Charnes and C. E. Lemke,[23] is also of fundamental importance, however, when the use of price guides is being considered. Indeed, unless separability is present then, as Whinston shows, [15] uncertainty may again be present—even though initially assumed away—and this may have to be dealt with by suitable organization devices before pricing can be relied upon as a guide to decentralized operations. That is, in the

---

[22] My own experience with "content analysis," for instance, has caused me to be considerably less sanguine concerning its use and prospects for improvement than appears to be the case for Haberstroh, especially when there are no readily available objective phenomena to tie into the analytical results. See, e.g., Haberstroh's paper in this volume and the references cited therein and then compare with Udy's study of rationalization etc., as cited above, and then also compare with the content analysis results of more subtle aspects of auditing in the field study which is reported elsewhere in this volume, in the paper I coauthored with Churchill and Sainsbury.

[23] Briefly a function is said to be separable when it can be written or transformed into a sum of functions each involving only one variable in its argument. See [18]. For further extensions and detailed exposition see [19].

absence of separability—and for other reasons, too—it may be necessary to consider a mixed system of prices and other devices for
guiding and controlling decentralized operations.

On the other hand, the issue of separability also suggests a way
of approaching the problems of formal organization, at least in part,
when price guides are being considered. Thus, for instance, when
the functions to be considered are only partially separable[24] they can
be used as a rather natural avenue for forming managerial hierarchies in that the separated parts can each be assigned to a manager
who, in turn, coordinates the activities associated with the variables
which are arguments in his own particular function.

As is suggested also, I think, in Balderston's paper, internal pricing or costing guides, to be really suitable, must accomplish something more than merely ensuring correct input and output decisions
with *given* production coefficients. It must also simultaneously ensure a correct choice of production coefficients and related capacity
alterations. To put this into a form that can be more easily understood, perhaps, we may utilize some industrial engineering terms
and say that production managers must decide on where, and how
much, method-time study to use and they must also decide on capacity alterations and related resource expenditures at the same time
that they are deciding the relevant mixes to schedule for current
production. This will, in general, produce a nonlinear problem but
it may be interest to note that when certain conditions of convexity
and separability are present then it is possible to utilize what are
called "repricing" and "reprocessing theorems". By means of
these theorems it is then possible to develop certain "bogus prices"
and "bogus production coefficients" for use in a linear model which
yields the "correct" solutions to the original nonlinear problem [20].

Arrow is right, of course, in insisting on the desirability of carefully considering prices as an object of inquiry (a) because this is
likely to provide new insights into the uses and limitations of pricing
per se and (b) because the results are likely to be of practical utility
especially as organizations grow larger and more complex. From
an information theoretic standpoint, such prices are useful devices
in which are impounded a great deal of information in a simple,
readily understood, manner. On the other hand, it must be remembered that such internal prices are usually intended to serve only as
a "unit of account" and therefore do not possess all properties of
market (money) prices. This raises enforcement questions such as
Shubik refers to in his game theoretic approach to the problems of

---

[24] If $f(x_1, x_2, x_3) = f_1(x_1) + f_2(x_2) + f_3(x_3)$, say, then the function, f, is
separable, but if $f(x_1, x_2, x_3) = \psi(x_1, x_2) + \phi(x_3)$ then f is only partially
separable.

accounting imputation[25] which, in turn, may produce game-like properties in his system; these, in turn, may require further controls, and so on.[26] In fact, given the usual managerial hierarchies etc., the assumptions of arms'-length transactions[27] and related ideas of accountancy break down so that consideration of further, alternative, controls is often necessary.

In the latter context we may again usefully recall Drucker's admonitions and Churchill's experimental results and especially so if we expect to accord some of the further properties of market (money) prices to these internal "units of account." For then we shall move close to a point where we shall be speaking of economic prizes and controls in the context of a system design so that it may not then be amiss to turn to the old muckraker and liberal, Lincoln Steffens, who also studied such system design problems—with insight, if not with the impeccability that one might desire in a social science field inquiry. Once queried by a California bishop on "how it [graft, corruption, etc.] all began," Steffens reports the following reply[28]

> "[So] you want to fix the fault at the very start of things. Maybe we can, Bishop. Most people, you know, say it was Adam. But Adam, you remember, he said it was Eve, the woman; she did it. And Eve said no, no, it wasn't she; it was the serpent. And that's where you clergy have stuck ever since. You blame that serpent, Satan. Now I come and I am trying to show you that it was, it is, the apple."

Perhaps it is now best to stop since this brings us back, once more, to the issues which Peter Drucker raised in his discussion of control, system design, measurement, and their related moralities.

BIBLIOGRAPHY

1. Shaw, G. B.: *Nine Plays by Bernard Shaw*, New York: Dodd, Mead, 1939, p. 478.
2. Dewey, John: "Unity of Science as a Social Problem," *International Encyclopedia of Unified Science*, vol. 1, no. 1, Chicago: University of Chicago Press, 1938, p. 29 ff.

[25] See the opening paragraph in Sec. 7 of Shubik's paper.

[26] Similar remarks may be made with respect to Hirshleifer's suggested use of a "neutral umpire." For further discussion of these problems see A. Whinston, "Price Guides in Decentralized Organization" Research Report, Cowles Commission for Research in Economics under ONR Task NR-047-006, 1962.

[27] These assumptions are related, of course, to the absence of force and fraud as assumed, usually in the theoretical analyses of market economics.

[28] *The Autobiography of Lincoln Steffens*, New York: Harcourt, Brace and World, 1931, p. 574.

3. Zipf, G. K.: *Human Behavior and the Principle of Least Effort*, Reading, Mass.: Addison-Wesley, 1949.
4. Churchill, N. C.: *Behavior Effects of an Audit:\An Experimental Study*, Ph.D. dissertation, Ann Arbor, Mich.: University of Michigan, 1962.
5. Stedry, A.: *Budget Control and Cost Behavior*, Englewood Cliffs, N. J.: Prentice-Hall, 1960.
6. Cooper, W. W.: "Some Implications of the Newer Analytic Approaches to Management," *California Management Review*, vol. 4, no. 1, pp. 51-64, 1961.
7. Becker, S., and D. Green, Jr.: "Budgeting and Employee Behavior," *Journal of Business*, vol. 35, no. 4, 1962.
8. Charnes, A., and W. W. Cooper: "Management Science and Managing," *Illinois University Quarterly Review of Business*, vol. 2, no. 2, pp. 7-19, 1962.
9. _____and A. Stedry: "Some Models of Organization Response to Budgeted Multiple Goals," Organization Research Report No. 1, Cambridge, Mass.: Massachusetts Institute of Technology, School of Industrial Management, 1962.
10. Udy, S. H., Jr.: *Organization of Work*, New Haven: HRAF Press, 1959, p. 121.
11. Bonini, C. P.: *Simulation of Information and Decision Systems of the Firm*, Englewood Cliffs, N. J.: Prentice-Hall, 1963.
12. Marschak, J.: "Economic Measurements for Policy and Prediction," in W. C. Hood and T. C. Koopmans (eds.), *Studies in Econometric Method*, New York: Wiley, 1953.
13. Forrester, J. W.: *Industrial Dynamics*, New York: Wiley, 1961.
14. Gruneberg, E., and F. Modigliani: "The Predictability of Social Events," *The Journal of Political Economy*, vol. 62, no. 6, pp. 465-478, 1954.
15. Whinston, A.: *Price Coordination in Decentralized Systems*, Ph.D. dissertation, Pittsburgh: Carnegie Institute of Technology, Graduate School of Industrial Administration, 1962.
16. Koopmans, T. C. (ed.): "Activity Analysis as an Efficient Combination of Activities," *Activity Analysis of Production and Allocation*, New York: Wiley, 1951.
17. _____: *Three Essays on the State of Economic Science*, New York: McGraw-Hill, 1957.
18. Charnes, A., and C. E. Lemke, "Minimization of Non-Linear Separable Convex Functionals," *Naval Research Logistics Quarterly*, vol. 1, no. 4, pp. 301-312, 1954.
19. _____ and W. W. Cooper: *Management Models and Industrial Applications of Linear Programming*, New York: Wiley, 1962, chap. 10.
20. _____ and _____: "Systems Evaluation and Repricing Theorems," *Management Science*, vol. 9, no. 1, pp. 33-49, 1962.